GROTESQUE AND PERFORMANCE IN THE ART OF AUBREY BEARDSLEY

Grotesque and Performance in the Art of Aubrey Beardsley

Evanghelia Stead

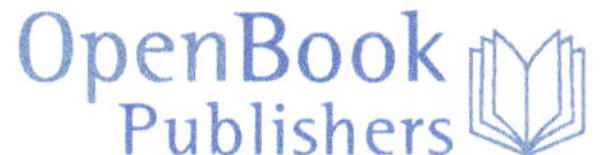

https://www.openbookpublishers.com

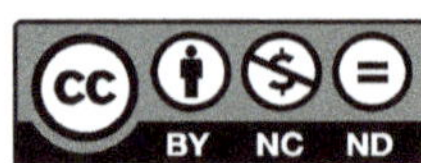 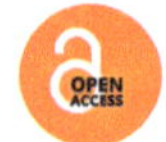

All external links were active at the time of publication unless otherwise stated and have been archived via the Internet Archive Wayback Machine at https://archive.org/web

Any digital material and resources associated with this volume will be available at https://doi.org/10.11647/OBP.0413#resources

ISBN Paperback: 978-1-80511-345-4
ISBN Hardback: 978-1-80511-346-1
ISBN Digital (PDF): 978-1-80511-347-8
ISBN Digital eBook (EPUB): 978-1-80511-348-5
ISBN HTML: 978-1-80511-349-2

DOI: 10.11647/OBP.0413

Cover design: Jeevanjot Kaur Nagpal

...there is no truer criterion of the vitality of any given art-period
than the power of the master-spirits of that time in grotesque

Thomas Hardy, *Far from the Madding Crowd*, 1874, Ch. XLVI

True grotesque is not the art either of primitives or decadents,
but that of skilled and accomplished workmen
who have reached the zenith of a peculiar convention

Robert Ross, *Aubrey Beardsley*, 1909, p. 49

Contents

List of Abbreviations

BM-FH + number	*Bon-Mots of Samuel Foote and Theodore Hook* (1894) + page number
BM-LJ + number	*Bon-Mots of Charles Lamb and Douglas Jerrold* (1893) + page number
BM-SS + number	*Bon-Mots of Sydney Smith and R. Brinsley Sheridan* (1893) + page number
BnF	Bibliothèque nationale de France, Paris, France
coll.	collection
Delaware	University of Delaware Library, Museums and Press, Newark, Delaware, USA
DocStAr	*Laboratorio di Documentazione Storico-Artistica*, Pisa, Italy
Early Work	*The Early Work of Aubrey Beardsley* (1899)
Fifty Drawings	Beardsley, *A Book of Fifty Drawings* (1897)
Five Drawings	Beardsley, *An Issue of Five Drawings Illustrative of Juvenal and Lucian* (1906)
Lucian's True History	*Lucian's True History, Translated by Francis Hickes* (1894)
MSL coll.	Mark Samuels Lasner collection, Delaware Library
PE coll.	Paul Edwards collection and scan
Pierrot of the Minute	*Ernest Dowson, The Pierrot of the Minute: A Dramatic Phantasy in One Act* (1897)
Posters in Miniature	*Posters in Miniature. With an Introduction by E. Penfield* (1896)
R<	replicated grotesque vignette, size reduced
R>	replicated grotesque vignette, size increased

Rape of the Lock	Alexander Pope, *The Rape of the Lock* [...] *Embroidered with Eleven Drawings by A. Beardsley* (1897)
Reade + number	Brian Reade, *Beardsley*, revised ed. (1987) + plate number
Uncollected Work	*The Uncollected Work of Aubrey Beardsley* (1925)
V&A	Victoria and Albert Museum, London, UK
Y90s	*Yellow Nineties 2.0*, Toronto Metropolitan University Centre for Digital Humanities
Zatlin + number	Linda Gertner Zatlin, *Aubrey Beardsley: A Catalogue Raisonné* (2016) + plate number

Introductory Note and Acknowledgements

The chapters in this book are based on various contributions previously published in French, mainly in edited volumes, a special issue, and a book chapter. My oldest piece on Aubrey Beardsley dates from the early 1990s, the latest from 2019. Yet this book is no mere collection of previously published work. All chapters correspond to revamped, rewritten, enlarged, and combined versions, elaborated in view of the various arguments put forward here.

In my literary explorations across cultures and printed material, Beardsley has always been one of my favourite artists. By no means an easily domesticated or uncomplicated travelling companion, he has trained my eye and taught me much about language and wit. Furthermore, revisions in this book have benefitted from my own previous work on books and prints as cultural objects and several collective ventures on the periodical press.

I warmly thank Paul Edwards, who many years ago patiently and thoroughly scanned the grotesque vignettes and other material from period publications in private collections; Corin Thorsby for her thorough editing of an earlier state of the manuscript, her critical eye and helpful questions; Margaret D. Stetz for a generous review; Alessandra Tosi for her confidence and interest in this book; Adèle Kreager for painstaking and patient copyediting; Cameron Craig for his clever layouts and work on images; Jeevanjot Kaur Nagpal for her skilful fortitude with images and an inventive conception of the cover; Mark Samuels Lasner and assistant Michael McShane for dedicated support with scans from Mark Samuels Lasner's first-rate collection of Beardsleyana; Gretha Arwas for authorising me to publish Alastair's colourful drawing; Lorraine Jansen Kooistra for images and elucidations from the *Yellow Nineties*

2.0; Éric Walbecq, Hélène Védrine and Clément Dessy for confirming details; and lastly the personnel of several institutions who responded to requests and questions with promptitude and grace.

Unless otherwise indicated, all translations from other languages into English are my own. In the absence of titles for Sidney H. Sime's and Marcus Behmer's grotesques, I have provided my own in captions as Linda Gertner Zatlin has done for Beardsley's in her *catalogue raisonné*.

Introduction : Breaking the Mould of Victorianism

"A New Poster" by Evelyn Sharp is a short story published July 1895 in the sixth volume of the *Yellow Book*. A piece of light social satire, it depicts a wealthy but rather unremarkable widow dithering over two suitors: an egotistical English artist and a matter-of-fact American businessman. The widow's naive view pits talent, intellect, and innovation against commerce and conventionality. Mrs Cynthia Milton, who adopts the arty name of Mrs Angelo Milton, deploys Aesthete tactics to break out of the world of trade and her own wealth from the commercial success of her deceased husband, manufacturer of the Milton Fountain Pen. The story would be of little concern here, had it not taken its subject (and title) from an up-to-the-minute poster advertising all over London this very pen. The billboard is designed by Cynthia's first choice of suitor, Adrian Marks, "a black and white artist, very new."[1] Adrian conceals his association with the poster from Cynthia in order to feign indifference to her fortune. Yet, if they marry, she will lose all her money. She finally marries the prosaic American businessman, her deceased husband's former associate, which ends her coveted foothold in fashionable avant-garde society and circles à la mode.

Adrian Marks resembles Aubrey Beardsley in no way: there are no common threads in age, manner, appearance, their intentions or behaviour. And yet a whiff of Beardsley's poster art seems to trigger and foster Sharp's story. The idea of a "new poster" gives the piece its title, and impels the plot. "Effete and decadent," Adrian, a "dandy artist,"[2] moves in good society and a cultivated set. He practises an

1 Evelyn Sharp, "A New Poster," *The Yellow Book*, 6 (June 1895): 123–66 (124).
2 *Ibid.*, 155 and 135.

 https://doi.org/10.11647/OBP.0413.00

art which, however exclusive, spurs a woman's modern dilemma in a quarterly journal from the 1890s. Several details draw on established fin-de-siècle clichés (awkward drawings, stark contrasts, interest in yellow as "peculiarly distinguished,"[3] flippancy, innuendo, dandified houses, impressive poses, witty remarks) to set them against the "commercial spirit"[4] from which Cynthia in vain strives to free herself. As a "new black and white artist," Adrian hence reads as Beardsley's fictionalised *alter ego* in a gently and innocuously ironic context.

Still, the billboard itself is not innocent. It has "a scarlet background with a black lady in one corner and a black tree with large roots in another corner, and some black stars scattered about elsewhere."[5] The off-the-cuff description (by an "ugly boy") disapproves of abstraction and teems with aesthetic qualms. It reads like a spoof of Beardsley's creations since "that nonsensical poster," "that ridiculous poster," "that hideous new poster"[6] makes no sense: "What has a black lady and a black tree to do with Milton or a fountain pen?" deliberates the boy, who "now at liberty, said it was howling cheek of the painter chap to stick different things on a scarlet sheet and call it an advertisement for something that wasn't there."[7] The blunt rebuff reflects regular reproaches and satires against strong flat colour, and its clever advertising of something absent on Beardsley's posters in the press, decrying the lack of perspective and rendering, choice of two-dimensionality, sparse colour scheme, flat tints and style.[8] The poster's conceptually abstract composition and its sharp contrasts recall both Beardsley's idea of the art of the hoarding and several of his own works.[9] Moreover, the Milton Fountain Pen it advertises is an ambiguous device: it bears the name of a successful American business;

---

3 *Ibid.*, 140.

4 *Ibid.*, 134.

5 *Ibid.*, 125.

6 *Ibid.*, 155, 160, and 140.

7 *Ibid.*, 126.

8 On Beardsley's poster art and negative reactions in the press, see Linda Gertner Zatlin, *Aubrey Beardsley: A Catalogue Raisonné*, 2 vols. (New Haven, Conn.: Yale University Press, 2016), II, 186, 188, 191 and 195.

9 Aubrey Beardsley, "The Art of the Hoarding," *The New Review*, 11 (July 1894): 53–55, collected in A. E. Gallatin, *Aubrey Beardsley: Catalogue of Drawings and Bibliography* (New York: The Grolier Club, 1945), 110–11; repr. in *Decadent Writings of Aubrey Beardsley*, ed. by Sasha Dovzhyk and Simon Wilson, MHRA Critical Texts 10, Jewelled Tortoise 78 (Cambridge: Modern Humanities Research Association, 2022), 188–89.

yet, more than once in the story, it is taken for an allusion to John Milton (and even competes with Shakespeare). Paradoxically, but as subtly as Sharp's adroit plot and fine irony, it shows that meaning should not be taken at face value. It arouses the desire to know more.

Sharp had certainly not penned such a description innocently. Spring of that same year, Beardsley had designed the cover, title page and initial key of her novel *At the Relton Arms* for the publisher John Lane's "Keynotes Series" (Zatlin 847). The story, of a "woman who refuses to marry and consequently loses the man she loves,"[10] belongs to the same pool of Sharp's women faced with life-changing decisions. Later on, in her book of reminiscences, Sharp would compliment both Beardsley and Lane: their fine edition supported her work, and, when her daring plots had faced dire criticism, Lane's "eye for a page and sense of the feel of a book" and Beardsley's cover design redeemed the publication to her critic's eyes.[11] "A New Poster" appeared in the *Yellow Book* after Lane had sacked Beardsley as art editor for his presumed association with the recently arrested Oscar Wilde. Two months after these events, Sharp's piece inevitably carried a veiled meaning. To put forward a black-and-white effete artist, suggestive of Beardsley's posture and artwork, shortly after his forced eviction from his first periodical, reads as an act of daring, even though the story itself – and its central character – are neither bold nor risky.

In fact, on close examination, various contributions to the *Yellow Book* after Beardsley's departure read as oblique defences of avant-garde writing and unconventional art that were the periodical's original aims.[12] Beyond Sharp, several contributions to volume six turn it into

10 Zatlin, *Catalogue Raisonné*, I, 506.

11 See Evelyn Sharp, *Unfinished Adventure: Selected Reminiscences from an Englishwoman's Life* (London: John Lane, 1933), 72. Qtd. by Zatlin, *Catalogue Raisonné*, I, 507.

12 See for instance Évanghélia Stead, "Les perversions du merveilleux dans la petite revue ; ou, comment le Nain Jaune se mua en Yellow Dwarf dans treize volumes jaune et noir," in *Anamorphoses décadentes, Études offertes à Jean de Palacio*, ed. by Isabelle Krzywkowski and Sylvie Thorel-Cailleteau (Paris: Presses de l'Université de Paris-Sorbonne, 2002), 102–39, revised version "Nain Jaune and Yellow Dwarf dans *The Yellow Book*: Un kaléidoscope," in É. Stead, *Sisyphe heureux. Les revues littéraires et artistiques, approches et figures* (Rennes: PUR, 2020), 195–218. In their general introduction to volume six of the *Yellow Book*, Dennis Denisoff and Lorraine Janzen Kooistra state that its editors "struggled to address the backlash against Wilde and Beardsley without eradicating the decadent bourgeois-baiting

a sophisticated reflection of the *Yellow Book*'s own reception, as well as Beardsley's. Two black-and-white drawings by Fred Hyland, for example, both read as imitations of Beardsley's own. First, Hyland's *The Mirror* pictures a woman facing her looking glass by candlelight without the slightest trace of makeup and against Japanese-inspired wallpaper, her hand ostensibly toying an absent piano.[13] It draws its idea from Beardsley's cover design for volume three of the *Yellow Book*, with a woman making herself up at her dressing table by street gaslight (Zatlin 901). Second, Hyland's *Keynotes* – an obvious reference to Lane's series designed by Beardsley – depicts another woman in ostensible outdoor garb playing the piano in a decorated drawing room while the upright case of the instrument assumes the oval shape of a fake mirror.[14] While it evidently refers to Hyland's preceding *Mirror*, it also reads as the reverse of Beardsley's title-page drawing for the first volume of the *Yellow Book* with a woman in a low-necked dress and hat playing the piano in an open field (Zatlin 888). This would later become Beardsley's poster for Singer sewing machines (Zatlin 971) – another "advertisement for something that wasn't there."

Both Hyland drawings represent such material that made young ladies blush and look with temptation and embarrassment at an open *Yellow Book* volume. Such is indeed the subject of a third picture, Gertrude D. Hammond's *The Yellow Book*, also published in volume six.[15] In this bold piece of art and in a clever *mise en abyme*, a man proffers an open volume of the periodical to a young lady in an Aesthetic interior decorated with Japanese fans. The tendered *Yellow Book* volume clearly bears Beardsley's designs on its front and back covers from issues of this very periodical before he was sacked. Beardsley, the *Yellow Book*'s

that had served as the periodical's hallmark of avant-gardism in the past." Kooistra and Denisoff, "*The Yellow Book*: Introduction to Volume 6 (July 1895)," in *The Yellow Book Digital Edition*, ed. by Dennis Denisoff and Lorraine Janzen Kooistra, 2012. *Yellow Nineties 2.0*, Ryerson University Centre for Digital Humanities, 2019, https://1890s.ca/yb-v6-introduction/

13 Fred Hyland, "Two Pictures: I. The Mirror," *The Yellow Book*, 6 (June 1895): 279. See *Yellow Book Digital Edition*, ed. by Denisoff and Kooistra, 2011–14. *Yellow Nineties 2.0*, Ryerson University Centre for Digital Humanities, 2020, https://1890s.ca/yb6-hyland-mirror/

14 Fred Hyland, "Two Pictures: II. Keynotes," *The Yellow Book*, 6 (June 1895): 281. See *Yellow Book Digital Edition*, https://1890s.ca/yb6-hyland-keynotes/

15 Gertrude D. Hammond, "The Yellow Book," *The Yellow Book*, 6 (June 1895): 119. See *Yellow Book Digital Edition*, https://1890s.ca/yb6-hammond-yellow/

recently dismissed art director, has again slipped into the picture. All three works carry a veiled celebration of the absent artist along with the periodical for which he was famous. Sharp's story joins in. Even though her effete Adrian Marks both resembles Beardsley and differs from him, Sharp's story invites us to gauge Beardsley's work in ways rendering visible concealed messages and handlings. In this book, I will often discuss hidden references and messages, details and oblique treatment, as well as the manner in which printed media take them on.

Beardsley's art is not to be taken at face value. It carries devious and playful meanings and reproves overt declarations. It further prompts clever artworks, stories that rejoice in coded messages, and hints at concealed significances. His covert presence in Sharp's "A New Poster" haunts a quarterly from which he had recently been banished. His spirit and stance became prevalent, indeed inescapable, within a year of his appointment as the *Yellow Book*'s art editor. His rapid advancement had been possible through printed books, posters, and the press. Adrian's poster design, obviously styled on Beardsley's, has coined a new currency in graphic art. The "ugly boy"'s glib dismissal of the fictitious poster suggests a new order of intelligence in art. The new poster is an essential part of modern life, with a commercial, tradable appeal for the fictitious artist. Nought distinguishes a dandified from a marketable stance, and Adrian embodies both. Sharp suggests that artistic and social principles are on the move: she herself and her adroit piece are part of the change. Her quip on Cynthia Milton, "mildly eccentric within the limits of conventionality," ironically signals predictable boundaries and limited elasticity within conformism. It recalls the phrase "popular in the better sense of the word," the original aim for the *Yellow Book* as announced in the magazine's first prospectus.[16] Yet boundaries have moved. "A New Poster" indirectly shows how Beardsley's work, aesthetically and thematically bold, exemplified a mould-breaking spirit. It had rocked the toed line to settle on metropolitan streets, straddling both the bohemian and the mainstream, like one of Cynthia's parties: "characteristic neither of Bohemia nor of South Kensington; she amused the one, puzzled the other, and received both."[17] Larger readerships, already Beardsley's own

16 Prospectus of *The Yellow Book*, 1 (Apr 1894). *Yellow Book Digital Edition*, https://1890s.ca/wp-content/uploads/YB1-prospectus.pdf

17 Sharp, "A New Poster," 123.

public, were newly confronted by a cutting-edge audacity, out to test their abilities of interpretation. It is Beardsley's art and persona as an embodiment of these paradoxes that this book seeks to explore.

Five months before his twenty-sixth birthday, Aubrey Vincent Beardsley, born in Brighton on 21 August 1872, died in Menton of tuberculosis on 15 March 1898. In less than six years, he had created over 1,000 drawings, had branded numerous texts with images now inseparable from his name, shaped two periodicals of literature and art, the *Yellow Book* and the *Savoy*, fashioned two series for Lane (the "Keynotes Series" and "Pierrot's Library"), drawn iconic posters, and designed several books. He had launched a style that was to spread throughout Europe and beyond, developed a highly recognisable and dynamic black-and-white technique, and galvanised a new artistic category. His flat, clear-cut graphics reproduced by line-block in print would undermine classic academic rankings of "high" and "low" art. By 1894, his friend Max Beerbohm had facetiously turned his truncated lifespan into an era: "the Beardsley period."[18] The phrase would be honoured in the title of Osbert Burdett's study from the 1920s.[19] His early death froze his mythic status, that of a young mischievous artist. He is still often seen as the representative *enfant terrible* of the English fin de siècle and regular exhibitions of his work since 1966 testify to his lasting appeal.

Already famous during his lifetime, Beardsley faced serious health problems. He fell ill as a child and throughout life knew his time was limited. There is an autobiographical element in much of his work, which speaks to the prospect of his premature end, but which he regularly downplayed with paradox, wit, and riddles. Creating an oeuvre to rival Mantegna's[20] within such a limited life expectancy required a unique daring and focus. Although critical approaches to his work form now

---

18 Max Beerbohm, "Diminuendo," first published as "Be it Cosiness," *The Pageant*, 1 (1896): 230–35, repr. in *The Works of Max Beerbohm, with a Bibliography by John Lane* (London: John Lane, The Bodley Head; New York: Charles Scribner's Sons, 1896), 160.

19 See Osbert Burdett, *The Beardsley Period: An Essay in Perspective* (London: John Lane, 1925).

20 On Beardsley and Mantegna, see Brigid Brophy, *Beardsley and his World* (London: Thames and Hudson, 1976), 44, 82–84; Stephen Calloway, *Aubrey Beardsley* (London: V & A Publications, 1998), 33–37, 53–54, 200–201, 220; and Matthew Sturgis, *Aubrey Beardsley: A Biography* (London: Harper Collins Publishers, 1998), 76, 95, 103.

a long list, many of his images still guard their secrets. This book aims at discussing some of them. Building on extensive knowledge of fin-de-siècle literature and art,[21] it endeavours to break new ground on Beardsley's grotesque oeuvre, aesthetics, and use of media.

I explore here several of Beardsley's significant contributions and lesser-discussed aspects of his art. First, I examine his renewal of the grotesque in the fin de siècle and his revitalisation of marginalia. The book seeks to give substance to his statement "If I am not grotesque, I am nothing" by reference to his grotesque drawings and self-portraits. I discuss for the first time the aesthetic importance of his *Bon-Mots* vignettes, often considered marginal in his oeuvre, and show how this graphic reservoir fostered the artist's liberation from the Pre-Raphaelite style. The book calls on histories of culture and aesthetics. It shows how Beardsley potently revamped the fin-de-siècle grotesque by reworking traditional images beyond recognition and by wittily recycling contemporary motifs; how he borrowed from and transformed iconic pieces of others' work, and how he shaped miniature bibelot books into innovative statements.

Second, I seek to illuminate Beardsley's distinguishing intellectual dandyism. His oeuvre is not limited to his drawings, a few posters and scarcer paintings. He also projected an image of the artist through performance – using his clothing, appearance, stance, and repartee – as a means of expression as vital as his graphic art. He shaped and promoted his images, bolstered by his skills as a writer, designer and raconteur in public space. He joked and provoked, retorted and bantered. "Have you heard of the storm that raged over No. 1?" he wrote to Henry James once the first volume of the *Yellow Book* was out. "Most of the thunderbolts fell on my head. However I enjoyed the excitement immensely."[22] He delighted in scandal and made good use of it, manipulating both an educated readership and a more commercial audience.

Third, I look at how border art and slight or minor creations attracted him, like textual fringes and odd details on monuments. His

21 See Évanghélia Stead, *Le Monstre, le singe et le foetus: Tératogonie et Décadence en Europe fin-de-siècle* (Geneva: Droz, 2004). Published version of a thesis defended in French in 1993 and awarded the 1994 Arconati-Visconti prize.

22 Letter to Henry James, 30 Apr 1894, *The Letters of Aubrey Beardsley*, ed. by Henry Maas, J. L. Duncan and W. G. Good (London: Cassell, 1970), 68.

art made that periphery central in bold ways, often questioning his contemporaries' perceptions of cultural and artistic hierarchies. This book discusses Beardsley's witty gallery of monstrous self-portraits and body art. It considers key pictures of his media performance: printed in periodicals as opposed to books, and as modern photographs expertly referring to medieval cathedrals. A differential comparison to related motifs by other writers and artists reveals his wit and avant-garde *forma mentis*.

Fourth, I seek to understand the under-scrutinised art of Beardsley's performances and show the innovative ways in which he manipulated printed media, and why such a feat was original at the time. "Like most artists who have thought much of popularity, he had an immense contempt for the public; and the desire to kick that public into admiration, and then to kick it for admiring the wrong thing or not knowing why it was admiring, led him into many of his most outrageous practical jokes of the pen," wrote Arthur Symons in the *Fortnightly Review* shortly after Beardsley's death.[23] The book shows how practical jokes also lie in his published portraits. However, his powerful image making sometimes also escaped his control, with dramatised pictures circulating in a manner he would rather have avoided.

Fifth, this book applies a broader perspective to the artist's reception, beyond Britain, with a lens that encompasses the breadth of Western cultural history. Beardsley was a draughtsman whose fame quickly spread beyond British borders: his style had a lasting impact on European and American graphic design, and yet he is still mostly considered in his British context and through British references. I probe Beardsley's presence and reception in Italy, France, the United States, and Germany through periodicals, a vital channel of communication in media-driven modernity, and show how the artist constructed his iconic image both at home and abroad.

Chapter 1, "Grotesque Vignettes and the 'All Margin' Book," extensively discusses the origins, meaning, and uses of Beardsley's grotesque vignettes. It showcases the 126 grotesques decking three tiny volumes of witticisms known as *Bon-Mots*, and contrasts them with the major commission of *Le Morte Darthur*, which Beardsley completed in

23 Arthur Symons, "Aubrey Beardsley," *The Fortnightly Review*, n.s., 69: 377 (1 May 1898): 752–61 (753).

parallel. I argue that the foundational spirit of such an early grotesque nucleus in Beardsley's work has been unduly neglected in scholarship. As a crucible of graphic forms, the grotesques cover a wide range of styles, radically transform motifs, and continually question meaning. Beardsley borrowed from closely contemporaneous artistic styles (Aesthete, Pre-Raphaelite, French), and then subverted them in a way that freed him from their very influence. His remodelling of the earlier grotesque tradition blurs or erases traces of paternity and affiliation beyond recognition. I relate calligraphic grotesques to adjacent textual quips, and highlight the relation between grotesques and naked bodies. This chapter evidences the vignettes' contribution to fin-de-siècle text-and-image relations (wry illustration, literal use of language). It shows how a new print culture bridged print categories and explores the fin-de-siècle idea of a book as "all margin." In a decisive reversal, with Beardsley, marginal creation becomes central.

Using new evidence, Chapter 2, "A Foetal Laboratory and Its Influence," investigates Beardsley's innovative foetus motif, from its earliest advent among the *Bon-Mots* vignettes to the end of his career. While previous scholarship has focused on the biographical origins of this motif, I focus on its aesthetic use and significance: its adaptability, cultural weight, shock value, and its particular resonances in the Decadent *zeitgeist*. By placing it within the Darwinian and biological preoccupations of the period, I show its bearing as a portrait of a generation and its potency as art manifesto. The chapter stresses the motif's graphic malleability, its effect on fin-de-siècle design, and its influence on three artists in Europe: the German Marcus Behmer (foetal variations), Dutch Karel de Nerée tot Babberich (*mises en abyme*), and Frenchman Henri Gustave Jossot (defending caricature as a superior form of deformation art).

Chapter 3, "A Dandy's Portico of Portraits," bridges the grotesque part of Beardsley's vignettes in the *Bon-Mots* and his monstrous self-portraits. Aplomb, caprice, and nerve characterise his dandified attitudes. A comparison between Beardsley and Beau Brummell shows an inherent versatility in his mischievous, disturbing, and progressively scandalous self-representations. Beardsley's dandyism became more intellectual under Baudelaire's influence. The chapter reveals how Beardsley deliberately placed himself at the margin of two related cultural monuments – the book and the cathedral – overturning the relationship between whole and part. I analyse his monstrous self-portraits in the *Yellow Book* and the *Savoy*, highlighting the subtlety of his humour and its manifesto-like potential, extending to typical fin-de-siècle tropes, parody, and replication. I further investigate Frederick H. Evans's photographic portraits of the artist, in which Beardsley posed as Charles Meryon's *stryge*[24] and a cathedral gargoyle, and compare them to the ancient practice of inscribing artists' "signatures" on a cathedral. Beardsley's clever use of Evans's platinum prints led to them becoming icons of fin-de-siècle visual culture, and a form of climactic grotesque expression that heralded body art. This gallery of eccentric depictions, fantasised or ludicrous images of the self, against an explicit background of monstrosity, call *in fine* for a revision of conventional assumptions about beauty and cultural hierarchies.

Chapter 4, "Beardsley Images and the 'Europe of Reviews,'" stresses the exceptional number of press articles devoted to Beardsley and how he worked them into shaping his image, having early grasped the importance of media in an artist's career. It follows Beardsley's images beyond the London scene and discusses his media performance in the Italian magazine *Emporium* as compared to other European periodicals. In this chapter, I differentially compare fine and applied arts journals aimed at the educated reader, mainstream periodicals for the general public, and avant-garde art and literature reviews. Beardsley's self-modelling of images comes to the fore, yet also apocryphal images conveyed by the press, replicating Beardsley's own practices. Considering periodicals in a network allows us to fathom not only an image's or a phrase's origins but also gauge the ever-increasing power of fin-de-siècle media.

Chapter 5, "Paris Performance Alive and Dead," explores Beardsley's reception in French periodicals and the press using new first-hand evidence. Unlike previous studies which have focussed on the textual element of reviews, I also look at the way Beardsley's artworks and portraits were reproduced in periodicals: I believe that images circulate more powerfully than text, make a stronger impact on the imagination

24 Based on Greek and Roman legendary creatures, the French term *strige* or *stryge* refers to the dead or sorcerers and sorceresses returning to suck their victims' blood. Famously used by artist and engraver Charles Meryon, it named one of the Notre-Dame gargoyles, on which more in Chapter 3. See also Fig. 3.9.

and prove crucial in evaluating reception. After recounting Beardsley's multiple connections to France, the chapter follows his reception in Jules Roques's *Le Courrier français*. It looks at the artist's likely deliberate choice of images for the publication as those that had most shocked the English public, his willing adaptability to commercial concerns, and his influence on French artists. Diverging from expected associations between Aesthete reviews either side of the Channel, I show how Beardsley's portrayal in the English *Savoy* was relayed by a large-circulation satirical paper in Montmartre, not the intellectual journals of the Parisian literary avant-garde. The chapter looks at how, after his death, touching tributes mixed with chauvinistic anecdotes borrowed from the English press. It shows that the artist was represented posthumously in ways he himself would not have approved.

This book aspires to show the importance of approaching artists in differential comparison. The concept is pertinently discussed by Ute Heidmann and has emerged from numerous seminars in the University of Lausanne with linguist Jean-Michel Adam, Hellenist and anthropologist Claude Calame, and philosopher Silvana Borutti.[25] It is myth-, genre-, and discourse-based and mainly applies to textual comparisons but I have often used it in my own work on images, reading books and prints as cultural objects, and the reception of major texts in visual and print culture.[26] Although this book is not a comprehensive study of Beardsley's global work, I stress the relations between his artwork approached in varying media and the spirit of the time. By showcasing his innovative approach to art, I analyse Beardsley's impact on a new artistic vocabulary and themes. I discuss his wide-ranging inspiration in differentiated contexts and also consider his influence on the work of fellow artists at the time. While not a monograph focused on a single man, this book's comparative and European perspective offers an approach applicable to other artists' work with analogous international appeal and impact

25 Ute Heidmann, "Pour un comparatisme différentiel," in *Le Comparatisme comme approche critique*, ed. by Anne Tomiche in cooperation with Kelly Morckel, Pauline Macadré, Léa Lebourg-Leportier *et al.*, Rencontres. Série Littérature générale et comparée (Paris: Classiques Garnier, 2017), 31–58.

26 See for instance Evanghelia Stead, "Introduction", in *Reading Books and Prints as Cultural Objects*, ed. by E. Stead, New Directions in Book History (Cham: Palgrave/ Macmillan, 2018), 1–30; and Evanghelia Stead, *Goethe's "Faust I" Outlined: Moritz Retzsch's Prints in Circulation*, Library of the Written Word. The Industrial World (Leiden: Brill, 2023).

on graphics and aesthetics. Its interdisciplinary methodology – bringing together art, literature, comparative studies, print culture and periodical studies – could easily adapt to other cases. The emphasis is on processes rather than finished products and fixed objects. I stress flux rather than stasis, interaction rather than stability and invariability, and procedures rather than Beardsley's finished pieces. In Beardsley's case, even paradox and oxymoron are exceptionally productive. His work aspired to a synthesis and activated the imagination. To re-read Beardsley is to revive him. How did he ingeniously break the mould of Victorianism while – in Sharp's words and through her fictional character – still remain acceptable to the "mildly eccentric within the limits of conventionality"?

1. Grotesque Vignettes and the "All Margin" Book

Barely twenty in late 1892, Aubrey Beardsley was hard at work on his first major assignment. He was to fully illustrate Thomas Malory's medieval narrative *Le Morte Darthur* and his undertaking pivoted on the Pre-Raphaelite style he would master, transform, and transgress. However, the artist quickly found the task both arduous and tedious and, in order to cheer him up, his publisher, Joseph Malaby Dent, further commissioned him to decorate three tiny volumes of puns and witticisms: the debonair, often humorous, gibes known as *bon mots* since the seventeenth century. The set of sketches Beardsley produced for this commission might seem marginal, but in this chapter I show how they became a seminal graphic laboratory for the emerging artist. These little grotesques – a multifarious combination of figures with blended body parts, hybrid animals, mythical creatures, foetuses, peacock feathers, one-eyed spiders, and endless other curious amalgamations and disturbing juxtapositions – almost form an artwork in their own right. They were small and sat on the edge of insignificant jokes. Yet, the visual and graphic marginality of such a peripheral creation gave Beardsley the opportunity to use the vignettes as a kind of breeding tank for forms that would occasionally feed into his "great" works.

The vignettes point to a significant turn in his work and prove to be a genuine crucible of graphic impulse as different styles are tried out, parodied, and revamped. This chapter will explore how Beardsley morphed and repurposed motifs launched by his contemporaries, such as the Pre-Raphaelites, Odilon Redon, and James McNeill Whistler, granting them new life in grotesque form. He inaugurated his "entirely new method of drawing," at times "founded on Japanese art but quite original in the main," and at other times "fantastic impressions treated

 https://doi.org/10.11647/OBP.0413.01

in the finest possible outline with patches of 'black blot.'"[1] The vignettes boldly engage in linear drawings enhanced by black-and-white contrasts. They play, alter, and convert. They are at once unnerving, erotic, and humorous. They prove to be that unique touchstone of "the smallest space and the fewest means" with which Beardsley achieved "the most."[2]

Beardsley usurped the earlier grotesque tradition to transmute it into something that felt shockingly contemporary. He twisted calligraphy and creatively explored scrawls. He morphed natural motifs into artistic riddles. He treated bodies like books and ornamented them with grotesque vignettes. He invented an ironic and wry way of illustrating, connecting his vignettes to literal meanings, nonsensical jokes, and verbal twists, skilfully manipulating words and expressions. Expanding into new print territories, his vignettes spread in the illustrated press. He even created a book genre his publisher would further capitalise on, parallel to the bibelot booklets cherished at the time. Compared to the medieval and Renaissance grotesques, which famously were peripheral ornaments in the margins of devotional missals and breviaries, his *Bon-Mots* vignettes introduced a style of book that was *all margin*. This chapter will show how, in an aesthetic reversal of order and hierarchy, the margin came to be crucial, predominant, and fundamental.

Birth and Critical Background of an Unexplored Set

The volumes that Beardsley illustrated, entitled *Bon-Mots*, were edited by Walter Jerrold within a year in 1893–94. Each of them featured the work of two authors. In volume one, Sydney Smith (1771–1845), founding editor of the *Edinburgh Review*, Anglican clergyman and liberal reformer, successful London preacher and lecturer, and author of a rhyming recipe for salad dressing, joined Richard Brinsley Sheridan (1751–1816), Irish satirist, politician, famed playwright, poet, profligate social climber, and womaniser. In volume two, Charles Lamb (1775–1834), the melancholic wit, essayist, and poet best known for his *Essays of Elia*, met with Douglas William Jerrold (1803–57), a master of epigram and retorts, professional

1 Letter to E. J. Marshall, [autumn 1892], *The Letters of Aubrey Beardsley*, ed. by Henry Maas, J. L. Duncan, and W. G. Good (London: Cassell, 1970), 34; letter to A. W. King, midnight 9 Dec [1892], *ibid.*, 37.

2 Osbert Burdett, *The Beardsley Period: An Essay in Perspective* (London: John Lane, 1925), 103.

journalist, *Punch* contributor, yet now forgotten dramatist. Samuel Foote (1720–77), comic playwright, actor, and theatre manager known as "the English Aristophanes," who had turned even the loss of his leg into a source for comedy, opened volume three. He teamed up with Theodore Edward Hook (1788–1841), composer and man of letters, best known for the Berners Street hoax, which he recalled in detail in their joint booklet. All texts, often of just a few lines, belong by nature to the periphery of these authors' works: they are spirited rejoinders from conversational sport or utterances of marksmanship that hit the bull's eye. Their droll anecdotes and amusing chitchat belong to the outer rim of *belles-lettres*, offered in these volumes for easy consumption to be readily repeated *ad nauseam*.

In autumn 1892, Beardsley wrote to his former headmaster at Brighton Grammar School, Ebenezer J. Marshall, who had founded *Past & Present*, the first school magazine ever published in England. Marshall had supported young Beardsley's artistic ambitions and published the artist's earliest drawings in *Past & Present* (Zatlin 135–44). Beardsley was anxious to impress Marshall in his letter, boasting of his feats with publishers, newly secured independence from salaried work, and the praise he had recently earned in Paris. He described the vignettes in a few brisk words and characteristic hurried style:

> Just now I am finishing a set of sixty grotesques for three volumes of *Bon-Mots* soon to appear. They are very tiny little things, some not more than an inch high, and the pen strokes to be counted on the fingers. I have been ten days over them, and have just got a cheque for £15 for my work – my first art earnings.[3]

The fledgling artist needed to take every opportunity to earn some money and build his reputation. He was proud to advertise his first profits, but stresses the triviality of these "very tiny little things." These lines immediately follow a description of the sumptuous grandeur of *Le Morte Darthur* commission. The latter description, however, is longer only by three-and-a-half lines. Even though Beardsley regards his vignettes as throwaway sketches, tossed off in ten days for a paycheck, the distinction between important and unimportant remains precariously balanced. Could the pre-eminence of *Le Morte Darthur* be questioned by the grotesques – if so, how and why?

---

3 Letter to Marshall, [autumn 1892], *The Letters of Aubrey Beardsley*, 34.

The *Bon-Mots* vignettes were indeed of Lilliputian size. The original drawings, some of which are minute (among the known originals, one of the smallest measures 3.8 x 5.4 cm and the largest 18.3 x 11.7 cm),[4] were often greatly reduced to fit into earmarked nooks and crannies in the printed versions. Ordinary copies of the booklets did not exceed 13.5 x 8.13 cm, and the large-paper edition, limited to one hundred copies, measured 16.4 x 9.9 cm. Whether ordinary or deluxe, the pages themselves, a standard 192 per volume, display a uniform printed surface never exceeding 9.85 x 5.3 cm. Reproduction further harmed their many subtleties. When printed, the vignettes seldom took up an entire page. Diminutive details became hard to decipher. Beardsley's work had greatly benefitted from line-block printing, i.e., reproduction of lines and dots against white background with no intermediate tones. The line-block process was cost-effective, fast and reliable in terms of printing text and image together, but had two shortcomings: it sometimes thickened fine lines and downgraded in places the compact blacks of Beardsley's designs. Several of the *Bon-Mots* grotesques fell victim to such processes. Layouts were not part of the artist's remit either. Although opinions vary,[5] Beardsley probably never saw proofs, Jerrold having assumed the task of checking them himself.

Initially the grotesques went relatively unadvertised in the *Bon-Mots*. First editions touted the title *Bon-Mots* in gilt capitals on their cream covers followed by the paired authors' names (Fig. 1.1a). The prominence and credit belonged to the text not the images. "Grotesques by Aubrey Beardsley" featured in small reddish type, next to a similarly coloured ornament of a fool with bauble and under a gilt peacock feather. Beardsley's renown having further expanded posthumously, it was only in 1904 that reissued volumes gave the lead to the artist: "with Grotesques by Aubrey Beardsley" girdled a cherub with two lilies (*Child Holding a Stalk of Lilies*, Zatlin 749, see Fig. 1.15a–b). Centrally placed on the cover, it ousted the authors whose names now took refuge on the

4 The smallest may be *Capped Head Gazing at a Fish* (Zatlin 730, see Fig. 1.13c), one of the largest is *Winged Baby in a Top Hat leading a Dog* (Zatlin 797, see Fig. 2.8c).

5 Linda Gertner Zatlin, *Beardsley, Japonisme, and the Perversion of the Victorian Ideal* (Cambridge: Cambridge University Press, 1997), 58–59, and Zatlin, *Aubrey Beardsley: A Catalogue Raisonné*, 2 vols. (New Haven, Conn.: Yale University Press, 2016), I, 424, does not grant him any authority, either of plan or layout. See *contra*, Malcolm Easton, *Aubrey and the Dying Lady: A Beardsley Riddle* (London: Secker and Warburg, 1972), 176, on the *Bon-Mots*: "The publisher allowed him every liberty. He could decorate the page as he wished."

narrow spines (Fig. 1.1b). The grotesque graphic core had become the book's most prominent feature.

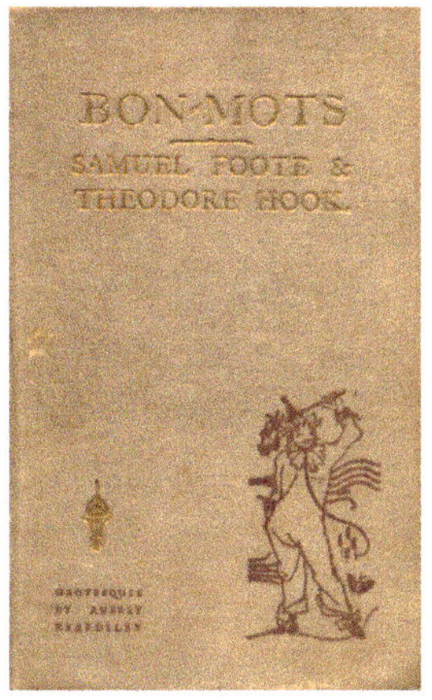

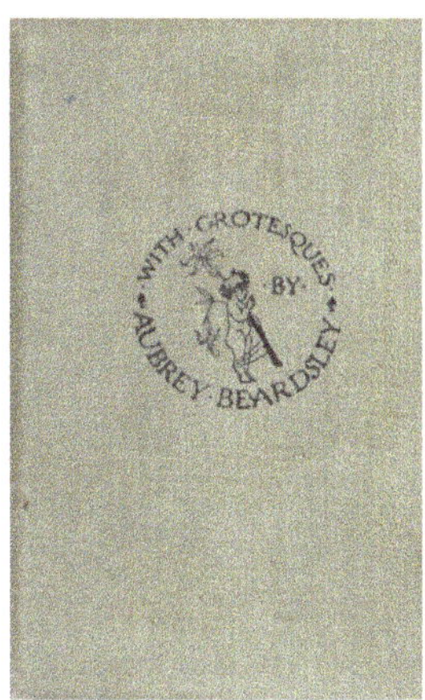

Fig. 1.1 a–b Successive *Bon-Mots* covers. 1.1a *Bon-Mots of Samuel Foote and Theodore Hook*, original edition with gilt title, peacock feather and fool with bauble. Courtesy of MSL coll., Delaware; 1.1b Later edition of the same promoting "Grotesques by Aubrey Beardsley." Author's collection

The lack of recognition of the vignettes in Beardsley's lifetime was partly a result of issues around the printing and reproduction of such small images, which hindered appreciation of their detailed features. In 1896, when Leonard Smithers considered including one in *Fifty Drawings*, Beardsley alerted him to the difficulty of reproducing its tenuous lines: "It will I am afraid make a very bad block as the line is so thin and broken."[6] Another note to Smithers further discouraged him from publishing the vignette: "As to the *Bon-Mot*, it is such a trifle."[7] In the end, the vignette (subject unknown) did not find its way into the volume.

Such remarks from Beardsley may well have taken a toll on these drawings' legacy: these "trifles" have been largely overlooked in scholarship. Even today, Beardsley is known as the art editor of the *Yellow Book* and the *Savoy*, and as the illustrator of *Le Morte Darthur*, *Salome*, and *The Rape of the Lock*. The foundational spirit of his early grotesques has remained in the shadows of his work. Brian Reade was a first exception in his 1967 *Beardsley*, which included a striking selection of eighty-seven untitled grotesques in sizeable reproductions and arresting contrast on the stark white pages of his

6 Letter to Smithers, [ca. 5 Sept 1896], *The Letters of Aubrey Beardsley*, 160.
7 Letter to the same, [ca. 20 Oct 1896], *ibid.*, 186.

catalogue.[8] Twenty years later, Ian Fletcher would comment on a few of them, followed in 1995 by Chris Snodgrass who focussed attention on some of Beardsley's recurring motifs: puppets, foetuses, Pierrot, Harlequin, and Clown, and grotesque dandies.[9] My own work and 1993 full catalogue (published in 2002) have remained unknown to Anglophone specialists and French connoisseurs alike.[10] The three volumes of *Bon-Mots* stayed "virtually undiscussed," as Linda Gertner Zatlin has put it.[11]

From one publication to the next, the total number of the vignettes varied, as in the figures given by Aymer Vallance and Albert Eugene Gallatin. Vallance presented them as "208 grotesques and other ornaments in the three volumes," totalling with the title page and cover decorations 211 designs.[12] Gallatin's catalogue, limited to a small global description, provided neither titles nor an account.[13] It counted 127 originals and two unused extras.[14] In turn, *The Letters of Aubrey Beardsley*, although referring to Gallatin, reckoned there are 130 drawings, described as "mostly small grotesques and vignettes."[15] The year 1998 marked the centenary of Beardsley's death, and the Victoria & Albert Museum celebrated it with an exhibition curated by Stephen Calloway, which toured in Japan. Princeton University Library commemorated the centenary more discreetly with its fine collection of Beardsleyana. At least thirteen publications were brought out, but several failed to offer new insights; this led Snodgrass to eagerly speculate if this was

8 Brian Reade, *Beardsley* (London: Studio Vista, 1967); revised ed. (Woodridge: Antique Collectors' Club, 1987), fig. 165–251 (hereafter abbreviated as Reade).

9 Ian Fletcher, *Aubrey Beardsley* (Boston: Twayne Publishers, 1987), 53–56. Chris Snodgrass, *Aubrey Beardsley, Dandy of the Grotesque* (New York, Oxford: Oxford University Press, 1995), 35, 165–66, 177–78, 181–84, 190, 198–99, 230–32.

10 The vignette catalogue was completed as an appendix to my 1993 PhD on monsters and the fin de siècle with descriptive titles. It was published, thanks to Paul Edwards, in a special issue of the Jarry-dedicated and confidential journal *L'Étoile absinthe* as "Les grotesques d'Aubrey Beardsley (*Bon-Mots*)," *L'Étoile-absinthe. Les Cahiers iconographiques de la Société des amis d'Alfred Jarry*, 95–96 (2002): 5–47, 132 fig., http://alfredjarry.fr/amisjarry/fichiers_ea/etoile_absinthe_095_96reduit.pdf

11 Zatlin, *Beardsley, Japonisme, and the Perversion of the Victorian Ideal*, 199.

12 "List of Drawings by Aubrey Beardsley, compiled by Aymer Vallance," in Robert Ross, *Aubrey Beardsley, with Sixteen Full-Page Illustrations and a Revised Iconography by Aymer Vallance* (London: John Lane, 1909), no. 65.

13 Albert Eugene Gallatin, *Aubrey Beardsley: Catalogue of Drawings and Bibliography* (New York: The Grolier Club, 1945), 37, nos. 642–771. Despite the high number, this corresponds to a short global entry.

14 *Ibid.*, 37–38, nos. 772–73.

15 *The Letters of Aubrey Beardsley*, 161.

"Tethering or Untethering a Victorian Icon?"[16] The grotesques were again outweighed by major drawings.

It wasn't until Zatlin's *catalogue raisonné* that we had a full reproduction of the grotesques, together with records, locations, measurements of the originals, uses, reuses, and commentary. Zatlin also provided names for each vignette, which I use in this book. Zatlin's project was first announced in 1997, and finally published in 2016.[17] This major accomplishment at last granted the grotesques the space and attention they deserved as individual creations. Using Zatlin as my base, this chapter offers a critical appraisal of these neglected drawings, exploring their significance in terms of the development of Beardsley's style and their impact on the artistic *zeitgeist*. Although trivial and marginal, I argue that such a body of work offers a rich insight into the artist's budding styles. They form a test bed for experimentations, freeing Beardsley from imposing motifs of the time, allowing him to modernise older grotesques, and representing new ideas on illustration, the use of the body in artworks, and the idea of the book itself.

Winning Freedom

Beardsley's minutiae were conceived on the side-lines of the two books that would establish him as one of the most talented and daring artists of the moment: Malory's *Le Morte Darthur* (1893–94), published by Dent; and the English translation of Oscar Wilde's *Salome* (1894), published by Lane. Both these publishers placed restrictions on Beardsley's creativity. Dent wanted *Le Morte Darthur* to rival Kelmscott Press's popular medievalism. The book was meant to be an exercise in imitation, offering readers photomechanical reproductions instead of costly originals under a sumptuous cover. Beardsley had wanted to translate *Salomé* into

16 Chris Snodgrass, "Beardsley Scholarship at His Centennial: Tethering or Untethering a Victorian Icon?," *English Literature in Transition*, 42:4 (1999): 363–99, reviewing thirteen titles. See also Anna Gruetzner Robins, "Demystifyng Aubrey Beardsley," *Art History*, 22 (1999): 440–44, discussing the following five: Stephen Calloway, *Aubrey Beardsley* (London: V & A Publications, 1998); Zatlin, *Beardsley, Japonisme, and the Perversion of the Victorian Ideal*; Jane Haville Desmarais, *The Beardsley Industry. The Critical Reception in England and France, 1893–1914* (Aldershot: Ashgate, 1998); Peter Raby, *Aubrey Beardsley and the Nineties* (London: Collins & Brown, 1998); Matthew Sturgis, *Aubrey Beardsley: A Biography* (London: Harper Collins Publishers, 1998).

17 Zatlin, *Catalogue Raisonné*, I, 421–83.

English from Wilde's original French that he had read and loved. His first plate on the play, published in *The Studio*, has a French quote from Wilde's initial published script (Zatlin 265). Instead, Alfred Douglas was entrusted with the word translation, and, furthermore, Lane chose to censor Beardsley's skilful yet shocking plates, which the artist intended as a daring visual translation.[18] Such restrictions and rebukes, also noticeable in Lucian's *True History*, issued by Lawrence and Bullen in 1894,[19] quickly wearied Beardsley.

The *Bon-Mots* grotesques formed in counterpart an untethered space of artistic freedom. Sketched in quick strokes but requiring several working sessions in 1892 and 1893, they would open the door to artistic experimentation and fuel Beardsley's graphic variety. The text featured in *Bon-Mots* lacked plot, discernible arrangement, introduction, or conclusion, and fostered the possibility for inventive and prospective design, amalgamation, and innovation. In this way, the vignettes were exonerated from the constraint of a text to respect, since the textual content was itself random, unhindered, and liberally delivered. They rarely related to the quips they peppered. Far from being literal illustrations, they were consonant reinterpretations of clever (or less clever) lines through visual means.

As little conundrums squared on tiny spaces, the *Bon-Mots* drawings engage interpretation and meaning as much as they short-circuit them and leave them suspended. As Fletcher suggests, they are apart from Beardsley's more famous work because they are inexplicable: "many operate as emblems requiring and at the same time defying interpretation in a way found elsewhere in the work, but never perhaps at such an extreme and so consistently."[20] They unquestionably form the largest and most diverse set of fin-de-siècle vignettes, and authenticate key statements by the artist. The press had christened Beardsley "An Apostle of the Grotesque,"[21] but he parodied the apostolic ideal. Instead of urging viewers to perfection,

18 See further on this, Évanghélia Stead, "*Encor Salomé*: entrelacs du texte et de l'image de Wilde et Beardsley à Mossa et Merlet," in *Dieu, la chair et les livres. Une approche de la Décadence*, ed. by S. Thorel-Cailleteau (Paris: Honoré Champion, 2000), 421–57, fig. 1–12, and "Triptyque de livres sur Salomé," revised and enlarged version in Évanghélia Stead, *La Chair du livre: matérialité, imaginaire et poétique du livre fin-de-siècle*, Histoire de l'imprimé (Paris, PUPS, 2012), 157–208, particularly 160–61, 163–64, 166–77.

19 On this, see Chapter 2.

20 Fletcher, *Aubrey Beardsley*, 54.

21 "An Apostle of the Grotesque," *The Sketch*, 9:115 (10 Apr 1895): 561–62.

sanctity, spiritual energy, and a holy life, he took great pleasure in confusing them with provocative drawings and mischievous titles. As the *enfant terrible* of the British fin de siècle, he inverted Saint Paul's proclamation "If I have the gift of prophecy and can fathom all mysteries and all knowledge, and if I have a faith that can move mountains, but do not have love, I am nothing" (1 Cor. 13, 2). While Saint Paul was nothing without love, Beardsley claimed, "If I am not grotesque, I am nothing."[22]

In this avowedly grotesque and early nucleus, free of textual imperatives, young Beardsley tested, formed, and enlarged a new artistic idiom, taking up a mock-apostolic mission. As I explore in the following section, he broke free from the Pre-Raphaelite influence, and toyed with Aesthetic symbols. He challenged their strongly artistic stasis. He borrowed from Japanese prints and appropriated doodles from past centuries. He adopted customary, misshapen forms (satyrs and aegipans), and implemented realistic drawings, quickly turning to his black-on-white compositions. His grotesque language bounced from fauns and imps to spidery fancies and arabesques to blur forms, combine, mix, and blend them: organs, genitals, breasts, ink stains, scrawls, bristles and hair, forked tongues, squiggly appendages, wings. The difficulty of giving his creations an accurate title is genuine, yet the renewal of grotesque certain: disturbingly physical, subversively erotic and ambiguous, they usher in fin-de-siècle symbols and manifestos such as the foetus vignettes analysed in Chapter 2. They form an altogether vital contribution to the renewal of the grotesque at the end of the nineteenth century, springing from the mobility and variety of patterns without head or tail.

Hijacked Innovation

Beardsley's vignettes in the *Bon-Mots* have a distinctive, incisive, impertinent spirit that hijacks existing motifs through pastiche and parody. Beardsley was proud, for example, of the impact of Japanese art on his graphics. He had just shown specimens of his new drawings to Puvis de Chavannes, then President of the Salon des Beaux-Arts in Paris, and reported to Marshall that Puvis liked them. *Past & Present*, his former school's magazine, had been prompt to broadcast Puvis's remark: "A

22 Arthur H. Lawrence, "Mr. Aubrey Beardsley and His Work," *The Idler*, 11 (Mar 1897): 198.

young British artist who does amazing work."[23] The comment referred to Beardsley's spatial illusion, characteristic of Japanese artworks, and the spidery lines that gave his compositions new verve. Likewise Beardsley challenged the creations of his innovative contemporaries. He appropriated Pre-Raphaelite motifs, the work of Walter Crane and his illustrated books, Whistler's hallmark butterfly (a symbol, seal and a signature all in one), typical images of the Aesthetic movement (the sunflower, the lily, the peacock feather), and even Redon's lithographs, as the following examples show.

Beardsley ably moved from traditional mythical themes to medieval depictions, leitmotifs of the Aesthetic movement, and fin-de-siècle patterns, all of which he altered in his signature style. A synthetic view of satyrs (Fig. 1.2a–g) shows how he used mythological motifs close to nature. He had peppered *Le Morte Darthur* vignettes and its dropped initials with cavorting fauns, evil terminal gods and voluptuous she-fauns smiling ambiguously. In the first volume of *Bon-Mots*, fauns and satyrs reappear as an especially predictable motif. A pouting and frowning Pan, holding a syrinx in his hairy paw, leans against a tree in *Pan Asleep*, named after Frederick H. Evans (Fig. 1.2a, Zatlin 710). Another, seen from the rear, rests against a tree stump, again with panpipes, in *Pan down by the River* (Fig. 1.2b, Zatlin 715, indeed "a sentimentalised version of the satyr in *Le Morte Darthur*").[24] A herm figure grins at us with a small faun perched on his shoulder, his belly covered by flowing fleece in *Terminal God Listening to a Satyr* (Fig. 1.2c, Zatlin 719). An evidently female version leaps around raising a trumpet in *Dancing Satyr*, a title that leaves gender unspecified (Fig. 1.2d, Zatlin 735). Another – bald, weary, and club-footed – closes the enigmatic parade of a skeleton in fancy dress and a sick man in an armchair, all perched on a peacock's feather in *Two Grotesques Approaching a Man with Gout* (Fig. 1.2e, Zatlin 736). An emaciated specimen, his pelvis covered in long hair, looks pensively at us atop a cliff in *Aged Satyr Seated on a Cliff* (Fig. 1.2f, Zatlin 757). And a stylish aegipan with a shepherd's staff collects rain or spring water in a vessel in *Faun with a Shepherd's Crook and a Bowl* (Fig. 1.2g, Zatlin 784).

23 Letter to E. J. Marshall, [ca. autumn 1892], *The Letters of Aubrey Beardsley*, 34. *Past & Present* clipping pasted into a 9 Dec [1892] letter to A. W. King, *ibid.*, 37: "*Un jeune artiste anglais qui fait des choses étonnantes.*"

24 Zatlin, *Catalogue Raisonné*, I, 438.

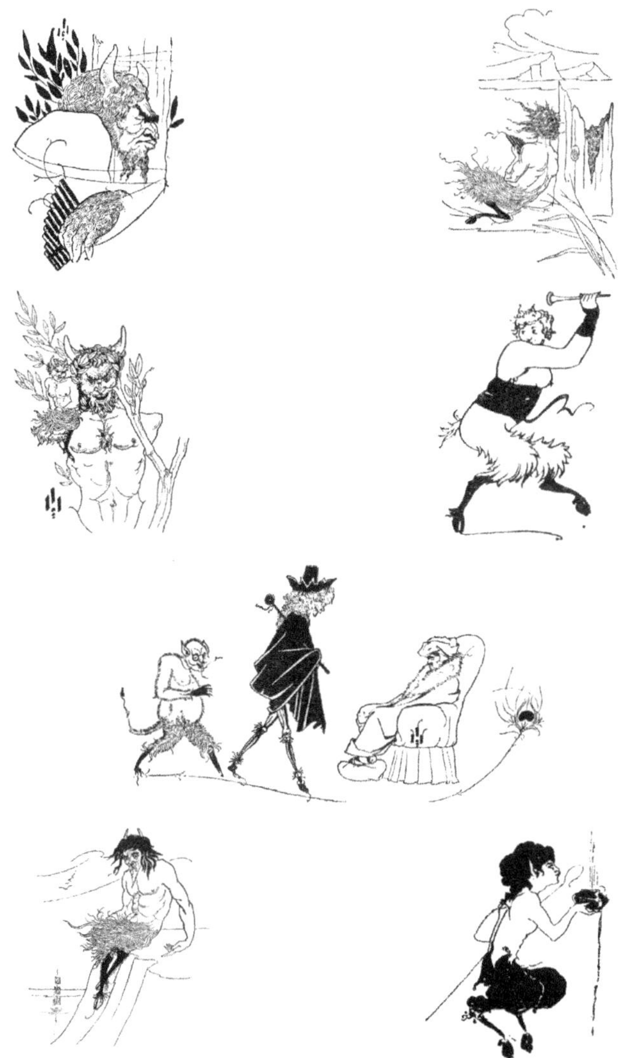

Fig. 1.2a–g Aubrey Beardsley, *Bon-Mots* grotesques based on satyrs. 1.2a *Pan Asleep*, BM-SS:51; 1.2b *Pan down by the River*, BM-SS:67, BM-LJ:141 (R<); 1.2c *Terminal God Listening to a Satyr*, BM-SS:79; 1.2d *Dancing Satyr*, BM-SS:117 (half-title vignette for "Sheridan"); 1.2e *Two Grotesques Approaching a Man with Gout*, BM-SS:119 (head vignette for "Bon-Mots of Sheridan"), BM-LJ:182 (head vignette); 1.2f *Aged Satyr Seated on a Cliff*, BM-SS:172, BM-LJ:99 (full page, R>); 1.2g *Faun with a Shepherd's Crook and a Bowl*, BM-LJ:108, BM-FH:62. PE coll.

The grotesque substance of these inveterate hosts of pastures, woods, and grottoes is heightened by the artist's graphic skills: abundant hair, wiry and flimsy lines, thin parallel or wavy strokes, dotted streaks, a towering unbalanced composition or the nascent stylisation of black shapes against white backgrounds offer different versions of a well-worn motif. Yet, although Beardsley varied and reworked the faun images in the *Bon-Mots*, he seems to have grown tired of them. Only three from volume one (Zatlin 715, 736, 757), all rather elaborate, are reused in volume two, yet only once, as if their grotesque essence and significance had already been exhausted. The very last, invented for volume two, is again reused only once in the third volume. Their limited usage suggests their restrained appeal on Beardsley's imagination.

Beardsley gleaned more long-lasting material from the Middle Ages, so cherished by the Pre-Raphaelites. There are numerous recurring figures in the *Bon-Mots* wrapped in loose cloaks, with faces hidden beneath a hood or cowl of medieval inspiration, which share a close resemblance to Edward Burne-Jones's androgynous pages or William Morris's similarly mysterious figures (Fig. 1.3a–g). With flesh bursting their tight-fitting garments, Beardsley's creations reveal strained joints and limbs terminating in thin, unpredictable arabesques. A typical example is *One-armed Man with a Sword* (Fig. 1.3a, Zatlin 693), which adorned the first volume's half-title, perhaps a playful allusion to the contents' slender or imaginary structure. *Seated Figure Tending a Steaming Cauldron* (Fig. 1.3b, Zatlin 754) may also be a wry comment on the volume's contents. Others, like the skeletal hairy monkey following a veiled man in *Grotesque Reaching for a Cloaked Figure* (Fig. 1.3c, Zatlin 738), may carry an armful of flowers as in *Pierrot Carrying Sunflowers* (Fig. 1.3d, Zatlin 707), or hold at arm's length a head dripping with blood as in *Cloaked Man Holding a Bleeding Head* (Fig. 1.3e, Zatlin 712). When they turn around, they disclose grimacing faces, covered in wrinkles. They combine with more modern figures, clowns and Pierrots, or become themselves jesters in small acts performed in silence, as in *Two Figures Conversing* (Zatlin 753) and *Jester with a Head on a String and a Disembodied Hand Holding a Cupid* (Fig. 1.3f, Zatlin 744), which have components in common.

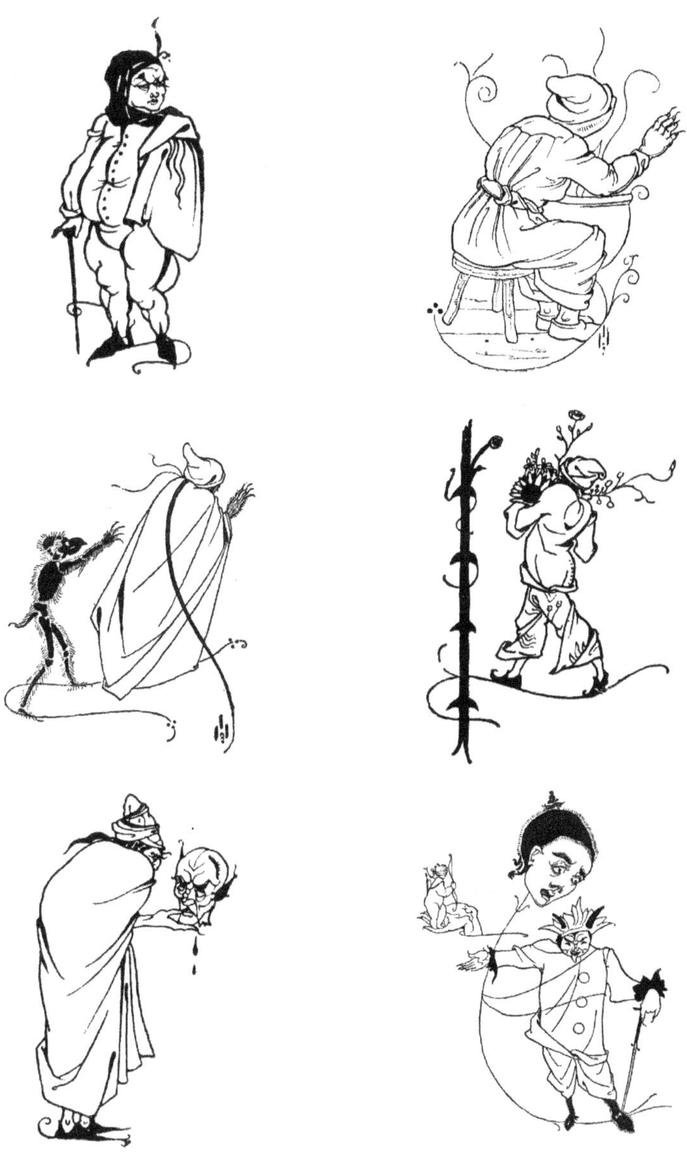

Fig. 1.3a–f Aubrey Beardsley, Medieval grotesques in the *Bon-Mots*. 1.3a *One-armed Man with a Sword*, BM-SS:1 (half-title vignette), BM-FH:38; 1.3b *Seated Figure Tending a Steaming Cauldron*, BM-SS:165, BM-FH:89 (full page, R>); 1.3c *Grotesque Reaching for a Cloaked Figure*, BM-SS:123; 1.3d *Pierrot Carrying Sunflowers*, BM-SS:44, BM-FH:174 (R<); 1.3e *Cloaked Man Holding a Bleeding Head*, BM-SS:58, BM-LJ:147 (full page, R>); 1.3f *Jester with a Head on a String and a Disembodied Hand Holding a Cupid*, BM-SS:139, BM-LJ:72 (R<). PE coll.

Pierrot and Jester (Fig. 1.4, Zatlin 711), which is reproduced three times in the *Bon-Mots* in two different sizes, enacts a scene of inexhaustible signification as Chris Snodgrass has noted. There are unlimited conceivable interactions between the clown on the left, the exotic bird he is presenting, the puppet head protruding from the larger clown-puppet on the right, and this very clown-puppet to the point that "the limits of the drawing's joke have become almost impossible to define." As Snodgrass suggests, uncertainty as to whether the grotesques are alive, puppets, or even life's puppets dominates. The joke rebounds to suggest to the viewer "the meeting of multiple mirror images, pet to pet, pet to puppet, puppet to puppet." We find ourselves at a loss: "Or is the joke that they [pets and puppets] *recognize* this truth, but they are nevertheless compelled to play out the game? Or that even though *they* recognize it, *we* do not, and thus do not understand that *we* are puppets looking at puppets looking at puppets? And on and on. The boundary line between fake and real, artificial and natural, frivolous and serious, are so confused that there is no way to stop the meaning from sliding almost endlessly."[25] Beardsley's love of theatre and music permeates these scenes that smack of drama, comedy, and farce. He himself performed at a very young age in drawing-room theatricals with his future actress sister Mabel. Here he hijacks and twists Pre-Raphaelite motifs by setting them in small arrangements and implausible combinations.

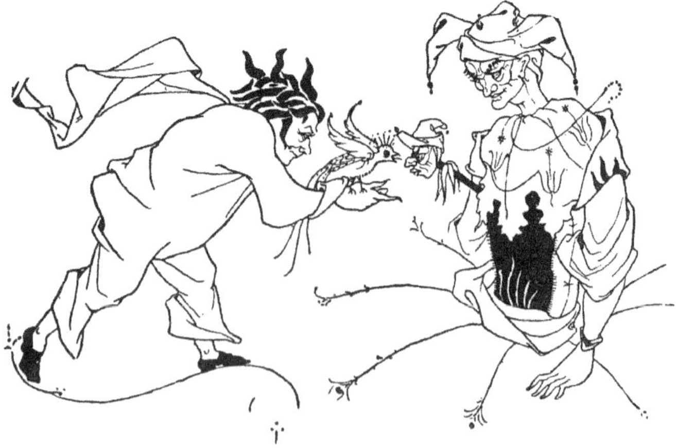

Fig. 1.4 Aubrey Beardsley, *Pierrot and Jester*, BM-SS:55, BM-LJ:132 (R<), BM-LJ:177. PE coll.

25 Snodgrass, *Aubrey Beardsley, Dandy of the Grotesque*, 166, author's emphasis.

The peacock feather, with its combination of barbs, filaments, and ocellus, is another recurring image lifted from the Aesthetic store and twisted (Fig. 1.5a–c). Its power lies in its contradictions: it is from the natural world, and yet it is also a symbol of sophisticated fashion. By 1878, it had made its way into the most elaborate interiors, such as Whistler's Peacock Room at 49 Prince's Gate in London, decorated for collector Frederick Leyland, which Beardsley had visited. In the *Bon-Mots*, the peacock feather hovers over grotesque scenes: during the painful extraction of a tooth, treated in Japanese fashion (*A Tooth Extraction*, Zatlin 697), it floats, underlined by a double arabesque, in the background of the scene like a bird or an insect (Fig. 1.5a). As the headpiece for "Bon-Mots of Sydney Smith" in volume one, the absurd episode projects surreal meaning onto the section contents.

When a stylish lady smilingly walks towards the viewer in *Woman in Evening Dress and a Fur-collared Jacket* (Zatlin 739), a triple peacock feather underlines the deceptive perspective (Fig. 1.5b): the black dado strip adorning the wall pierces her bodice to form a high belt, yet also a slightly shifted dado fragment penetrating her coat. Both arrangements suggest that the peacock feather rules instability and the deflection of forms and plans, as if the ocellus's iridescence irradiated the composition to undermine use of space and meaning and trick perception.

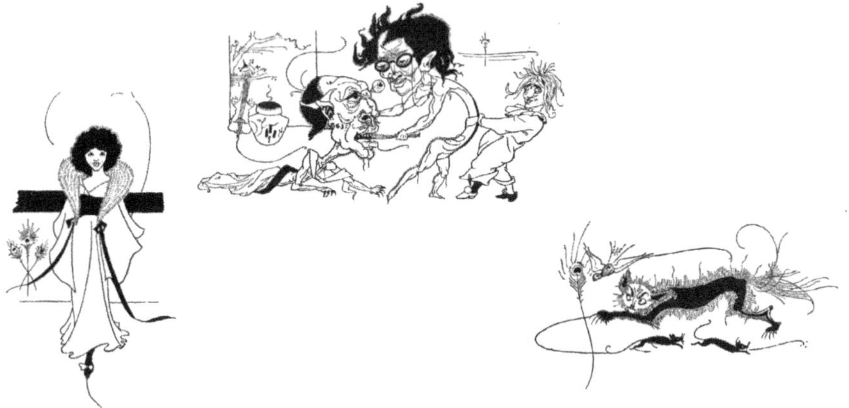

Fig. 1.5a–c Aubrey Beardsley, *Bon-Mots* grotesques involving a peacock feather. 1.5a *A Tooth Extraction*, BM-SS:17 (head vignette for "Bon-Mots of Sydney Smith"), BM-LJ:120 (R<); 1.5b *Woman in Evening Dress and a Fur-collared Jacket*, BM-SS:126, BM-LJ:1 (half-title vignette, R<), BM-LJ:87 (full page, R>); 1.5c *Cat Chasing a Bird and Large Mice*, BM-SS:7 (head vignette for "Introduction"), BM-LJ:84 (R<). PE coll.

In, for example, the vignette *Cat Chasing a Bird and Large Mice* (Zatlin 694), the cat is hunting the mice around a peacock feather (Fig. 1.5c). The feather's stem vertically counterbalances the arabesque traced horizontally by the hunt, but also threatens to throw it off balance. Flying over the bristling cat, the bird deflects the graphic paradigm of the feather and encourages dispersal: the bird's body carries an eye motif that mirrors the feather while its tail imitates the feather's barbs. Its flight distracts the cat. It might chase the bird and forget about the mice. The mice may well go out to play, jests Beardsley – and one does, breaking free from the arabesque chase and darting towards a new curve, which ends in three small dots.

In *Molière Holding Three Puppet Heads* (Zatlin 716), the peacock feather turns into a triple stem mastered by Molière's disembodied and enlarged hand (Fig. 1.6a). On the stems, three figures act out the comedy of a husband being cuckolded. Refined, the stems are speckled with ink dots in *Three Grotesque Heads* (Fig. 1.6b, Zatlin 723), a vignette reworking the same scene. In the first version, the characters are clearly recognisable: the cuckold wears horns, and his wife smiles at her lover, perhaps a painter, judging by his artist's cap. In the second, the characters are more sexually and socially ambiguous. They certainly owe something to Jean-Jacques Grandville's *Fleurs animées* (1846), Crane's *Flora's Feast: A Masque of Flowers* (1889), or even Redon's *La fleur du marécage, une tête humaine et triste* (from the portfolio *Hommage à Goya*, 1885), but it is hard to say which figure is feminine and which masculine, and whether they belong to the real world or to the imagination of the grumpy old fool, out of whose horned skull they spring.

The vignette *Two Grotesque Heads and a Winged Female Torso on Vines* (Zatlin 724), which follows in Smith and Sheridan's *Bon-Mots*, is yet another version of the same, by now abstract and fantastical (Fig. 1.6c): the basic pattern is identical, the cast similar, but the scene, resolutely fantastic and eroticised, features surreal beings.[26]

26 BM-SS (London: J. M. Dent and Company, 1893), 92–93.

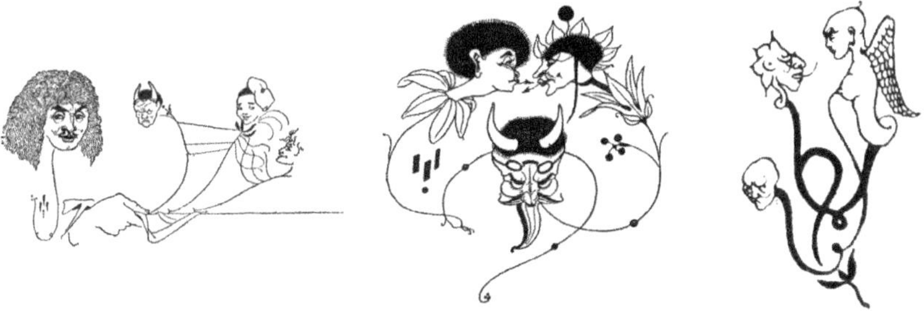

Fig. 1.6a–c Aubrey Beardsley, Three versions of the comedy of the cuckold husband. 1.6a *Molière Holding Three Puppet Heads*, BM-SS:70, BM-FH:119; 1.6b *Three Grotesque Heads*, BM-SS:92, BM-LJ:17 (R<), BM-FH:28 (R<); 1.6c *Two Grotesque Heads and a Winged Female Torso on Vines*, BM-SS:93, BM-LJ:180 (R>). PE coll.

Another image that Beardsley tampers with is taken from Redon's *L'Araignée souriante* ("The Smiling Spider"), a well-known image at the time, which featured in Huysmans's *À Rebours* in 1884 as "a ghastly spider lodging a human face in the midst of its body" ("*une épouvantable araignée logeant au milieu de son corps une face humaine*").[27] Beardsley knew the novel well: he had modelled his lodgings at 114 Cambridge Street after the main character, Jean des Esseintes's interior. Redon's charcoal drawing of 1881 had in 1887 been lithographed in twenty-five copies (Fig. 1.7) and Beardsley is known to have seen them in Evans's shop.[28] A number of Beardsley's vignettes draw on this image (Fig. 1.8a–e). The first is *Spider and Bug Regarding Each Other* (Fig. 1.8a, Zatlin 706), whose spider resurfaces in the larger composition *La Femme incomprise* (Zatlin 264). The first time it appears in the *Bon-Mots*, it is printed sideways, in the middle of an anecdote on Smith annoyed by a young man's familiarity.[29] The context grants it an illustrative tinge: the spider could well be Smith ogling the young man. Its half-humorous, half-threatening aspect calls to mind a satire of Redon's work, portrayed as Pancrace Buret in *Les Déliquescences d'Adoré Floupette*, a fin-de-siècle spoof by Gabriel Vicaire and Henri Beauclair: "A giant spider which carried, at the end of each of its tentacles, a bunch of eucalyptus flowers and whose body consisted

27 Joris-Karl Huysmans, À *Rebours* (Paris: G. Charpentier et Cie, 1884), 85.

28 Sturgis, *Aubrey Beardsley: A Biography*, 99.

29 BM-SS, 41.

of an enormous, desperately pensive eye, the sight of which alone made you shudder; no doubt, another symbol."[30]

Beardsley's *Spider and Bug Regarding Each Other* reads at first glance like a simple, naturalistic scene: the spider stares with its single eye at a black insect, which looks up at it in dread. As in Redon, the fantastic image of the spider, as opposed to the rather realistic rendering of the bug, comes from its rotund body with legs and its glaring eye, embedded, as in several Redon lithographs, in a round form. Still, Redon's spider has two eyes and a predatory mouth. It paces in indefinite space while Beardsley's lies implanted in text. On closer examination, Beardsley's minute episode is in no way naturalistic: the spider has six legs, like an insect, whereas it should have eight, like any arachnid worthy of the name (Redon's has ten). As for the bug, it has... nine (four on one side, five on the other). It is therefore as improbable as the spider: we are presented with a double *lusus naturae*, two freaks of nature, which, like Floupette's *Déliquescences*, is based on the sophisticated parody of *artistic*, not nature-based motifs.

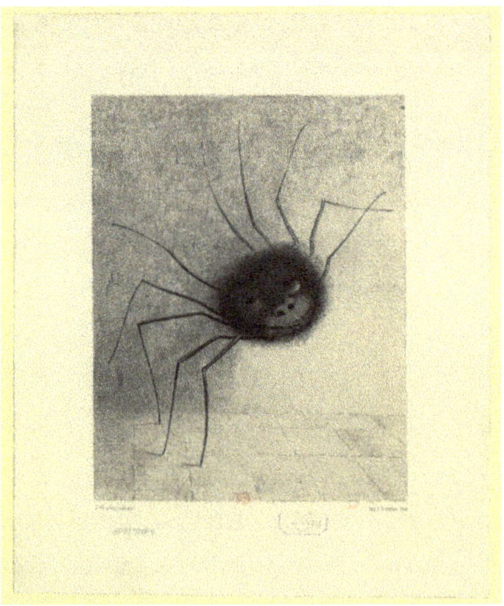

Fig. 1.7 Odilon Redon, *L'Araignée souriante* (originally 1881), lithograph (1887). © BnF, Paris

30 *Les Déliquescences, poèmes décadents d'Adoré Floupette, avec sa vie par Marius Tapora* (Byzance: Chez Lion Vanné [*sic* for Paris: Léon Vanier], 1885), xl: "*Une araignée gigantesque qui portait, à l'extrémité de chacune de ses tentacules, un bouquet de fleurs d'eucalyptus et dont le corps était constitué par un œil énorme, désespérément songeur, dont la vue seule vous faisait frissonner; sans doute, encore un symbole.*"

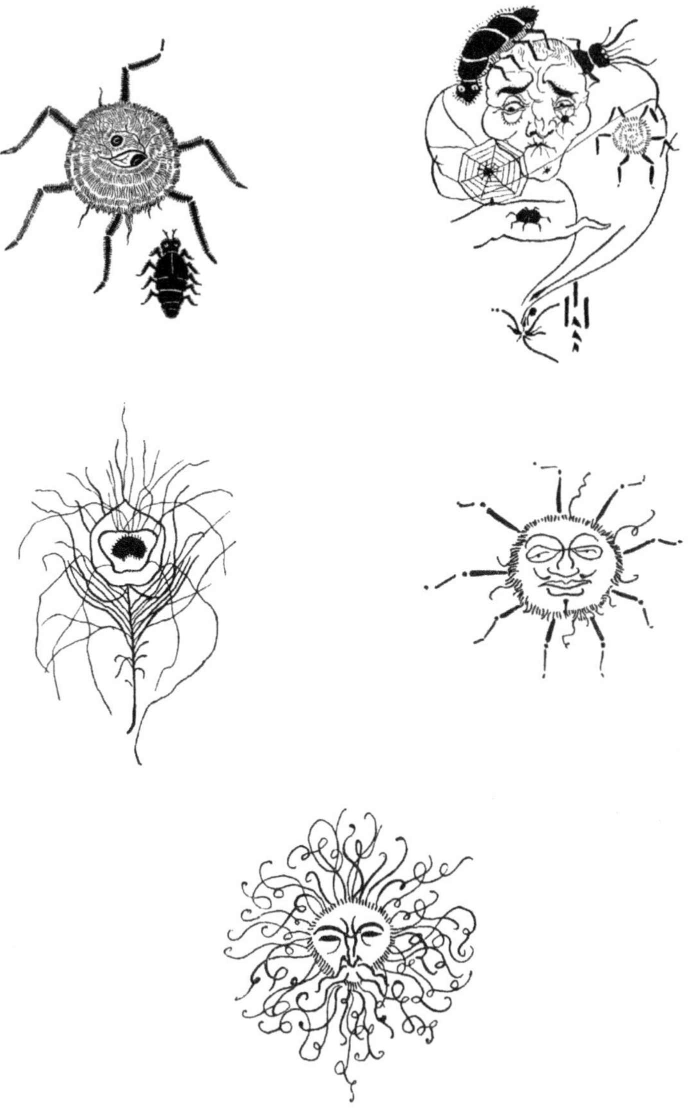

Fig. 1.8a–e Aubrey Beardsley, *Bon-Mots* grotesques with spiders and webs. 1.8a *Spider and Bug Regarding Each Other*, BM-SS:41 (repr. on the side), BM-LJ:13 (R<); 1.8b *Head Overlaid with Bugs and a Spiderweb*, BM-SS:131, BM-LJ:168 (R>); 1.8c *Large Peacock Feather*, BM-SS:190, BM-FH:145; 1.8d *A Spider*, BM-SS:177; 1.8e *The Sun*, BM-SS:113. PE coll.

Both the spider and its web multiply in Beardsley's *Head Overlaid with Bugs and a Spiderweb* (Fig. 1.8b, Zatlin 741). Beardsley read French well and would have been familiar with the expression "*avoir une araignée au plafond*" (literally "to have a spider on the ceiling"), commonly used to refer to someone's eccentricity or derangement as in "to have bats in the belfry." There is a connection between spiders and madness in several other languages: *spinnen* means both "to weave" and figuratively "to ramble" in German, and in English *cobweb* can signify "subtle fanciful reasoning" as in "to blow away the cobwebs." In Beardsley's vignette, the wrinkled grinning human head beset by arachnids and insects reflects madness, melancholy, or arachnophobia, as much as it is a dusty mask on which spiders spin webs. How many spiders, webs, and bugs are out there? It is hard to say: a strand has just been cast from the right to the left, the whole scene may soon be covered in a spider's netting, unless it itself becomes a part of a bigger web. The image keeps interpretation at bay.

Beardsley also connects the peacock's feather to the spider's net. In *Large Peacock Feather* (Zatlin 765), a plume turns into a ragged web (Fig. 1.8c). There is something alarming in seeing such an Aesthetic symbol fall apart, as if art did not hold together any longer in the face of nature and time. In further metamorphosis, *A Spider* (Zatlin 758) rather humorously wears a nose clip (Fig. 1.8d). Redon's smiling, carnivorous beast has become a man's head with an indolent, almost idiotic, gaze in its bespectacled eyes. Another grotesque mask set in curly filaments (Fig. 1.8e), oddly named *The Sun* in the *catalogue raisonné* (Zatlin 732), extends the motif, and the layout of the first volume grants it a function similar to *A Spider*. Placed centre page, both grotesques interrupt a joke.[31] But it may well be that *The Sun* is merely born from a calligraphic doodle.

Such motifs, borrowed from his creative contemporaries and treated with subversive vivacity and humour, highlight the quick evolution and visual dynamism of Beardsley's style. Once he uses a motif, it is then refracted and burgeons further. The vignettes initially derive from disrespectful appropriations, but then also stem from each other,

31 *The Sun* is featured first, BM-SS, 113, among quips by Smith, and *A Spider* is featured second, 177, among witticisms by Sheridan.

pushing their visual potential to new extremes. They are flexible graphic gestures, open to suggestiveness. They hold in store playful wonders for the viewer despite their minute size. A graphic resource from which the artist may draw at any time, they parody or distance themselves from their subjects, including old established favourites of the grotesque tradition.

Unrecognisable Legacies

While seizing and distorting recent trends (Aestheticism, Japonisme, Pre-Raphaelites, Redon, Whistler), Beardsley also borrowed from older traditions. Several depictions refer to the origin of the grotesque, starting with the title-page frame (Zatlin 692), identical in all three *Bon-Mots*: an arabesque assortment of forms surrounds a spacious square held in reserve for the title lettering (Fig. 1.9). The grotesques lodge in the whorls and coils or emerge from them as in the finest tradition of the "nameless ornament," inspired by the sixteenth-century findings at Domus Aurea, Nero's excavated palace in Rome. Taken up and refashioned by numerous artists during the Renaissance, often engraved in sets, they were copied from one workshop to the next.[32] Yet Beardsley replaces all the expected shapes with Aesthetic or Japanese components: three Whistlerian butterflies on the left, another on the right above a grotesque with a sunflower hat perched on a peacock, at the very top two tiny masks stemming like Japanese lanterns from a small monster, at the bottom a grimacing satyr with long leaves mimicking hair, and brawny, strapping grotesques in varied attitudes.

32 See Nicole Dacos, *La Découverte de la Domus Aurea et la formation des grotesques à la Renaissance* (London: The Warburg Institute; Leiden: E. J. Brill, 1969); Cristina Acidini Luchinat, "La grottesca," in *Storia dell'arte italiana*, 11, 3, *Situazioni, momenti, indagini*, 4. *Forme e modelli*, ed. by Federico Zeri (Turin: Einaudi, 1982), 159–200; André Chastel, *La Grottesque. Essai sur l'"ornement sans nom"* (Paris: Le Promeneur, 1988); Philippe Morel, *Les Grotesques. Les Figures de l'imaginaire dans la peinture italienne de la fin de la Renaissance* (Paris: Flammarion, 2001).

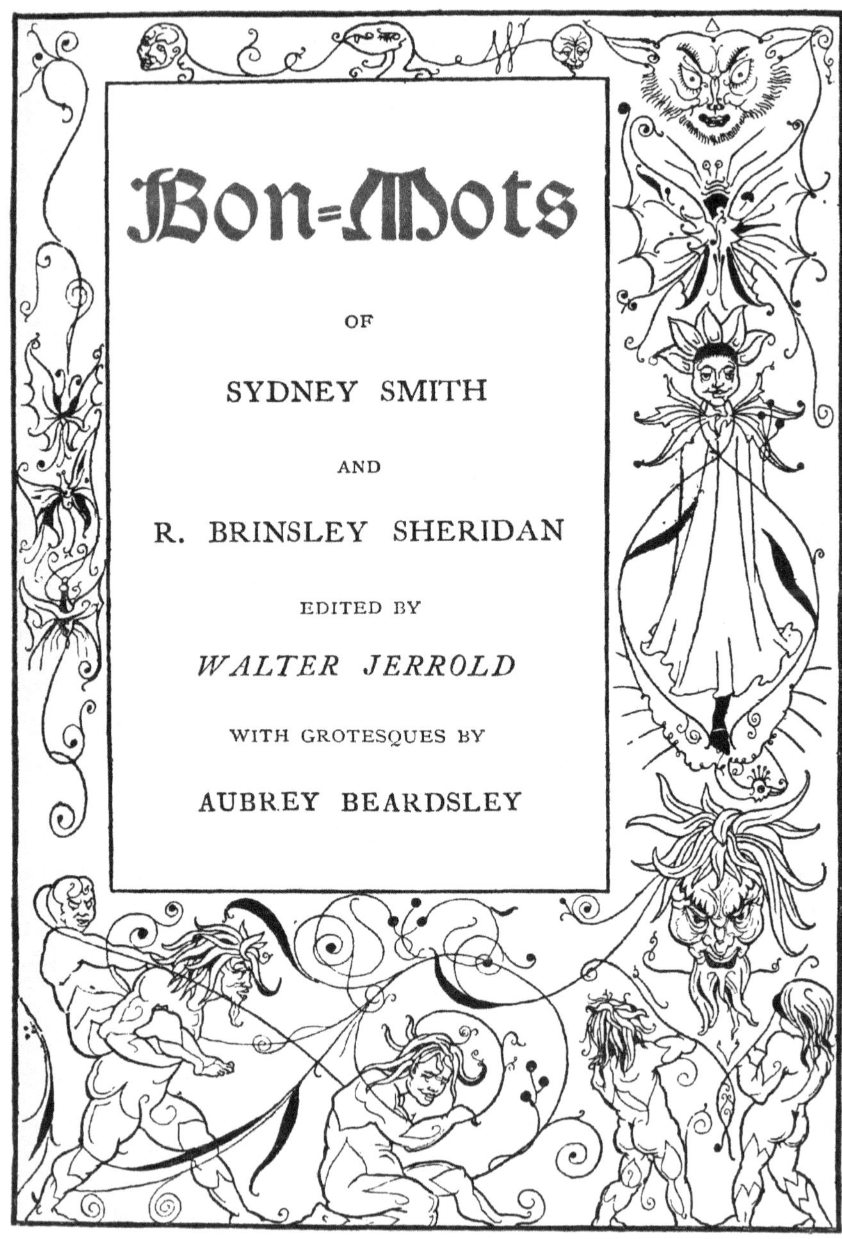

Fig. 1.9 Aubrey Beardsley, Title page for BM-SS (1893), identical frame for all three *Bon-Mots*. PE coll.

Borrowing from other sources and blending forms are characteristic of this protean art, in which even skilful or scholarly identification is often at a loss. The remodelling of forms, modernity of garb, attribute, and attitudes blur or erase their origins. Take for instance the horned *Grotesque on a Camp Stool* (Zatlin 801), printed only once (Fig. 1.10a).[33] Beardsley uses as his basis a tower demon from Paris's Notre-Dame, the very one depicted by Charles Meryon and known as *Le Stryge* in his 1853 portfolio *Eaux-fortes sur Paris* (see Fig. 3.9). Frequently pirated in woodcuts, its shape had already become a vignette as early as 1865 in *A History of Caricature and Grotesque*, Thomas Wright's famous historical compilation, which Beardsley must have known. As opposed to other demons, which may be considered as ridiculous or even humorous, this grotesque embodies for Wright the very *Spirit of Evil* (Fig. 1.10b): "It is an absolute Mephistopheles, carrying in his features a strange mixture of hateful qualities – malice, pride, envy – in fact, all the deadly sins combined in one diabolical whole."[34]

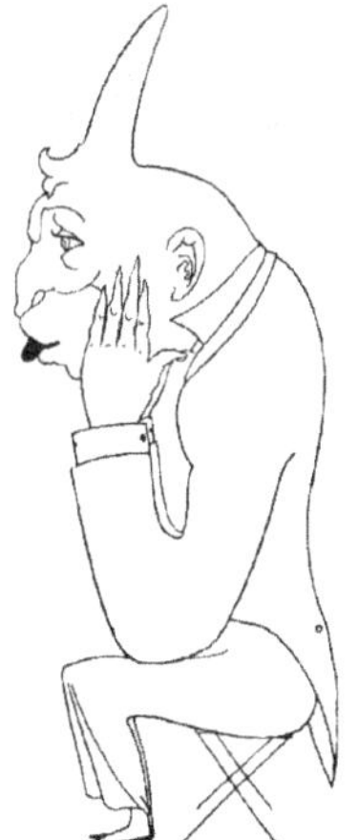

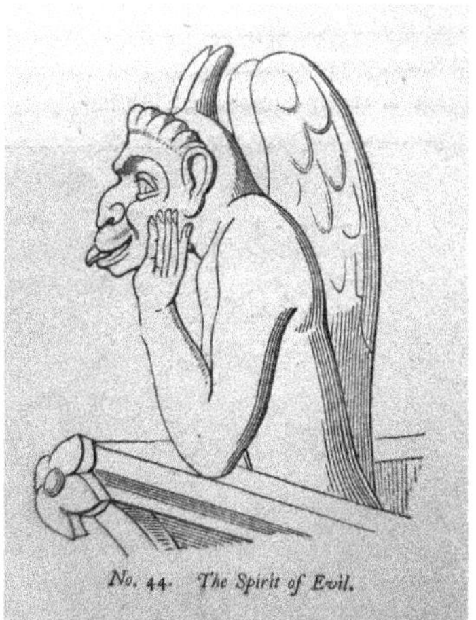

Fig. 1.10a–b Aubrey Beardsley reshaping traditional grotesques. 1.10a Beardsley, *Grotesque on a Camp Stool*, BM-FH:31. PE coll.; 1.10b F. W. Fairholt, Meryon's *Le Stryge* captioned *Spirit of Evil*, in Wright, *A History of Caricature and Grotesque*, 74 (detail). Author's photograph

33 BM-FH (London: J. M. Dent and Company, 1894), 31.

34 Thomas Wright, *A History of Caricature and Grotesque in Literature and Art* (London: Chatto & Windus, 1875), 74, fig. 44. First published (London: Virtue Brothers, 1865); trans. into French by Octave Sachot with a note by Amédée Pichot, 2nd ed. (Paris: A. Delahays, 1875).

Beardsley neutralises the demon through indolence. Its stuck-out tongue, single forehead horn, and hand on the cheek draw closely on the sculpted demon (whether the original, Meryon's etching, its pirated reproductions, or Wright's vignette), while the profile is finely outlined. As will be discussed further in Chapter 3, Beardsley himself would be photographed in 1894 by Frederick H. Evans in two poses advertised as grotesque, one adopting this very posture (see Fig. 3.10).[35] And yet, the full evening dress, the court slippers, the aloofness of the horned grotesque, apathetically perched on its fold-up seat, transform it to the extent that even Zatlin, the great Beardsley scholar, missed its inspiration. She originally saw it as conveying either desire or inaction, and related it to Beardsley's social criticism of his contemporaries.[36] Due amendments were made in her *catalogue raisonné* thanks to Matthew Sturgis's input.[37]

Triple-faced Grotesque (Zatlin 790) transforms into an egg-shaped figure (Fig. 1.11a) another monstrous being of earlier origin, reproduced by Frederick William Fairholt in Wright as a vignette captioned *The Music of the Demon* (Fig. 1.11b).[38] The original is Erhard Schön's *Des Teufels Dudelsack* (*The Devil's Bagpipe*), a coloured woodcut from ca. 1530–35 and one of the best known caricatures in the history of the Reformation. Wright sees in it a satirical attack on Martin Luther, whose head features as the bagpipes into which the devil blows (Fig. 1.10c), an interpretation carried on in manuals and schoolbooks, yet recently contested.[39] Beardsley's new creation conforms to wry humour similar to Schön's. He moves the grinning face that Schön had rendered on the devil's pelvis on top of the creature's head, with a Humpty Dumptyian scowl and lolled-out tongue. A smiling face appears now on the pelvis. The middle bagpipes have given way to a ludicrous sulking burgher staring ahead from under a tiny top hat. It is doubtful whether Reade's relating it to "certain types of schizophrenic drawing" and Zatlin's suggestion of Hokusai and Victorian hypocrisy are helpful.[40] Instead,

35 See Chapter 3.

36 Zatlin, *Beardsley, Japonisme, and the Perversion of the Victorian Ideal*, 203.

37 Zatlin, *Catalogue Raisonné*, I, 473.

38 Wright, *A History of Caricature and Grotesque in Literature and Art*, 252, fig. 145.

39 See Christophe Pallaske, "Luther – kein Teufels Dudelsack | zur Fehlinterpretation einer Karikatur," *Hypotheses: Historisch Denken | Geschichte machen*, https://historischdenken.hypotheses.org/5409

40 Reade, 330, n. 229. Zatlin, *Beardsley, Japonisme, and the Perversion of the Victorian Ideal*, 204, and Zatlin, *Catalogue Raisonné*, I, 468.

it is more useful to acknowledge the image's heritage and see that Beardsley's elusive modernity has taken over an old-style grotesque. He has radically transformed it by replacing the hybrid animal forms with clear-cut shapes, and adopting modern apparel together with languid, tongue-in-cheek postures.

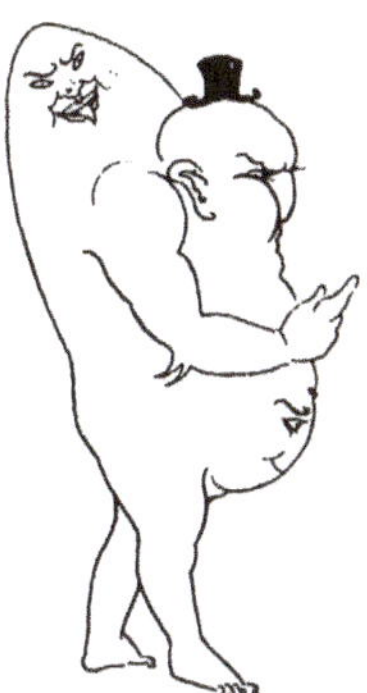

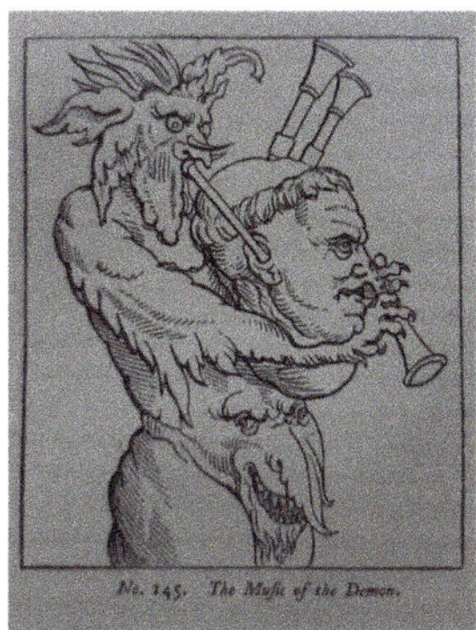

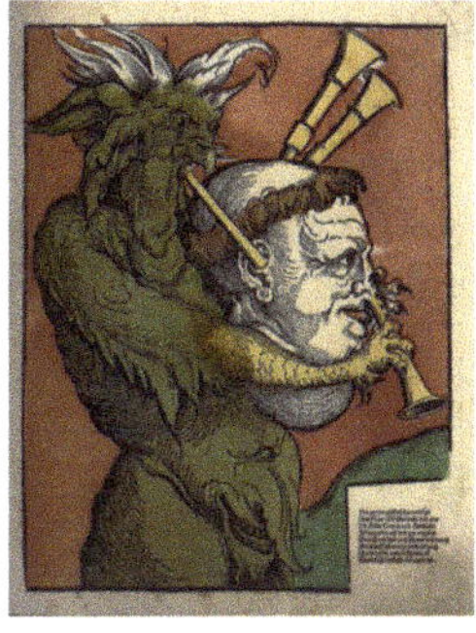

Fig. 1.11a–c Aubrey Beardsley reshaping traditional grotesques. 1.11a Beardsley, *Triple-faced Grotesque*, BM-LJ:156, BM-FH:22 (R<). PE coll.; 1.11b F. W. Fairholt, Vignette captioned *The Music of the Demon*, in Wright, *A History of Caricature and Grotesque*, 252 (detail). Author's photograph; 1.11c Erhard Schön, *Des Teufels Dudelsack* (ca. 1530–35), coloured woodcut. Wikipedia, https://commons.wikimedia.org/wiki/File:Teufels_Dudelsack.gif#/media/File:A_monk_as_devil's_bagpipe_(Sammlung_Schloss_Friedenstein_Gotha_Inv._Nr._37,2).jpg

In Beardsley's work, innovation is both a matter of breaking new graphic ground and flouting tradition. He plays on the fine contours of outline, on curlicues, festoons and flourishes, threadlike lines, small dots, squiggles, doodles, feathers, bristles, tassels or strands of hair, which he mixes with the most predictable grotesque motifs: forked hooves, arrow-like tongues, horns, clawed paws, bristly pelts. His complex language also addresses nakedness. It subverts Victorian puritanism by introducing disturbing images of nudity and the human body. Beardsley implants on his grotesques a potpourri of human shapes, but figures rarely appear whole. Revamped organs, bones and limbs slide, shift and reposition. Nipples and breasts grow on cheeks, skulls, and occiputs. Bodies morph, genders mutate, and amputated limbs melt away. The little grotesques look at the viewer with a sneer, stick out their tongues mischievously, pull faces, and smile: they call for attention, invite deciphering, and then evade interpretation.

Curlicues, Letters, and Bodies

Beardsley himself slyly slipped in among his grotesques several self-portraits, in a mocking, buffoonish, even disconcerting manner, including as a foetus.[41] This discreetly assertive but ironic presence, this demanding stance that promptly beats a retreat, is often accompanied by a Japanese mark, Beardsley's signature, made up of three vertical strokes and a few dots (which become inverted hearts in *Salome*). Such a moniker accompanies, for example, a slumbering head on the extreme left of *Four Heads in Medieval Hats* (Zatlin 695), which is Beardsley's own clandestine portrait (Fig. 1.12); it becomes a decorative motif on the vase in *A Tooth Extraction* (Zatlin 697, see Fig. 1.5a); or even, close to the foetus itself, it balances the abortive/phallic instrument in *Two Figures by Candlelight Holding a Fetus*, one of the grotesques most often reproduced (Zatlin 700, see Fig. 2.1).

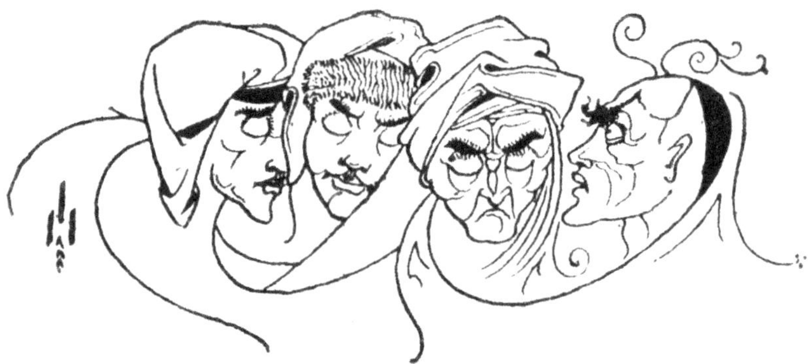

Fig. 1.12 Aubrey Beardsley, *Four Heads in Medieval Hats*, BM-SS:13 (cul-de-lampe for "Introduction"), BM-FH:5 (R>). PE coll.

Other forms of Beardsley's signature sometimes appear on his grotesques, as well as numerous scribbles, doodles, and squiggles lifted from penmanship manuals.[42] Skilful engraver and calligrapher Edward Cocker (1631–76) and his intricate compositions in *The Pen's*

41 See Reade, 325, n. 167; Milly Heyd, *Aubrey Beardsley: Symbol, Mask and Self-Irony* (New York: Peter Lang, 1986), 55–67; Zatlin, *Beardsley, Japonisme, and the Perversion of the Victorian Ideal*, 209–16; and my own analysis in the following chapter.

42 As recorded by Reade, 327, n. 189 and n. 191; 328, n. 199; and 329, n. 212.

Transcendencie, or Fair Writing Labyrinth (1657) and *The Pen's Triumph* (1658) acted as potential models for Beardsley. For Cocker, however, the perfection of writing proves the excellence of being, itself a reflection of the creator's flawlessness mirrored in the long programmatic titles of his manuals. In the title page of *The Pen's Transcendencie, or Fair Writing Labyrinth*, a rhyming quatrain comments unequivocally the title: "Wherein faire Writing to the Life's exprest, | in sundry Copies, cloth'd with Arts and Vest. | By w[hi]ch, with practice, thou may'st gaine Perfection, | As th' Hev'n taught Author did, without direction."[43] In *The Pen's Triumph*, the short title is expanded as follows: "Being a Copy-Book, Containing variety of Examples of all Hands Practised in this Nation according to the present Mode; Adorned with incomparable Knots and Flourishes Most of the Copies consisting of Two Lines onely, and those containing the whole Alphabet; being all distill'd from the Limbeck of the Authors own Brain, and an Invention as Usefull as Rare. With a discovery of the Secrets and Intricacies of this Art, in such Directions as were never yet published, which will conduct an ingenious Practitioner to an unimagined Height." All examples for exercising calligraphy are moral maxims or exhortations. "Flourishing" (prospering, thriving) and "making flourishes" go hand in hand, states Cocker, playing on the word's double intent: "Some sordid Sotts | Cry downe rare Knotts, | Whose envy makes them currish | But Art shall shine, | And Envie pine, | And still my Pen shall flourish."[44]

For Beardsley, on the other hand, calligraphy turns into doodles housing unexpected shapes (Fig. 1.13a–f). By knotting itself, the line comes to be a letter. The penmanship grotesque is meshed and breeds new forms in its twisted loops. The letters, when decipherable in the drawing, are also tails, moustaches, hair, breasts, muzzles, wings, and paws. Shapes echo the anecdotes described in the text. *The Hairy Grotesque* (Fig. 1.13a, Zatlin 752) may playfully reflect amusing accounts of Sheridan's hopeless hunting, or again comment on wondrous rhetoric dispensed on futile subjects such as Foote's dissertation on a cabbage

43 *The Pen's Transcendencie, or Fair Writing Labyrinth* (London: Samuel Ayre, 1657), n.p. See https://www.numistral.fr/ark:/12148/bpt6k94009620.image

44 This aphorism is printed on the plate with calligraphic figures from *The Pen's Triumph* (London: Samuel Ayre, 1658), n.p. See https://books.google.fr/books?id=iyICAAAAQAAJ&printsec=frontcover&hl=fr#v=thumbnail&q&f=false

stalk.[45] Flourishes, instead of a head's crown, in *Man in a Calligraphic Hat with a Long Tongue and Breasts on his Cheek* (Fig. 1.13b, Zatlin 727) may spiritedly picture Sydney Smith's "absence of mind" or comment on the double meaning of "flourish" in a quip by Foote.[46] *Capped Head Gazing at a Fish* (Fig. 1.13c, Zatlin 730) could represent Smith's comment on platitudes or a topsy-turvy carousal, when turned sideways.[47] The wriggly lines of *Calligraphic Owl* (Fig. 1.13d, Zatlin 756) compete perhaps with skilled rhetoric on endless bills.[48] And the *Calligraphic Grotesque* (Fig. 1.13e, Zatlin 763) could be a mischievous gloss on a trick played by Sheridan.[49] Such matches highlight the kinship between writing and drawing, both from a similarly writhing pen.

Likewise, flourishes stray into initials. The *Long-necked Grotesque* (Fig. 1.13f, Zatlin 742) with its extended neck, womanly chest, round hips, and peacock's head, may have inspired Max Ernst.[50] Hermaphrodite and maimed, it recalls the grotesques with endless necks in Hokusai's *Manga*.[51] It pulls a thread-like strand with its beak, and ends in two squiggles: one stands for its foot, the other for its hand, but may also be read as the designer's own initials, AB. Just below, three small black rings form an elusive face under a bulging hairdo. AB himself signs his creature while glancing at the spectator, as if in awe at such boldness.

45 BM-SS, 160–62, see https://archive.org/details/bonmotsofsydneys00smit/page/160/mode/2up; BM-FH, 85–87, see https://archive.org/details/bonmotsofsamuelf00foot/page/86/mode/2up.

46 BM-SS, 101, see https://archive.org/details/bonmotsofsydneys00smit/page/100/mode/2up; BM-FH, 101, see https://archive.org/details/bonmotsofsamuelf00foot/page/100/mode/2up.

47 BM-SS, 109, see https://archive.org/details/bonmotsofsydneys00smit/page/108/mode/2up; BM-FH, 142–43, see https://archive.org/details/bonmotsofsamuelf00foot/page/142/mode/2up.

48 BM-SS, 170, see https://archive.org/details/bonmotsofsydneys00smit/page/170/mode/2up.

49 *Ibid.*, 186, see https://archive.org/details/bonmotsofsydneys00smit/page/186/mode/2up.

50 Max Ernst, etching for Tristan Tzara, *Où boivent les loups* (Paris: Éditions des Cahiers libres, 1932). There were only ten copies made of the etching, on Japanese pearly paper. Repr. in Max Ernst, *Écritures, avec cent vingt illustrations extraites de l'œuvre de l'auteur* (Paris: Gallimard, 1970), 400. I thank Anne Larue for this suggestion.

51 Zatlin, *Beardsley, Japonisme, and the Perversion of the Victorian Ideal*, 183 and 187 (fig. 89), 204, and 207 (fig. 102).

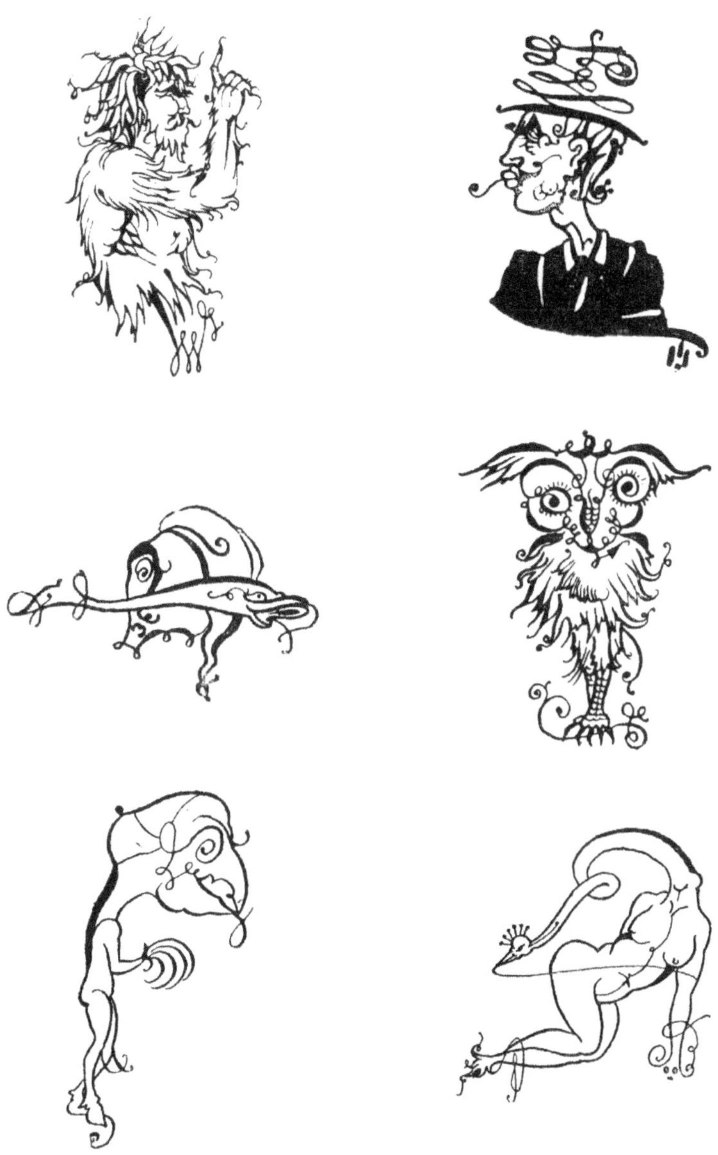

Fig. 1.13a–f Aubrey Beardsley, calligraphic grotesques in the *Bon-Mots*. 1.13a *Hairy Grotesque*, BM-SS:160, BM-FH:86; 1.13b *Man in a Calligraphic Hat with a Long Tongue and Breasts on his Cheek*, BM-SS:101, BM-FH:101; 1.13c *Capped Head Gazing at a Fish*, BM-SS:109, BM-FH:142 (repr. vertically); 1.13d *Calligraphic Owl*, BM-SS:170; 1.13e *Calligraphic Grotesque*, BM-SS:186, BM-FH:98; 1.13f *Long-necked Grotesque*, BM-SS:133. PE coll.

Beardsley's grotesques and flourishes recede into the background, such is their peculiarity and charm: while offering themselves to be scrutinised and deciphered as amalgams and debris of forms, they are also elusive. To speak of them in terms of a "grammar" (Fletcher)[52] or "types" in a socio-critical perspective ("not individualized characters but types," Zatlin),[53] hardly tackles the issue since they do not form a reliable ensemble of meaning.

Often somatic and eroticised, the grotesques also bridge the difference between book and body. In his unfinished novel, *Under the Hill*, Beardsley's description of the costumes and trappings of Venus's guests borrow from his own grotesques. Even more significantly, Paul Chatouilleur De La Pine,[54] his fictional painter (previously Jean Baptiste Dorat in bowdlerised published versions), actually adorns the bodies of the party guests themselves with grotesques:

> Then De La Pine had painted extraordinary grotesques & vignettes over their bodies, here and there. Upon a cheek, an old man scratching his horned head, upon a forehead, an old woman teased by an impudent amor, upon a shoulder, an amorous singerie, round a breast, a circlet of satyrs, about a wrist, a wreath of babes,[55] upon an elbow, a bouquet of spring flowers, across a back, some surprising scenes of adventure, at the corners of a mouth, tiny red spots, & upon a neck, a flight of birds, a caged parrot, a branch of fruit, a butterfly, a spider, a drunken dwarf, or, simply the bearer's initials. But most wonderful of all were the black silhouettes painted upon the legs, & which showed through a white silk stocking like a sumptuous bruise.[56]

52 Fletcher, "A Grammar of Monsters: Beardsley's Images and Their Sources," *English Literature in Transition, 1880–1920*, 30:2 (1987): 141–63.

53 Zatlin, *Beardsley, Japonisme, and the Perversion of the Victorian Ideal*, 202 ff.

54 Literally "Tickler of the Dick," using French to both conceal and enhance the erotic meaning.

55 Beardsley had initially written "unborn children." In the same chapter, the list of masks includes masks "of little embryos & of cats." See *Decadent Writings of Aubrey Beardsley*, ed. by Sasha Dovzhyk and Simon Wilson, MHRA Critical Texts 10, Jewelled Tortoise 78 (Cambridge: Modern Humanities Research Association, 2022), 76 and 35.

56 After the original manuscript, in *Decadent Writings of Aubrey Beardsley*, 36. The January 1896 *Savoy* text, the 1904 Lane edition, and the Smithers 1907 edition for private circulation all have Dorat. To note, the last sentence, "But most wonderful of all were the black silhouettes painted upon the legs, & which showed through the white silk stocking like a sumptuous bruise," was not printed either in the

Aesthetics are reversible as the body turns into a book of tattooed grotesques, while the *Bon-Mots* use bodies as a fulcrum of monstrous application. The ultimate bid of the to-and-fro movement between body and book is Beardsley's own body, pictured as monstrous in photographs (see Chapter 3). Such a bold move radically reviews the relation of images to text while opening a new perspective on fin-de-siècle print culture.

Wry Illustration and the Use of Language

Beardsley's grotesques are generally seen as largely irrelevant to the text they accompany. Commenting on the first volume, *The Studio* suggested their symbolic rather than illustrative capacity: "as an attempt to symbolise the jokes rather than as pictorial illustrations they will repay study."[57] Despite this, there has been a tendency to neglect the booklets' content when thinking about Beardsley, and consider his designs independently of the text. Reade, for example, offers an interpretation of *The Birth of Fancy* (Zatlin 748, named after Evans) by resorting to tentative psycho-erotic analysis of a presumable female despite the grotesque's androgyny (Fig. 1.14):

> A startling allegory perhaps of Romantic Music, whereby the grotesque "notes" are bred in the mind of Woman by the mental energy of Man, which fecundates her aural sense by means of an ear. This is one of the most effective of Beardsley's foetal drawings, in spite of the calligraphic flourish for the sleeve, which academic draughtsmen might deprecate.[58]

Savoy or in Aubrey Beardsley, *Under the Hill, and Other Essays in Prose and Verse* (London/New York: John Lane, 1904), 23, which circulated widely and is readily available on the internet.

57 "New Publications," *The Studio*, 1 (15 July 1893): 167. This review of the first *Bon-Mots* is published parallel to the first instalment of *Le Morte Darthur*.

58 Reade, 328, n. 203.

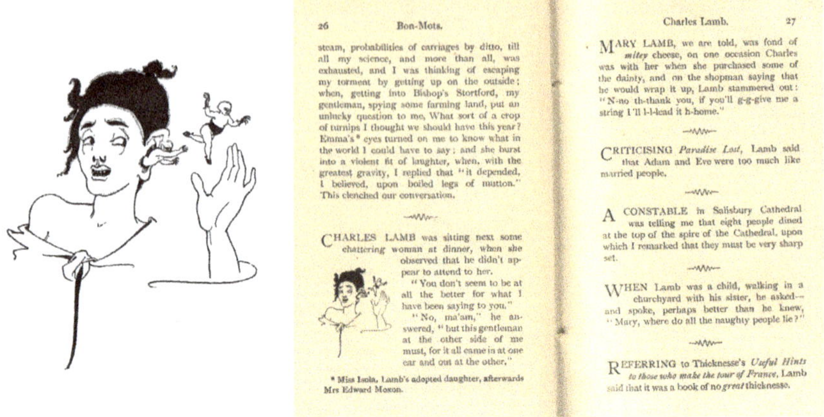

26 Bon-Mots.

steam, probabilities of carriages by ditto, till all my science, and more than all, was exhausted, and I was thinking of escaping my torment by getting up on the outside; when, getting into Bishop's Stortford, my gentleman, spying some farming land, put an unlucky question to me, What sort of a crop of turnips I thought we should have this year? Emma's* eyes turned on me to know what in the world I could have to say; and she burst into a violent fit of laughter, when, with the greatest gravity, I replied that "it depended, I believed, upon boiled legs of mutton." This clenched our conversation.

CHARLES LAMB was sitting next some chattering woman at dinner, when she observed that he didn't appear to attend to her.

"You don't seem to be at all the better for what I have been saying to you."

"No, ma'am," he answered, "but this gentleman at the other side of me must, for it all came in at one ear and out at the other."

* Miss Isola, Lamb's adopted daughter, afterwards Mrs Edward Moxon.

Charles Lamb. 27

MARY LAMB, we are told, was fond of *mitey* cheese, on one occasion Charles was with her when she purchased some of the dainty, and on the shopman saying that he would wrap it up, Lamb stammered out: "N-no th-thank you, if you'll g-g-give me a string I'll l-l-lead it h-home."

CRITICISING *Paradise Lost*, Lamb said that Adam and Eve were too much like married people.

A CONSTABLE in Salisbury Cathedral was telling me that eight people dined at the top of the spire of the Cathedral, upon which I remarked that they must be very sharp set.

WHEN Lamb was a child, walking in a churchyard with his sister, he asked—and spoke, perhaps better than he knew, "Mary, where do all the naughty people lie?"

REFERRING to Thicknesse's *Useful Hints to those who make the tour of France*, Lamb said that it was a book of no *great* thicknesse.

Fig. 1.14a–b Aubrey Beardsley, grotesque vignette *The Birth of Fancy*. 1.14a *The Birth of Fancy*, BM-SS:150, BM-LJ:26 (R<); 1.14b The same in context with the Lamb anecdote, BM-LJ:26–27. Courtesy of MSL coll., Delaware

Reade's suggestion that this is an allegory of music (born perhaps in his mind from a jokey allusion of the related anecdote to "a wine composer and importer of music" in the first *Bon-Mots*)[59] may seem arbitrary, especially since, when replaced in the second *Bon-Mots*, this grotesque has a clearly illustrative value. In the accompanying story, Charles Lamb replies to his chatty neighbour, who reproaches him for not paying attention to what she says, by noting that his own table neighbour is listening to her, almost despite himself: the words are entering one of Lamb's ears and leaving through the other.[60] Beardsley's drawing reflects precisely this facetious response with his typical gender twist: Lamb has become sexually indeterminate while the plump grotesques have rounded hips and long black gloves together with masculine bald heads and cloven hoofs. Evans's title, *The Birth of Fancy*, similarly occults their tongue-in-cheek relation to the text and vests the composition with an allegory.

In contrast, some of the foetal vignettes are wry, whimsical illustrations, as in the penmanship vignettes. They adorn the witty sayings of the *children* of the anthologised authors, not the authors themselves – the foetuses, as in Sheridan's case at the very end of

59 BM-SS, 150–51.

60 BM-LJ (London: J. M. Dent and Company, 1892), 26.

volume one. The last two pages offer young Tom Sheridan's ripostes to his father on marriage and money next to the vignette of *Fetus Figure Seated on a Peacock Feather with a Lily between its Feet* (Zatlin 766, see Fig. 2.2a). The offspring's clever replies match the genitor's, Tom being "emphatically the son of his father."[61] In the vignette, the lily, the very symbol of innocence, ironically faces a foetus, a depiction of Tom as Sheridan's *enfant terrible*, his pointy tongue standing for his sharp retorts (Fig. 1.15a). In another anecdote, Jerrold compares a minor poet to "the smallest of small beer over-kept in a tin mug – with the dead flies in it."[62] Set in the middle of the story, the same vignette of the wide-eyed, half-dead, half-alive foetus facing the lily grows into a wry illustration of Jerrold's comparing the minor poet to "the kitten with eyes just opened to the merits of a saucer of milk." (Fig. 1.15b). Several portraits of the fin-de-siècle generation, discussed in the next chapter, also refer to the foetus as offensive model. In the three *Bon-Mots* cases, instead of allegory, Beardsley preferred a witty literality, plumbing the potential of language as shown in his own self-portrait, *A Footnote* (see Chapter 3).

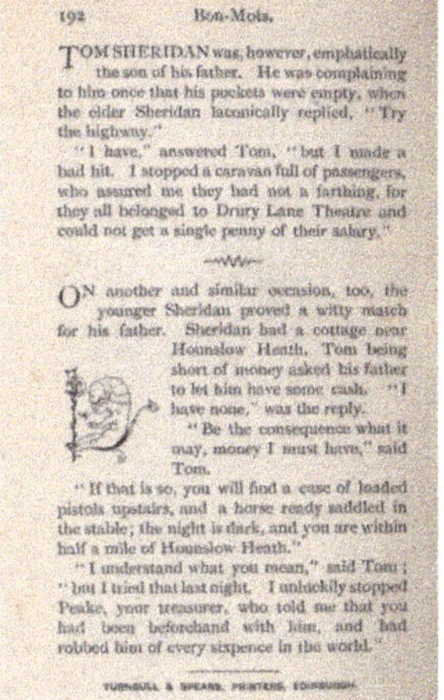

192 Bon-Mots.

TOM SHERIDAN was, however, emphatically the son of his father. He was complaining to him once that his pockets were empty, when the elder Sheridan laconically replied, "Try the highway."

"I have," answered Tom, "but I made a bad hit. I stopped a caravan full of passengers, who assured me they had not a farthing, for they all belonged to Drury Lane Theatre and could not get a single penny of their salary."

ON another and similar occasion, too, the younger Sheridan proved a witty match for his father. Sheridan had a cottage near Hounslow Heath. Tom being short of money asked his father to let him have some cash. "I have none," was the reply.

"Be the consequence what it may, money I must have," said Tom.

"If that is so, you will find a case of loaded pistols upstairs, and a horse ready saddled in the stable; the night is dark, and you are within half a mile of Hounslow Heath."

"I understand what you mean," said Tom; "but I tried that last night. I unluckily stopped Peake, your treasurer, who told me that you had been beforehand with him, and had robbed him of every sixpence in the world."

TURNBULL & SPEARS, PRINTERS, EDINBURGH.

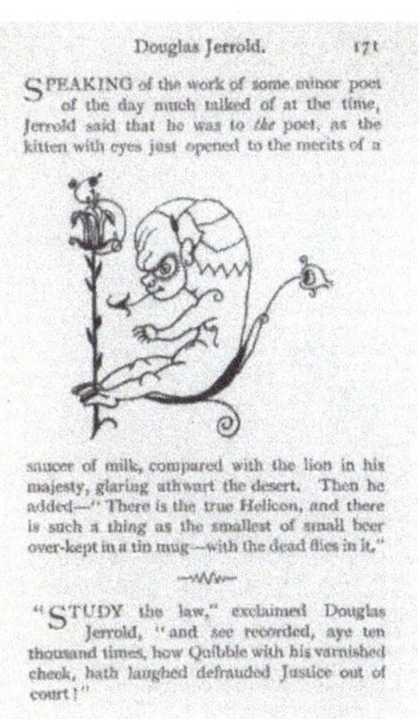

Douglas Jerrold. 171

SPEAKING of the work of some minor poet of the day much talked of at the time, Jerrold said that he was to *the* poet, as the kitten with eyes just opened to the merits of a saucer of milk, compared with the lion in his majesty, glaring athwart the desert. Then he added—"There is the true Helicon, and there is such a thing as the smallest of small beer over-kept in a tin mug—with the dead flies in it."

"STUDY the law," exclaimed Douglas Jerrold, "and see recorded, aye ten thousand times, how Quibble with his varnished cheek, hath laughed defrauded Justice out of court!"

Fig. 1.15a–b Aubrey Beardsley, *Bon-Mots* foetal grotesques as wry illustration. 1.15a *Fetus Figure Seated on a Peacock Feather with a Lily between its Feet*, shown in context, BM-SS:192 (last page); 1.15b the same in context, BM-LJ:171 (R>)

61 BM-SS, 192.
62 BM-LJ, 171.

Such divergence in interpretation stresses how hard it is to identify and evaluate the grotesques' fin-de-siècle importance and meaning as opposed to their Romantic and post-Romantic heritage. The tradition of hallucination, reverie, or nightmare breeding monsters, the "sick dreams" (*aegri somnia*) or "dream of painting" (*picturae somnium*) was an explanation ingeniously advanced by Daniele Barbaro in 1567, at the height of what André Chastel named the "quarrel on the grotesques," to justify the extravagance of such creations.[63] Dreams and hallucinations were also favoured throughout the nineteenth century to justify incidences of the incongruous and ugly. Numerous texts, including E. T. A. Hoffmann's *Fantasiestücke in Callots Manier* (1814–15), Aloysius Bertrand's *Gaspard de la Nuit* (1842), Théophile Gautier's "Le Club des Hachichins" (1851), the Goncourt brothers' "Un visionnaire" based on Charles Meryon (1856), and Robert Murray Gilchrist's "A Pageant of Ghosts," the conclusive narrative of his *Stone Dragon and Other Tragic Romances* (1894), called up monsters and grotesques through the tropes of dreams, phantasms, or madness.

Something of this idea lingers in Fletcher's approach to Beardsley's vignettes, which he sees "as in a nightmare."[64] Yet the three *Bon-Mots* break away from such Romantic and post-Romantic tradition thanks to their humorousness and resourceful use of language. They are essentially a series of jokes based on verbal misperception, gibes founded on mix-ups, paronomasia, homophonies, verbal twists, and reductions of metaphors to their literal significance; they manipulate meaning and words. Beardsley's images embody this farcical spirit. Rather than dismissing the textual quips as insipid (although some of them are indeed dull), we should rather ask whether it is not precisely from linguistic discrepancies (particularly by Lamb), characterised by mystification or nonsense (a particularly British genre familiar to all), that Beardsley draws practices that reinforce and enrich his innate

---

63 See Chastel, *La Grottesque*, 12–18 and 47–52; Elisheva Rosen, *Sur le grotesque: l'ancien et le nouveau dans la réflexion esthétique* (Saint-Denis: Presses Universitaires de Vincennes, 1991), 11–18.

64 Fletcher, *Aubrey Beardsley*, 55.

inclination for paradox. His own collection of aphorisms, edited by Lane as "Table Talk," is a testament to his interest in the practice.[65]

In such absurdist works, discrepancy occurs at several levels: between the grotesques and the modern or older motifs they rework, but also between text and image, reason and linguistic madness, sense and nonsense: no salt of the earth, but end-of-the-century spicing. To base three booklets only on paradox is a feat, but this is the essence of fin-de-siècle art. As a side trend (*para*) to a common or established belief (*doxa*), paradox is the perfect expression of grotesque as in Snodgrass's refined definition:

> The grotesque is a true paradox. It is both a fiction of autonomous artistic vision, operating by laws peculiar to itself, and a reflection of laws and contradictions in the world – paradoxically both "pure" and impure, autonomous and dependent, fictional image and mimetic mirror – in effect, incarnating the same contradictions that are central to art itself.[66]

It is then hardly surprising that young Beardsley should form his artistic language here, discovering at the borders of his grand illustrated books the heart of discrepancy. Such a limbo provides him with a luxuriant fauna. A few of his grotesques will resurface in large, well-known drawings. Most stem from experiments that promptly provide him with full command of his art, a fine virtuosity in such limited space, with such limited means.

Fin-de-siècle Choice Booklets, Mass Print Culture, and the "All Margin" Book

Marginal as they may be, Beardsley's vignettes are a unique contribution to fin-de-siècle print culture. They appeared in two types of publications, which targeted different audiences in the 1890s: refined booklets appealing to bibliophiles and collectors of limited editions; and general-interest magazines for a large bourgeois readership. The three *Bon-Mots*, with their covers decorated by Beardsley, gilt top edges, and

65 Aubrey Beardsley, "Table Talk," in *Under the Hill, and Other Essays in Prose and Verse* (London and New York: John Lane, 1904), 63–65.

66 Snodgrass, *Aubrey Beardsley, Dandy of the Grotesque*, 165.

a large-paper edition of one hundred copies per volume, were designed as deluxe fin-de-siècle collectables. French publishing had favoured such dainty trifles, as in the cute Elsevier collections of short stories by Catulle Mendès, René Maizeroy, or Charles Aubert. Yet these were designed on an altogether different template, laid on Holland paper, and opened onto a content-related frontispiece engraving, beneath a colourfully illustrated cover.[67] They were conceived as unique editions, never to be reprinted. Beardsley's *Bon-Mots* strongly differed not only in their production but also in their irreverent content and irrational layout. And, notwithstanding the narrow reader category they targeted, they were frequently reprinted: Smith and Sheridan totalled five reissues by 1904.[68]

Moreover, they founded a *type of book* in Great Britain, the fin-de-siècle collection of (more or less memorable) past sayings decked with modern grotesques. Witness Dent's *Bon-Mots of the Eighteenth and Bon-Mots of the Nineteenth Century*, again edited by Walter Jerrold, this time "with grotesques by Alice B. Woodward." Woodward, who at the time exhibited fine watercolours and contributed illustrations to several collections and the illustrated press thanks to Joseph Pennell (Beardsley's patron and first critic), would later be best known for her striking children's books with black-and-white illustrations for Blackie and Son and the first illustrated version of Peter Pan's story, *The Peter Pan Picture Book* (1907).[69] She had adopted Beardsley's distinctive black-and-white style but, unlike his, her grotesques were primarily illustrative. The astute publisher Dent used the template previously established with Beardsley for *his* three *Bon-Mots* to shape the two

67 See Catulle Mendès, *Monstres parisiens*, 2nd series (Paris: Chez tous les libraires, 1883–85), ten booklets printed in Elzevir type on laid Holland paper; Mendès, *Tous les baisers* (Paris: Chez tous les libraires, 1884), four booklets; René Maizeroy, *Les Amours défendues* (Paris: Chez tous les libraires, 1884), five booklets; Charles Aubert, *Péchés roses* (Paris: Chez tous les libraires, 1884–85), five booklets. Publisher Thomas Bird Mosher in Portland, Maine, also issued ten works as "tall slender volumes, 'modeled on the Aldine Books, and, like them entirely printed in Italics'" in his "Bibelot Series", 1893–97. See Jean-François Vilain and Philip R. Bishop, *Thomas Bird Mosher and the Art of the Book* (Philadelphia, Penn.: F. A. Davis, 1992), 12–13 (12).

68 Zatlin, *Catalogue Raisonné*, I, 423.

69 Geoffrey Beare, "Alice B(olingbroke) Woodward (1862–1951)," *Yellow Nineties 2.0*, ed. by Lorraine Janzen Kooistra, https://1890s.ca/wp-content/uploads/woodward_bio.pdf

new booklets she illustrated. They looked identical to Beardsley's from layout to cover and format while inside Woodward peppered the eighteenth- and nineteenth-century witticisms with her own illustrative grotesques. Cream covers replicating Beardsley's design proffered "Grotesques by Alice B. Woodward" next to Beardsley's fool with bauble and under his gilt peacock feather in duplicate colours.[70] The typography and printer are identical (Turnbull and Spears in Edinburgh), the format (13.6 x 8.4 cm) and the dimensions of the printed page (9.2 x 5.3 cm) close. Only the number of pages varies (195 for the first volume, 189 for the second) as the publication was probably starting to lack material.

Placing grotesques in a beautifully produced and refined-looking volume shifts their meaning and creates a whole new category of publications. Irregularity and disorder are no longer an indefinable marginal game but they perform at the core. Édouard Pelletan, a publisher deeply committed to the revival of fine book printing along classical lines at the time, professed that "the true magnificence of a book must be understood as the superiority of the written work, the beauty of the illustration, the suitability of the typesetting, the perfection of the printing, the quality of the paper and the limited number of copies."[71] However, he also published grotesques: in 1907 he produced a deluxe edition of *Le Triomphe du grotesque* by Fredh, decorated with 113 original compositions. The cover and the identical title page are again paradoxical: two naked women, their hair, legs, and breasts ending in folly bells, hold out two laurel wreaths to a pot-bellied middle-class man strolling atop the page (Fig. 1.16). It is odd, to say the least, to see Thucydides's famous phrase "*ΚΤΗΜΑ ΕΣ ΑΕΙ*" ("a treasure forever"),[72] shifted from reported facts and history as the eternal asset of mankind to Pelletan's trademark to crown a fin-de-siècle book on the grotesque.

---

70 See https://archive.org/details/jerroldbonmotseig00jerr (*Bon-Mots of the Eighteenth Century*) and https://archive.org/details/bonmotsofninetee00jerr (*Bon-Mots of the Nineteenth Century*).

71 Motto of the *Almanach du bibliophile pour l'année 1898* (Paris: Se vend aux Éditions d'Art chez Édouard Pelletan, 1898). The *Almanach* ran for ten issues (1898–1905).

72 Thucydides, *The Peloponnesian War*, I, 22.

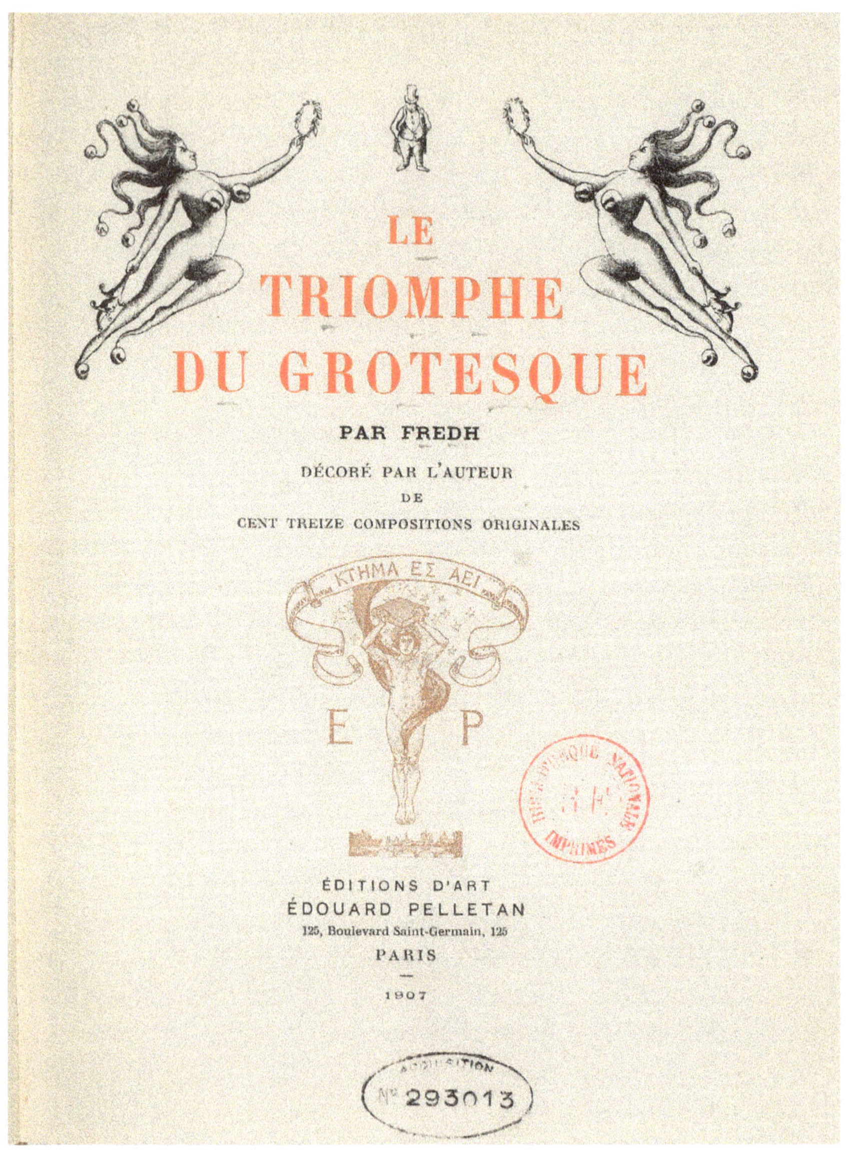

LE

TRIOMPHE

DU GROTESQUE

PAR FREDH

DÉCORÉ PAR L'AUTEUR

DE

CENT TREIZE COMPOSITIONS ORIGINALES

ΚΤΗΜΑ ΕΣ ΑΕΙ

E P

ÉDITIONS D'ART

ÉDOUARD PELLETAN

125, Boulevard Saint-Germain, 125

PARIS

1907

Fig. 1.16 Fredh, *Le Triomphe du grotesque, décoré par l'auteur de cent treize compositions originales* (Paris: Éditions d'Art, Édouard Pelletan, 1907), title page. © BnF, Gallica, Paris

The grotesque vignette also straddled new print territories. Beardsley was perhaps the first artist to extend this type of drawing into more general, high-circulation periodicals, with four of his vignettes published in *St. Paul's Magazine* in March and April 1894. Catalogued as *Music* (Zatlin 333), *Seated Woman Gazing at a Fetus in a Bell Jar* (Zatlin 334), *The Man that Holds the Watering Pot* (Zatlin 335), and *Pierrot and a Cat* (Zatlin 336), they all read thematically and stylistically close to the *Bon-Mots*, although larger.[73] *Masked Pierrot and a Female Figure* (Zatlin 933), first published on 28 April 1894 and in five subsequent issues in *To-Day*, the weekly "magazine-journal" founded and initially edited by Jerome K. Jerome, also relates to the *Bon-Mots* vignettes, with its Pierrot figure displaying a foetal head.

A series of Beardsley's followers were quick to publish similar work, still mostly unchartered. Sidney Herbert Sime's drawings for *Eureka*, also called *The Favorite Magazine*, or the *Pall Mall Magazine* echo Beardsley's style.[74] Between April and December 1899, Sime supplied the latter publication with a fine series of vignettes, accompanying the writing of George Slythe Street, the author of the Wilde satire *The Autobiography of a Boy*. Street, under the heading "In a London Attic," published a news column that closed each issue. Another series of grotesques by Henry Mayer[75] and Dion Clayton Calthorp[76]

73 Reade lists the last of these as a headpiece published in *St. Paul's*, 20 July 1895 (*Beardsley*, 338, n. 294), which disagrees with Zatlin's catalogue listing "four drawings" made for *St. Paul's* and recorded as published in the March and April 1894 issues (I, 221–23). The periodical is to be identified as *St. Paul's Magazine: An Illustrated Journal for the Home*, ed. by Mary C. Rowsell (Mar 1894–6 Jan 1900) but it has proved impossible to check further.

74 Mostly known for his full-page illustrations of Lord Dunsany's books, Sidney H. Sime (1865–1941) published numerous drawings and illustrations with fantastic themes in *Pick-Me-Up*, the *Idler* (which he also briefly owned), and the *Pall Mall Gazette*. See Frank Harris, "Lord Dunsany and Sidney Sime," *Contemporary Portraits, Second Series* (New York: The Author, n.d. [1919]), 141–57; George Locke, *From an Ultimate Dim Thule: A Review of the Early Works of S. H. Sime* (London: Ferret Fantasy, 1973), and *The Land of Dreams: A Review of the Work of Sidney H. Sime, 1905 to 1916* (London: Ferret Fantasy, 1975); *Sidney H. Sime, Master of Fantasy*, compiled by Paul W. Skeeters (Pasadena: Ward Ritchie Press, n.d. [1978]); and Simon Heneage and Henry Ford, *Sidney Sime, Master of the Mysterious* (London: Thames and Hudson, 1980).

75 Born in Germany, Henry Mayer (1868–1954), the son of a Jewish merchant from London, worked as a magazine illustrator in Munich, Paris, and London (*The Pall Mall Gazette*). He emigrated to the United States in 1886, became a political cartoonist for the *New York Times* from 1904, and worked on children's books, the illustrated press and several films.

76 Dion Clayton Calthorp (1878–1937) started out as a painter and cartoonist and co-edited the *Idler* magazine with Sidney Sime. From 1906 he devoted himself to his own books and essays.

were published a year later, also in the *Pall Mall Magazine*. Beardsley's influence also spread internationally: Claude Fayette Bragdon's marginal vignettes and full-page designs for the American *Chap-Book*, a magazine published in Chicago by Stone and Kimball and often referring to Beardsley, sometimes recall the Englishman's grotesques.[77] In Germany, the designs of Marcus Behmer were also inspired by Beardsley, as shown in the next chapter.

Sime's case forms an endpoint beyond which it would be difficult to go. His vignettes frequently feature the drama of creation (Fig. 1.17a–f). In one of them, Sime has abandoned his palette in front of an unfinished painting and turns away (Fig. 1.17a); in another, a yawning author with donkey's ears points to an arabesque-bordered void while an imp runs away with a manuscript (Fig. 1.17b); in another, an author at his table, lacking inspiration, verve, and cash, has nothing to sink his teeth into but his own wastepaper basket, filled with the abortive crop of his pen (Fig. 1.17c); in another, a company of miniature imps sharpens a gigantic quill on a grindstone (Fig. 1.17d); in yet another, a black fiend squeezes paint from a tube onto an oversized palette in front of a tiny laurel-wreathed artist, now enclosed in black whirls that end up in a peacock feather (Fig. 1.17e). As if to confess to Beardsley's stimulus, a last vignette reworks the comedy of the cuckolded husband (Fig. 1.17f) as in Beardsley's two puppets manipulated by Molière's hand and its transformation (Zatlin 716 and 723, see Fig. 1.6a–b). Likewise, in his accompanying column, Street often admitted that he had nothing to say and simply let his pen wander.

77 Claude Fayette Bragdon (1866–1946) is mainly recorded as an American architect related to the Prairie School, writer, and stage designer. His work as an illustrator is unexplored.

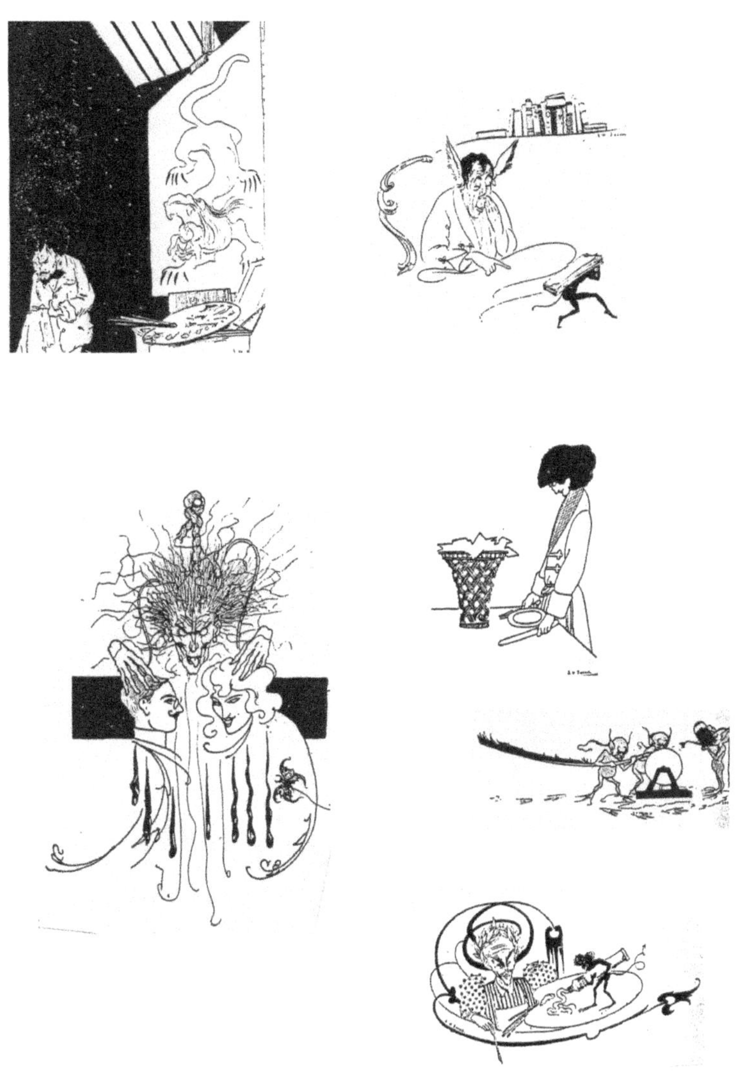

Fig. 1.17a–f Sidney Herbert Sime, Grotesque vignettes published in the *Pall Mall Magazine*. 1.17a *Sime Abandons his Palette* (July 1899): 430a; 1.17b *Yawning Author and Imp* (April 1899): 576; 1.17c *Author and Wastepaper Basket* (July 1899): 430b; 1.17d *Miniature Imps Sharpening a Gigantic Quill* (June 1899): 288b; 1.17e *Black Fiend and Tiny Laurel-wreathed Artist* (July 1899): 432b; 1.17f Sime's version of Beardsley's *Comedy of the Cuckold Husband* (May 1899): 140b. Taken from the *Pall Mall Magazine*

It is in this contrasting context, at once luxurious and cheap, sophisticated and silly, soliciting and denying meaning, that Beardsley's vignettes inaugurated a new type of the book. Contrary to the tradition of the medieval or Renaissance grotesque, which acted as peripheral ornamentation *in the margins of* the main text,[78] each *Bon-Mots* volume is a book that is, in essence, *all margin*. The medieval or Renaissance grotesque appeared in the borders and at the line ends of a manuscript or a book. Unruly curios at the fringe of pious texts, these earlier grotesques adorned psalters, missals, collections of exempla, and sermons. A striking example is the *Book of Hours* of Emperor Maximilian I, adorned by Albrecht Dürer and his colleagues. The demons and grotesques await – on the edges and rims – those who stray from the straight and narrow path set by the text, to either prompt the pious reader to return to the holy text, or perhaps to charm and entertain them in their moment of distraction. The *Book of Hours* richly adorned by Jean Pucelle for Jeanne d'Évreux (1325–28) measures less than 9.5 x 6 cm and is filled with a mixture of horror and grace. Its nearly 900 grotesques threaten to drown the pages and cover the prayers with their juxtaposed profanity, as Jurgis Baltrušaitis has shown.[79]

Beardsley's three booklets have a similar sense of excess and contradiction, but unlike this medieval border art, they are a product of media-driven modernity. They featured in industrially-printed booklets and were created using the mechanical line-block reproduction process, spreading even further in mass-produced magazines. They offered contemporary types, fashionable clothing, and of-the-moment motifs. They were marginal by virtue of their futile, anecdotal and disjointed content, and their grotesques nestle in retorts and quips that rarely conquer a full page, resurfacing without system or plan. Such a book genre was well known to fin-de-siècle sensibility, from the large paper copies meant for bibliophiles to the end of the century's fascination with the blank, unwritten page. It may seem odd to relate them to John Gray's *Silverpoints* in 1893, which offered poems in minute italics on expensive

78 See Jurgis Baltrušaitis, "Le Réveil du fantastique dans le décor du livre," *Réveils et Prodiges: le gothique fantastique* (Paris: A. Colin, 1960), 195–234. His dating slightly differs from the following.

79 *Ibid.*, 206–07 and 208 (fig. 8). See also Jean Pucelle, *Les Heures de Jeanne d'Évreux, reine de France* (ca. 1324–28), *Metropolitan Museum of Art*, https://www.metmuseum.org/fr/art/collection/search/470309

laid paper and a distinguished elongated format. Yet, in an adroit comment full of wit, Ada Leverson invited Wilde to prolong Gray's collection by a book she called "all margin:"

> There was more margin; margin in every sense of the word was in demand, and I remember, looking at the poems of John Gray (then considered the incomparable poet of the age), when I saw the tiniest rivulet of text meandering through the very largest meadow of margin, I suggested to Oscar Wilde that he should go a step further than these minor poets; that he should publish a book *all* margin; full of beautiful unwritten thoughts, and have this blank volume bound in some Nile-green skin powdered with gilt nenuphars and smoothed with hard ivory, decorated with gold by Ricketts (if not Shannon) and printed on Japanese paper; each volume must be a collector's piece, a numbered one of a limited "first" (and last) edition: "very rare."
>
> He approved.
>
> "It shall be dedicated to you, and the unwritten text illustrated by Aubrey Beardsley. There must be five hundred signed copies for particular friends, six for the general public, and one for America."[80]

Beardsley's *Bon-Mots* are a bold realisation of this same idea, not due to the utmost blank of margins invading and cancelling the text, but by the fact that the conjunction of text and drawings is by nature marginal. The three booklets were undoubtedly born of the chance meeting of a publisher's idea with the verve of a talented young illustrator. A literally off-centre triumph of the eccentric become central, the vignettes transform nonsense into a book, and an illustrated book at that. Grotesque, inane, facetious: paralanguages, where the "all margin" boldly takes permanent shape between deluxe editions, newspapers, magazines, and other ephemera, drawing its graphic sense from incongruous textual meaning.

80 Ada Leverson, *Letters to the Sphinx, from Oscar Wilde, with Reminiscences of the Author* (London: Duckworth, 1930), 19–20.

2. A Foetal Laboratory and Its Influence

This chapter considers an innovative, if disturbing, motif in Beardsley's oeuvre: the foetus. He used this image first in the *Bon-Mots* vignettes and then throughout his brief career. Brian Reade and Malcolm Easton have both suggested that Beardsley's repeated depiction of the foetus could be a biographical reference to his sister Mabel's surmised abortion or miscarriage.[1] They also considered it as a minor motif that the artist would leave behind as his work and designs moved to other forms. Yet I see its significance as going far beyond the biographical, and in this chapter I show how it became the artist's most strikingly characteristic and formally innovative emblem.

At the very moment Beardsley was developing his own style and forming his artistic language through the *Bon-Mots*, he plied the foetus into baroque minutiae. He used the shock value of juxtaposition, combining the foetus with what were promoted as more Aesthetic forms, and in doing so pitted himself against the Pre-Raphaelite aesthetics that had nurtured him. As an early manifesto, claiming rights to life and a new existence, he also used it as a provocative metaphor for his own artistic emergence. It came to represent Beardsley's creative and cultural bearings. The foetus also embodied the "elderly youngster," blending the old and decrepit with the extremely young, a common fin-de-siècle motif associated with artistic Decadence. Beardsley's depiction of writer and artist Max Beerbohm as a foetus – complete with top hat and walking stick – is a revealing example of this Decadent figure. The foetal

1 Easton, *Aubrey and the Dying Lady: A Beardsley Riddle* (London: Secker and Warburg, 1972), 156–207, discusses the influence on Beardsley of Mabel's interrupted pregnancy, as well as the hypothesis of incest between brother and sister. Reade had already alluded to Mabel's miscarriage, revised ed., 22.

 https://doi.org/10.11647/OBP.0413.02

motif also burgeoned throughout his later career (drawings for Lucian's *True History*, "A Kiss of Judas," *Salome*, *The Rape of the Lock*, and even a *Savoy* cover) showing an ability for this image to evolve in a way that reflected Darwinian theories of the time. In a telling shift from biology to aesthetics, the foetus exemplifies the power to adapt and differ in style, extending through architecture and caricature. Three instances from German, Dutch, and French contexts prove Beardsley's immediate effect on fin-de-siècle graphic design and its adoption by artists across the Continent.

Foetal *Bon-Mots*

Of Beardsley's seventy-five vignettes in the first volume of *Bon-Mots*, three depict foetuses. *Two Figures by Candlelight Holding a Fetus* (Zatlin 700) is an important yet elusive scene given its dimensions and complexity. It features two grotesques either side of the central foetus figure (Fig. 2.1).

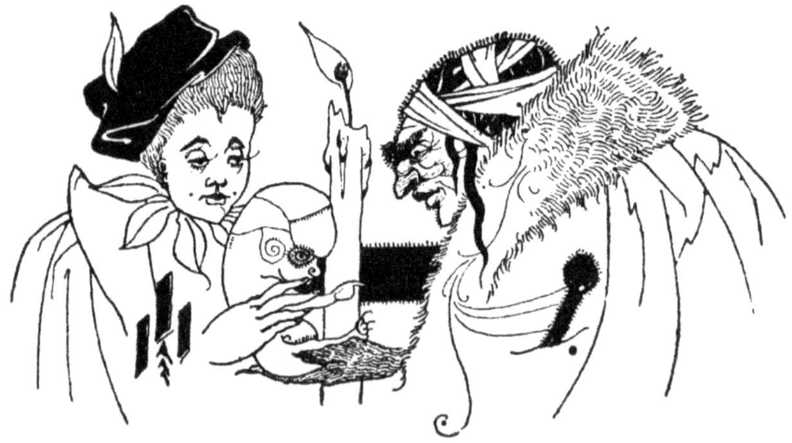

Fig. 2.1 Aubrey Beardsley, *Two Figures by Candlelight Holding a Fetus*, BM-SS:26, BM-LJ:123 (full page, vertically), BM-LJ:151 (R<), BM-FH:165 (R<). PE coll.

A scowling witch-like person stands on the right (although some critics have read it as a frowning man) and a tall candle burns bright in the middle, a frequent Beardsley signature. The scene could be an obscure recollection of a witches' Sabbath. It could also depict an abortion, or perhaps a foetus's nightmarish baptism. The eyes of the female figure on the left certainly droop in weariness above her floral collar. Her fedora hat sits askew on her head as she holds the foetus with one hand. The foetus lifts its arm and points an accusatory finger at the witch. Indescribable expressions and ornate outfits obfuscate what could be connivance or conflict between the hatted woman and the abortionist/witch. Even the device protruding from the right-hand figure's pocket is equivocal: probably an abortive device, it is also phallic, as Reade points out.[2] Yet, under such unclear circumstances and between unreadable figures, the foetus itself stands as a grotesque and unnerving presence. Taken perhaps from an anatomy or embryology plate with additional jots, lines, and dots, this is a new way of drawing the foetus, tense and rich in elusive gist. The fantastic scene is both poised and obsessive, as confirmed by its use throughout the three volumes.

If, as Easton argues, Beardsley was indeed free to arrange the *Bon-Mots* vignettes as he liked,[3] the artist repeats this very scene four times in the three volumes, a privilege afforded to only three grotesques. Its importance is heightened all the more as one is a full-page reproduction.[4] But even if the art direction is not Beardsley's, the vignette certainly made a strong impression on whoever took care of the layout.

In the two remaining vignettes, the foetus lends itself to whimsical treatment and the vagaries of line drawing. The skull stitches become decoration in *Fetus Figure Seated on a Peacock Feather with a Lily between its Feet* (Fig. 2.2a, Zatlin 766). They include Beardsley's Japanese signature in *Memento Mori and a Butterfly above a Fetus Eating its Pointed Tail* (Fig. 2.2b, Zatlin 722).

---

2 Reade, 326, n. 172, compares it to the phallic candle.

3 Easton, *Aubrey and the Dying Lady*, 176.

4 Once in BM-SS, 26; twice in BM-LJ, 123 (full page) and 151; once in BM-FH, 165. This also occurs for *Winged Demon in Evening Dress* (Zatlin 728) and *Child Holding a Stalk of Lilies* (Zatlin 749), which will serve as cover grotesque in later editions (see Fig. 1.1b).

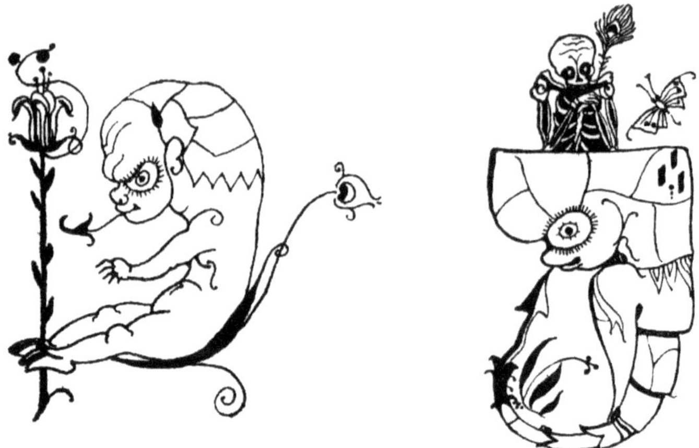

Fig. 2.2a–b Aubrey Beardsley, Two foetal vignettes. 2.2a *Fetus Figure Seated on a Peacock Feather with a Lily between its Feet*, BM-SS:192 (last vignette), BM-LJ:171; 2.2b *Memento Mori and a Butterfly above a Fetus Eating its Pointed Tail*, BM-SS:88. PE coll.

Both involve Aesthetic motifs violently colliding with the foetus as baffling companion. The foetus itself takes on random animal shapes (a shrimp or a crustacean), details from mythical creatures (forked feet) or other unnerving physical features (arrow-like tongue, claws, prickly tail). Such mocking mimicry of traditionally grotesque beings (fauns) or magical symbols (the ouroboros eating its own tail) seeks to recast the imaginary, and mythology itself, by means of new shapes. The foetus's gruesome connection with a skeleton in *Memento Mori* links the end of life to its origin. It is probable that Beardsley's own sense of approaching demise influenced the image. Yet, its aesthetic power goes far beyond the biographical. In Beardsley's work, the foetus also takes on Pre-Raphaelite motifs (a peacock feather, a lily) and a Whistlerian butterfly. Beardsley ironically uses these newly established emblems, still perceived as avant-garde, in an unexpected visual clash with the foetal form. He would eventually elevate the foetus to an aesthetic credo and manifesto on par with these other motifs.

The first and third of these grotesques return in the second volume of *Bon-Mots* (the first appears twice) as part of a set of seven, four of which are new and two full-page. After settling into volume one, the odd shape takes root and proliferates. *Seated Grotesque with a Skull on its Forehead* (Zatlin 789), original in its frontal posture, is more evocative of anatomy samples in jars than of medical plates showing foetuses in profile (Fig. 2.3). The autobiographical explanation of the motif could be both confirmed and mocked by this sulky homunculus. Its protuberant head could allude to two "very different skulls," the first comic, the second diverse, as in Jerrold's pun (skull/scull) above it, alluding to his and a friend's different minds (see Fig. 2.4). The layout of the second *Bon-Mots* brings this vignette and *Two Figures by Candlelight Holding a Fetus* face to face in the same opening (Fig. 2.4).[5] The volume's amiable flippancy reveals images that are intentionally provocative. Zatlin has commented on this foetus's fingers under its protuberant belly, creating "the outline of the head or skull of an animal, possibly a fox, whose snout forms the creature's penis and tiny genitalia or the skull's eyes, nose and upper lip."[6] As with its multiple deformed toes, the bloated shape swells with anomalous bodies.

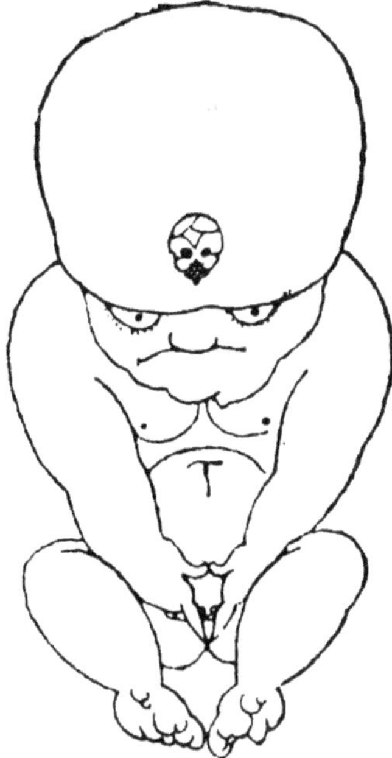

Fig. 2.3 Aubrey Beardsley, *Seated Grotesque with a Skull on its Forehead*, BM-LJ:150, BM-FH:50 (R<). PE coll.

5 BM-LJ, 150–51.

6 Linda Gertner Zatlin, *Aubrey Beardsley: A Catalogue Raisonné*, 2 vols. (New Haven, Conn.: Yale University Press, 2016), I, 468.

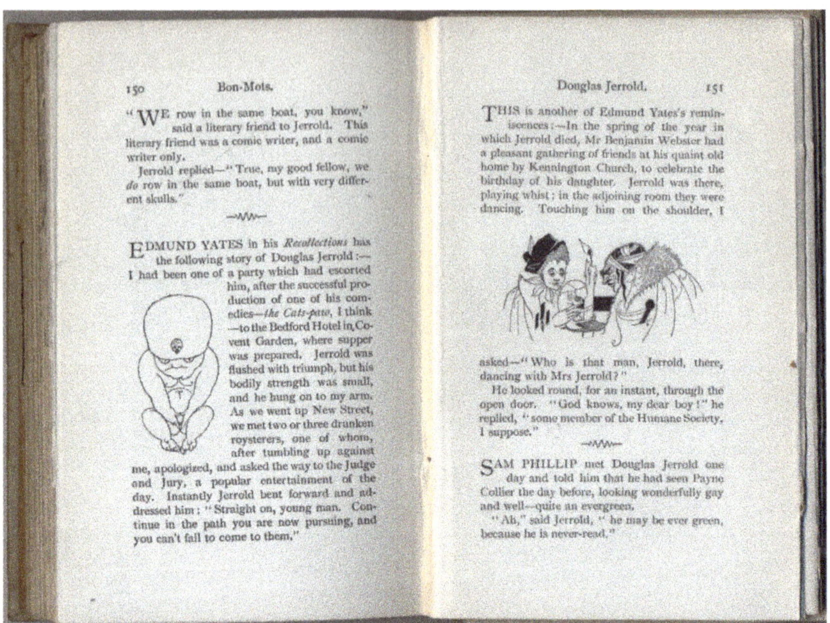

150 Bon-Mots.

"WE row in the same boat, you know," said a literary friend to Jerrold. This literary friend was a comic writer, and a comic writer only.

Jerrold replied—"True, my good fellow, we *do* row in the same boat, but with very different skulls."

EDMUND YATES in his *Recollections* has the following story of Douglas Jerrold:—I had been one of a party which had escorted him, after the successful production of one of his comedies—*the Cats-paw*, I think—to the Bedford Hotel in Covent Garden, where supper was prepared. Jerrold was flushed with triumph, but his bodily strength was small, and he hung on to my arm. As we went up New Street, we met two or three drunken roysterers, one of whom, after tumbling up against me, apologized, and asked the way to the Judge and Jury, a popular entertainment of the day. Instantly Jerrold bent forward and addressed him: "Straight on, young man. Continue in the path you are now pursuing, and you can't fail to come to them."

Douglas Jerrold. 151

THIS is another of Edmund Yates's reminiscences:—In the spring of the year in which Jerrold died, Mr Benjamin Webster had a pleasant gathering of friends at his quaint old home by Kennington Church, to celebrate the birthday of his daughter. Jerrold was there, playing whist; in the adjoining room they were dancing. Touching him on the shoulder, I asked—"Who is that man, Jerrold, there, dancing with Mrs Jerrold?"

He looked round, for an instant, through the open door. "God knows, my dear boy!" he replied, "some member of the Humane Society, I suppose."

SAM PHILLIP met Douglas Jerrold one day and told him that he had seen Payne Collier the day before, looking wonderfully gay and well—quite an evergreen.

"Ah," said Jerrold, "he may be ever green, because he is never-read."

Fig. 2.4 Aubrey Beardsley, shocking layout in BM-LJ:150-51, showing left *Seated Grotesque with a Skull on its Forehead*, and right *Two Figures by Candlelight holding a Fetus*. Courtesy MSL coll., Delaware

The second volume of *Bon-Mots* acts as an arena for new experiments. The foetal form becomes the basis for a new series of limp and adaptable, often epicene beings (a feature deriving from the embryo's undefined gender). In this volume, Beardsley eschews his typical arabesque and hairy-line style in favour of the black-and-white contrast that heralds the *Yellow Book* drawings. His new style inspires further innovation. The foetus's characteristic bulging head and distinctly domed skull is a key to *Caricature of Max Beerbohm* (Zatlin 770), a grotesque in black evening dress with cape I will come back to (see Fig. 2.8a). Thanks to graphic mutation, the foetus escapes the abortive or decorative context to enter a gallery of fin-de-siècle types, of which the second *Bon-Mots* provides three examples: the foetal dandy, the cloaked and masked hermaphrodite, and the man in a ballerina's tutu. The *Masked Pierrette in a Cape and a Ruff*, classified as female (Zatlin 788), is the most baffling of all three (Fig. 2.5a).

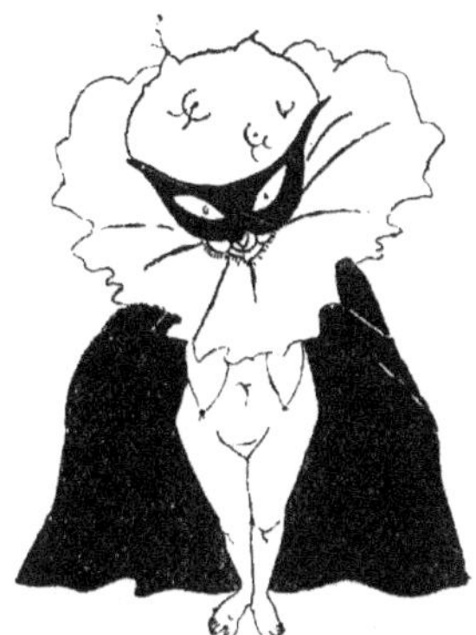
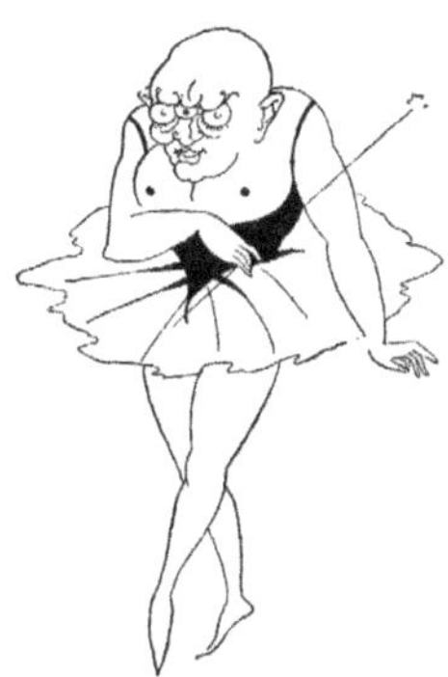

Fig. 2.5a–b Aubrey Beardsley, Foetal fin-de-siècle types from the second *Bon-Mots*. 2.5a *Masked Pierrette in a Cape and a Ruff*, BM-LJ:138; 2.5b *Bald-headed Figure in a Short Tutu*, BM-LJ:162, BM-FH:130 (R<). PE coll.

A bloated head covered in hirsute breasts, growing anarchically over a wide ruff, crowns a feminine body whose chest is flaccid. An evil grin lurks under its mask, but the creature is also a bearded Pierrot, a figure recurrent in Beardsley's work, to whom Laforgue ascribes an "air of hydrocephalic asparagus" in *L'Imitation de Notre-Dame la Lune*, a collection organised as the very space of barrenness where the foetus appears twice.[7] Laforgue and Beardsley shared a similar sensibility and Jacques-Émile Blanche recorded their intellectual kinship.[8] A *Bald-headed Figure in a Short Tutu* (Fig. 2.5b, Zatlin 792) closes the series in her dashing garb, perhaps a reminder of the monsters in Léon Genonceaux's novel *Le Tutu: mœurs fin-de-siècle*,[9] but the lure of her luscious bare breasts

7 Jules Laforgue, "Pierrots, I," in Laforgue, *L'Imitation de N.-D. la Lune* (Paris: Léon Vanier, 1886 [1885]); Laforgue, *Poésies complètes*, ed. by Pascal Pia, Poésie (Paris: Gallimard, 1979), 28: "*un air d'hydrocéphale asperge.*" Beardsley, who certainly knew Laforgue's collection, refers to one of his drawings as *Notre Dame de la Lune* (Zatlin 196). See *The Letters of Aubrey Beardsley*, ed. by Henry Maas, J. L. Duncan, and W. G. Good (London: Cassell, 1970), 19.

8 Blanche, "Aubrey Beardsley," *Antée: Revue mensuelle de littérature*, 2:11 (1 Apr 1907): 1114–15 and 1122. They did not know each other, states Blanche.

9 Princesse Sapho [Léon Genonceaux], *Le Tutu: mœurs fin de siècle, avec une planche de musique céleste et une composition symbolique de Binet* (Paris: L. Genonceaux, 1891).

is at odds with her scowling, masculine, Cyclopean head. Monstrosity incarnate beckons to us.

The motif progresses again in the third volume of *Bon-Mots* with nine foetal vignettes out of sixty-six (Fig. 2.6a–d). Beardsley's more traditional themes are clearly receding as the volumes progress. Fauns or satyrs, for instance, are common in the first, decline in the second, and hardly appear in the last volume. Conversely, the foetal grotesque grows all the more prominent, as only twenty-five out of the sixty-six vignettes are new, one fifth of which are foetal. I will comment later on the *Winged Baby in a Top Hat Leading a Dog* along with the dandy foetus (both being Max Beerbohm caricatures, see Fig. 2.8a and 2.8c), to group here the *Skeleton in an Evening Frock* (Fig. 2.6a, Zatlin 803), the *Bald Dandy Doffing his Hat to a Lady*, whose ballooning head discloses pointed ears (Fig. 2.6b, Zatlin 798), and the *Devil in Morning Coat*, which may also be described as a hydrocephalic horned fop (Fig. 2.6c, Zatlin 810).

Some of the titles that have been given to the works minimise the creatures' oddity and mask their foetal nature. Yet all of them depict a bloated head, occasionally with a frown, that is characteristic of the foetus. The ballooning head rounds off silhouettes of indisputable modernity, all stamped by some incongruity: a skeletal arm, a faun's ear, a sneering mask or a horn. Reduced to pure outline, devoid of arabesques or interlacing, the contour boosts their strangeness. The reason is their grotesque nature: the foetal inspiration merges both dead and living parts. Yet in this last volume former macabre references start to recede. The *Dual-sex Grotesque* exploits previous forms to show the astonishingly plastic potential of sprouting foetal bodies (Fig. 2.6d, Zatlin 815). Here the foetal element both governs the figure and nourishes its parts. Its posture is in profile rather than frontal, its head domed, its swollen occiput covered in breasts and nipples, its skull stitches dotted. Its hermaphroditism is patent, its body shrivelling, its limbs prawn-like. Mutation is complete. A being is born that resists description or identification.

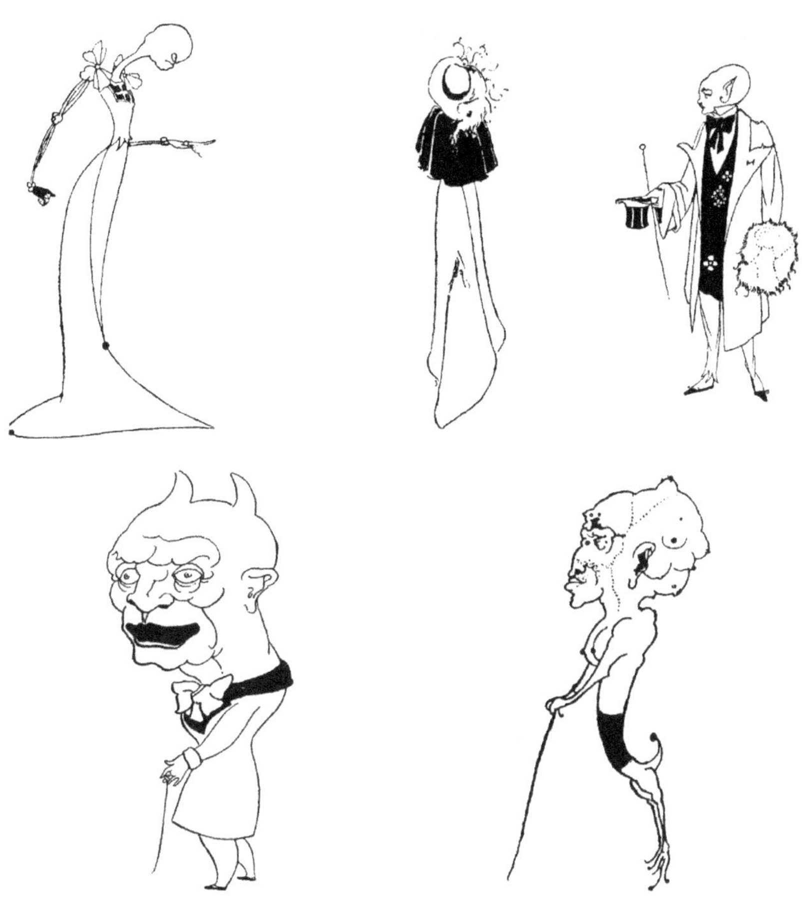

Fig. 2.6a–d Aubrey Beardsley, Foetal grotesques in the third *Bon-Mots*. 2.6a *Skeleton in an Evening Frock*, BM-FH:44; 2.6b *Bald Dandy Doffing his Hat to a Lady*, BM-FH:17; 2.6c *Devil in Morning Coat*, BM-FH:104; 2.6d *Dual-sex Grotesque*, BM-FH:148

Surfacing in just three vignettes in the first *Bon-Mots*, Beardsley's foetal grotesque appears seven times in the second (three old, four new), and nine in the third (four repeated, five new). It has clearly proliferated from one volume to the next although new grotesques decrease and old ones are profusely reused. It conquers key spaces including half-titles and even full-page spreads. The foetus may well partly be a private obsession of Beardsley, based on incidents in his life, but it also represents a revolutionary medium. A quick look at key scientific theories of the time explains why.

Monstrous Embryology

Embryology had emerged as a science in the nineteenth century and had made a major contribution to Darwinian theory. *On the Origin of Species* (1859) referred to Karl von Baer's principle of embryonic resemblance between mammals, birds, lizards, serpents, and chelonians. Darwin had him pronounce the following statement, filled with captivating uncertainty:

> [...] in my possession are two little embryos in spirit, whose names I have omitted to attach, and at present I am quite unable to say to what class they belong. They may be lizards or small birds, or very young mammalia, so complete is the similarity in the mode of formation of the head and trunk in these animals.[10]

Furthermore, Darwin used the structure of the embryo rather than the adult's as a classification basis.[11] A parallel between the similarity of the embryonic structure and similarity of descent allowed him to formulate the hypothesis of all species originating in the same ancestor: "some ancient progenitor, which was furnished in its adult state with branchiae, a swim-bladder, four fin-like limbs, and a long tail, and fitted for an aquatic life."[12] Darwinian theory did not explicitly concern the human embryo. Yet Ernst Haeckel's controversial comparative figures of tortoise, fowl, dog, and human embryos in *Natürliche Schöpfungsgeschichte* (1868, translated into English as *The History of Creation*, 1876) made the point, further popularised in Haeckel's *Anthropogenie* (1874). Haeckel openly stated that in only an advanced state of development does it become possible to distinguish between human and animal shapes. In *The General Morphology of Organisms* (*Generelle Morphologie der Organismen*, 1866), he formulated the catchy axiom "ontogeny is an abridged and accelerated recapitulation of phylogeny." He meant that the growth and development of an individual organism recapped the evolutionary history of a species. Although this was far from a full-blown theory, it implied that, during the intra-uterine period, the human embryo undergoes all the stages involved in the evolution of species.

10 Charles Darwin, *On the Origin of Species by means of Natural Selection, or the Preservation of Favoured Races in the Struggle for Life* (London: John Murray, 1859), repr. 1900, 605.

11 *Ibid.*, 617.

12 *Ibid.*

Though incorrect, the theory fascinated the fin-de-siècle imagination.[13] The foetus potentially contained all forms. It was individualised by science and also existed in a state of gestation. It was concurrently a synopsis of the evolution of the species, a possible mould for the monster, and a form by nature subject to transformation. Beardsley transferred its transformative ability to his work. In his vignettes, the foetus embraces a variety of graphic languages (fine outline, hairy-line style, arabesque, black-and-white contrast). An inherently pliant image, it lends itself to new creations. It is the dominant motif of a new conception of the grotesque, the very emblem of a budding new – indeed, embryonic – artform.

An Aesthetic Proposal

Beardsley's *Incipit Vita Nova* (Fig. 2.7, Zatlin 243) is an Indian ink and white gouache drawing on brown paper. Zatlin dates it to May 1892, which precedes the *Bon-Mots* by four months, and differs from them in size, technique and meaning. It shows a woman and a foetus with a book in between them. The woman belongs to the Pre-Raphaelite type frequent in Dante Gabriel Rossetti's work, which Beardsley caricatures. Her streaming hair on the left and a lonely curl on the right claim the central book as her own. On the open page of the book is written "Incipit vita nova" ("Here begins a new life"), which, we assume, refers to the foetus, its wide-open eye, demanding gesture and jutting-out foot pulling the book towards it. The phrase is taken from the first paragraph of Dante's *Vita Nova*, translated into English by Rossetti between 1846 and 1847, and already twice published in *The Early Italian Poets from Ciullo d'Alcamo to Dante Alighieri* (1861) and *Dante and His Circle* (1874). Beardsley, who must have known it,[14] appropriates it by transferring it to his own creature, who claims a right to its own atypical life.

13 Further on this, see Évanghélia Stead, *Le Monstre, le singe et le fœtus: Tératogonie et Décadence dans l'Europe fin-de-siècle* (Geneva: Droz, 2004), 420 ff.

14 Beardsley had previously drawn inspiration from Dante's relation to Beatrice Portinari, referenced through Rossetti's work and the Pre-Raphaelites' relation to Dante's *Vita Nova*. See Beardsley's *Annovale della Morte di Beatrice* (Zatlin 228) as well as his *Dante in Exile* (Zatlin 185) and *Francesca di Rimini (Dante)* (Zatlin 184).

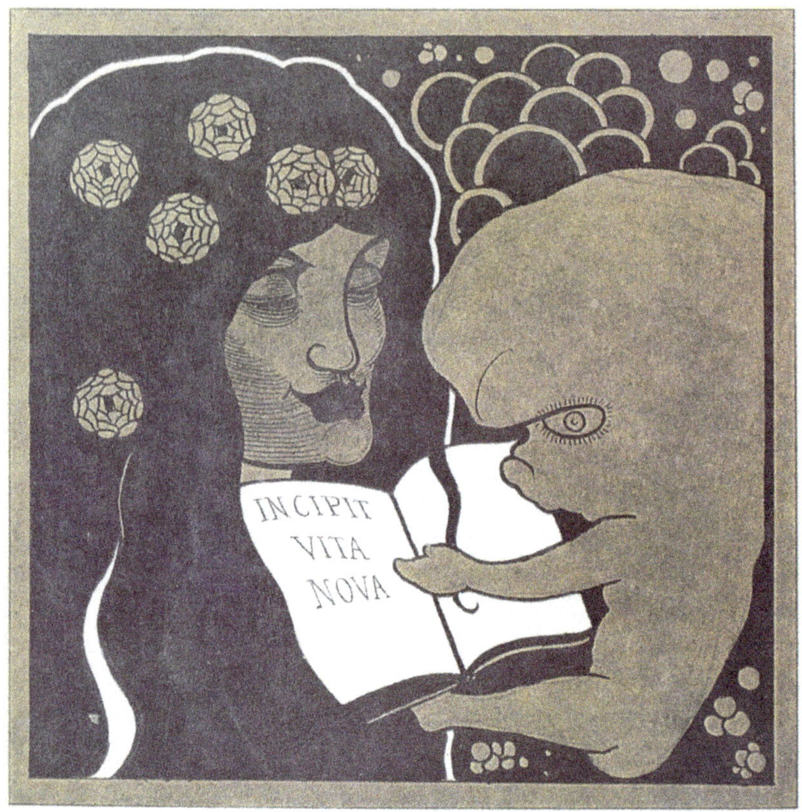

Fig. 2.7 Aubrey Beardsley (May 1892), coll. Linda Gertner Zatlin; WikiArt, Visual Art Encyclopedia, https://www.wikiart.org/en/aubrey-beardsley/incipit-vita-nova

Beardsley was fascinated by the Pre-Raphaelites in his early days. He visited Edward Burne-Jones in person and excitedly discovered eleven Rossetti paintings in the collection of Frederick Leyland, a major Pre-Raphaelite patron.[15] He was certainly familiar with one of Rossetti's most famous works, *Beata Beatrix*, which was acquired by the Tate Gallery in 1889. This Beatrice is the only one of her Rossetti namesakes to be pictured with her eyes closed, a detail referring to the last sentence of the *Vita Nova*, as Rossetti himself specified in a letter of March 1873: "Beatrice is rapt visibly into Heaven, seeing as it were through her shut lids (as Dante

15 *The Letters of Aubrey Beardsley*, 19.

says at the close of the Vita Nuova): 'Him who is blessed throughout all ages.'"[16] Rossetti had even unscrupulously changed the last sentence in the *Vita Nova*, *"quella benedetta Beatrice la quale gloriosamente mira..."* ("that blessed Beatrice, who gloriously beholds..."), to include the title of his own painting (*"beata Beatrice"*) in his *New Life of Dante Alighieri*.[17]

Beardsley's female figure in *Incipit Vita Nova* may be a caricature of the generic Pre-Raphaelite type cast by Rossetti (sensual lips, flowing hair, voluptuous expression), and Zatlin has argued, based on hairstyles, that there is a kinship between Beardsley's drawing and four Rossetti pictures in Leyland's collection.[18] However, her shut eyelids link her specifically with *Beata Beatrix*. Beardsley would thus combine the opening formula (*Incipit vita nova*) with the final phrasing of Dante's text while challenging the Pre-Raphaelites' very leader, Dante's namesake and English translator. Indeed, far from being a harmless skit, his drawing is a subversive manifesto addressed to an image acquired by national collections.

"Here begins a new life" is to be taken in the literal sense. The mystical and exalted dimension of Dante's original disappears in favour of a literal pun, a matter-of-fact interpretation of metaphor, typical of fin-de-siècle style.[19] It "brings Dante's tale of ideal love down to earth with a bump" in Zatlin's felicitous phrase.[20] Facing the caricature of one of the most famous Pre-Raphaelite paintings of the time, the sullen foetus, indignantly clenching its fist and gesticulating as in many vignettes, claims the right to ultimately come of age into grotesque *aesthetic* existence. Such is this very drawing but also the *Bon-Mots* vignettes, as they freed the artist from the Kelmscott Press philosophy and choices, inflicted on him by the illustration of Malory's *Le Morte Darthur*. The incongruous foetus rebels here against the overwhelming Pre-Raphaelite mother. Reade, referring to Art Nouveau designs by Peter Behrens, argues that the motif holds promise of "stylized economies of

16 Letter dated 11 Mar 1873, in *The Pre-Raphaelites* (London: The Tate Gallery / Penguin Books, 1984), 209.

17 *The New Life of Dante Alighieri. Translations and Pictures by Dante Gabriel Rossetti* (New York: R. H. Russell, 1901), 12.

18 Zatlin, *Catalogue Raisonné*, I, 139.

19 On this, see Stead, *Le Monstre, le singe et le fœtus*, 39–40, 43, 70, 128, 209, 233–38, 248.

20 Zatlin, *Catalogue Raisonné*, I, 140.

form and tone."[21] As in the vignettes, pliability and formal invention exemplify a new grotesque vocabulary with the foetus as emblem.

Without overlooking the personal or emotional weight it may have for Beardsley, I consequently argue that the foetus represents above all a graphic, symbolic, and aesthetic crucible. It persists in Beardsley's work until at least 1896. Since the artist died in March 1898 aged twenty-five, frequent blood losses hardly allowing him to work during the last year, it could well be that the unusual motif, either primary or secondary, colonised three to four of the six short years of his production. A quick examination of Beardsley's work, with the exception of *Le Morte Darthur*, shows the motif's regular return. It features, for example, in two of the four drawings published in *St. Paul's* in 1894 (Zatlin 333–36). It re-emerges in the plates for several texts, Lucian's *True History* (1894), X. L.'s narrative "The Kiss of Judas" (1893), the English translation of Oscar Wilde's *Salome* (1894), and Alexander Pope's heroic-comic *The Rape of the Lock* (1896). It transcends genre. Each of these incidences has its own weight and deserves consideration. We face a motif capable of readily transforming itself and blending with others. It is no accident the foetus embodied genesis and development, concepts strongly emphasised by evolutionary theories of the time. It even became the basis of a collective Decadent identity.

Portrait of a Generation

Despite its Dantean title, Ezra Pound's "'Siena mi fé; disfecemi Maremma'" is an account of the Yellow Nineties and English fin de siècle. The poem begins by describing Victor Plarr, "Among the pickled foetuses and bottled bones, | Engaged in perfecting the catalogue" of the Royal College of Surgeons, of which he was a curator from 1897.[22] In the corresponding short collection *Hugh Selwyn Mauberley* (1919), Pound mentions several other figures of the day: Ernest Dowson, the Rhymers' Club, Lionel Johnson, Selwyn Image, and, last but not least, Beerbohm in "Brennbaum," the poem immediately following "'Siena mi fé.'" *Hugh Selwyn Mauberley* includes, as John J. Espey has shown, a collective

21 Reade, 335, n. 269.

22 "'Siena mi fé, disfecemi Maremma,'" *Hugh Selwyn Mauberley by E. P.* (London: The Egoist Ltd., 1919). Qtd. in Ezra Pound, *Poems and Translations*, ed. by Richard Sieburth, The Library of America 144 (New York: The Library of America, 2003), 553.

generational portrait and an elliptical painting of degeneration[23] in which Beerbohm's effigy is favoured:

> The sky-like limpid eyes,
> The circular infant's face,
> The stiffness from spats to collar
> Never relaxing into grace;
>
> The heavy memories of Horeb, Sinai and the forty years,
> Showed only when the daylight fell
> Level across the face
> Of Brennbaum "The Impeccable."[24]

Like Pound's verses, Beardsley's vignettes depict a flawlessly elegant Beerbohm as a foetus in black evening dress with a fake collar (Fig. 2.8a, Zatlin 770), or as a winged infant in a top hat, with a stick and dog-leash in hand (Fig. 2.8c, Zatlin 797). There is a striking resemblance between this Beerbohm-as-foetus and the opening vignette that Maurice Mac-Nab published with his poem "Les Fœtus," issued in Paris in his 1886 collection *Poèmes mobiles* (Fig. 2.8b).

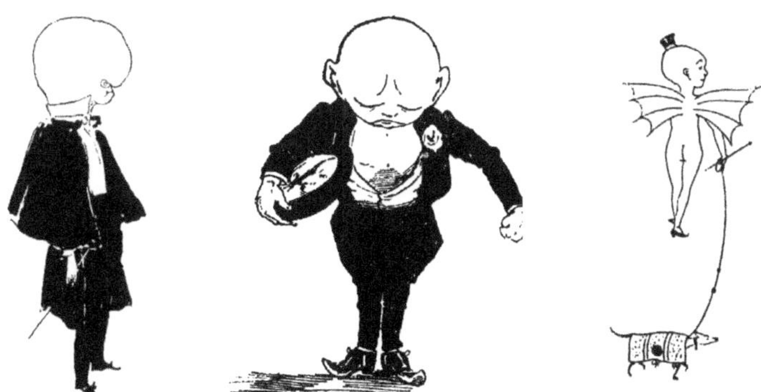

Fig. 2.8a–c Aubrey Beardsley, Beerbohm as foetus, and Mac-Nab's foetus vignette. 2.8a Beardsley, *Caricature of Max Beerbohm*, BM-LJ:23, BM-FH:156; 2.8b Mac-Nab, *Foetus Vignette in Evening Dress, Poèmes mobiles* (1886), 17; 2.8c Beardsley, *Winged Baby in a Top Hat Leading a Dog*, BM-FH:15 (half-title vignette for "Samuel Foote"). PE coll.

23 John J. Espey, *Ezra Pound's "Mauberley:" A Study in Composition* (Berkeley and Los Angeles, Calif.: University of California Press, 1955), 15 and 91–93.

24 Pound, *Poems and Translations*, 554. The references to Horeb and the Sinai in relation to Beerbohm are enigmatic. Beerbohm was not Jewish, although his name may be taken as such.

Mac-Nab's foetus bows in a black suit, and Beardsley may have reworked this form, emphasising the bloated head, black garb, and shirtfront, and increasing the black-and-white contrast. Mac-Nab himself performed the poem as a monologue in deadpan style at the Chat Noir cabaret, of which he was an early star, contributing to its tongue-in-cheek entertainment and humour.[25] The satirical magazine *Les Hommes d'aujourd'hui* published on its cover a full-length portrait of Mac-Nab carrying a protesting foetus in a green jar under his arm in 1887.[26] The cover of the following issue pictured Stéphane Mallarmé as a faun. Respected symbolist poets and cabaret performers met in the press. In such context, the foetus had become an iconic image related to the mischievous avant-garde. Beardsley, who first visited Paris in 1892 and referred to the Chat Noir in an 1893 letter, may have seen such drawings.[27] He certainly spent time with the Pennells at the Chat Noir and other Parisian cabarets in 1893.[28] As for Beerbohm, he was certainly aware of his two grotesque "portraits" by Beardsley, since he depicts the latter in *Caricatures of Twenty-Five Gentlemen* (1896), trailing a pet dog on wheels,[29] as Beerbohm himself dragged a pet puppy behind him in the Beardsley vignette.

But why would Beerbohm become a grotesque with a foetal head? And why a foetus-dandy portrait in Pound's verse several years later? Perhaps for the very same reason that Beerbohm provides a rather unusual portrait of himself in a January 1895 *Sketch* interview with Ada Leverson (Fig. 2.9).

---

25 Maurice Mac-Nab, "Les Fœtus," in Mac-Nab, *Poèmes mobiles: Monologues, avec illustrations de l'auteur et une préface de Coquelin cadet* (Paris: Léon Vanier, 1886), 15–22, with vignettes.

26 Pierre et Paul [Léon Vanier], "Maurice Mac-Nab, dessin de Fernand Fau," *Les Hommes d'aujourd'hui*, 6:295 (1887): 1, https://gallica.bnf.fr/ark:/12148/bpt6k11924086/f369.item.zoom

27 *The Letters of Aubrey Beardsley*, 53 (letter to John Lane, postmarked 12 Sept 1893).

28 See Elizabeth Robins Pennell, *The Life and Letters of Joseph Pennell*, 2 vols. (Boston: Little, Brown, and Co, 1929), I, 253.

29 Max Beerbohm, *Caricatures of Twenty-Five Gentlemen, with an Introduction by L. Raven-Hill*, London, Leonard Smithers, 1896, 12. See https://archive.org/details/bub_gb_RsIrAQAAMAAJ/page/n35/mode/2up?view=theater

A FEW WORDS WITH MR. MAX BEERBOHM.

Mr. Max Beerbohm left Oxford only last term to plunge into the delights of literature in London. In that short space of time, by his curious contributions to the *Yellow Book*, he has gained a more than merely esoteric fame. Indeed, he may be said to occupy in literature somewhat the same position as does Mr. Aubrey Beardsley in art. The success of each has been a success of astonishment. Both are essentially modern, and "implected," to borrow some of Mr. Beerbohm's own favourite phrases, with a love of the "mysteries of style," a passion for "paradox and marivaudage"—in fact, for "all unusual things." The style of each, moreover, is wonderfully sure and complete for artists so very young.

I went with a letter of introduction to Mr. Beerbohm's house some time ago. It is one of that row of houses known as Hyde Park Place. Its windows command a charming view of the Park—a place which, as Mr. Beerbohm remarked to me, is "quite as nice as the country, and not half so provincial." The room in which Mr. Beerbohm received me and spends most of his time is the same room in which Kinglake wrote his famous history of the Crimean War. I could not help wondering what

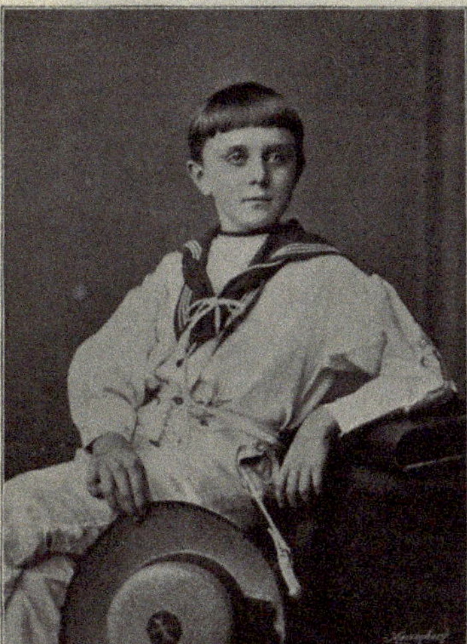

MAX BEERBOHM IN BOYHOOD.

Kinglake would have thought of his youthful successor's History of George the Fourth. Youthful certainly he is—not, indeed, quite as youthful as he is seen in the portrait which he gave me for reproduction in *The Sketch*, and which, he explained, is the only one that has been taken in recent years. He has altered very little since then, though he no longer wears a fringe and has exchanged the frivolities of the white and blue sailor suit for the sterner realities of the frock-coat and high collar. His inscrutable, somewhat cynical, expression heightens his appearance of youthfulness, and his manners are studiously urbane.

"I am afraid," he said, in his gentle, musical voice, in answer to my request, "that there is very little to tell about my life so far. I have done the ordinary things. I went to Charterhouse when I was twelve, but I don't know that I enjoyed myself much there. I agree with that cosy writer, Mr. James Payn, who has so often pointed out that boys are not a nice race. They are bullies or cowards, according to their size. Not that there was 'bullying' in the accepted sense—that has all been suppressed, along with highway robbery and town-and-gown rows. Boys, nowadays, indulge in a kind of social terrorism among themselves that is far more objectionable than the roasting and tossing of the good old days. The snobbishness of boys is amazing. The gossip and the scandal that go on at a public school would alarm a dowager. But Oxford—Oxford is the perfect city. I shall never have such a happy time as I had there."

"What are your plans now? Are you going in for literature wholly?"

"No; I intend to draw as well—always caricatures. You may have seen my series in *Pick-Me-Up* and the *Pall Mall Budget*. One or two of those drawings have been thought rather cruel, I believe. I can't understand how anyone can resent a mere exaggeration of feature. The caricaturist simply passes his subject through a certain grotesque convention. That the result is not a classically beautiful figure proves nothing about the personal appearance of the subject. There is no such thing as a good or a bad subject for caricature. To the true caricaturist Adonis or Punchinello is equally good game. I never pretend that my caricatures are meant for portraits. And I do not think that the men themselves whom I have drawn have ever been offended."

"Perhaps their wives have been? Now tell me, Mr. Beerbohm, about your writing. Tell me about the article on 'Cosmetics'—the best-abused thing in the first number of the *Yellow Book*—or about your white-washing of George IV."

"My article on 'Cosmetics' was a very good joke, but—I thought when I wrote it—rather obvious. I was surprised the critics did not see it at once. It is not often a new writer has to complain of being taken too seriously. 'George IV.' was received in a far more reasonable manner. My point of view was more nearly understood. I meant all I said about George, but I did not choose to express myself quite seriously. To treat history as a means of showing one's own cleverness may be rather rough on history, but it has been done by the best historians, from Herodotus to Froude and myself. Some of my 'George' was false, and much was flippant; but why should a writer sit down to be systematically serious, or else conscientiously comic. Style should be oscillant."

"Oscillant? Is that one of your queer words, of which we have heard so much? Do you intend to abandon them, as an affectation?"

"Certainly not. They are not affected. At times there is no word in the English dictionary by which I can express my shade of meaning. I try to think of a French, or Latin, or Greek one. If I can't, then I invent a word—such as 'pop-limbo' or 'bauble-tit'—often a compound of some well-known English word with an affix or prefix to point its significance. Sometimes I invent a word merely because the cadence of a sentence demands it."

"And are you writing much now?"

"I am doing some work for the new *Saturday Review*, and I am in treaty with a publisher to produce a little book of studies and essays. At this moment I am writing a treatise upon 'The Brothers of Great Men,' including a series of psychological sketches of Mr. Willie Wilde, Mr. Austin Chamberlain, and others."

"You are a brother of Mr. Beerbohm Tree, I believe?"

"Yes; he is coming into the series!"

HOW THE MAILS ARE STOPPED IN CENTRAL AFRICA.

Who ever heard of a flea being capable of such important transgressions as to actually hinder the delivery of her Majesty's mails? And yet the thing has occurred quite recently in British Central Africa. This horrid little beastie has, it appears, certain corkscrew capabilities with which it insinuates its unwelcome presence, principally in the victim's foot, and this lively traffic in humanity has lately become so general that many of the native postmen have been lamed, and so considerable delay has occurred in transmission of the mails. Locusts are also a power to be reckoned with in the land, coming in uncountable myriads and picnicking on native plantations. So far, they have avoided the tea and coffee shrub grown largely in the Shiré province, and have disdained European crops generally, to the surprised satisfaction of the settlers. But how long it will take them to cultivate a false appetite is another question quite; and one vigorous young colonist, writing home, piously assures me that there is a fortune for any of "those inventive fellows who can produce a remedy or antidote against the inroads of these blankety blank locusts," or still more, no doubt, the doubly blanked "jigger." Speaking of fleas brings one naturally to flies, and here is an interesting photograph of the proboscis of a fly, taken by Mr. Richard Smith, of Hovis Bread fame.

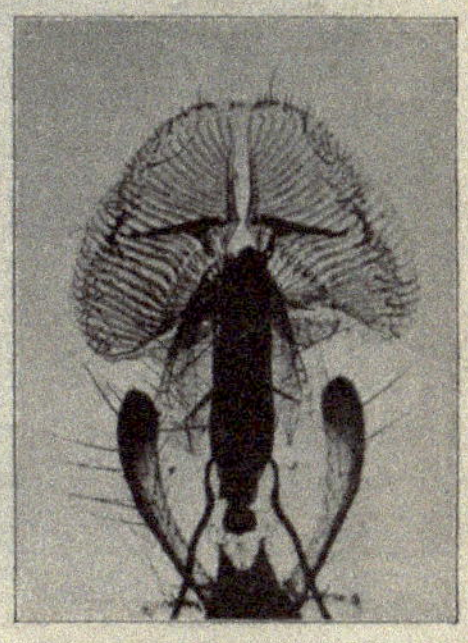

THE PROBOSCIS OF A FLY.

From a Photograph taken by Mr. R. Smith, of Hovis Bread fame.

Fig. 2.9 Beerbohm's portrait in a sailor's suit, "A Few Words with Mr. Max Beerbohm," *The Sketch*, 8:101 (2 Jan 1895): 439. University of Minnesota Libraries

In a sailor's collar, he is only ten years old, and the text emphasises his extreme youth – shared with Beardsley:

> Youthful certainly he is – not, indeed, quite as youthful as he is seen in the portrait which he gave me for reproduction in *The Sketch*, and which, he explained, is the only one that has been taken in recent years. He has altered very little since then, though he no longer wears a fringe and has exchanged the frivolities of the white and blue sailor suit for the sterner realities of the frock-coat and high collar. His inscrutable, somewhat cynical, expression heightens his appearance of youthfulness, and his manners are studiously urbane.[30]

Was he not a premature genius? His photograph testified to this. Similarly, period accounts on Beardsley by Dugald Sutherland MacColl and Evelyn Sharp stressed his own boyish personality.[31] Beardsley, at the height of his fame, gave *Sketch* a photograph of himself at eleven and a half in April 1895 (see Fig. 4.6).[32] The British public craved posturing more than facts, and extreme youth was one of the fashionable poses. The paradox of a fresh yet cynical being, young yet experienced, youthful yet elderly, resurfaces in Holbrook Jackson's *The Eighteen Nineties*, a rich record of English Decadence. It relates, at least in part, to having an upper-crust British education: Beerbohm was an eminent Old Carthusian, still honoured at Charterhouse public school. However, the fresh yet cynical fellow, youthful yet elderly, was also a common fin-de-siècle type, associated with the Decadents. Jackson's portrait of Beerbohm, for example, references W. S. Gilbert's trope of the "precocious baby":

> Max Beerbohm gives the impression of having been born grown-up – that is to say, more or less ripe when others would be more or less raw and green. One can well imagine such a youth a few years earlier filling,

30 "A Few Words with Mr. Max Beerbohm," *The Sketch*, 8:101 (2 Jan 1895): 439.

31 MacColl starts with the expression "that extraordinary boy" (17) and frequently repeats the word. See D. S. MacColl, "Aubrey Beardsley", in *A Beardsley Miscellany*, ed. by R. A. Walker (London: The Bodley Head, 1949), p. 15–32 (21, 22, 29). See also Evelyn Sharp, *Unfinished Adventure: Selected Reminiscences from an Englishwoman's Life* (London: John Lane, 1933), 60: "Aubrey Beardsley, who rather liked to pose as a very youthful genius."

32 See further Chapter 4.

in a more elegant way, the part of Sir W. S. Gilbert's immortal "Precocious Baby,"[33] who was born, it will be remembered, with

"A pipe in his mouth, and a glass in his eye,
A hat all awry,
An octagon tie,
And a miniature-miniature glass in his eye."[34]

Similarly Paul Verlaine describes several fin-de-siècle men of letters as "eyeglass kids" ("*Mômes-monocles*"), so named because of their young age and the monocle they share with Beerbohm, "the cherished emblem of the upcoming generation of this decadence."[35] Verlaine goes on to portray Édouard Dubus as "hairless and pale," and Dauphin Meunier and Julien Leclercq as "glamorous, presumptive, beardless."[36] The profile returns in "Silhouettes décadentes," a series of written portraits broached by the little-known Pierre Vareilles for the review *Le Décadent*: "Razor-sharp, beardless as a virgin, and hairless, here comes Georges Toulouse."[37] Even the coterie in Charles Buet's novel *Saphyr* is made "of beardless Decadents and elderly Parnassians."[38]

A fin-de-siècle type emerges: the Decadent wears an eyeglass (as Beerbohm and the "*Mômes-monocles*"); he looks exceptionally young, and is therefore hairless or beardless; and he is born both adult and premature. It makes sense that Beardsley depicts Beerbohm in the guise of a foetus. Two standard expressions in French refer to this paradoxical figure: the "elderly youngsters" (*les vieux-jeunes*) and the "Decadent foetuses." The foetus, to which all such features silently refer, combines extreme youth with great old age: according to Mac-Nab, it

33 See "The Precocious Baby, A Very True Tale (To be sung to the Air of the 'Whistling Oyster')," *Fun*, n.s. 6 (23 Nov 1867).

34 Holbrook Jackson, *The Eighteen Nineties: A Review of Art and Ideas at the Close of the Nineteenth Century* (London: Grant Richards, 1913), repr. 1922, 118.

35 Paul Verlaine, "Gosses [Mômes-monocles]," *Art et Critique*, 2:76 (8 Nov 1890); *Œuvres en prose complètes*, ed. by J. Borel (Paris: Gallimard, 1984), 227: "*l'emblème chéri de cette décadence-ci.*"

36 *Ibid.*, "*glabre et pâle*" (227); "*superbes présomptifs imberbes*" (230).

37 Pierre Vareilles, "Silhouettes décadentes: I. Georges Toulouse," *Le Décadent*, 1 (10 July 1886): 2: "*Figure tranchante comme une lame de rasoir, imberbe comme celle d'une vierge, et glabre, c'est Georges Toulouse.*"

38 Charles Buet, *Saphyr* (Paris: Calmann-Lévy, 1897), 14: "*les Décadents imberbes et les Parnassiens très âgés.*"

is "dead before [it] was born"[39]– a mischievous, subversive picture of a generation.

Such vocabulary pointed to fin-de-siècle literature as well as imagery. One of the copious French allusions to the phenomenon includes *Physiologies parisiennes* by Albert Millaud, who, reviving in 1886 the long tradition of *physiologies* under the pen name of Labruyère, offered a portrait of the "Decadent," a "species" described in curtailed and jarring verse as the unnatural or abortive outcome of a hybrid genealogy:

> He is the son of the modernist,
> Grandson of the idealist,
> Nephew of the impassive,
> Great-nephew of the parnassian [*sic*],
> A bit of a bastard of the realist,
> And twelfth cousin of the old romantic.
>
> *Il est fils du moderniste,*
> *Petit-fils de l'idéaliste,*
> *Neveu de l'impassible,*
> *Arrière-neveu du parnassien,*
> *Un peu bâtard du réaliste,*
> *Et cousin au douzième degré de l'ancien romantique.*

By a significant inversion of roles, it was no longer the muse who gave birth to verse but the Decadent who "gave birth" to poetry (and also "set her low" thanks to a pun on the French expression *mettre bas*). He generated – against all logic – a fascinating lineage:

> Still, the Decadent, however low he has set poetry, is not yet the last. He has beneath him a tadpole, which now starts to exhibit itself under the name of "deliquescent." It is the beginning of a grand series, which will go from the "infused" to the "putrefied" via the "liquefied."
>
> *Toutefois, le décadent, si bas qu'il ait mis la poésie, n'est pas encore le dernier. Il a sous lui un têtard qui commence à s'exhiber sous le nom de "déliquescent." C'est le commencement d'une suprême série, qui ira des "influsés" aux "putréfiés," en passant par les "liquefiés."*[40]

Such an *Incipit vita nova* would have delighted Beardsley. It gave full meaning to his foetus frowning and lifting its fist against a Pre-Raphaelite

39 Mac-Nab, "Les Fœtus," 20, v. 42: "*mort avant de naître.*"

40 Labruyère [pseud. of Albert Millaud], "Le Décadent," in Millaud, *Physiologies parisiennes: 120 dessins de Caran d'Ache* (Paris: À la Librairie Illustrée, 1886), 175 and 178.

caricature and a national heritage picture. The foetus exemplified the new generation. It was a proclamation exemplifying Decadent intentions, style and tone.

Much of Beerbohm's literary career illustrates such foetal poetics. Extremely young (and old) at twenty-four in 1896, he published *The Works of Max Beerbohm*. The ostentatious title materialised as a tongue-in-cheek slim booklet of just seven articles previously issued in avant-garde periodicals, followed by an eighteen-page bibliography of their slightest occurrences and variations, and John Lane's biography of this (ironically) prolific writer. Lane described Beerbohm as a Decadent in his youth (1894), and a historian in his maturity, i.e., but a year later (1895), whose voluminous work had led to the recent extension of the National Archives. The Decadent period was represented by "A Defense of Cosmetics," and his "historical work" by two articles of about thirty pages on two "suspect" periods, that of Aestheticism ("1880") and that of an effeminate king ("King George the Fourth"). The booklet closed with "Diminuendo," in which Beerbohm, declaring that he belonged to "the Beardsley period," would prepare for his exit and, exhausted by such demanding literary labour, step down in favour of the youngsters.

A joint project between author and publisher, the booklet is a good example of the art of making books from rudiments. The seven youthful articles read inconsistent with the grandiose title and swollen bibliography. Rules of common sense are perverted and the joke might have been limited to an amiable prank. However, although his decadence passed with his youth, the titles of Beerbohm's later collections still bear the memory of it. Over a period of twenty-five years they apologetically echo his "Diminuendo" promise: *More* in 1899, *Yet Again* in 1909, *And Even Now* in 1920. Such loyalty to his youthful pose as a "Decadent foetus" illuminates in retrospect the meaning of "elderly youngsters."

In a serial *Punch* skit entitled "Letters from a Débutante," Leverson also pictured a juvenile socialite under the name of Baby Beaumont, probably a reference to the phrase *le beau monde*, i.e., the refined upper crust. Paradox has him "really almost nineteen, but wonderfully well preserved, very clever, and so cynical that he is quite an optimist."[41] Unsurprisingly "*gay and decadent*," and deemed to be the author of *The Mauve Camellia*,[42] he

41 "Letters from a Débutante," *Punch*, 107 (6 Oct 1894): 168.

42 "Letters from a Débutante," *Punch*, 107 (13 Oct 1894): 180, emphasised.

displays the same ironic discrepancy as the French foetal Decadents, dead before they were born. Precocity and youth corresponded to a less morbid British version. As Osbert Burdett put it, "the very children were living in an age of experience" in Beardsley's time.[43]

Leverson's sketch pre-empts Edward Frederic Benson's novel *The Babe B. A.* (1897) whose first much shorter version was published in instalments in the Cambridge student magazine *Granta*.[44] The magazine imitated Beardsley's designs at least twice.[45] Describing trivial incidents of Cambridge life, the novel intends to be a futile narrative on an anti-heroic protagonist, the Babe. The character and looks of this "cynical old gentleman of twenty years of age," as angelic as beardless when "waltzing gaily about among rough-bearded barbarians," are that of the quintessential Decadent.[46] His age is equivocal ("old in everything else, but not in years") and his sexuality ambiguous (he cross-dresses and is often compared to women).[47] Yet because of his youth no one takes his transgressions seriously. He tries to grow old by adopting a bulldog as escort (a jocular allusion to Beerbohm and Beardsley pictured with pet dogs) and reading the *Yellow Book*, each volume of which is supposed to add twenty years to the reader's age.[48] Links with Decadence are ironic, as Benson, with a wilfully silly sense of humour, pastiches three fin-de-siècle figures – Wilde's Salomé, Walter Pater's Mona Lisa, and Gustave Flaubert's Saint Anthony – by transferring their reactions or phrases to the Babe.[49]

---

43 Osbert Burdett, *The Beardsley Period: An Essay in Perspective* (London: John Lane, 1925), 104.

44 See E. F. Benson, "Scenes from the Life of the Babe at Cambridge" (originally only eight chapters), published weekly in *The Granta* 9:175–82 (18 Jan–10 Mar 1896). Benson's *The Babe* was no confidential publication and even had a popular edition (London: William Heinemann, 1911).

45 Once for a Beardsleyesque version of the cover by Cam, *Design for New Cover of the "Granta." (à la BEARDSLEY)*, *The Granta*, 8:155 (23 Feb 1895), 212; and S. T., *A Cambridge Night-Piece (with Apologies to Mr. Aubrey Beardsley)*, 9:169 (2 Nov 1895), 37. The latter cheekily replaces with Cambridge dons Beardsley's streetwalker from his drawing *Night Piece*, published in *The Yellow Book*, 1 (Apr 1894): 127.

46 Edward Frederic Benson, *The Babe B.A., Being the Uneventful History of a Young Gentleman at Cambridge University* (London and New York: G. P. Putnam's Sons, 1897), 30 and 31.

47 *Ibid.*, 88 (age), and 43, 165, 202 and 283 (comparisons with Clytemnestra, Sarah Bernhardt, Œnone, Alice in Wonderland, and Danaë).

48 *Ibid.*, 38.

49 *Ibid.*, 100, 168 and 193.

Such a network of mocking allusions points at gleeful dissipation. The Babe could well be a disguised reference to the fin-de-siècle foetus: the model was Herbert J. Pollitt, a hardly angelic friend of Wilde, a devotee of Beardsley's more daring drawings and, later still, Aleister Crowley's disciple in black magic. Beardsley knew Benson's novel sufficiently well to write to Leonard Smithers on 19 February 1897 that it mentioned his own name three times.[50] A week later, in a letter to André Raffalovich, he identified Pollitt as one of Benson's models for the Babe.[51] Beardsley was friendly enough with Pollitt to mark out as a gift for him *Bookplate of the Artist* (Zatlin 1065), the ex-libris design he intended as his own but had never used. Close in conception to *Enter Herodias*, the drawing depicts a foetal creature lifting a heavy tray of books in front of a fleshy, naked woman selecting suitable reading (Fig. 2.10). It is possible that Benson's novel inspired Beardsley in choosing a bookplate for Pollitt.

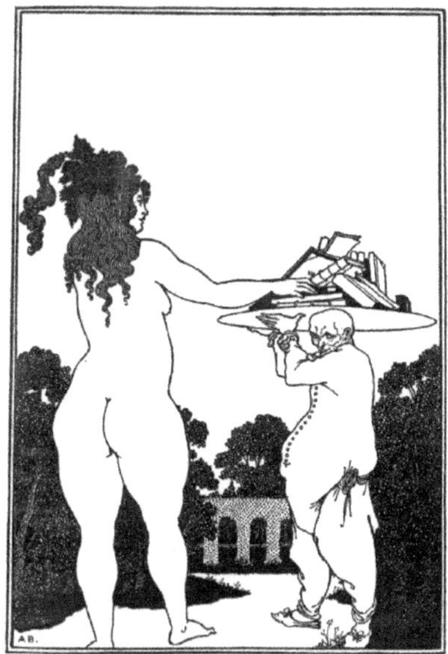

Fig. 2.10 Aubrey Beardsley, *Bookplate of the Artist* (Sept 1896), Harvard Art Museums / Fogg Museum, Cambridge, USA, repr. from *Fifty Drawings*, 195

There is a further very direct reference to Beardsley in Benson's novel, in which the Babe expresses a desire to be drawn by him: "He looks like a man out of the *Yellow Book* by Aubrey Beardsley. I wish I could

50 *The Letters of Aubrey Beardsley*, 254.
51 *Ibid.*, 261.

look as if Aubrey Beardsley had drawn me."[52] Would such a desire have been projected onto the foetal creature of the plate Beardsley imparts to Pollitt? There is no answer to the question in the twenty-eight letters from Beardsley to Pollitt in the artist's published correspondence. But the second to last of these, dated 10 January 1898, speaks of a child and giving birth two months before Beardsley's end:

> My dear pretty Pollitt,
>
> I will make you the most adorable Bambino as soon as ever I can say "finished" of Volpone. Continue to light candles for my safe delivery.[53]

Ironically enough, *Volpone* would be a volume that was indeed aborted due to Beardsley's untimely passing. Yet his bookplate, assigning a foetal creature to his library, calls for an investigation of the foetal motif in books on which Beardsley had left his stamp.

In Lucian's Steps

On 9 December 1892, the publishers Lawrence and Bullen commissioned Beardsley to illustrate Lucian of Samosata's short second-century novel, *True History*. These would have constituted about thirty full-page plates, according to a letter to Arthur William King.[54] Conceived, however, in parallel with the *Bon-Mots* grotesques, they are described in a 15 February 1893 letter to George Frederick Scotson-Clark as "thirty little drawings to do for it 6 inches by 4" (ca. 15.3 x 10.2 cm). Lucian's fantastic narrative, which includes the first literary voyage to the moon, had plenty to seduce Beardsley, who described his drawings as "the most extraordinarily things that have ever appeared in a book both in respect to technique and conception," adding "they're also the most indecent."[55] Did such boldness stay the publishers in prudish Victorian England? Or was Beardsley overwhelmed with work? The book, issued in 1894, contained only sixteen plates, with just two by Beardsley, *A Snare of Vintage* (Zatlin 270) and *Dreams* (Zatlin 271). A third plate, the first version of *A Snare of Vintage* (Zatlin 269), was inserted only in fifty-four copies on Japanese vellum. The fourteen remaining are by William

52 Benson, *The Babe*, 101.
53 *The Letters of Aubrey Beardsley*, 422.
54 *Ibid.*, 38.
55 *Ibid.*, 44.

Strang and J. B. Clark, who would continue to work for Lawrence and Bullen. Beardsley, however, did not. The hypothesis of the publishers censoring a shocking production seems plausible, especially since two plates, *Lucian's Strange Creatures* (Zatlin 272) and *Birth from the Calf of the Leg* (Zatlin 273), were published after the artist's death by Smithers in *An Issue of Five Drawings Illustrative of Juvenal and Lucian* as "too free in design for general circulation." Of these five, three relate to the foetus.

Three passages struck Beardsley when he read Lucian's novel: the sailors' couplings with the vine-women at the beginning of Book I, twice rendered in the two versions of *A Snare of Vintage*; the customs of the moon-dwellers (Bk. I, § 22); and the arrival at the Isle of Dreams (Bk. II, § 32–35), also treated twice. I follow Milly Heyd's suggestion that we may successively read in them coitus, birth, and adoration of the child, yet all of unnatural devising.[56] The *Birth from the Calf of the Leg* (Zatlin 273) depicts marriage and births on the moon, the land of men who do not even know the name of woman (Bk. I, § 22). Francis Hickes's translation of Lucian cautiously omits a detail from the Greek, which I have completed within square brackets below. The passage, however, is explicit enough for Beardsley to have based his plate on it:

> they [the children] are not begotten, of women, but of mankind: for they have no other marriage but of males: the name of women is utterly unknown among them: until they accomplish the age of five and twenty years, they are given in marriage to others: from that time forwards they take others in marriage to themselves: [they carry the child not in the womb, but in the calf of the leg] for as soon as the infant is conceived the leg begins to swell, and afterwards when the time of birth is come, they give it a lance and take it out dead: then they lay it abroad with open mouth towards the wind, and so it takes life: and I think thereof the Grecians call it the belly of the leg, therein they bear their children instead of a belly.[57]

By mischievously recalling the pederast practices of Greek Antiquity, Lucian mocks the story of Bacchus born from Jupiter's thigh. He takes literally the word *gastroknēmia*, "calf" in Ancient Greek, and breaks it up in its two components, "belly" (*gastēr*) and "leg" (*knēme*). Here, it is not the function that creates the organ, but language itself. Decadent

56 Heyd, *Aubrey Beardsley: Symbol, Mask and Self-Irony* (New York: Peter Lang, 1986), 61–62.

57 *Lucian's True History, Translated by Francis Hickes, Illustrated by William Strang, J. B. Clark and Aubrey Beardsley* (London: Privately Printed [Lawrence and Bullen], 1894), 61–62.

monstrous creation had taken ample advantage of such linguistic sleight-of-tongue as I have shown elsewhere.[58] Similarly, in *Birth from the Calf of the Leg* (Fig. 2.11), Beardsley breaks with personal trauma. The image may reflect his latent homosexuality or an interruption of pregnancy, as Reade and Easton have argued,[59] but here I am interested in the ambivalent signs surrounding the foetus's extraction at birth. The incision in the thigh (not the calf) recalls the pubic area and an open vagina. Beardsley multiplies the signs of cruel and bloody delivery (a knife, dots for blood on the foetus and hands), even castration (scissors pointing to an absent organ), but caricatures the foot and the little finger, alleviating tension and trauma. The presence of an elegant toilet table and the drapery cast doubt on the sex of the person whose thigh is incised. In Lucian, the child comes into the world dead, which reactivates the spectre of the unborn foetus. Beardsley's newborn characteristically frowns in discontent with eyes wide open. It does not take much for the relentless extraction to turn into a killing.

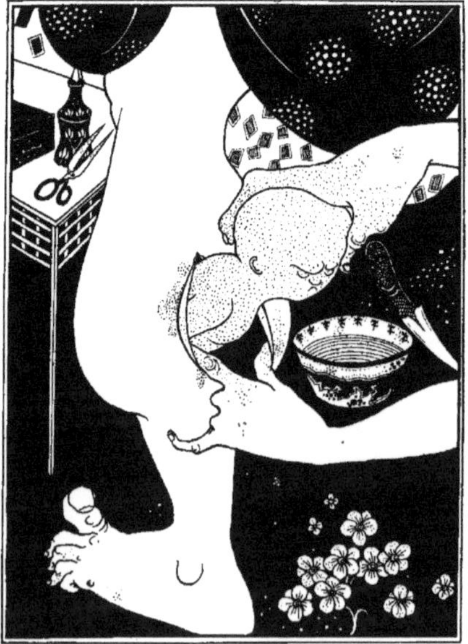

Fig. 2.11 Aubrey Beardsley, *Birth from the Calf of the Leg* (Dec 1892–March 1893), repr. from *Five Drawings*, no. 5

58 See Stead, *Le Monstre, le singe et le fœtus*, 28, 36–40, 70, 128, 205, 228–29.

59 Reade, 333; Easton, *Aubrey and the Dying Lady*, 178–79, following Reade but also opening a new perspective through embryology. See also Stephen Calloway, *Aubrey Beardsley* (London: V & A Publications, 1998), 65, referring to Reade and the motif of "irregular births."

Heyd's "adoration of the child" is based on Lucian's Island of Dreams, populated by all sorts of reverie, as shown in Hickes's translation:

> These dreams are not all alike either in nature or shape, for some of them are long, beautiful and pleasing: others again are as short and deformed. Some make show to be of gold, and others to be base and beggarly. Some of them had wings, and were of monstrous forms: others set out in pomp, as it were in triumph, representing the appearances of kings, gods and other persons.[60]

An attentive and passionate reader, Beardsley scrupulously singles out monstrosity and pictures only the ugly. The first *Dreams* plate (Zatlin 271), positioned opposite this very extract, is invaded by spidery lines, bats or butterflies, spiky, grimacing, and dragon-like forms, close to the *Bon-Mots* grotesques and *Le Morte Darthur*, his Japanese-style signature, and roving parts of bodies (Fig. 2.12). Yet, in this brief deformed vision, gazes converge on a well-known central scene: the hand presenting the aborted foetus as in *Two Figures by Candlelight Holding a Fetus* (see Fig. 2.1), although the foetus now looks more resigned to its fate. There are lines and patterns superimposed in a way that the disturbing scene may go unnoticed. Such is not the case in the second version, cautiously entitled *Lucian's Strange Creatures* (Zatlin 272). In this, the strong black-and-white contrast makes forms more explicit although endowed with a fluid, dream-like quality (Fig. 2.13). A woman's hand blatantly presents the protesting foetus, but this time nobody is watching. Lightly layered over each other and turned towards the viewer, the peripheral figures hover and float in a characteristically vague vision. They glide and drift, which promotes a mimetic spreading of the foetal form to the bloated head of a masked Pierrot – recalling the *Masked Pierrette in a Cape and a Ruff* (Zatlin 788, see Fig. 2.5a) –, here split into two, himself and a lithe hermaphrodite whom the Pierrot tickles. At the very top, the foetus, stark white on an inky background, turns into a nucleus of black-and-white art while various caricatures of contemporary individuals also crowd the plate. The sexual ambiguity that reigns in these drawings, thanks to the inherently ambiguous and potentially erotic nature of the dream, will be elevated to a system in Beardsley's plate for "A Kiss of Judas."

60 *Lucian's True History*, 209–11.

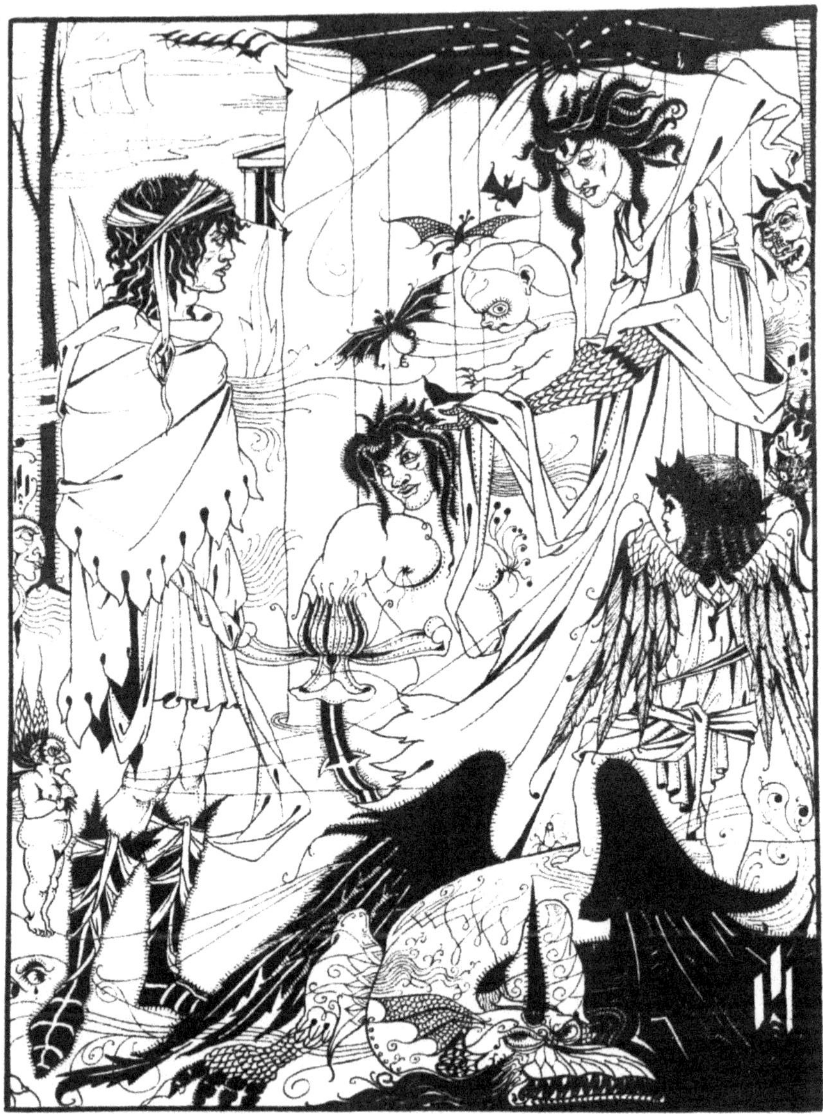

Fig. 2.12 Aubrey Beardsley, *Dreams* (Dec 1892–March 1893), Harvard Art Museums / Fogg Museum, Cambridge, USA, repr. from *Lucian's True History*, facing p. 209

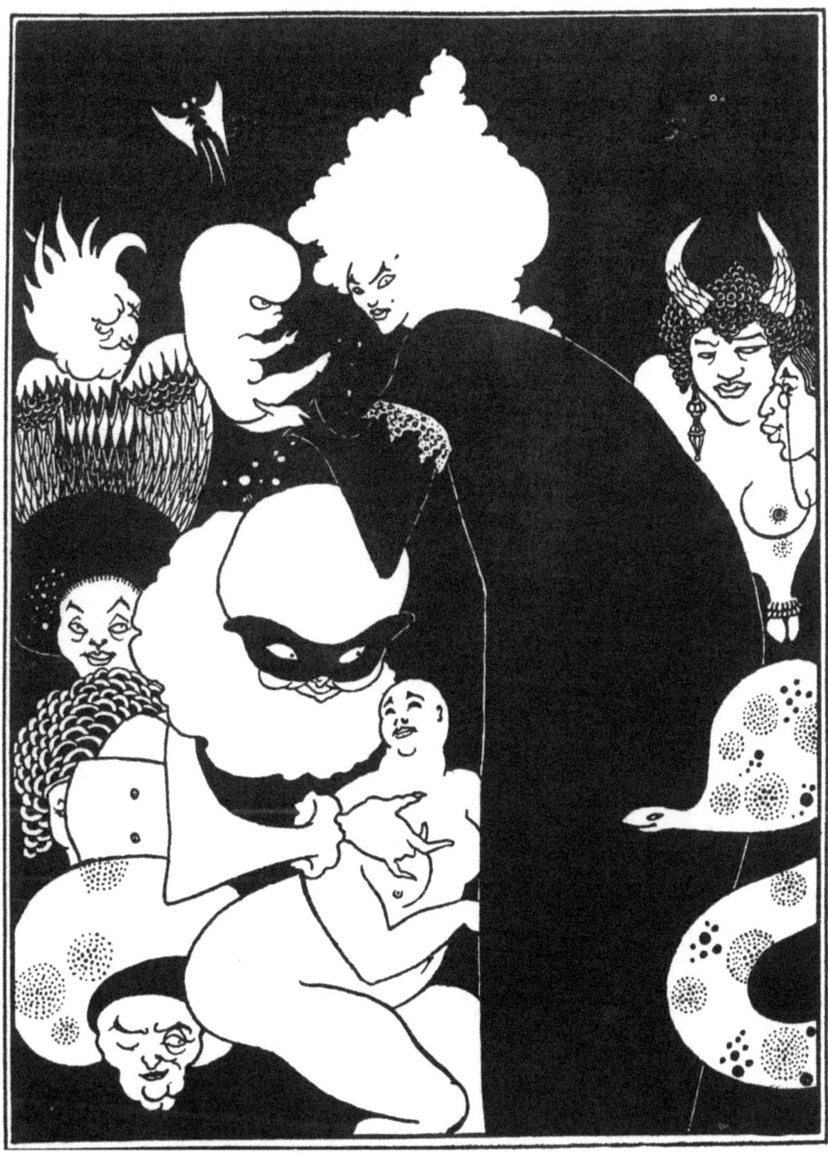

Fig. 2.13 Aubrey Beardsley, *Lucian's Strange Creatures* (Dec 1892–March 1893), repr. from *Five Drawings*, no. 4

Judas, Mary, and the Foetus

In his book on vampires, Christopher Frayling identified the American writer Julian Osgood Field as the author of the short story "A Kiss of Judas," originally published under the pseudonym X. L. in the *Pall Mall Magazine* in 1893.[61] Beardsley granted it a parodic and enigmatic plate, named *The Kiss of Judas* after the story (Fig. 2.14, Zatlin 313). Field's text emphasises the parody of a Christian rite[62] and the mysterious appearance of a beautiful woman.[63] His story offers a vampiric treatment of Judas's kiss when betraying Jesus in the Garden of Gethsemane, and reads as the antipode of Christ's sacrifice to save humanity from its sins. It is based on a Moldavian legend of the Children of Judas, who are inversions of Christ: they are branded by unparalleled ugliness, hate their fellow men instead of loving them, and commit suicide instead of sacrificing themselves for them. Their suicide entitles them to return to Hell, reincarnate and come back in the form best suited to their vengeance on mankind but not as a female. This vengeance takes the form of a deadly kiss. The mark XXX on the victim's body refers to the Gospels' thirty pieces of silver (Matthew 27, 3–6), the "price of blood."[64]

Such is the fate of the story's protagonist, Colonel Hippy Rowan, who causes the wrath of one of the Children of Judas, Isaac Lebedenko, having discovered his hideous face, ferret-like muzzle, and wet, slimy mouth. Field's long description[65] must have interested Beardsley, all the more as the Child of Judas, a monster, commits suicide and – contrary to the legend – transforms into a woman (repeatedly likened by Field to the Madonna) as dispenser of the fatal kiss. Beardsley referred in a letter to T. Dove Keighley, the *Pall Mall Magazine*'s editor, to "an awfully striking legend" which he proposed to treat in a drawing that "should contain in one decorative scheme – the strange form kissing its victim (as the centre), with the other incidents (such as the diabolical

61 Christopher Frayling, ed., *Vampyres: Lord Byron to Count Dracula* (London: Faber & Faber, 1991), 221.

62 X. L. [Julian Osgood Field], "A Kiss of Judas," *The Pall Mall Magazine*, 1:3 (July 1893): 339–66 (351).

63 *Ibid.*, 364.

64 *Ibid.*, 350.

65 *Ibid.*, 344.

commission, the suicide and victim after death) worked round it."[66] However, the drawing he sent from Paris a few days later[67] omits the peripheral incidents, retaining only the kiss that a foetus-like creature is about to lay on the forearm of another figure, no less ambiguous, lying under a tree.

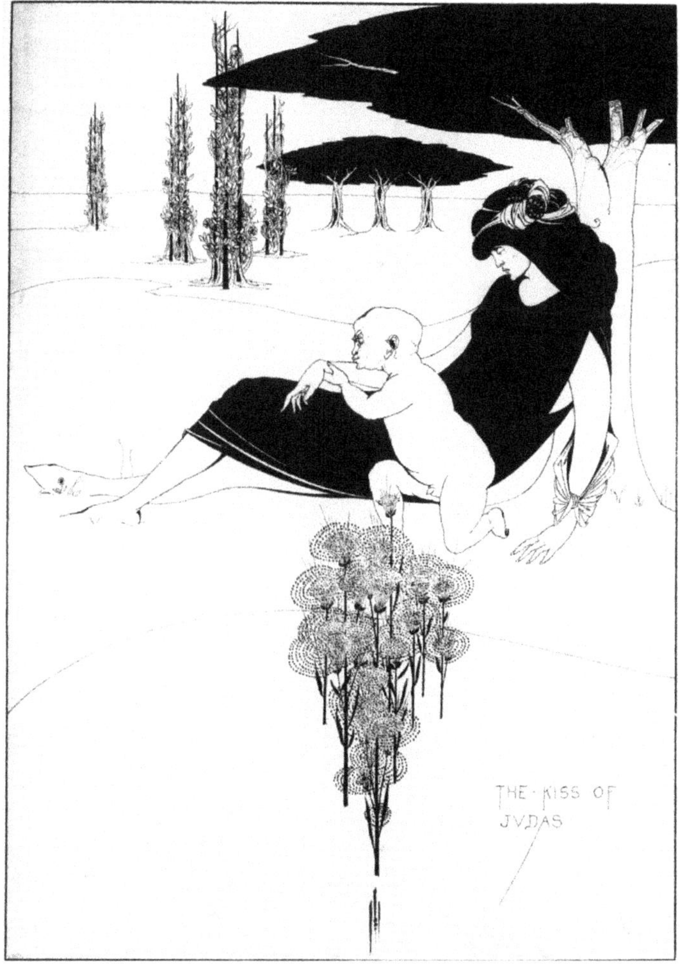

Fig. 2.14 Aubrey Beardsley, *The Kiss of Judas* (ca. 18 May 1893), Victoria and Albert Museum, London, *The Pall Mall Magazine*, 1:3 (July 1893), facing p. 339; repr. from *Early Work*, no. 16

66 *The Letters of Aubrey Beardsley*, 48.

67 *Ibid.*, 48–49.

Building on a parody of the Christian rite that is central to the tale, Beardsley reworks the kiss in the Garden of Gethsemane. In his drawing, vertical trellises in the back and the Judas tree flowers in the foreground represent the garden. The figure under the tree would be Christ with Judas at his side, or rather the "Child of Judas," an expression taken literally: a kind of monstrous infant. The interpretation responds to the various forms taken by Judas's offspring and its repulsive ugliness: the foetus, able to assume all forms, summarises an ideal monstrosity. The text calls Lebedenko a "monster," a "hostile monster," a "monster not born of woman."[68] Beardsley instead chooses the being *par excellence* born of woman, creating a bold new take on this figure.

Although the legend depicted the Children of Judas as Christ's opposites, Field inverts this by projecting Christ's sufferings onto Lebedenko: at the mercy of Hippy Rowan, who would have whipped him and relentlessly nailed his hands to a tree,[69] the Child of Judas endures flagellation and crucifixion. Foetal in the image, monstrous in the text, reincarnated in a woman likened to the Madonna, he is also both Jesus and Judas. Beardsley's aged infant serves a multiple monstrosity, a compound of ugliness, animalism, vampirism, and hermaphroditism. It is the perfect medium to depict the contradictory roles and status of Field's character, and shows that the artist read text far more subtly than is commonly thought.

This is further shown in the figure beneath the tree, a decidedly feminised Christ, since Beardsley assigns him the "all black" garment worn in the novella by the Marian figure, "as that of a member of some religious order" enclosing the face in "a covering not unlike a cowl."[70] Such complexity borders on confusion in Beardsley's *The Kiss of Judas*. The monstrous Lebedenko has returned as a Madonna figure, and the plate reflects such doubling up by that of a Judas/foetus and feminised Christ. The object of Lebedenko's vengeance, Hippy Rowan, has disappeared. We are faced with two monsters, one virginal, the other foetal, and a doubly disturbing message: if the Judas of the text has Christ-like aspects, the Christ of the image is

68 X. L. [Julian Osgood Field], "A Kiss of Judas," 344, 345, 354.

69 *Ibid.*, 352–53.

70 *Ibid.*, 363.

like Mary. If the foetus is also Jesus, the Christ is also a Madonna. According to Field, Lebedenko's reincarnation and return resemble a ghostly masquerade on a night close to Christmas.[71] Beardsley's drawing could, in this light, be read as a kind of grotesque Nativity scene.

The kiss of Judas, here that of the foetus to its mother, is just another expression of the grotesque foetus's wrath, as previously discerned in its clenched fist. The foetus takes revenge on the mother in a vampiric, possibly incestuous, way. Furthermore, from a formal point of view, *The Kiss of Judas* is akin to *A Platonic Lament*, one of Beardsley's plates for Wilde's *Salome* (1894), in which a black-clad figure leans over another before a floral background (Zatlin 868).[72] The first version of Beardsley's *Enter Herodias* (Zatlin 870) already looms large.

In *Enter Herodias*, my interest lies with the hydrocephalic monster on the left (Fig. 2.15), a *Bon-Mots* offspring, as shown by its nipple-covered neck and pointed thumbnail. The figure does not raise its fist as it has in previous works, but stands erect in front of a ripe, provocative Herodias. Although masked by its loose clothing, the creature's erection is underscored by the candle's flame and echoed by the three phallic candlesticks at the foot of the image. Still, the naughty detail escaped the publisher's notice. Reade, who tracked the history of the original and its two subsequent versions, has shown that Lane censored Beardsley's plate (reproduced here) to mask the genitals of the young man on the right.[73] No changes whatsoever were made to the foetal creature, which is not only an iconographic novelty, but also carries a covert and disturbing spirit, playfully superimposing desire and tension.

---

71 *Ibid.*, 361.

72 On Beardsley's *Salome*, see my article "*Encor Salomé*: entrelacs du texte et de l'image de Wilde et Beardsley à Mossa et Merlet," in *Dieu, la chair et les livres. Une approche de la Décadence*, ed. by S. Thorel-Cailleteau (Paris: Honoré Champion, 2000), 421–57, fig. 1–12, and "Triptyque de livres sur Salomé," revised and enlarged version, in Stead, *La Chair du livre: matérialité, imaginaire et poétique du livre fin-de-siècle* (Paris: PUPS, 2012), 157–203.

73 Reade, "Enter Herodias: Or, What Really Happened?," *Los Angeles County Museum of Art Bulletin*, 22 (1976): 58–65.

Rich Foetal Avatars

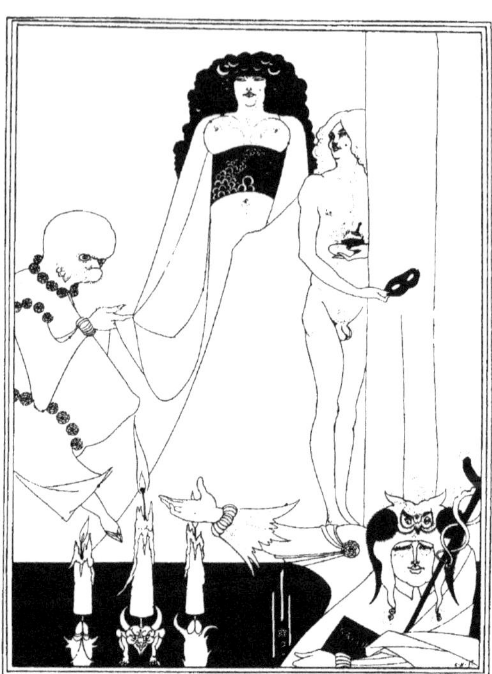

Fig. 2.15 Aubrey Beardsley, *Enter Herodias* (late autumn 1893), Los Angeles County Museum of Art, Los Angeles, USA, repr. from Reade, 285

Enter Herodias is in this sense resumed in the first (rejected) version of *The Toilette of Salome*, also intended for Wilde's drama (Fig. 2.16, Zatlin 871). In this work, the nappy around the frail foetus on the front left-hand shelf of Salomé's dressing table might also hide another erection. A small vase with a pointed protuberance seems to endorse the assumption. The Japanese perspective and furniture also recall the misshapen Japanese figurines present in fin-de-siècle texts such as Pierre Loti's "human embryos with octopus tentacles."[74] The biblical dancer is in the hands of a Pierrotic and foetal hairdresser who owes much to *Masked Pierrette in a Cape and a Ruff*, classified as female (Zatlin 788, see Fig. 2.5a). A clash between sundry cultural references is mirrored on the table itself, a crucial piece of furniture in Beardsley's work according to Easton.[75]

74 Pierre Loti, *La Troisième Jeunesse de Madame Prune* (Paris: Calmann Lévy, 1905), 167: "*embryons humains ayant des tentacules de poulpe.*"

75 Easton, *Aubrey and the Dying Lady*, 121–26.

A gloss on femininity and coquetry, the dresser carries a fossil that would better suit the Natural Science museum. The foetus has become a decorative, removable article, and sits amongst pomade jars, ointments, a powder compact and a jewel case. The books stacked under Salomé's dressing table – including two then scandalous titles, Baudelaire's *Les Fleurs du Mal* and Zola's *La Terre* – add a final touch to this curiosity cabinet to stress the weight of incongruity in fin-de-siècle culture. The dressing table turns bookshelf and display case. Gustav-Adolf Mossa's watercolour *Le Fœtus* (1905) may have referenced Beardsley's invention in an exaggerated version: it shows a gigantic ornate jar with a tiny foetus bathing in its liquid in the foreground while its mother powders her nose in front of her mirror in the background, ready to depart with a supercilious suitor.[76]

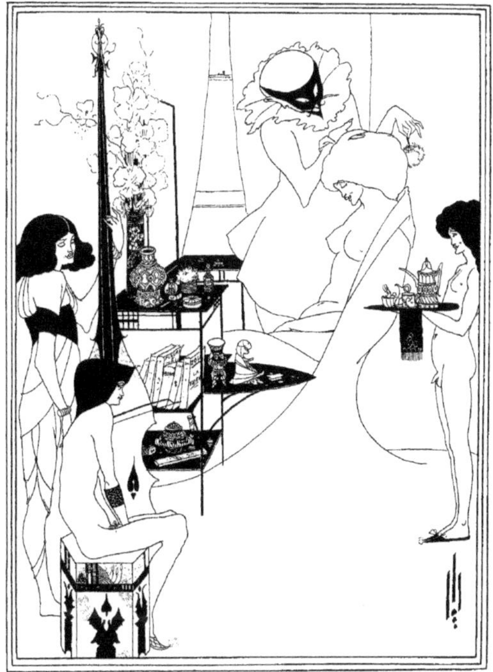

Fig. 2.16 Aubrey Beardsley, *The Toilette of Salome*, first version (summer 1893), coll. Marie Mathews, Key West, Fl., USA, repr. from Reade, 287

76 Gustav-Adolf Mossa, *Le Fœtus* (ca. 1905), watercolour, graphite, ink, gouache relief and gilding on paper, 50 x 32 (34 x 19) cm, Nice, Musée des Beaux-Arts. See *Gustav Adolf Mossa. Catalogue raisonné des œuvres "symbolistes"* (Paris: Somogy, 2010), 152–53 (A 68).

Richness and variety mark Beardsley's treatment of the foetal motif, though critics like Reade and Fletcher have downplayed its significance. Although Reade frequently evokes the foetus in his comments, he describes it as a "minor obsession." Fletcher does not recognise the motif in Beardsley's work after 1893.[77] Yet, it is well and fivefold present in the most complex rococo-influenced plate of 1896, *The Cave of Spleen* (Zatlin 983), after Pope's *The Rape of the Lock*. Beardsley's attention is indeed drawn by the same detail in Pope as in Lucian:

> Unnumber'd Throngs on ev'ry side are seen
> Of Bodies chang'd to various Forms by Spleen.
> Here living Teapots stand, one Arm held out,
> One bent; the Handle this, and that the Spout:
> A Pipkin there like Homer's Tripod walks;
> Here sighs a Jar, and there a Goose-pye talks;
> *Men prove with Child*, as pow'rful Fancy works,
> And Maids turn'd Bottles, call aloud for Corks.[78]

Two male figures in the lower left-hand corner of *The Cave of Spleen* exhibit such unusual pregnancies (Fig. 2.17). In the swollen, transparent belly of the first, stylised female genital apparatus and a foetus appear in profile – the one external to the other. The second figure carries the foetus in a part of the "body" resembling the thigh, as in Lucian. This would have sufficed for a hemistich. Yet, in the heart of the picture, to the left of the turbaned figure looking at us, a third foetal form emerges in profile from the very vapours of spleen, a literal response to the second hemistich "as pow'rful Fancy works." Finally, two dandies (akin to the foetuses in the grotesque vignettes) sit in a lantern and a jar in the lower right-hand corner. Such proliferation does not belong to a morbid spirit, absent from Pope's text, but to graphic caprice. Indeed, unlike Beardsley's "pictured" books or volumes "embellished with drawings," *The Rape of the Lock* is "embroidered," as states its subtitle "embroidered with eleven drawings by Aubrey Beardsley." Wreaths, ringlets, loops, festoons, broken lines, dots and all

---

77 Reade, 22; Fletcher, "A Grammar of Monsters: Beardsley's Images and Their Sources," *English Literature in Transition, 1880–1920*, 30:2 (1987): 141–63 (147).

78 Alexander Pope, *The Rape of the Lock*, ed. by Geoffrey Tillotson, 3rd ed. (London, Methuen Educational Ltd., 1971), Canto iv, v. 47–54, my emphasis.

the subtleties of openwork, crochet and filigree create such embroidery. Versatile and pliable, the foetal form generates and invades them, the viewer no longer knowing what is foetal and what not. *The Cave of Spleen*'s probable influence on artists such as Alan Odle and Alastair[79] – and Marcus Behmer as presented below – shows the plastic potential of the foetal shape.

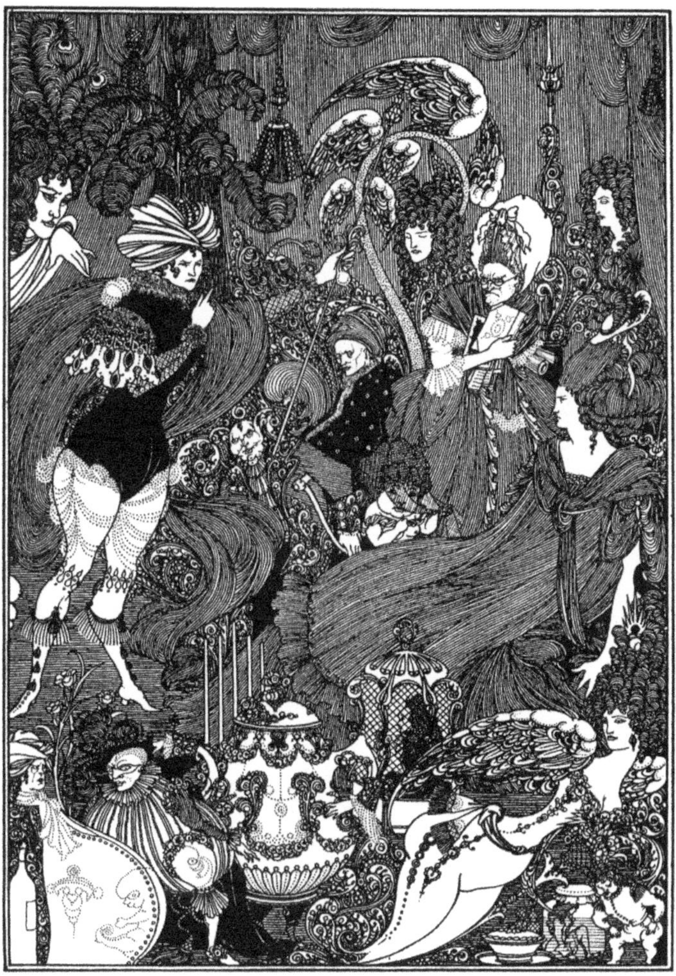

Fig. 2.17 Aubrey Beardsley, *The Cave of Spleen* (ca. 6 March 1896), Bigelow coll., Boston Museum of Fine Arts, Boston, USA, repr. from *Rape of the Lock*, facing p. 24

79 Reade refers to Alan Odle's early works, 353, n. 410.

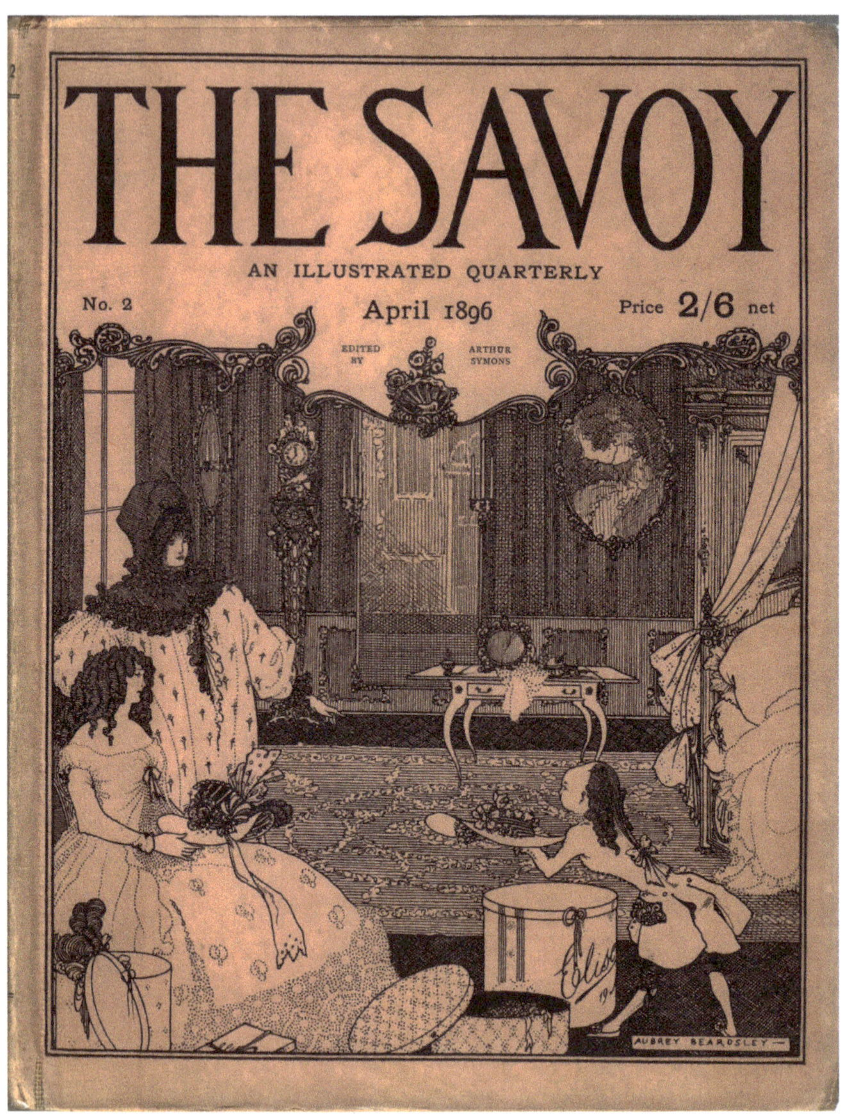

Fig. 2.18 Aubrey Beardsley, *Choosing the New Hat* or *Cover and title page for issue No. 2* (by last week of March 1896), repr. from *The Savoy*, 2 (Apr 1896). Courtesy MLS coll., Delaware

In *Choosing the New Hat* (Fig. 2.18), his April 1896 cover for the *Savoy*, catalogued as *Cover and Title Page for Issue No. 2* (Zatlin 1003), Beardsley uses a style close to the Pope plates. In the image, two women try on hats proffered by a pageboy. "The little creature handing hats,"

Beardsley wrote in a letter to Smithers, emphasising negation, "is *not* an infant but an unstrangled abortion."[80] If we are to follow him, many other beings still in the limbo of existence pervade his work: the three musicians in the foreground of the third *Comedy-Ballet of Marionettes, as Performed by the Troupe of the Théâtre-Impossible, Posed in Three Drawings, III* (Zatlin 897a); the creature carrying a tray of books on the bookplate later given to Pollitt (see Fig. 2.10); even the monkey in *The Lady with the Monkey* (Zatlin 1050) following Reade, who sees in it "perhaps an unconscious *revenant* of the foetuses of 1893, in more plausible terms."[81] I will not attempt to list them all, but one thing is certain: the only image of reassuring, blossoming motherhood in Beardsley's oeuvre appears nestling between the symbolically protective legs of the letter M (alluding to Mother),[82] an initial letter designed for Ben Jonson's *Volpone* (Zatlin 1084r), under the empty gaze of two figures with multiple breasts (Diana of Ephesus-like), half-women, half-statues. Too late: that book would remain unfinished and be published posthumously.

Beardsley's Sway on Fin-de-siècle Art

Beardsley's uniquely rich body of foetal work is no doubt related to his precarious state of health. It cannot be excluded that he turned the foetus into a kind of *alter ego*, as Heyd and Zatlin have both proposed.[83] Yet, such a view is also strangely restrictive. I would argue that it conceals two more powerful considerations: the role of the foetus in the post-Darwinian Decadent imagination; and the part it played in fin-de-siècle graphic design. A morbid myth of "species" origins was emerging at the time, of which the foetus was the most striking corollary.[84] Beardsley's graphic art saw in the foetus a pliable shape apt to impregnate and pollinate his creativity. It further spread into other artists' work as in three examples from the German, Dutch, and French context, each revealing

80 *The Letters of Aubrey Beardsley*, 120.

81 Reade, 364, n. 492.

82 Contrariwise, in the published version of *Volpone*, the initial is that of Mosca (London: Leonard Smithers, 1898), 82 (Act III, scene I).

83 Linda Gertner Zatlin, *Beardsley, Japonisme, and the Perversion of the Victorian Ideal* (Cambridge: Cambridge University Press, 1997), 58–67; Heyd, *Aubrey Beardsley*, 212–17.

84 See Stead, *Le Monstre, le singe et le fœtus*, 419–510.

a different paradigm. The motif would be spelled out varyingly, nurture complex *mises en abyme*, and associate with caricature as a superior form of deforming art.

Beardsley's art was sufficiently significant at the end of the nineteenth century for Burdett to name his book on the English fin de siècle *The Beardsley Period*, turning Beerbohm's originally droll quip into a significant scholarly study.[85] Beyond Britain, several European countries, including Italy, France, and Germany, welcomed his graphic work. As the last chapter in this book shows in detail, several of his drawings were published in Jules Roques's *Le Courrier français* from 1894 onwards, then in *La Plume* and *L'Ermitage*. The question of his reception in France, attempted by Jacques Lethève, was again addressed by Jane Haville Desmarais,[86] and will be further discussed based on new evidence. In Germany, Franz Blei in *Pan*, Otto Eckmann in *Die Kunst*, and Emil Hannover in *Kunst und Künstler* praised him in Berlin art magazines between 1899 and 1903. Julius Meier-Graefe followed suit in his notable study on the evolution of modern art.[87] Volumes on Beardsley were included in prestigious series: "Die Kunst" issued by the Berlin publisher Julius Bard and "Moderne Illustratoren" published by Reinhard Piper.[88] These are but a few examples of a genuine craze. Critics acclaimed and hailed his unique designs.

Beardsley's work was particularly reflected and expanded upon Marcus Behmer, a German water-colourist, talented draughtsman, engraver, illustrator and original book artist. Fascinated by Beardsley, Behmer learned English to read his idol's few literary remains in the

85 Beerbohm, "Diminuendo," in Beerbohm, *The Works of Max Beerbohm, with a Bibliography by John Lane* (London: John Lane, The Bodley Head; New York: Charles Scribner's Sons, 1896), 160. Beerbohm wrote "I belong to the Beardsley period." Osbert Burdett, *The Beardsley Period: An Essay in Perspective* (London: John Lane, 1925).

86 Jacques Lethève, "Aubrey Beardsley et la France," *Gazette des beaux-arts*, 68:1175 (Dec 1966): 343–50; Jane Haville Desmarais, *The Beardsley Industry: The Critical Reception in England and France, 1893–1914* (Aldershot: Ashgate, 1998).

87 Julius Meier-Graefe, "Aubrey Beardsley and his Circle," *Modern Art: Being a Contribution to a New System of Aesthetics*, trans. by Florence Simmonds and George W. Chrystal, 2 vols. (New York: G. P. Putnam's Sons; London: William Heinemann, 1908), II, 252–66.

88 See Rudolf Klein, *Aubrey Beardsley* (Berlin: Julius Bard, [1902]), already at its second edition; and Hermann Esswein, *Aubrey Beardsley* (Munich and Leipzig: R. Piper & Co., [1908]).

original.[89] He decorated the walls of his Charlottenburg studio with photographs of the Englishman, knew the *Yellow Book* and the *Savoy* well, owned Beardsley's published work in reproduction, and commented ironically on the blunders of a German edition of his letters.[90] Between 1900 and 1902, his drawings for the art and literature review *Die Insel* widened the orbit of Beardsley's foetal grotesques, as did some of his own major designs.

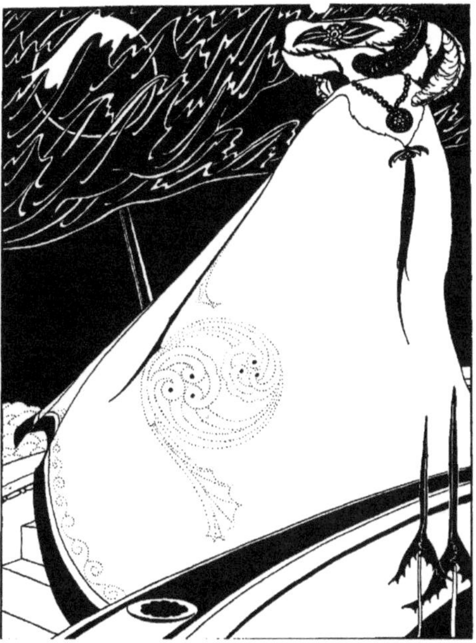

Fig. 2.19 Marcus Behmer, 9th plate [Herod or Herodias?], in *Salome, Tragödie in einem Akt von Oscar Wilde,* Übertragung *von Hedwig Lachmann* (1903), after the 1999 reprint, priv. coll.

Behmer's ninth plate for Wilde's *Salome*, translated into German in 1903, is both a tribute to Beardsley and a highly original work (Fig. 2.19). A fishtailed arabesque dotting a character's ample cloak with embryonic shapes recalls the genitalia and foetuses of the transparent wombs in Beardsley's *The Cave of Spleen* (see Fig. 2.17). In Behmer, the motif

89 Martin Birnbaum, "Marcus Behmer," in Birnbaum, *Jacovleff and Other Artists* (New York: Paul A. Struck, 1946), 153–54.

90 Marcus Behmer and Max Meyerfeld, "Beardsleybriefe," *Kunst und Künstler*, 7:3 (1909): 134–38, particularly 137–38.

sustains gender uncertainty, now relating to Wilde's play. We may waver to recognize in this figure either Herod hurrying away from the terrace, or Herodias repeatedly accused in the text of sterility.[91] Amplified and transformed, the borrowed foetal motif also gains new graphic heft as it reflects the half-hidden lunar disc. Behmer thus unexpectedly reinterprets Beardsley's *The Woman in the Moon* (Zatlin 864), a *Salome* plate wittily referring to Wilde's homosexuality, while feminising the German folklore figure of the man in the moon. In his graphics for the German *Salome*, Behmer assumed the place and role of his English counterpart. His inverted B, used as his signature, literally mirrors Beardsley's initial in several plates and honours his debt with a twist. The *Salome* plates were a consecration of both Beardsley and Behmer's graphic achievements.

In the monthly *Die Insel*, Behmer's foetal grotesques meet in turn with his expert entomological knowledge to create a series of beings (Fig. 2.20a–g). The grotesque lies in the juxtaposition of two monsters – laughable yet terrible – a shapeless newborn babe and a fly (Fig. 2.20a). The design turns the infant into a bundle of flesh, a body *plastic*, an adjective which fin-de-siècle culture understood as "likely to take various forms." In another drawing, Behmer's morbid imagination takes over, placing the foetus in the arms of a skeleton swathed in black (Fig. 2.20b). No more cloven feet or arabesques, just beings fitting one and the same hydrocephalic species, depicted in outline with characteristic black-on-white economy of means, as Beardsley had promoted: a spindly diver suspended in mid-air (Fig. 2.20c); an oversize silhouette crossing a landscape (Fig. 2.20d); an enigmatic figure in a black mantle (Fig. 2.20e). Even the full-page illustration for Paul Ernst's short story "Der Schemen" bears the mark (Fig. 2.20f): the bulging skull and profile posture come from Beardsley's work, especially the *Bon-Mots* foetuses. Last but not least, a hydrocephalic Pierrot bites into a mask with eyes rolling upwards while his long scrawny arm falls victim to the frame's very edge (Fig. 2.20g). Its eerie appearance, the uncertain forms within folds and lines (is it one or two figures?), the stark contrast of black and white recall the creatures hovering on the left-hand side of *Lucian's Strange Creatures* (see Fig. 2.13), Beardsley's bold version of *Dreams*.

91 See further on this Stead, *La Chair du livre*, 192–203.

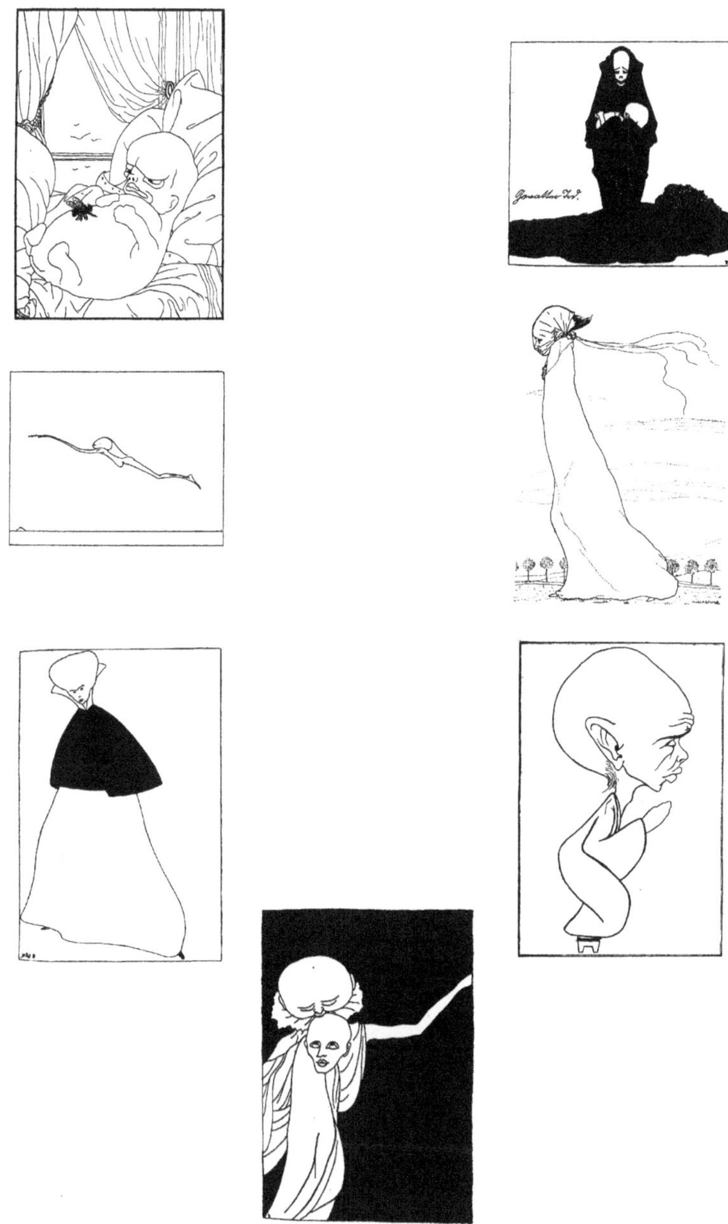

Fig. 2.20a–g Marcus Behmer, Foetal Grotesques from *Die Insel.* 2.20a *Newborn Babe and Fly, Die Insel,* 2.4:10 (July 1901): 127; 2.20b *Fœtus and Skeleton, Die Insel,* 3:10 (July 1902): 107; 2.20c *Spindly Diver, Die Insel,* 1.3:7 (Apr 1900): 93; 2.20d *Oversize Silhouette, Die Insel,* 1.3:9 (June 1900): 375; 2.20e *Figure in Black Mantle, Die Insel,* 3:7–8 (Apr-May 1902): 135; 2.20f Full-page Illustration for Paul Ernst, "Der Schemen," *Die Insel,* 2.1:1 (Oct 1900): 81; 2.20g *Hydrocephalic Pierrot Biting into a Mask, Die Insel,* 3:5 (Feb 1902): 245

Even more daringly, the Englishman's influence on Karel de Nerée tot Babberich, known as "the Dutch Aubrey Beardsley," plays with the very idea of the foetus and the book, perhaps a foetal book. De Nerée's drawing *Sourire* (1901) sets eye to eye on the cover of an open volume an elegant mother with a disgruntled foetus complete with umbilical cord (Fig. 2.21). The drawing, inspired by the prose and verse collection *Witte Nachten* (*Sleepless Nights*) by de Nerée's friend Henri van Booven, engages in a series of subtle *mises en abyme* with Beardsley's *Incipit Vita Nova* as the overt inspiration (see Fig. 2.7). First, a male character in female attire (reminiscent of Beardsley's *The Black Cape*), holding the book open, postures as the reader. Instead of looking at the volume, he stares at the viewer. While a book is involved in a first *mise en abyme*, two potential readers of van Booven's volume consider each other in de Nerée's drawing.

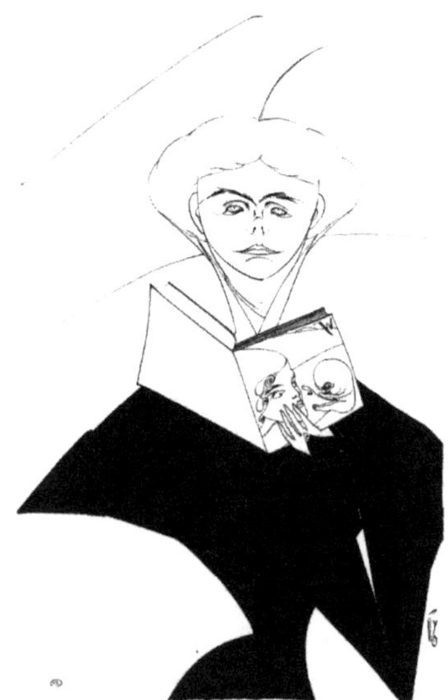

Fig. 2.21 Karel de Nerée tot Babberich, *Sourire* (1901), Paris, Musée d'Orsay, inspired by Henri van Booven, *Witte Nachten*. © PE for a high-resolution scan made from a © RMN photograph acquired in 1990

Upper right-hand on the book cover, besides Beardsley's reworked characters, the corner monogram WN refers to van Booven's title. *Witte Nachten* opens with a significant preface, a literary manifesto celebrating deliverance. It recalls the renaissance of Dutch letters at the end of the nineteenth century and marks van Booven's distance from two *Tachtigers*, i.e., members of the 1880s generation, Willem Kloos, secretary of the *Nieuwe Gids* review, and Herman Gorter, professor of classics and author of the *School der poezie*, from whose influence van Booven had since freed himself. His liberation, in the form of verse emancipated from established forms, amounts to the birth of a poet. In stressing such a fact, the preface uses a familiar phrase in small caps: "INCIPIT VITA NOVA."[92] Here we witness a second *mise en abyme*: van Booven's book is the content of the Beardsley drawing on its cover, but also its container, since the preface ends with the title of Beardsley's drawing now summarising the volume's meaning. Redrafting Beardsley, de Nerée projects on van Booven's book a foetus. A tribute to Beardsley, the image takes up the challenge of Beardsley's 1892 drawing to transpose it onto van Booven's text. Here is a new poet who revolts and comes to life to join Pound's foetal-like depiction of the English Nineties and Verlaine's "eyeglass kids."

In an article published after de Nerée's death, which remains a valuable source of information on this self-taught artist, van Booven repeatedly refers to the influence of Beardsley on his friend, who also died from tuberculosis. He shows him "sitting propped by pillows, browsing in Beardsley's 'Early Work,'" a book he himself had given him.[93] It was in it that de Nerée had discovered *Incipit Vita Nova* as reproduction no. 34, now entwined with *Witte Nachten*. Even though, in de Nerée's drawing, neither Beardsley's woman nor the foetus has moved from the book cover, the meaning of the image has changed. The young woman, eyes wide open, looks perplexed at a foetus that turns away with arm raised in protest but umbilical cord afloat. Her wonder is stressed by de Nerée's androgynous reader's hand that has entered the space of Beardsley's drawing in yet another *mise en abyme*. In de Nerée's drawing, the hand is there in principle to hold the book, but its tapered ringed fingers also

92 Henri van Booven, *Witte Nachten* (Haarlem: Gebrs. Nobels, 1901), XII, small caps in text.

93 Booven, "Karel de Nerée," *Elsevier's Geillustreerd Maandschrift*, 21:42 (July–Dec 1911): 18: "*Nog zie ik hem zitten overeind in de kussens, bladerend in Beardsley's 'Early Work'.*" On Nerée and van Booven, see also Sander Bink, *Carel de Nerée tot Babberich en Henri van Booven: Den Haag in het fin de siècle, met een voorwoord van Caroline de Westenholz* (Zwolle: WBOOKS, 2014); and Bink, "Konlookerarel de Nerée tot Babberich's Forgotten Torture Garden," *The Rijksmuseum Bulletin*, 68:4 (2020): 335–58.

belong to the young mother herself, marvelling at the foetus confronting her. The Dutch artist's drawing enters that of the Englishman to modify it. In a clearly Decadent kaleidoscope, the foetus signals both a problematic domain and the innovative state of a text in limbo.

Henri Gustave Jossot also turned to the foetus. The French caricaturist, illustrator, poster designer, painter, writer, and rebellious thinker, was fascinated by deformation and the arabesque. He created exaggerated interpretations of Art Nouveau, marked by inflated forms and extreme distortion. In 1897 he published in Édouard Pelletan's art review, *L'Estampe et l'Affiche*, a leading article on posters and caricature decked *inter alia* with two drawings of monsters and a tailpiece of stylised jumping frogs.[94] He was sufficiently involved in the periodical to be entrusted with a coloured composition and the back-cover vignettes to three volumes bringing together all the issues of this short-lived venture.[95] Jossot's article protested against a widespread view, namely that his twisted shapes and warped figures were not art, and claimed new vigour for decoration and poster bills based on deformity. Keen to "assault the viewer's gaze," and even stun the onlooker by his "grotesque drawing, pushed to the point of monstrosity,"[96] Jossot used thematic and linguistic violence in both text and drawings as well as formal disparity. His highly flavoured defence of abnormality and contortion assaulted Baudelaire's verses on beauty in his well-known homonymous poem, turned by Jossot himself into a commonplace:

> Baudelaire lost a rich opportunity to put down his pen and roll a cigarette the day he wrote:
>
> I hate the movement that shifts the lines,
> And I never cry, and never laugh.
>
> It was he who brought us the band of the symbol-brokers with their straight and forthright females, (oh so very forthright!) holding stiff lilies (hieratically, my dear!) in their rigid-fingered hands.
>
> *Baudelaire a perdu une riche occasion de poser sa plume et de rouler une cigarette, le jour où il* écrivit*:*
>
> *Je hais le mouvement qui déplace les lignes,*
> *Et jamais je ne pleure, et jamais je ne ris.*

94 Jossot, "L'Affiche caricaturale," *L'Estampe et l'Affiche*, 10 (15 Dec 1897): 238–40.

95 See Philippe Di Folco, "*L'Estampe et l'Affiche*, une revue méconnue (1897–1899)," *La Revue des revues*, 52:2 (2014): 24–35.

96 Jossot, "L'Affiche caricaturale," 239: "*violenter les regards du passant*," "*mon dessin grotesque, poussé jusqu'au monstrueux*."

> *C'est lui qui nous a amené la bande des symbolos avec leurs bonnes femmes droites et longues, (longues, oh combien!) tenant des lys tout droits (hiératiquement, ma chère!) dans leurs mains aux doigts longs.*[97]

In Jossot's work, the deliberate deformation of line is rooted in a rough draft of the human form. As an undefined shape of the creature-to-be, the foetus fostered the deforming power of his pencil. Rich in variance and mutation, evolution had engendered the monster at the end of the nineteenth century. In a pamphlet entitled *Le Fœtus récalcitrant* (*The Reluctant Foetus*), Jossot drew on the foetus's unwillingness to leave the womb and be in the world, in order to scourge forced education on children, pit a war machine in dissecting social flaws, and promote the development of a critical mind.[98] Monstrosity in his case was regarded as a sure sign of revitalisation. The editors of *L'Estampe et l'Affiche* defended Jossot's work: "he has renewed caricature, decoration and the art of the poster." They saw his direct lineage in Castel Béranger at 14 Rue La Fontaine, architect Hector Guimard's first Art Nouveau building in Paris.[99] Such lineage was based on Jossot's line, and such a line was foetal, as architect Adolf Loos would soon show.

Loos's famous essay and lecture *Ornament and Crime*, originally published as *Ornament und Verbrechen* (1910), criticised excessive ornamentation of objects and interiors. It opened with an eloquent evolutionary pattern: "The human embryo goes through all the animal evolution phases while in its mother's body."[100] In so doing, Loos succinctly establishes a parallel with the process of design, which evolves in gestation, but tolerates no redundancies for ultimate fitness to purpose.

Rather than breaking with Loos's conception of criminal embellishment and over-ornamentation, many artists of the late nineteenth century focused with fascination on the mystery of wombs, where the future of races and the superfluity of deforming decoration both came to life. The foetal form looked both backward and forward,

97 *Ibid.*, 238.

98 Jossot, *Le Foetus récalcitrant*, ed. by Henri Viltard ([Bordeaux]: Finitude, 2011).

99 La Direction, "Nos Illustrations. Jossot," *L'Estampe et l'Affiche*, 10 (15 Dec 1897): 233: "*Il a renouvelé la caricature, la décoration, l'affiche.*"

100 Adolf Loos, "Ornament und Verbrechen," in Ulrich Conrads, *Programme und Manifeste zur Architektur des 20. Jahrhunderts* (Bauwelt: Fundamente, 1964), 15–21: "*Der menschliche embryo macht im mutterleibe alle entwicklungsphasen des tierreiches durch.*" Loos's essay deliberately omits capital lettering current in German.

promising growth and harbouring decay. Likewise, the fin de siècle oscillated between birth and demise, deformation and germination. Deformation was often the very name given to *Jugendstil* and Art Nouveau shapes and designs. Evolution had met regression while the foetus captured and condensed a key vacillation between existence and annihilation.

In the first of Jossot's drawings for *L'Estampe et l'Affiche*, a hydrocephalic monster with webbed feet, a cock's tail, and a second head growing out of its breastbone, bites into an infant's limp body (Fig. 2.22a). It performs as the aggressive version of Beardsley's sophisticated *Triple-faced Grotesque* (Fig. 2.22b, Zatlin 790), itself redrafting Erhard Schön's *Des Teufels Dudelsack* (see Fig. 1.11a–c). A third creature may be compared to them: a monster named "Epignathus," from Christian Friedrich Schatz's *Die Griechischen Götter und die menschlichen Mißgeburten* (*Greek Gods and Human Abortions*), in which, by congenital malformation, one foetus swallows another (Fig. 2.22c).[101] In 1901, Schatz organised the contents of his book as a parallel between typical Greek monsters and anomalous creations of the womb, all explained as Cyclops, mermaids, harpies, and centaurs. Three reproductions of a bodiless, an anidian,[102] and a headless foetus were proposed as Medusa prototypes.[103] In such endeavours, a time-honoured tradition of mythological monsters was coming to an end. Fifteen years after Charles Gould had sought to explain monsters by geology, evolution, and philology in *Mythical Monsters*,[104] Schatz opened up a new perspective with his womb anomalies. The congenitally malformed monster Epignathus, as Schatz purported, explained the myth of Saturn and Jupiter devouring their children.[105] When compared to Beardsley's and Jossot's foetal creatures, the formal analogy is striking. Beardsley's *Triple-faced Grotesque*, an oval shape from

101 An epignathus is in fact a tumour affecting the sphenoid bone, the palate, the pharynx, tongue, and jaw, but is used here in a wider sense.

102 An anidian (formless) embryo or foetus is an amorphous cluster of hair, teeth, bone, cartilage, muscle tissue, etc.

103 Dr Christian Friedrich Schatz, *Die Griechischen Götter und die menschlichen Mißgeburten. Vortrag gehalten im Docentenverein der Universität Rostock am 3. Mai 1901, mit 62 Abbildungen im Text* (Wiesbaden: J. F. Bergmann, 1901), fig. 30, 51, and 53, https://archive.org/details/diegriechischen00schagoog/page/n2/mode/2up

104 Charles Gould, *Mythical Monsters, with Ninety-three Illustrations* (London: W. H. Allen & Co., 1886).

105 Schatz, *Die Griechischen Götter und die menschlichen Mißgeburten*, 32, fig. 43.

which emerge three heads and an arm, Jossot's hydrocephalic monster, and Schatz's Epignathus all sit at the crossroads of Decadent grotesque with monstrous obstetrics.

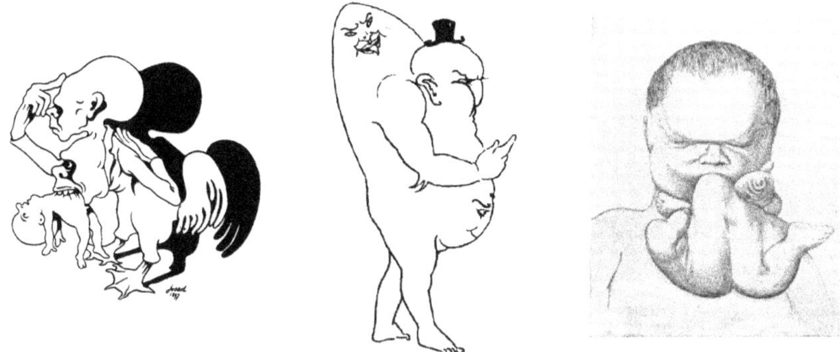

Fig. 2.22a–c Three Grotesques in Comparison. 2.22a Jossot, Two-headed Monster Biting into a Child's Body, *L'Estampe et l'Affiche*, 10 (15 Dec 1897):240 (detail); 2.22b Beardsley, *Triple-faced Grotesque*, BM-LJ:156, BM-FH:22 (R<). PE coll.; 2.22c Dr Schatz, "Epignathus," in *Die Griechischen Götter und die Menschlichen Mißgeburten* (1901), no. 43

Teratological imagination was an integral part of Decadent Aestheticism and such aesthetic issues reached out, well beyond the realm of Beardsley's vignettes and drawings, to the arts in general. Beardsley's complex oeuvre had given the kick-off to such extensive use of the foetal motif. In his art, the motif broadly permeated scenes and shapes. Others appropriated it in creative assimilation. However, his ingenious imagination was also held in check by a polished intellect. He completed his grotesque art with refined posturing and the stance of a dandy. Delighting in play and extravagance, he would incorporate the grotesque to his natural love of notoriety and his own portraits.

3. A Dandy's Portico of Portraits

Fame or Bust

On leaving Westminster Abbey, little Aubrey is said to have quizzed his mother: "Mummy, shall I have a bust or a stained-glass window when I am dead? For I may be a great man some day." When asked what he would prefer, he added: "A bust, I think, because I am rather good-looking."[1] A singular beauty, to say the least, enhanced by elaborate outfits and a dandified stance; and an early intuition of his own looming end. Beardsley would propel his tongue-in-cheek perception of himself onto the public stage via the emerging mass press, even projecting his own creative habits into his work. By drawing his tall thin candlesticks with tapering candles, he insinuated that he worked only by candlelight with curtains drawn. He repetitively shocked the Victorian ruling classes in interviews, conversations, and declarations, promoting his French posture and love of France. It takes several facets to make a bust and Aubrey had grasped three of them prematurely: scandal, rumour, and genius. To earn himself a statue and become the icon we all know, he owed it to himself to work quickly.

Five months before his twenty-sixth birthday, Aubrey Beardsley died of tuberculosis. In less than six years, he had established an impressive oeuvre, and marked a whole era as "the Beardsley period." No recollection of the British fin de siècle was ever going to escape his oeuvre or his moniker, let alone his persona. In due course, he swapped the bust for a gallery of his own images. His visage has been remembered through his cabinet portraits, prancing or mischievous *alter egos*, and press photographs. His portraitists, from Max Beerbohm to

1 Brigid Brophy, *Beardsley and his World* (London: Thames and Hudson, 1976), 5.

 https://doi.org/10.11647/OBP.0413.03

Jacques-Émile Blanche, sought to represent the main qualities defined by their model: aplomb, caprice, and nerve. Aplomb translated into his self-confidence in the most demanding situations. Caprice, into his changeable moods and flippant behaviour. And nerve, into his insolent styling of himself.

The Gallery

To start with, aplomb. Beardsley's early ambition to one day be rendered in a bust is hinted in a self-portrait in profile, with contours sharply delineated in outline, on stark white, dating from March 1895 (*A Portrait of the Artist*, Zatlin 951). The figure's erect head projects his gaze into the far distance (Fig. 3.1). His outfit, curtailed at waist level, swells exaggeratedly at the torso as if the figure was ready to stand in the sculpture gallery. Voicelessly, the portrait has turned into a museum bust on a pedestal, if not for the lace collar, shirred with a double black ribbon, and the pleated shirtfront (or is it a ruffle?). The garment takes the artist back in time and gives him an androgynous elegance. The style favours the linear harmony of the Old Masters, cherished by Beardsley, a trait that, Walter Crane believed, would give the subject construction and character.[2]

Beardsley's portrait might well be styled on Beau Brummell brazenly wearing his Regency suit. In a well-known portrait by Richard Dighton (1805), Brummell with his Titus hairstyle wears a dark double-breasted cutaway tailcoat with a stand-up collar, an elaborately knotted cravat, and watch fobs. In Beardsley's *A Portrait of the Artist*, there is no tailcoat, yet a fitted waistcoat; no watch fobs, yet a buttonhole to be adorned and a lapel pin; no Titus hairstyle, yet smooth hair parted at the front; and the high cravat has been tempered by a tiny earring. However, all in all, the wide lapels and the neat white linen are similar. Beardsley has modelled on Brummell a fin-de-siècle replica for posterity: his auspicious outline

2 Regarding outline, Crane abundantly praised *Hypnerotomachia Poliphili*, attributed to Francesco Colonna and printed by Aldus Manutius in Venice (1499), as with designs "in outline, and want[ing] nothing else." He also stressed the charm, simplicity, and "broad effect" of outline in modern publications. See Walter Crane, *Of the Decorative Illustration of Books Old and New* (London: George Bell and Sons, 1896), 62–71 and 223.

has made it to the frontispiece of more than one modern biography.[3] And yet there lurks a hardly noticeable tension between petrification and action, immutability and mutability, as if the figure were to come to life and transform again.

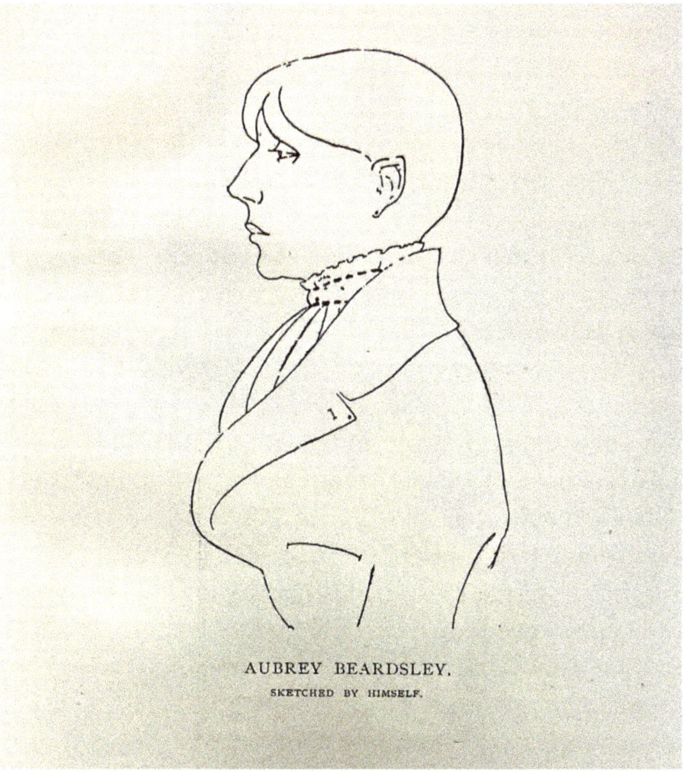

Fig. 3.1 Aubrey Beardsley, *A Portrait of the Artist* (Mar 1895), repr. from *Posters in Miniature*, with the title *Aubrey Beardsley. Sketched by Himself*. Courtesy MSL coll., Delaware

The same occurs with Jacques-Émile Blanche's splendid portrait of Beardsley in the National Portrait Gallery (1895), and the impression of movement it conveys. Strikingly stylish, boutonnière with flower, stick in gloved hands, the figure – in a grey suit, which brings out his light eyes, pallid skin, red hair and fine features – is firmly seated. Only

3 This drawing serves as frontispiece in Brigid Brophy, *Beardsley and his World*. It also faces the "Introduction" in Matthew Sturgis, *Aubrey Beardsley: A Biography* (London: Harper Collins Publishers, 1998).

the scenery behind him stirs. Yet, the portrait suggests motion and transformation, as when Walter Sickert captured Beardsley in 1894, turning away, hat and stick in hand, at the unveiling of Keats's bust in Hampstead.[4] Beardsley's portraits seize an inherent versatility. They became progressively more disturbing, mischievous, and provocative in the printed black-and-white portraits and the photographs by Frederick H. Evans, which I discuss below.

Caprice, then. In his first self-portrait, we face Beardsley's back (Fig. 3.2). He is perched on a high stool at a desk with a massive open book – working, we assume, on some thankless task (he had to earn a living in an architect's office, then an insurance broker's, before he could establish himself as a designer). Written above him is the French inscription "Le Dèbris [*sic*] d'un poète," which gives the drawing its title (Zatlin 244), literally, "The remains of a poet." At first glance, we understand it as a pathetic appeal. It stems, however, from Flaubert's caustic comment on Léon, Madame Bovary's first lover, ready to spurn their love affair to better establish himself professionally and socially: "The most mediocre libertine has dreamed of sultanas; every notary carries within him the remains of a poet."[5] Beardsley had read Flaubert's novel in the original and the quote brings with it the ironic barb Flaubert aimed at Léon. Apparent self-pity conceals a twist. The ostensible defeatism and resignation carry no despair, quite the opposite. It would not take long before such mocking self-commiseration would become bravado, panache, with the growing aura of scandal, of that Victorian din and clamour which Beardsley took advantage of. The distanced character would gradually appear centre stage, and then quickly turn into a cheeky celebrity.

---

4 Walter Sickert, "Portrait of Aubrey Beardsley," *The Yellow Book*, 2 (July 1894): 223, in *The Yellow Book Digital Edition*, ed. by Dennis Denisoff and Lorraine Janzen Kooistra, 2011–14. *Yellow Nineties 2.0*, Ryerson University Centre for Digital Humanities, 2020, https://1890s.ca/YB2-sickert-aubrey-beardsley/; Brophy, *Beardsley and his World*, 57.

5 Gustave Flaubert, *Madame Bovary: mœurs de province, édition définitive suivie des requisitoire, plaidoirie et jugement intenté à l'auteur* (Paris: G. Charpentier, 1877), 321: "*Le plus médiocre libertin a rêvé des sultanes; chaque notaire porte en soi les débris d'un poète.*" (2nd Part, Chapter VI).

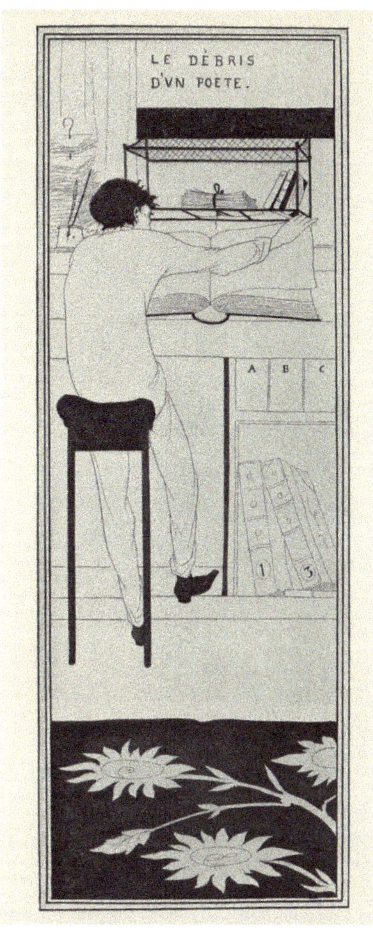

Fig. 3.2 Aubrey Beardsley, *Le Dèbris* [*sic*] *d'un Poète* (June 1892), Victoria and Albert Museum, London, UK, repr. from *Uncollected Work*, no. 12. Courtesy MSL coll., Delaware

Beardsley certainly struck poses, not necessarily to show off, nor simply to have fun. His self-portraits have nerve. In a game of heads or tails, it could be argued that the Brummell bust (heads) is the obverse of the reversely monstrous portraits (tails): a provocative alternative to dandyism. If dandyism relied on good looks, Beardsley had a gaunt, hardly attractive physique. Yet sophisticated and urbane ugliness, relying on the din of the metropolis, would be an alternative to dandyism, also resonant with nascent psychology and its allusion to Jekyll and Hyde.

Appearance and New Aesthetics

Beardsley was very tall, cut a sharp thin profile, and spoke in a dry, staccato voice. He dressed primly, and moved with a bouncing gait in a nervous, agitated manner. Oscar Wilde described "a face like a silver hatchet, and grass green hair."[6] Most terms referring to his persona and work gravitated around *strange, weird, quaint, peculiar*, at times *freakish*. Feverishness was another recurrent descriptor: a liveliness that changed from haste to abruptness as he moved from the most recent work to the next, from one style to the other. He gloated when he shocked, overflowing with capricious mischief. To his near twin, Beerbohm,[7] he had given a photograph of himself by Frederick Hollyer, caricatured in watercolour (*Self-caricature*, Zatlin 939).[8] And Beerbohm satirised him nine times, sharpening his angular profile, magnifying his restless-fingered hands, twisting his crossed legs high. He made him drag a doggie on wheels in response to his own skit as an angelic babe with stylish puppy at his heels (see Fig. 2.8c). Beardsley knew he didn't have long to live. To amaze and grandstand, he started with his close friends before his renown reached the general public. He determined to be a dandy with composure.

From 1892, Beardsley started to see dandyism in a more intellectual light relating to his Francophilia. Bust apart, his dandyism was no longer that of Brummell, but of Charles Baudelaire as Matthew Sturgis recorded. Not that he was turning away from the trappings of dress: at the spring 1893 opening of the Parisian Salon, he sported a grey suit, grey gloves, a golden tie, a stick, and a straw hat; he would have loved "a white overcoat with a pale pink lining" from his first *Yellow Book* earnings in 1894.[9] But, like Baudelaire in his essay on Constantin Guys, "The Painter of Modern Life,"[10] he understood dandyism, to use

6 Sturgis, *Aubrey Beardsley*, 160.

7 Beardsley and Beerbohm were both born in August 1872, Beardsley being the elder by three days.

8 Brophy, *Beardsley and his World*, 49.

9 Sturgis, *Aubrey Beardsley*, 136–37, 202.

10 Charles Baudelaire, "Le peintre de la vie moderne," *Le Figaro* (26 and 29 Nov, 3 Dec 1863); collected in *L'Art romantique* (1868); *Œuvres complètes*, ed. by Claude Pichois, 2 vols. (Paris: Gallimard, 1976), II, 683–724.

Baudelaire's words, as "the last glow of heroism in decadent times,"[11] when heroes had been overpowered by the growing masses. Modern heroism lay no more in physical strength and moral integrity but in artful difference. The scrupulous distinction of spanking clean attire, the attention to grooming and dress code "were for the perfect dandy but a symbol of the aristocratic superiority of his spirit." Sartorial feats had become intellectual. Baudelaire would have recognised in Beardsley the desire to enjoy the "pleasure of astonishing and the haughty satisfaction of never being astonished."[12]

In order to astonish, Beardsley had drawn lessons from James McNeill Whistler's public assertions through his famous lawsuit against John Ruskin, control of his work, artistic philosophy, and Wilde's parade of aphorisms. He revered wit and witticisms, as evidenced by his polysemous captions and multifaceted statements. The illness that plagued him, the bodily appearance that might have been a disservice to him, he made glow and shine in weirdness. Invited to give a speech on the occasion of the *Yellow Book*'s launch, he began with "I am going to talk about an interesting subject, myself."[13] His gallery of portraits playfully introduced this particular self as a monster.

Margin in Books and Minsters

Several of Beardsley's self-portraits ironically celebrate a monstrosity apparent from his physical appearance, in feigned attitudes, scripts in drawings, or his own captions. To display one's self in one's own work as an anomaly, to stage oneself as a monster, implied both a jeering distancing from one's identity, and a consented banishment from the rest of humanity, even the artistic community. The dominant

---

11 Baudelaire, "Le peintre de la vie moderne," 711: "*Le dandysme est le dernier éclat de l'héroïsme dans les décadences.*"

12 *Ibid.*, 710: "*Ces choses ne sont pour le parfait dandy qu'un symbole de la supériorité aristocratique de son esprit.*" "*C'est le plaisir d'étonner et la satisfaction orgueilleuse de ne jamais être étonné.*" On Beardsley and Baudelaire, see also Sturgis, *Aubrey Beardsley*, 96–97.

13 Sturgis, *Aubrey Beardsley*, 192.

culture took normality for granted, and desired its artists to present an idealised version of themselves. Instead, Beardsley constructed and delivered images, which, at their heart, are not only provocative but also humorous. As in the foetal likenesses of fin-de-siècle dandies and Decadents discussed in the previous chapter, the margin this artist claimed was not so much social as artistic. It was determined by the disparity he created between the audience's desires and what he delivered. In the images discussed here, margin frequently becomes a play on distance and dimensions. Yet, it is also a border, a fringe that calls upon the history of culture and aesthetics. It may be defined in relation to a text, in terms of printed pages, or to a piece of architecture that relates to text in multiple ways. It frequently refers to two monuments of culture, opposed in size but linked in the imaginary: the book and the cathedral.

Margin traditionally welcomes monsters and grotesques, which brim and flourish at the rim of Western books, from the *babewyns* of medieval manuscripts as Jurgis Baltrušaitis has commented,[14] to Albrecht Dürer and his fellow artists' famous *Randzeichnungen*.[15] These were interlaced motifs and marginal drawings in Emperor Maximilian I's *Book of Hours*, interspersed with scrawls, oddities, and grimaces. They had been lithographed by Johann Nepomuk Strixner at the beginning of the nineteenth century and fascinated the Romantics.[16] The margin plays spontaneous home to grotesques, André Chastel's "nameless ornament."[17] It appears in the very first example analysed by Chastel, a passage from Montaigne's *Essays* (chap. XVII). Chastel

14 Jurgis Baltrušaitis, "Le réveil du fantastique dans le décor du livre," in Baltrušaitis, *Réveils et Prodiges: le gothique fantastique* (Paris: A. Colin, 1960), 195–234.

15 See Hans Christoph von Tavel, *Die Randzeichnungen Albrecht Dürers zum Gebetbuch Kaiser Maximilians* (Munich: Prestel Verlag, 1966).

16 See Richard Benz, *Goethe und die romantische Kunst* (Munich: R. Piper & Co., 1940), 146–55; Arthur Rümann, *Das illustrierte Buch des XIX. Jahrhunderts in England, Frankreich und Deutschland, 1790–1860* (Leipzig: Im Insel-Verlag, 1930), 294. And more recently, Cordula Grewe, *The Arabesque from Kant to Comics* (New York: Routledge, 2021).

17 André Chastel, *La Grottesque. Essai sur l'"ornement sans nom"* (Paris: Le Promeneur, 1988), 9. See also Philippe Morel, *Les Grotesques: Les Figures de l'imaginaire dans la peinture italienne de la fin de la Renaissance* (Paris: Flammarion, 2001).

goes on to state in his study: "We are literally at the margins, and margins are always and everywhere the realm of permissiveness."[18]

And it is again in the cathedral's periphery and decoration that the gargoyles and monsters reside, storming that medieval monument often dubbed the "great book of stone." While the minster is erected as the figurative sum total of the Christian doctrine, the demons and monsters, discarded from the didactic programme, inhabit its borders, protuberances, and pinnacles. The parallel is arresting: a paper margin, filled with demons, tritons, and aberrations for the book; a sculpted margin, full of gargoyles and chimaeras for the cathedral. And the relation between the two is no invention. The striking metaphor of the cathedral as book of stone appeared in the writings of Saint Bernard of Citeaux and still survives in commonplace forms today. In 1884, Ruskin called the Amiens Cathedral "the Amiens Bible," cementing a direct analogy between architecture and the book. The façade of any cathedral is a "written page" (to be deciphered) and the monsters "words uttered by [the] sculptors" in Joris-Karl Huysmans's short text "The Monster."[19] By the end of the nineteenth century, the striking image had become a cliché, as Jean de Palacio has shown.[20]

As we shall see in this chapter, Beardsley claimed to be a part of both the book and the book of stone. The press saluted him as "An Apostle of the Grotesque,"[21] indeed the prophet of a new era, illustrating his assertion: "If I am not grotesque, I am nothing."[22] Whilst Beardsley made these statements to shock the media, his actual artistic practices were far more revolutionary than a soundbite. By setting himself up as an anomaly, he attempted to reshape the artistic canon through wit, aloofness, and discrepancy. By deliberately placing himself at the margin of cultural monuments (either book or cathedral), he inverted the relationship between main text and note, whole and

18 Chastel, *La Grottesque*, 42: *"Nous sommes au sens propre dans le marginal, et le marginal est toujours et partout le domaine de la permissivité."*

19 Joris-Karl Huysmans, "Le Monstre," in Huysmans, *Certains* (Paris: Tresse et Stock, 1889), 142.

20 See Jean de Palacio, "La cathédrale hystérique: monstre hybride et repaire de monstres," in *La Cathédrale*, ed. by Joëlle Prungnaud (Lille: UL3, Travaux et Recherches, 2001), 142–43.

21 "An Apostle of the Grotesque," *The Sketch*, 9:115 (10 Apr 1895): 561–62.

22 Arthur H. Lawrence, "Mr. Aubrey Beardsley and His Work," *The Idler*, 11 (Mar 1897): 198.

part, leading and secondary discourse, magnum opus and fragment. Yet, concurrently, the force of jest at the heart of his work led to both their parody and their imitation by others. Beardsley's self-portraits inspired other works, which also referenced the period's key texts such as Wilde's *The Picture of Dorian Gray* that poses, among others, the crucial question of representation. These parodies highlight both the subtlety and power of Beardsley's humour and its manifesto-like potential.

This chapter also looks at portraits taken of Beardsley by the photographer Frederick H. Evans, in which the artist poses as a cathedral gargoyle. Such images reassess the artist's relationship to the monument and ironically comment on the ancient practice of the "signature," updated in the nineteenth century. By magnifying the monstrous detail, the photographs achieve a form of climactic expression that heralds modern practices closer to us, for instance using one's own body in art or as art. The humour of this series of fantasised or ludicrous images of the self, against an explicit background of monstrosity, calls *in fine* for a revision of cultural hierarchies.

In what follows, both book and minster appear in typical fin-de-siècle form. The book, regularly seen as a major testimonial, is swapped for ephemeral periodicals, although these may be choice art and literature reviews playing with the idea of the book (such as the *Yellow Book*). Thanks to the formidable expansion of the press, a new media era had risen. New printing technologies had enhanced Beardsley's linear graphics. The periodical press had made his work known, and he would make a gallery of self-images to match. As for the cathedral, it turns out to be ultimately fragile, conquered by its most anomalous parts.

Humour in Periodicals' Borders

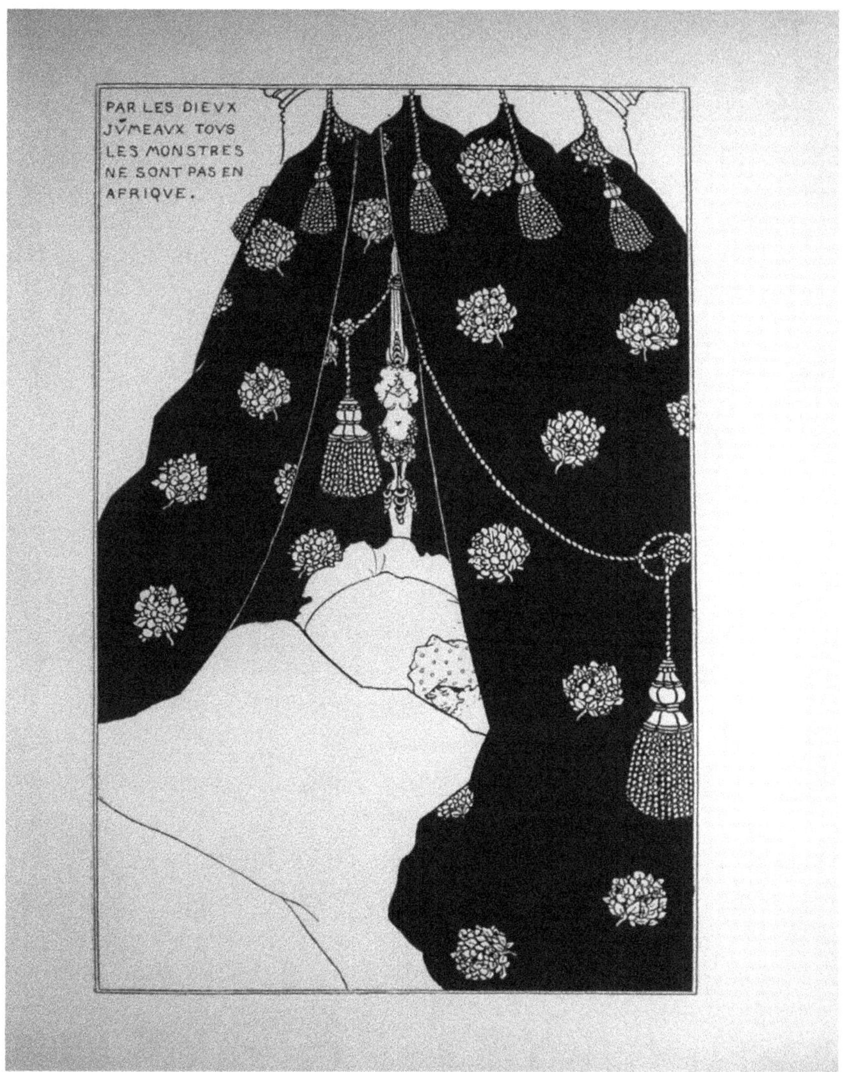

Fig. 3.3 Aubrey Beardsley, *Portrait of Himself* (late summer–autumn 1894), repr. *The Yellow Book*, 3 (Oct 1894): 51. Courtesy Y90s

Portrait of Himself (Fig. 3.3, Zatlin 906), the first of Beardsley's cheeky self-portraits in periodicals on gaining fame, was published in 1894 in the third volume of the *Yellow Book* when Beardsley himself was its art editor.[23] It already shows a man who scrutinises his ego ironically. There is a dry detachment in the capitalisation of the caption "Himself," a virtually honorific title, which speaks of the conflict between the artist and his persona. As if to enhance its own oddity, the drawing bears in French the inscription "*Par les dieux jumeaux tous les monstres ne sont pas en Afrique*" ("By the twin gods not all monsters are in Africa"), the opening sentence of Cyrano de Bergerac's comedy *Le Pédant joué* (1654). An 1895 interview with Beardsley would also picture him in his black-and-orange studio with "an exquisitely bound *exemplaire*" of this very comedy,[24] known for its creative language, numerous sexual allusions, impracticable communication, bizarre scenes, and monologues with no connection to the plot.

The uncurved lettering calls to mind chiselled antique stone slabs or commemorative pillars, bringing Beardsley into kinship with a far-off Antiquity peopled by monsters and prodigies. The twin gods may refer to Castor and Pollux, the Dioscuri, literally "sons of Zeus," a couple accumulating ambiguities. The twin nature of the half-brothers is based on irregular birth: Castor and Pollux spawn from one of Leda's eggs, inseminated on the same night by Zeus metamorphosed into a swan and by husband Tyndareus. Although sharing the same egg, the twins are distinct, Pollux being considered Zeus's son, and Castor Tyndareus's. Divided between divinity and humanity, they oscillate, even after the death of one of them, between immortality and the underworld. As for Africa, it refers (like Libya, often used as a synonym) to that margin of the ancient world that was seen to harbour "abnormality," which many a weird and wonderful ancient travelogue had offered to "civilised" eyes.

Inversely, by way of antiphrasis, *Portrait of Himself* presents the artist, already a hot new topic in the London press, as a modern-day monster at the heart of the metropolis, in a sumptuous and ornate setting, far from exotic lands. The oversized décor contrasts with his microscopic figure. Dressed in a nightgown, he peeks beneath an enormous frilly nightcap with ruched brim and the quilt of a giant bed, a catafalque or throne, whose canopy is adorned with formal bouquets and suggests the oriental skirts of an overbearing female. Despite the affectation

23 *The Yellow Book*, 3 (Oct 1894): 51.
24 "An Apostle of the Grotesque," 561.

of the capitalised "Himself," the artist is losing substance within the invasive folds of fabrics and drapes which seem to undermine his virility. The bold perspective grants him a choice place in the giantess's lap (the bulging canopy). Miniaturisation is equally disturbing: the plump forms of a she-faun, both arms severed, under a dishevelled grinning head, adorn the aptly placed bedpost. An equivocal ornament, she acts as a symbol of the artist's ambiguous sexuality, and her amputation signals removal or loss of some part of *his* body. By playing on the margins of the civilised world ("Africa") and the distance from Antiquity, humour brings back to the hub of civilisation an artist not only mockingly monstrous but also minuscule.

Barely two years later, Beardsley re-styles his own self in a new portrait and titles it *A Footnote* (Fig. 3.4). After John Lane had dismissed him as art editor of the *Yellow Book*, he again signs his likeness, this time in the *Savoy* (Zatlin 1004r).[25] The artist has now matured. Grown to a spectacular size and equipped with a gigantic quill, he figures centre stage. Although moved to the open, he sports the same refined dress as in *Portrait of Himself*, in clinging breeches and a fancy open-necked shirt fringed with flowers. Yet his monstrousness and flippancy are brazenly on display. The she-faun has tailed him, converted into a horned and armless herm fetish, a deity of boundaries, with protruding, rounded hips, his muscular back turned to us. The artist himself is a faun: his ears are exaggeratedly sharp and pointed, his gaze slides under a middle parting over an impish triangular face. Devoted to the small, maimed Pan, he is tied by a rope to his pillar, a replacement for the bedpost. His tether gives him little leeway or room for manoeuvre, and he offers his custodian a slanting, pouting glance. We may have expected the herm god's blatant sexuality to state itself to the fore, but the statuette shies away. Playfully, the monstrosity – and the artist's persona – recalls its ties to the margin, obvious in the title's pun on "footnote." Indeed, the *Savoy* drawing is a gloss, a note, a below-the-text comment on a previous achievement, the earlier *Portrait of Himself*.

25 *The Savoy*, 2 (Apr 1896): 185.

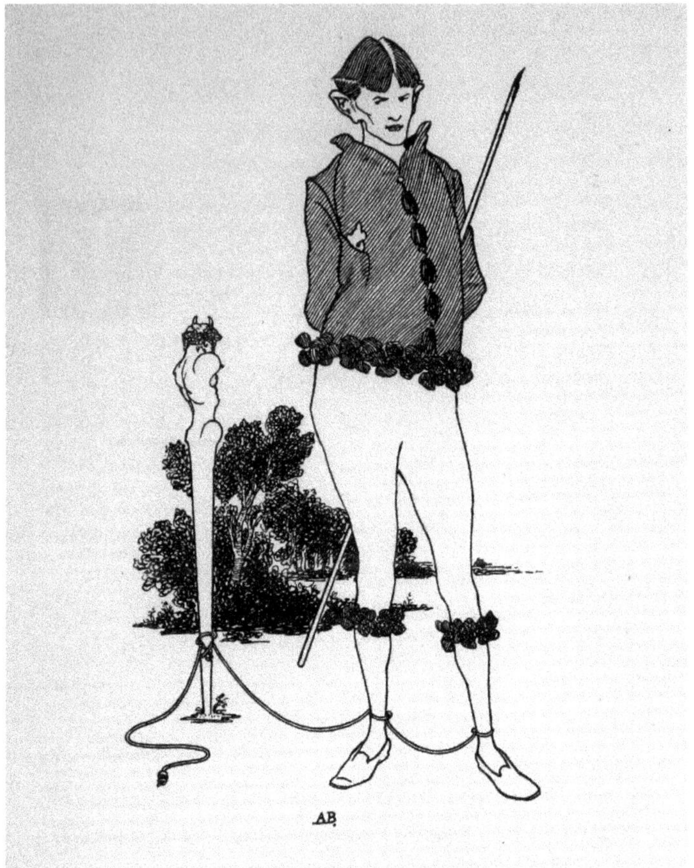

Fig. 3.4 Aubrey Beardsley, *A Footnote* (by last week of Mar 1896), repr. *The Savoy*, 2 (Apr 1896): 185. Courtesy Y90s

Both self-portraits possess a status of oblique manifesto, each to its own fin-de-siècle periodical. They provokingly set the artist within the periodical he edits, as a challenging part of his aesthetic and artistic choices, claiming monstrosity as an asset, and at the same time fuelling press excitement. Yet the *Savoy* drawing is also a literal interpretation of the title's two components, *foot* and *note*, a "footnote" materialised in the rope chaining the artist to Pan's pillar by the ankles. A footnote figures by definition at the bottom edge of a text, just as the cord secures the artist's foot. By reducing the figurative expression to its literal sense, humour is now based *on* the margin itself. Together they have brought the monstrous artist to the forefront with a bump. It is worth noting, that such humour went largely unnoticed. The image, considered shocking, was censored as early as 1899, the god's torso erased, and the rope removed. Gilt stamped, what remained of it featured on the red cover of *A Second Book of Fifty Drawings*, published 1899 by Smithers, who was not a man shy of taking risks. Now Beardsley seemed to pose with an inexplicable unadorned stake on the left (Fig. 3.5).

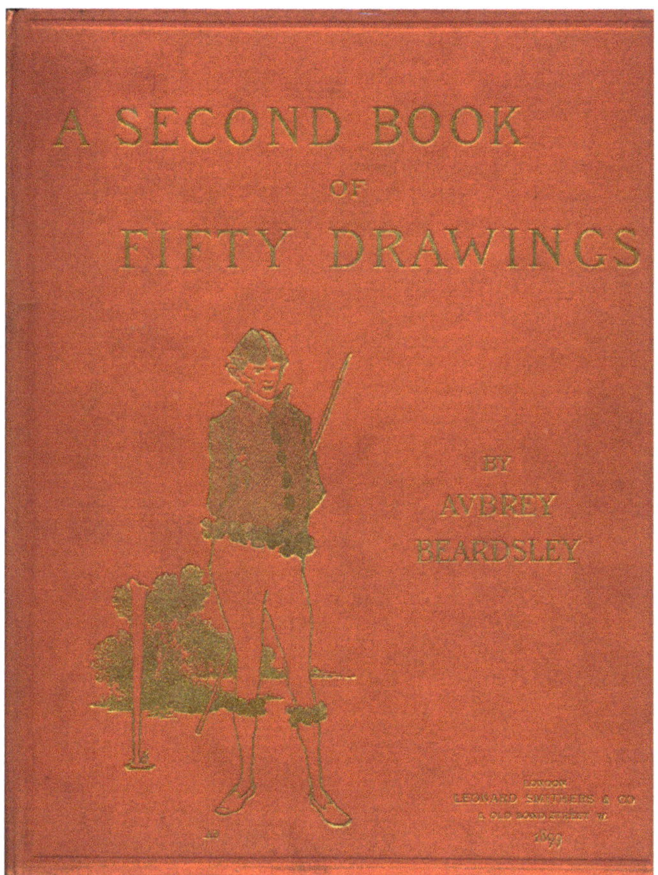

Fig. 3.5 Cover of *A Book of Fifty Drawings by Aubrey Beardsley* (London: Smithers, 1897) with *A Footnote* altered. Courtesy MSL coll., Delaware

Mock and Genuine Impersonations

Fin-de-siècle art was often steeped in pile-on parody, and Beardsley's *Yellow Book* self-portrait inspired further takes on the artist's contrived monstrosity. An unsigned spoof of *Portrait of Himself* by Edward Tennyson Reed (Fig. 3.6) was published in *Punch*, the humorous weekly, in the month following the *Yellow Book* issue. Adopting playful pseudonyms, such as Mortarthurio Whiskersly or Whiskersley, Danby Weirdsley, or "Yellow Book" Impressionist, Reed regularly reworked Beardsley's drawings between 1893 and 1895, offering inflated distortions which often out-parodied parody to form a body of work parallel to Beardsley's own and rich in alternative significance. He aped Beardsley's style but also promoted it, contributing to its spread and ascendancy. In this drawing, the ornamental posies on the drapes have turned into scowling faces that besiege a frightened figure cowering under the sheets. Beardsley's own grimacing creatures now ogle the artist in bed. His wickedness attacks its creator and his monstrous identity is both dependent on his graphics and ruled by them.

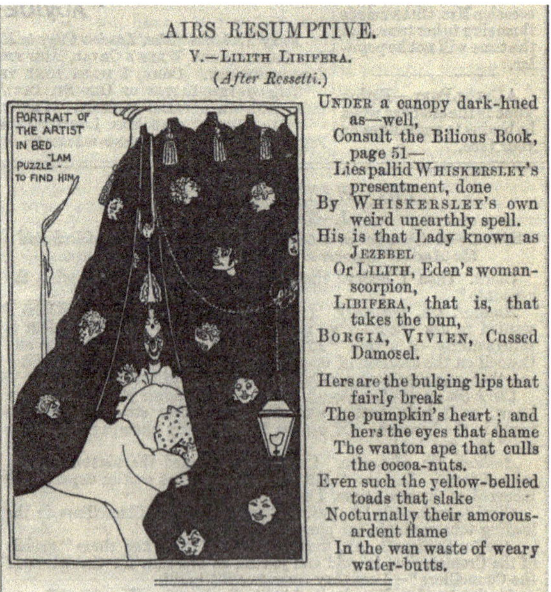
AIRS RESUMPTIVE.

V.—LILITH LIBIFERA.

(*After Rossetti.*)

UNDER a canopy dark-hued as—well,
Consult the Bilious Book, page 51—
Lies pallid WHISKERSLEY'S presentment, done
By WHISKERSLEY'S own weird unearthly spell.
His is that Lady known as JEZEBEL
Or LILITH, Eden's woman-scorpion,
LIBIFERA, that is, that takes the bun,
BORGIA, VIVIEN, Cussed Damosel.

Hers are the bulging lips that fairly break
The pumpkin's heart; and hers the eyes that shame
The wanton ape that culls the cocoa-nuts.
Even such the yellow-bellied toads that slake
Nocturnally their amorous-ardent flame
In the wan waste of weary water-butts.

Fig. 3.6 [Edward Tennyson Reed], unsigned pastiche of Beardsley's *Portrait of Himself*, repr. *Punch, or, the London Charivari*, 107 (3 Nov 1894): 205 (detail). University of Minnesota Libraries

Yet, despite the clever drawing, what accompanies the image reads flat, as if the humour permeating the original were its secret impervious force, tolerating distortion only at the cost of demoted meaning. The inscription "Portrait of the Artist in Bed-lam, puzzle – to find him" propounds an easy joke: Bed-lam refers first to the bed, then to Bethlem Royal Hospital, nicknamed Bedlam, the famous psychiatric asylum. Moreover, an unsigned sonnet supplements the image, Owen Seaman's "Lilith Libifera," which, under pretence of a pastiche of "Lilith," one of Dante Gabriel Rossetti's most beautiful sonnets,[26] parodies Rossetti's "Sibylla Palmifera" closely associated with "Lilith."[27] Both works were composed in parallel to the homonymous *Lady Lilith* (1866–68) and *Sibylla Palmifera* (1866–70), two oil paintings on canvas with nearly identical dimensions, indeed considered a diptych by Rossetti himself, who renamed them "Body's Beauty" and "Soul's Beauty." In *Punch,* they no longer point at beauty, but ironically at monstrosity, both of body (as in *Portrait of Himself*) and soul (as in the bed drapes' distorted imaginings). Pointedly, Rossetti's "Sibylla Palmifera" glorified beauty in a broad allegory.[28] The beard (of Beard-sley) being replaced by whiskers in the pastiche, "Lilith Libifera," ascribed to Whiskersley's parodied portrait, now crowns her a monster in the place of Beauty. As in the reworked drawing, in the poem next to the skit, she is surrounded by abnormal spawn, exclusively female.[29] The female figures targeted are not, however, Beardsley's but Rossetti's, whose several paintings and poems are easily recognisable. "Cussed Damosel" parodies "The Blessed Damozel," "Borgia" refers to the watercolours *Borgia* and *Lucrezia Borgia Administering the Poison-Draught*, and Vivien is a favourite figure of the Pre-Raphaelites (including Frederick Sandys, Edward Burne-Jones, and Henry R. Rheam). Seaman's heavy parody has, moreover, little in common with Beardsley's witty humour. In its vehemence, pompous style, and triviality, it aligns satirised images and a lewd toxic bestiary. It reads as a war machine. Originally marginal and idiosyncratic, oddity has become outrage.

Beardsley's drawing fared much better in the hands of Hans-Henning von Voigt, known as Alastair, a man of letters, polyglot translator, set and costume designer, dancer, actor and circus performer, who himself

26 Dante Gabriel Rossetti, "Lilith (For a Picture)," in *Poems* (London: F. S. Ellis, 1870), republished as "Body's Beauty" within the section "The House of Life," in *Ballads and Sonnets* (London: Ellis and White, 1881).

27 Later entitled "Soul's Beauty," this sonnet precedes "Lilith" in both collections.

28 Rossetti, "Sibylla Palmifera," v. 1–10.

29 [Owen Seaman], "Lilith Libifera (*After Rossetti*)," *Punch, or The London Charivari,* 107 (3 Nov 1894): 205; later collected in *The Battle of the Bays* (London and New York: John Lane, 1896), 57 (with variants).

loved theatrical attitudes and posturing.[30] His version helps to highlight the image's rich semantic potential when combined with an equally rich text. In a drawing from the 1920s (Fig. 3.7), in which *Portrait of Himself* is unmistakably the source of inspiration, a figure lies again in bed with plume-decorated drapes and elaborately carved bedposts. Is this yet another monster?

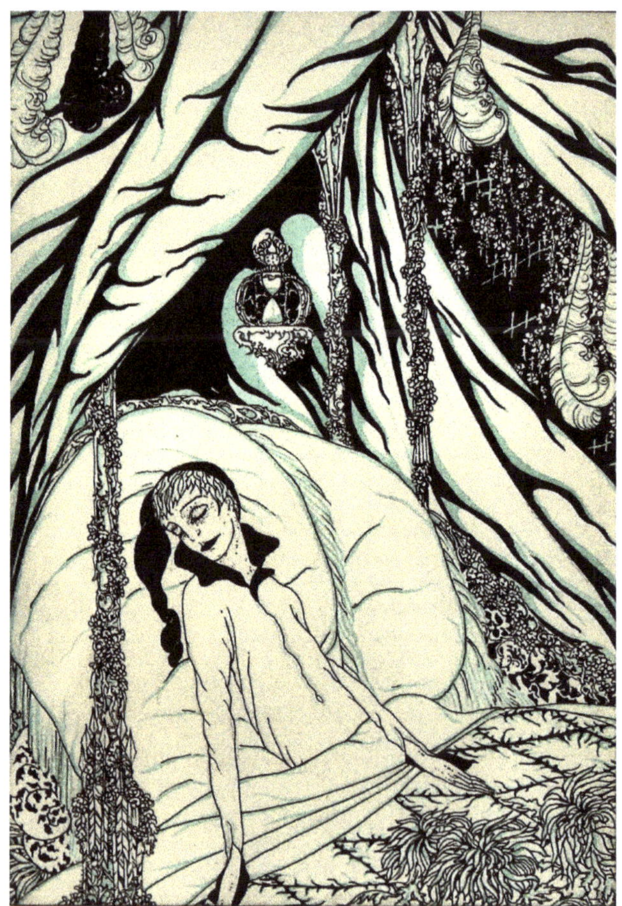

Fig. 3.7 Alastair, *The Picture of Dorian Gray* or *Dorian Gray in Catherine de Medici's Mourning Bed* (early 1920s), Victor and Gretha Arwas coll., London, UK. Courtesy and © Gretha Arwas

30 See Victor Arwas, *Alastair: Illustrator of Decadence* (London: Thames and Hudson, 1979); Ines Janet Engelmann, ed., *Alastair. Kunst als Schicksal* (Halle: Stiftung Moritzburg Halle, Kunstmuseum des Landes Sachsen-Anhalt, 2004); Engelmann, ed., *Alastair. Kunst als Schicksal* (Munich: Bayerische Akademie der Schönen Künste, 2007).

The title, given by Victor Arwas as *The Picture of Dorian Gray*[31] and also known as *Dorian Gray in Catherine de Medici's Mourning Bed*, endorses the guess, yet designates not the creator but the creation, conceived here again in between text and image. Alastair knew Beardsley's and Wilde's work well. He provided drawings for three editions of Wilde's writings, namely *The Sphinx Decorated by Alastair* (John Lane, 1920),[32] *Salomé* republished in the original French (Les Éditions G. Crès et Cie, 1922), and *The Birthday of the Infanta* in French translation (The Black Sun Press, Éditions Narcisse, 1928). He went on to translate Wilde's novel into German in 1948,[33] and he certainly picked the title in full awareness. However, Dorian Gray's picture is not only a portrait, as claims *Le Portrait de Dorian Gray*, its French title in translation, but also a work of art, a representation infused with its self-governing life. Alastair's drawing is no mere illustration either, but an opus in its own right. Its author, a multi-talented draughtsman-cum-polyglot-translator combines a complex fin-de-siècle novel[34] and the monstrous overtones of *Portrait of Himself* that he repurposes in a composition halfway between beauty and monstrosity. The bedstead's she-faun has been replaced by an hourglass in which time drifts unescapably – a key motif in this image since the portrait earns Dorian eternal youth, bringing time and age to an abrupt stop. Once on canvas, Dorian, the epitome of beauty and grace at the beginning of the novel, takes on every alteration of age, and Wilde presents his picture as "the hideous thing," "this monstrous soul-life," "the living death of his own soul."[35] As in Seaman's pastiche, humour has here utterly vanished, along with eccentric life in the margins. The character (or his representation) features centrally as a half-body figure. Still, in strong contrast to Seaman's polemic, Alastair crowns a beautiful monster hallowed by a fin-de-siècle oxymoron, a subtle summary of the novel, and an icon on his deathbed.[36]

---

31 Arwas, *Alastair: Illustrator of Decadence*, 86, no. 71.

32 See https://archive.org/details/TheSphinxDecoratedByAlastaiOscarWilde/mode/2up

33 Oscar Wilde, *Das Bildnis des Dorian Gray, Roman aus dem Englischen übertragen von Alastair* (Konstanz: Lingua Verlag, 1948). No images.

34 On Wilde's novel and its complexity, see for instance Catherine Rancy, *Fantastique et Décadence en Angleterre, 1890–1914* (Paris: Éditions du CNRS, 1982), 25–47.

35 Wilde, *The Picture of Dorian Gray* (Harmondsworth: Penguin Books, 1949), repr. 1981, 245, 247, 245.

36 There is a series of Catherine de Medici's beds in the Loire Valley castles; the bed she is said to have died on is in the Chateau of Blois.

Fin-de-siècle Minster Signatures

Such a complex relationship between the monster and the artist is intensified when we move from paper to stone. The cathedral or abbey allows for a new enquiry on the relation of artist and monument, part and whole, fraction and entity in the fin-de-siècle imaginary, as evidenced in texts by Félicien Champsaur and Jules Vallès, with Victor Hugo's *Notre-Dame de Paris* novel as background. "Signature" by Champsaur, a sonnet first published in his novel *Dinah Samuel* (1882) and collected among the poems of his *Parisiennes* (1887), offers an ideal portrait of the artist facing his own work. Culminating his art at the end of a fulfilled life, the anonymous "artist," representing his stone-mason's credo and privilege, carves his own image in granite, destined for the "pinnacle balcony" whence he will contemplate his creation to the end of time, as shows the following prosaic English translation of a French sonnet:

> The artist, also a man of virtue,
> once he had completed his lofty cathedral,
> and made the central rose window sparkle,
> and sawed the marble as fine as a chaff,
>
> once he had erected the pointed turret,
> and turned the staircase into a narrow spiral,
> when all was filled with sepulchral majesty,
> and every choir wall was clad in gold,
>
> took his cold chisel, and ere the last knell,
> in a block of granite, he hewed himself,
> that he might be seated on the pinnacle balcony,
>
> and, as he neared his last hour,
> he placed the statue so that he would behold,
> his masterpiece of stone for all eternity.[37]
>
> *L'artiste, en même temps un homme de vertu,*
> *lorsqu'il eut achevé sa haute cathédrale,*
> *qu'il eut fait resplendir la rosace centrale,*
> *qu'il eut scié le marbre aussi fin qu'un fétu,*
>
> *lorsqu'il eut fait surgir le clocheton pointu,*
> *et tourner l'escalier en étroite spirale,*

37 Félicien Champsaur, "Signature," *Parisiennes* (Paris: A. Lemerre, 1887), 93.

lorsque tout fut empli de grandeur sépulcrale,
que chaque mur du chœur fut en or revêtu,

prit son ciseau froid, puis, avant le glas suprême,
dans un bloc de granit, il se tailla lui-même,
pour qu'au balcon du faîte on le pût accouder,

et, comme il approchait de son heure dernière,
il plaça la statue, afin de regarder,
pendant l'éternité, son chef-d'œuvre de pierre.

When first published in *Dinah Samuel*, Champsaur associates this sonnet with "Erwin von Steinbach's likely effigy" at the foot of the octagonal tower of Strasbourg Cathedral's spire.[38] He thus draws on the history of the cathedral (Erwin von Steinbach had presented its plans to Conrad, Bishop of Lichtenberg, as Champsaur recalls) and a monument on which such "signatures" are notable and multiple.[39]

Champsaur's idea is part of a distinctly mythical, historical, and cultural context at the end of the nineteenth century. During Eugène Viollet-le-Duc's monumental restoration of Notre-Dame in Paris, a statue destroyed in 1792 had been newly erected at the foot of the spire among the apostles. A well-known "signature," it was the portrayal of Viollet-le-Duc himself by French sculptor and goldsmith Victor Geoffroy-Dechaume.[40] While the other apostles contemplate the city, Viollet, in the guise of Thomas, is turned towards the spire, the only one to consider the cathedral itself, and particularly the spire, his *magnum opus*, using his hand as a shade. Now Thomas the Apostle may well be the patron saint of architects,[41] with whom Viollet wished no doubt to identify, but was also the disbelieving and sceptical disciple. Intended to highlight the character's awe in front of the edifice, does the gesture signal only admiration? Could it indicate disbelief, or simply a wish to see more clearly? In Thomas's story, Doubt had penetrated the Revelation.

38 Champsaur, *Dinah Samuel*, ed. by Jean de Palacio (Paris: Séguier, 1999), 413.

39 The statue of architect Ulrich von Ensingen gazing up at the spire may be seen in the Musée de l'Œuvre Notre-Dame in Strasbourg. In the south transept, another architect leaning on the railing, marvelling at the Last Judgement pillar, probably represents Hans Hammer (1486). See Robert Walter, *Histoire anecdotique de la cathédrale de Strasbourg* (Strasbourg: Erce, 1992).

40 With thanks to Joëlle Prungnaud for this suggestion.

41 Thierry Crépin-Leblond, *La Cathédrale Notre-Dame* (Paris: Éditions du Patrimoine, 2000), 46–47, with a photograph by Étienne Revault.

Likewise, Jules Michelet ironically commented on the earthing wire of the lightning rod fastened to Strasbourg Cathedral's spire: it roots down in the tomb of the Steinbach family![42] Artistic signatures already beset the cathedral with warped intentions in the nineteenth century.

Champsaur's sonnet itself, based on antithesis and oxymoron, is included in his section "La Petite Légende des siècles," ("The *Little* Legend of the Ages," my emphasis) by reference to Victor Hugo's foremost collection *La Légende des siècles* (1859–83), keen to depict humanity's history across time. Champsaur suggests that neither Hugo's famous *Notre-Dame de Paris* novel, nor his extensive poems, may be henceforth achieved except in a sonnet (etymologically "little song"), decidedly in miniature. Compared to *La Légende des siècles*, Champsaur's "Signature" stands indeed for the counterpart of Hugo's "The Seven Wonders of the World," wherein the monuments speak. Already in Hugo's work, this section leads to a poem entitled "The Epic of the Worm," announcing the end of all civilisation.

On his side, Jules Vallès had already given the theme unexpected treatment back in 1866, having seen one of the best-known artists of the time as a funambulist and acrobat rehearsing on the cathedral itself. On leaving Gustave Doré's studio, his imagination was not stirred by the artist's "powerful fecundity" (Doré had by then already illustrated the epic, comic, and tragic masterpieces that had made him famous) but his athletic performance: "He engaged in *an arm-wrestling contest* [un bras de fer] up there on the Notre-Dame towers."[43] While placing the artist at the spot assigned by Champsaur, Vallès turns him into a showman whose irreverent juggling act is performed under the Creator's nose: "Gustave Doré, for his part, had let go of his feet, gripped by the hands, and slowly rising to himself, had tightened his body like a sword, and perhaps even cut a caper [*battu un entrechat*] under God's eye and shaken the dust from his shoes onto the believers' heads."[44]

42 Qtd. by Roland Recht, *La Cathédrale de Strasbourg* (Strasbourg: La Nuée bleue, 1993), 17.

43 Jules Vallès, "Les Exercices du corps," *L'Événement* (5 Feb 1866): 3c: "— *Il a fait le* bras de fer *là haut sur les tours de Notre-Dame*," his emphasis.

44 *Ibid.*: *"Gustave Doré, lui, avait lâché les pieds, s'était accroché par les mains, et se relevant lentement, il avait tendu son corps comme une épée, et même peut-être, il avait battu un entrechat sous l'œil de Dieu et secoué sur la tête des croyants la poussière de ses souliers."*

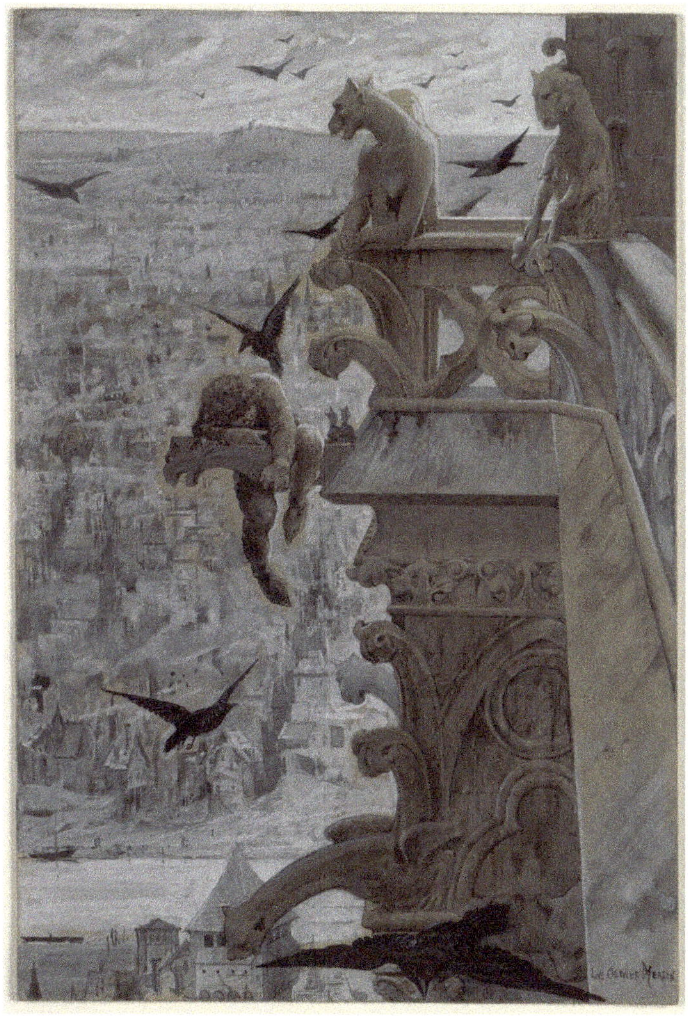

Fig. 3.8 Luc-Olivier Merson, *Notre-Dame de Paris* (ca. 1881), The Cleveland Museum of Art, Cleveland, Oh., USA. The CMA Open Access Initiative, https://www.clevelandart.org/art/2008.359

Now, such an account can only recall a monstrous character in the literal sense, one who, crouching among the misshapen statues, is the soul, demon, and spirit of the Notre-Dame Cathedral he haunts. Doré, seen by Vallès, is akin to Quasimodo as interpreted by a host of painters and artists at the time, including Luc-Olivier Merson (Fig. 3.8), the great illustrator of Hugo's novel.[45] Merson was inspired by "a *strange dwarf* atop one of the towers who climbed, snaked, crawled, on all fours, stepped down over the abyss, jumped from ledge to ledge, and went to burrow into the belly of some carved gorgon," "*a sort of living chimaera*," "*a ghastly shape* wandering on the frail, lacy balustrade that crowns the towers and borders the apse."[46] Similar to the artist-juggler (Doré by Vallès), this monstrous Quasimodo and his kind could appropriate the place devoted by Champsaur to the anonymous and pious sculptor. Indeed, the fin-de-siècle cathedral, a massive work of art, stands for a "hybrid monster and den of monsters" in Decadent imagination.[47] For philosopher Vladimir Jankélévitch, it sums up "the allegiance both to the colossus and the trinket."[48] The antithesis that governs it breaks it up into a mass of grotesques that forever perpetuate its fragmented image. All-powerful, the margin takes the monument by storm. Indeed, the best-known visions of Notre-Dame in fin-de-siècle iconography neglect its general view in favour of monstrous details, gargoyles or demons. In his richly illustrated novel *Lulu* (1901), Champsaur transforms them into the cursed deities of end-of-the-century Paris: the second book of the novel opens with the chapter "Les Gargouilles" ("The Gargoyles") and closes with "Chœur de gargouilles" ("Gargoyles' Choir"). The monsters' dialogue and in-text images frame the text.[49]

---

45 Merson illustrated the two-volume deluxe edition of Hugo's novel for the publisher A. Ferroud in 1889–90 following the composition reproduced here. A chapter heading repeats this motif with a modified perspective in Victor Hugo, *Notre-Dame de Paris, illustrations de Luc-Olivier Merson*, 2 vols. (Paris: A. Ferroud, 1889–90), I, 227. The work reproduced here was published in Alfred Barbou, *Victor Hugo et son temps* (1881), a volume frequently republished. It introduces the chapter devoted to *Notre-Dame de Paris*. I thank Mrs Danielle Molinari, former general curator of the House of Victor Hugo and Hauteville House, for her help tracing this image's career.

46 Victor Hugo, *Notre-Dame de Paris* [1831] (Paris: Garnier-Flammarion, 1967), Bk. IV, Chapter III, 177, my translation and emphasis: "*un* nain bizarre *qui grimpait, serpentait, rampait, à quatre pattes, descendait en dehors sur l'abîme, sautelait de saillie en saillie, et allait fouiller dans le ventre de quelque gorgone sculptée,*" "une sorte de chimère vivante," "*on voyait errer* une forme hideuse *sur la frêle balustrade découpée en dentelle qui couronne les tours et borde le pourtour de l'abside.*"

47 Such is the subtitle of Jean de Palacio's article, "La Cathédrale hystérique: monstre hybride et repaire de monstres."

48 Vladimir Jankélévitch, "La Décadence," *Revue de métaphysique et de morale*, 4 (1950): 337–69 (345): "*à la fois la tendance au colosse et la tendance au bibelot.*"

49 Champsaur, *Lulu, roman clownesque* (Paris: Eugène Fasquelle, 1901), 41–50 and 249–52.

The etching known as *Le Stryge*, one of Charles Meryon's *Eaux-fortes sur Paris* (1853), was instrumental in establishing such imagery (Fig. 3.9). It was reproduced in the most popular illustrated editions of Hugo's novel and was frequently pirated by woodcuts and vignettes in, for instance, the two volumes of the "new illustrated edition" of *Notre-Dame de Paris* published by Eugène Hugues in 1876–77. In this, *Le Stryge* and *La Galerie Notre-Dame*, engraved by Méaulle after Meryon, form an appropriate setting for Quasimodo to appear.[50] Yet Beardsley is not far off either.

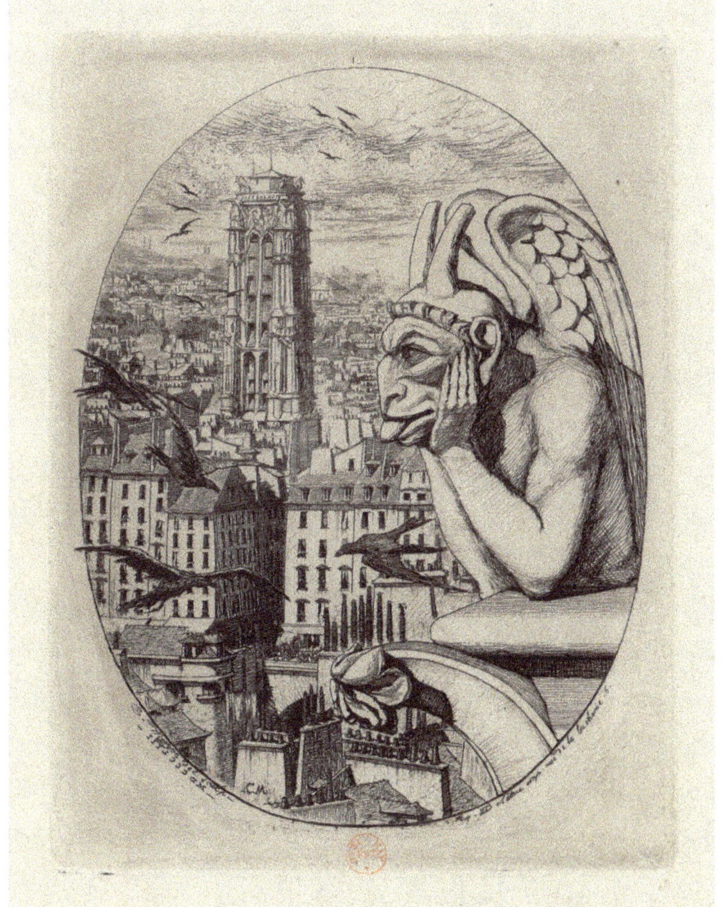

Fig. 3.9 Charles Meryon, *Le Stryge*, engraving, 5th state, in portfolio *Eaux-fortes sur Paris*, 1853, pl. 6, numbered 1. © BnF, Estampes, Paris

50 Victor Hugo, *Notre-Dame de Paris : 1482* (Paris: Eugène Hugues, 1876–77), 148–49. See online https://gallica.bnf.fr/ark:/12148/bpt6k9941148/f168.item and https://gallica.bnf.fr/ark:/12148/bpt6k9941148/f169.item

In the Margin of the Book of Stone

Beardsley himself tracked such posturing thanks to photography, that deceptively realistic art. Two of his photographic portraits spiritedly mould themselves on such icons. The first (Fig. 3.10) is openly modelled on Meryon's *Le Stryge*, the second (Fig. 3.11a) was named *The Gargoyle*.

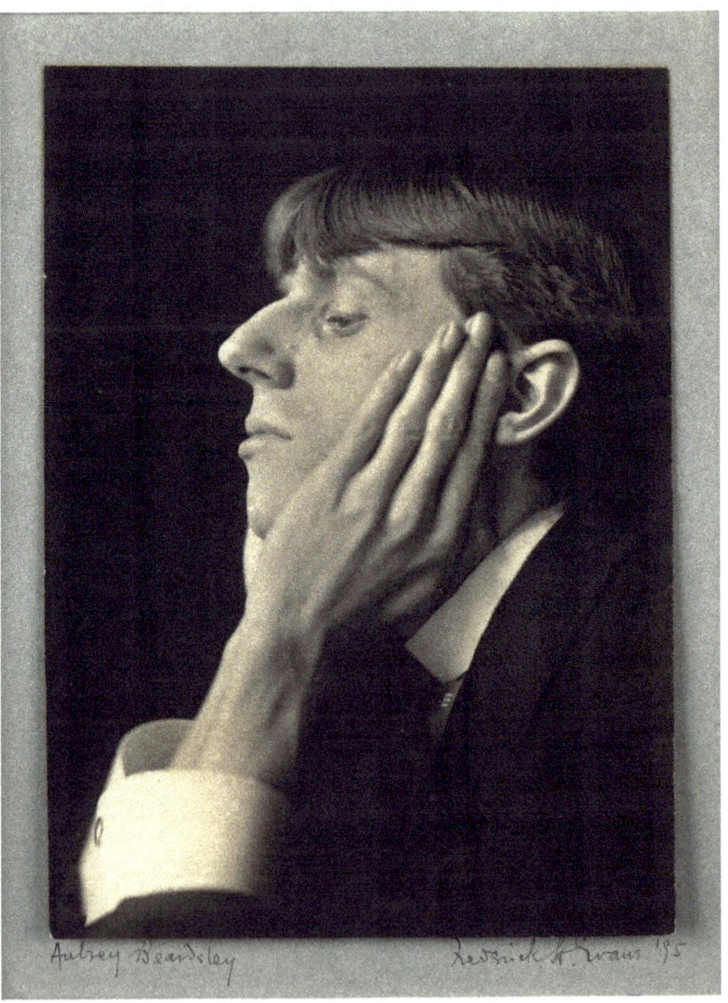

Fig. 3.10 Frederick H. Evans, framed photograph of Aubrey Beardsley as *Le Stryge* (1894), platinum print, signed, titled and dated by Evans. © GrandPalais-RMN (Musée d'Orsay) / Christian Jean

As early as summer 1894, Beardsley had dressed impeccably for the expert lens of his friend Frederick Henry Evans. Famous for his platinum prints of English and French cathedrals, Evans used a unique chromatic and luminous gradation. As anecdote has it, he teased Beardsley for looking like a gargoyle and challenged him to pose as the demon famously depicted by Meryon: "He [Beardsley] said he was sure he could and immediately put his hands up to his face. I only had to draw back his cuffs so as not to hide any of his marvelous hands and wrists, and then draw his chin a bit forward for its shadow and contour to be obvious and voila, there you are! The often-pirated success!"[51]

It is worth stressing that Evans usually spent a long time (up to two weeks) capturing the soul of a monument. He practised an "untouched realism" that refused smoothing adjustments. He often photographed partial views and details of these monuments and his vast oeuvre was regularly exhibited from 1890.[52] Beardsley as *Le Stryge* and *The Gargoyle* photograph (Fig. 3.11a) were both meant to be seen as cathedral fragments, chimaeras used to advertise the artist's eccentricity. Particularly pleased with the result, Beardsley wanted them "on cabinet boards."[53] He also meant to exhibit them: the one after *Le Stryge* was shown at the Salon Exhibition in October 1894 and was subsequently used as a frontispiece to *The Later Work of Aubrey Beardsley* (1901). The other appeared in the periodical press with the caption *The Gargoyle* as the conclusive photograph of an article with three pieces of Beardsley's work (Fig. 3.11b). It served as a signature piece to the whole.[54]

51 Qtd. from ms. Wilde E92LM466 in William Andrews Clark Memorial Library, University of California, Los Angeles, by Linda Gertner Zatlin, *Aubrey Beardsley: A Catalogue Raisonné*, 2 vols. (New Haven, Conn.: Yale University Press, 2016), I, 200.

52 See Beaumont Newhall, *Frederick H. Evans: Photographer of the Majesty, Light and Space of the Medieval Cathedrals of England and France* (New York: Aperture, 1973); and Anne M. Lyden, *The Photographs of Frederick H. Evans, with an Essay by Hope Kingsley* (Los Angeles, Calif.: The J. Paul Getty Museum, 2010).

53 *The Letters of Aubrey Beardsley*, ed. by Henry Maas, J. L. Duncan, and W. G. Good (London: Cassell, 1970), 73: "Dear Evans, I think the photos are splendid; couldn't be better. I am looking forward to getting my copies. I should like them on cabinet boards if that's not too much trouble."

54 See Herbert Small, "Book Illustrators: X. Aubrey Beardsley," *The Book Buyer*, n.s., 12:1 (Feb 1895): 26–29.

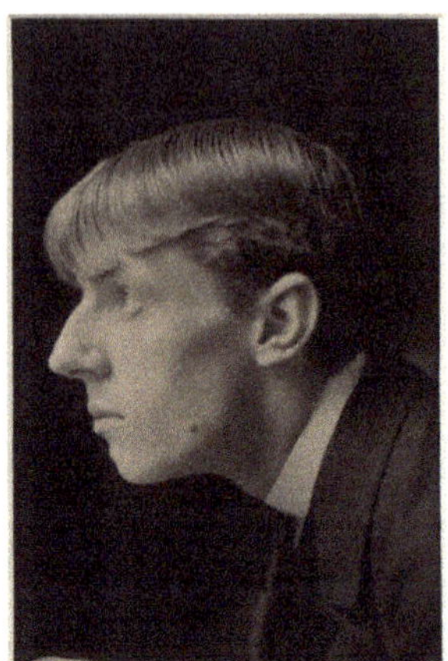

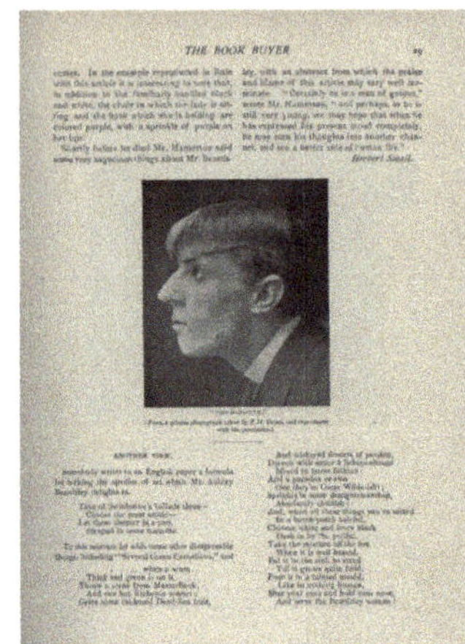

THE BOOK BUYER

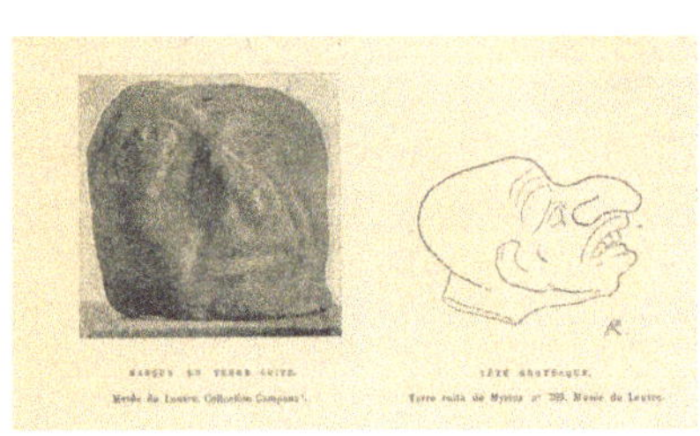

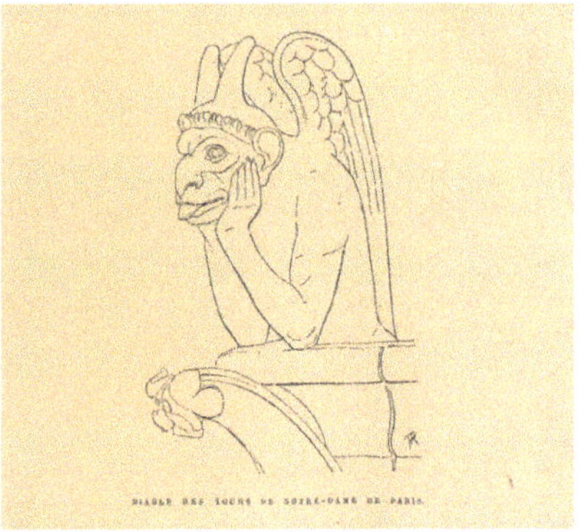

Fig. 3.11a–d Frederick H. Evans, photograph of Aubrey Beardsley as *The Gargoyle* in comparison. 3.11a Beardsley photograph (1894), platinum print, © GrandPalais–RMN (Musée d'Orsay) / Christian Jean; 3.11b The photograph captioned *The Gargoyle*, repr. *The Book Buyer*, n.s. 12:1 (Feb 1895): 29. University of Minnesota Libraries; 3.11c *Grotesque Head*, in Jean-Martin Charcot and Paul Richer, *Les difformes et les malades dans l'art* (1889), 9 (detail). BnF, Gallica; 3.11d Meryon's *Le Stryge*, repr. in Charcot and Richer, 7 (detail). BnF, Gallica

The Gargoyle photograph brings out in profile Beardsley's beak-like nose, chin with lump, tapering ear, upturned gaze. Drooped, the sweeping fringe drapes the forehead. The gargoyle looks up, ready to spew out the waters of heaven. The chin's round lump further underlines unevenness. In 1889, the doctors Jean-Martin Charcot and Paul Richer had published an illustrated treatise entitled *Les difformes et les malades dans l'art* (The *Deformed and Sick in Art*). In this, the terracotta head no. 769 from the Myrina excavations which had entered the Louvre collections (Fig.

3.11c), reproduced in the opening pages, shows a close resemblance to Beardsley's profile but for the hermetically shut mouth and the refined features. The artist's peculiar physique and his illness were styled as artworks modelled on past examples. In the same volume, the terracotta head was duly preceded by a reproduction of the Notre-Dame stryge (Fig. 3.11d).[55] A matching subtlety is to be read in Evans's strygian portrait of Beardsley (see Fig. 3.10). Meryon's stone monster, sticking out its tongue at the city (see Fig. 3.9), is swapped for a face resting between drawn-out, beautiful, manicured hands, wearing a haughty air, distant gaze, and perhaps condescending pout.

Both photographs operate yet another aesthetic reversal. Panoramic and topographic views of cathedrals were frequent in the nineteenth century. Beardsley's portraits invert the paradigm. They offer a detailed, individualised and monstrous view of the artist instead. By superseding the gothic sanctuary, they erect a new definition of the self as an unruly detail that obliterates the whole. Detached from the cathedral's medieval cultural background, the artist is a monster in his very flesh, a good twenty years before body art emerged as such. Upon visiting Westminster Abbey with his mother, the stained-glass window had been an option for little Aubrey, we remember, but he had preferred the bust. His pictorial effigies now force themselves onto the disintegrated building. Modernity cast the artist himself into a new plastic paradigm. Effigies in paper and platinum prints had replaced stone. Evans's two shots frame the introduction to *The Early Work of Aubrey Beardsley* (1899, posthumous), propelling the artist himself as the anomalous preamble to his work. John Lane, Beardsley's crafty publisher, knew what he was doing.

Beardsley's enduring interest in such marginal and atypical art had already devised yet another ironic aesthetic credo. A drawing published in the *Pall Mall Budget* on 4 January 1894 pictured the American illustrator and art critic Joseph Pennell, the first to promote him in the April 1893 *Studio*, with the title *Mr Pennell as "The Devil of Notre Dame."* (Fig. 3.12a).

55 Jean-Martin Charcot and Paul Richer, *Les difformes et les malades dans l'art* (Paris: Lecrosnier et Babé, 1889), 7 and 9.

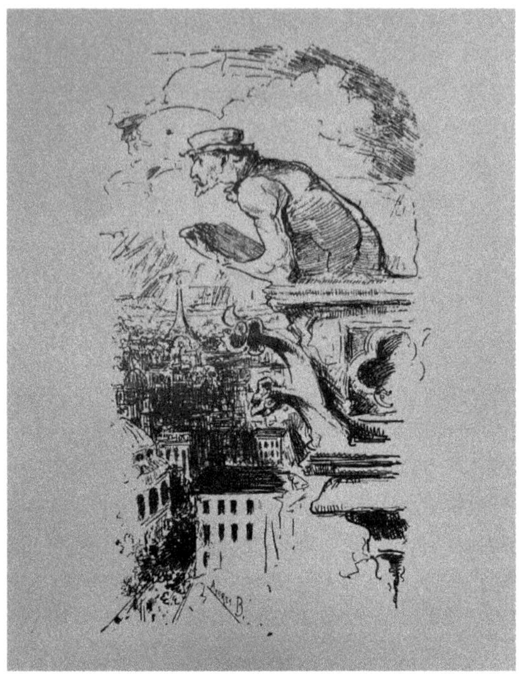

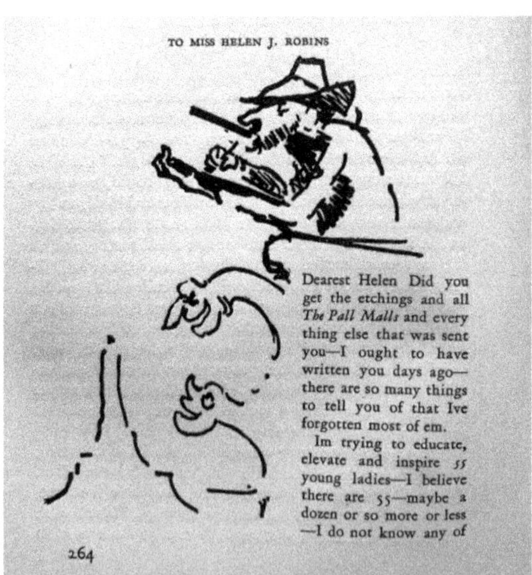

TO MISS HELEN J. ROBINS

Dearest Helen Did you get the etchings and all *The Pall Malls* and every thing else that was sent you—I ought to have written you days ago—there are so many things to tell you of that Ive forgotten most of em.

Im trying to educate, elevate and inspire 55 young ladies—I believe there are 55—maybe a dozen or so more or less—I do not know any of

264

Fig. 3.12a–b Aubrey Beardsley sketching Joseph Pennell as Meryon's *Stryge*. 3.12a Beardsley, *Mr Pennell as "The Devil of Notre Dame," The Pall Mall Budget* (4 Jan 1894): 8, repr. from *Early Work*, pl. 155. Courtesy MSL coll., Delaware; 3.12b Pennell, humorous sketch of himself after Beardsley, repr. in Elizabeth Robins Pennell, *The Life and Letters of Joseph Pennell* (1929), I, 264. Author's photograph

In the *catalogue raisonné* this drawing has been retitled *A New Year's Dream, after Studying Mr Pennell's "Devils of Notre Dame"* and dated May 1893 (Zatlin 312). In the *Pall Mall Budget*, the Beardsley reproduction closely followed publication of Pennell's own gargoyles of Notre-Dame issued in two instalments in this very magazine's Christmas issue where they profusely illustrated a text by Robert A. M. Stevenson.[56] Beardsley's drawing originates from the artist's second stay in Paris with the Pennells, and Joseph preparing a series of etchings on the cathedral demons.[57] Beardsley (as Evans himself) had climbed the towers more than once to meet Pennell who had spent part of the summer and autumn 1893 in the so-called Notre-Dame gallery, often receiving his friends there as guests. In a 24 December 1893 letter to his sister-in-law Helen J. Robins, Pennell had even jokingly depicted himself as Meryon's *Stryge* after Beardsley's drawing (Fig. 3.12b). He reproduced Beardsley's artwork opposite his own etched interpretation of *Le Stryge* in his memoirs and even declared: "Beardsley, who was with me in Paris in 1893, climbed up too [in the Notre-Dame tower], and made me into a chimera."[58] In his good-humoured version, Pennell depicts himself nonchalantly smoking a giant cigar and sketching the city from the cathedral's very tower.[59] As his wife put it in his biography, published with numerous letters and sketches, "Viollet-le-Duc oppressed him" and "His happiest hours were on the roof among the devils and monsters."[60] However, Beardsley represented his patron bending over the city as a gargoyle and artist in one: his clawed paw gripped a portable sketch board, and his gaze eagerly scanned the city

56 See "The Devils of Notre-Dame, by Mr Joseph Pennell with a Comment by R. A. M. Stevenson," *The Pall Mall Budget* (14 and 21 Dec 1893). Also separately published in 1894 as a deluxe elephant folio folder on Japanese paper, limited edition of seventy copies with only fifty for sale. See *The Devils of Notre-Dame, A Series of Eighteen Illustrations by J. Pennell, With Descriptive Text by R. A. M. Stevenson* (London: Pall Mall Gazette, 1894).

57 Sturgis, *Aubrey Beardsley*, 135.

58 Joseph Pennell, *The Adventures of an Illustrator, mostly in Following his Authors in America & Europe* (Boston, Mass., Little, Brown and Company, 1925), 204, reproductions *ibid.*, 218–19.

59 See Elizabeth Robins Pennell, *The Life and Letters of Joseph Pennell*, 2 vols. (Boston: Little, Brown, and Co, 1929), I, 264; and Michael Pantazzi, "Du stryge au gratte-ciel," *Livraisons de l'histoire de l'architecture*, 20 (2010): 91–112, fig. 17, https://doi.org/10.4000/lha.261

60 Pennell, *The Life and Letters of Joseph Pennell*, I, 253.

for a view worthy of depiction. Beardsley's drawing is no humorous caricature. He provides Pennell with petrified fingers and a frozen body, which may ironically exhibit his conventional realistic aesthetic and attachment to life drawing. Only his face, painter's bonnet, and flopping necktie belong to the modern world. And yet, instead of the medieval city that Luc-Oliver Merson reconstructs (see Fig. 3.8) or the Middle Ages recalled by Meryon's inclusion of the St. Jacques tower in his *Stryge* (see Fig. 3.9), Beardsley pictures the nascent Eiffel Tower in the background, a detail that Pennell's jesting sketch takes on. The modern city of sky-high memorials (and photographic portraits) breathes beneath this conservative depiction of Pennell. Modernity invites again the artist to formulate new aesthetic rules. Beardsley grants an animated life to the stone ornaments below Pennell: one of them opens up like a flower, the other has acquired an eye avidly looking at the city. Pennell again follows light-heartedly, his own ornament jokingly conversing with one of its fellows. By contrast to Pennell's self-parody, Beardsley's mordant humour pictures Pennell as half-fossilised, a rigidified remnant of the past.

Body Art

Evans's photographic portraits are much more than portraits. Champsaur imagined the artist as a meticulous sculptor and the supreme master of the vast monument he had created. Vallès saw Doré, his 1866 contemporary, as an athlete and clown, defying God himself on Notre-Dame. Some thirty years later, for Evans and Beardsley the artist identifies not with the main body of the cathedral, but with a monstrous detail of the disintegrating whole. Both of Evans's platinum prints relate also to Beardsley's deviant self-portraits, *Portrait of Himself* and *A Footnote*. These images offer striking proof of Beardsley's deliberate monstrosity, displaying his physical appearance as deformed, without artifice or artistry, as a substitute for the long-desired bust. Evans's photographs ultimately record Beardsley's very form as an early manifestation of body art. The systematic use of the body in artistic performances dates from the 1960s–70s. Among its forerunners, it is customary to mention the pioneering works of Frank Wedekind, Filippo Tommaso Marinetti, and Oskar Kokoschka (1909),

Egon Schiele (1910), David Burliuk and Vladimir Mayakovsky (1914), or Marcel Duchamp (*Tonsure*, 1920, and *Belle Haleine, eau de voilette*, 1921), all of which post-date Beardsley by at least fifteen years.[61]

Nonetheless, art had already broken out of the picture frame and infused life itself at the end of the nineteenth century. Only three years before Evans took his photographs of Beardsley, the satirical writer Alphonse Allais was describing similarly conceptual forms of art. In his short story "Le Bon Peintre" ("The Good Painter"), Allais describes an artist putting postage stamps on an envelope, "taking great care that the tones were well arranged – *so that it wouldn't look too gaudy.*" He even pastes a last superfluous stamp at the very bottom "*to have a touch of blue.*"[62] Not only does he treat postage stamps like palette colours to paint with, but also the food he consumes: "For nothing in the world [...] would [the same painter] drink red wine while eating fried eggs, because it would have made him an ugly tone in the stomach."[63] Like Beardsley, Allais's painter treats his own body as a work of art in a way that is likely intended as an amusing dig at the art world.

Beardsley's humour opened the way to innovation. It was a form that allowed for the critical freedom of the imagination. In these far-reaching fin-de-siècle experiments, creation turned to life itself with the artist in person as support and expression. Beardsley's grotesque self-portraits wittily exploited all the possibilities opened up by humour and margin. Between dominant culture and protest, humour drives a rift. It speaks a language that assails hierarchy and order. The margin, packed with rejected elements surging at the periphery, de-centred as eccentric, ends by invading text, whether script or stone incision, to invert their relationship. By exploring such breaches as so many salutary cracks in the hermetic house of norms, humour and margin save culture from the presumption, smugness, and pride it is bound to bear within it. Robert Ross had acutely discerned the

61 See *L'Art au corps: Le Corps exposé de Man Ray à nos jours* (Marseille: RMN, 1996); and Lea Vergine, *Body Art e storie simili* (Milan: Skira, 2000).

62 Alphonse Allais, "Le Bon Peintre," (*Œuvres anthumes*) *À se tordre, histoires chatnoiresques* (Paris: Ollendorff, 1891), 139–41; repr. in *Œuvres anthumes*, ed. by François Caradec (Paris: Robert Laffont, 1989), 50–51: "*verticalement, en prenant grand soin que les tons s'arrangeassent* – pour que ça ne gueule pas trop", "pour faire un rappel de bleu." (Allais's emphasis).

63 *Ibid.*, 50: "*pour rien au monde il ne buvait de vin rouge en mangeant des œufs sur le plat, parce que ça lui aurait fait un sale ton dans l'estomac.*"

inversion when he wrote on Beardsley: "True grotesque is not the art either of primitives or decadents, but that of skilled and accomplished workmen who have reached the zenith of a peculiar convention."[64]

64 Robert Ross, *Aubrey Beardsley with Sixteen Illustrations and a Revised Iconography by Aymer Vallance* (London: John Lane, The Bodley Head; New York: The John Lane Company, 1909), 49.

4. Beardsley Images and the "Europe of Reviews"

Aubrey Beardsley aroused exceptional critical interest, resulting in an extraordinary number of entries, interviews, and articles in newspapers and periodicals. In 1989, Nicholas Salerno collected and commented on more than 1,500 bibliographical references in *Reconsidering Aubrey Beardsley*.[1] A good part of these were articles written in Beardsley's lifetime.[2] Despite some inaccuracies, Salerno's list proves that Beardsley enjoyed outstanding critical fortune, which, by virtue of the space and standing it assured him, became a sturdy foundation of his oeuvre. Beardsley's ascension was reliant not only on his innovative artwork but also on the broadcasting of ideas and controversies. The artist was acutely aware of the press's power as mentor and tastemaker, and he was able to partly mould the media's depiction of him. However, as reviews and articles spread, they invested his images with strong mythical value that was beyond his control, making Beardsley a meteor in the European art constellation of the time. His works have the aura of shooting stars: still irradiating the artistic sky long after they have passed. Twenty-seven obituaries appeared on his death in the British press alone. In an early French article of 1897, Henry-D. Davray echoed the phenomenon beyond Britain, from the buzzing heart of Paris: "If, following the example of

1 Nicholas A. Salerno, "An Annotated Secondary Bibliography," in *Reconsidering Aubrey Beardsley*, ed. by Robert Langenfeld (Ann Arbor, Mich./London: U.M.I. Research Press, 1989), 267–493.

2 This would have been more apparent if a chronological (instead of an alphabetical) order had been adopted as in Jane Haville Desmarais, *The Beardsley Industry: The Critical Reception in England and France, 1893–1914* (Aldershot: Ashgate, 1998), 132–48, and Linda Gertner Zatlin, *Aubrey Beardsley: A Catalogue Raisonné*, 2 vols. (New Haven, Conn.: Yale University Press, 2016), II, 481f, particularly for the years 1893–1900.

 https://doi.org/10.11647/OBP.0413.04

Mr. Whistler, he were to publish all his newspaper clippings, it would certainly form a most interesting and instructive collection. For he was proclaimed, discussed and vilified beyond words."[3]

Beardsley had early on grasped the importance of the media to advancing an artist's career. Each press article not only assessed his artistic value but, even when censuring or complaining about him, also served to expand his notoriety. He therefore skilfully steered magazines from behind the scenes, and readily put himself forward through intriguing, distancing, and ironic postures. Magazines embodied the very spirit of media modernity. They were numerous, diverse, and each called for differentiated attention, if maximum effect was to be achieved. In promoting avant-garde work in a transitional era with numerous conservative proclivities, Beardsley had to embrace older paradigms, adapting them to his vision in order to gain widespread notoriety. Such was the first major commission he accepted, the illustration of Thomas Malory's *Le Morte Darthur*. Although the book was in theory following the model of hand printing and craftsmanship set by William Morris's Kelmscott Press, its publisher J. M. Dent had tailored it to photomechanical printing and commercial distribution. Industrialised reproduction in magazines was also representative of the spirit of modernity, and these mass-produced formats allowed Beardsley's images to be seen by an ever-increasing viewership.

This chapter looks at the presentation of Beardsley in the press, and the images associated with these articles – their original significance, and Beardsley's and others' repurposing of them within new contexts. I take into consideration the layout of the articles and images, showing that the display and array can speak a language as expressive as the artwork itself. I am also interested in how Beardsley's representation differed depending on the country and type of periodical he appeared in. His fortunes emerged between distinct categories of cultural magazines: those meant for the general public, those specific to fine and applied arts, and those shaped as select art and literature reviews. The chapter focuses primarily on the Italian *Emporium*, which gathered its

3 Henry-D. Davray, "L'Art d'Aubrey Beardsley," *L'Ermitage*, 14 (Apr 1897): 253–61 (254): *"Si suivant l'exemple de M. Whistler, il publiait toutes ses coupures de presse, cela formerait certainement un recueil des plus intéressants et plein d'enseignements. Car il fut proclamé, discuté et vilipendé au-delà de tout dire."*

material from across the European press. But first, it looks at the earliest representations of Beardsley in the English journal *The Studio*, which set a blueprint for the selection of his work and its positive reception.

It then gauges Beardsley's reception in Italy against a matrix of images and ideas in a variety of international publications, including the British *Sketch*, the American *Art Student*, the French *Le Livre et l'Image*, the German *Kunst und Künstler*. As we will see, Italian articles partly shape each other while reflecting ideological, artistic, and aesthetic points of view of national specificity. They also reveal a vast network of journals in Europe. However, comparison and the spreading of images do not explain everything: it is also necessary to look at Beardsley's own plying of the press and his self-modelling. To illustrate the artist's input to his own representation, I turn primarily to the British *Sketch*, in which a hoax by Beardsley himself was naively taken on by *Emporium*. In the next chapter on the French press, we will see how the artist's image was also appropriated in ways well beyond Beardsley's control. Indeed, two complementary forces drive image making in the fin de siècle: clever stage-managing of one's own iconography, and unstoppable dissemination by the media.

What then of critiques, polemics, and facetious taunts? Are we to take all objections to Beardsley as negative reactions? Are they all outright condemnations and *ad hominem* attacks? As shown in the previous chapter, Edward Tennyson Reed mimicked and parodied Beardsley in *Punch* under mock pseudonyms, but his spoofs were also vital in making Beardsley known, calling attention to his work, and broadcasting his style. The American *Chap-Book* contributed to such assortment by mock-hallowing and nicknaming Beardsley, and repurposing his work in overtly commercial ways.

This chapter also considers periodicals in a network that includes small, medium, and larger publications. My reticular approach stresses circulation and exchanges. It puts individual creations in perspective: not only as unique inventions but in a distribution flow and in conversation with others. Such give-and-take is not only intellectual. It depends on marketing, relies on relations, and carries symbolical and emotional weight. A media-driven era is an age in which publications are not merely stable objects *per se*, but shared practices and processes through which individual artists and communities engage, barter, and trade.

Framing Beardsley in England

The Studio, an English fine and applied art periodical, which was to become hugely influential and ran until 1964, introduced and established Beardsley: the first article to make him known was the centrepiece of its very first issue in April 1893. That month, the promising but little-known artist, hitherto hardly published, had been commissioned by Dent to illustrate *Le Morte Darthur* with the first instalment issued in June. The work's requirements appealed to Joseph Pennell, the American engraver, lithographer, and illustrator. Pennell was an authority on illustration and a promoter of process engraving. By supporting Beardsley through *The Studio*, he meant to deal a blow to traditional art criticism and hierarchy, which tended to consecrate artists only once they were dead.[4] By contrast, his protégé was at the outset of his career and extremely young. Images were a major instrument in such a campaign. Beardsley's novel iconography was carefully reproduced in this first *Studio* article, with seven pages of illustrations encompassing the three pages of Pennell's text. His artwork contrasted with others' drawings in the same issue, which tended to be realistic and hastily sketched.

The layout of the article added to the surprise effect, a metaphor for the images' sudden, indeed abrupt, emergence. The first materialised at the end of a piece by R. A. M. Stevenson on "The Growth of Recent Art" (against Decadence). It was a miniature reproduction of Beardsley's *The Procession of Joan of Arc* (Zatlin 241) and would lead to a full replica of this exceptionally long pencil drawing, folded and mounted in *The Studio*'s second issue. Next to it, a full-page display featured *Siegfried, Act II* (Zatlin 246), an elaborate drawing that thrilled Edward Burne-Jones who owned it. Pennell's text only started after these two images, and shared the first page with Frank Brangwyn's "Letters from Artists to Artists: Sketching Grounds." It either sat next to Beardsley's designs or was framed by an impressive layout of *Le Morte Darthur* covering a double page spread. Drawings in the hairline style such as *The Birthday of Madame Cigale* (Zatlin 266) took up a page, introducing Beardsley's Japanese manner. Pennell defended "an artist whose work is quite

4 Joseph Pennell, "A New Illustrator: Aubrey Beardsley," *The Studio*, 1:1 (Apr 1893): 14–19.

as remarkable in its execution as in its invention." He also upheld mechanical engraving, the excellence of Beardsley's pen line, and decoration as specific drawings per individual pages. To crown it all, quality reproductions turned *The Studio* itself into a technical benchmark of reproductive excellence.

The Studio article was a double debut, in which the periodical and the artist set foundations by helping each other. Beardsley had designed the *Studio*'s cover (Fig. 4.1, Zatlin 308b) and partly fashioned its graphic identity, drawing from it lessons for the art and literature reviews he would later direct. In turn, the *Studio* showcased an artist representative of two fields it clearly defined as its own and in contrast to the hierarchies of the art establishment, that is, the fine and applied arts. Their double passport, however, is based on what could be described as safe aesthetic choices. Promoting, close to Burne-Jones and the Pre-Raphaelites, a Beardsley recently engaged by Dent to illustrate a late medieval text on the model of the Kelmscott Press, but without its requirements of craftsmanship and manual labour, the periodical championed a medieval-inspired style and design that was fashionable rather than forward-looking. Indeed, medievalism was more associated with bourgeois complacency than the daring and provocative images that Beardsley was already developing. The disturbing side of his art nevertheless emerges in the *Studio* article in the last full-page drawing which includes a French quote, "*J'ai baisé ta bouche Iokanaan, J'ai baisé ta bouche*" ("I have kissed your mouth, Iokanaan, I have kissed your mouth") (Zatlin 265). The citation is from Oscar Wilde's original version of *Salomé* (in French), which had just been published not in England but in France. It presented Beardsley as a connoisseur of daring French literature. The drawing would earn him another prestigious commission (for the English edition of *Salome* by John Lane, 1894), whose audacity led to a much more controversial reception. Already in this choice, the first *Studio* article showed how Beardsley's artistic identity had broken free from the medieval mould in which his first major commission might have ensnared him.

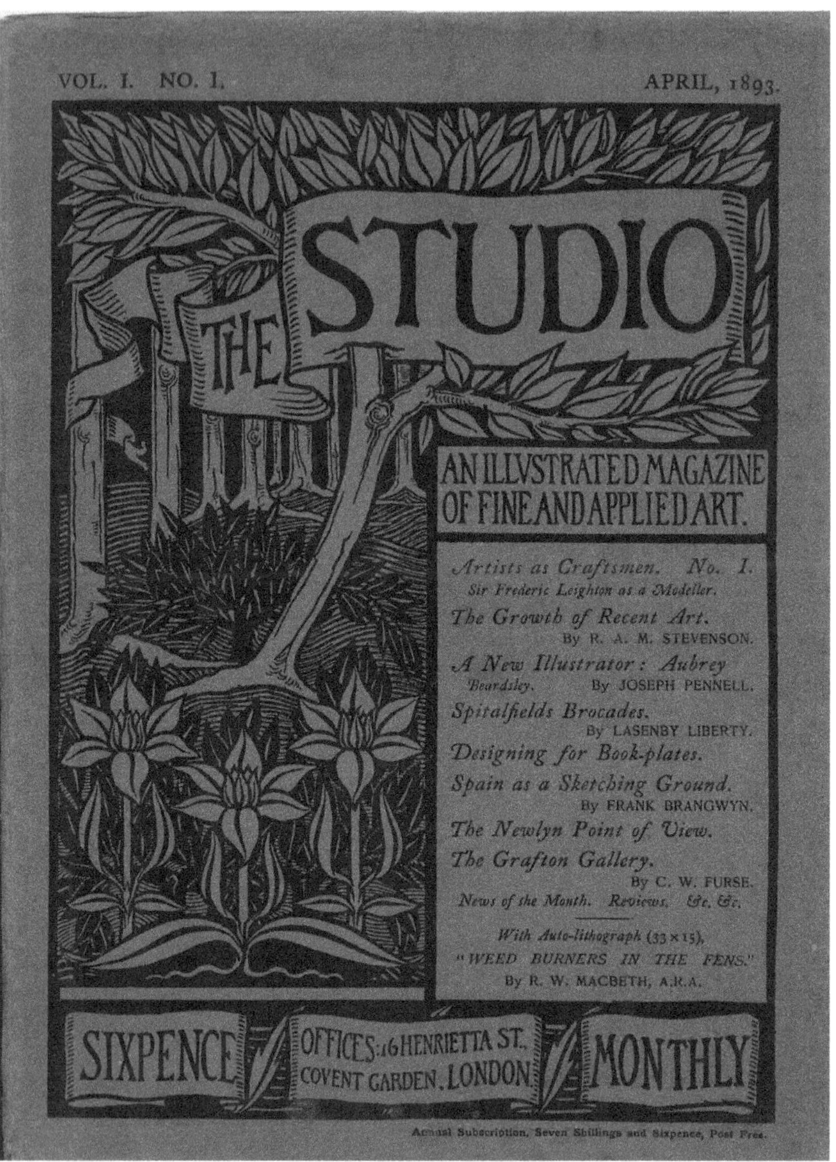

Fig. 4.1 Aubrey Beardsley, *Cover Design of the "Studio"*, 1:1 (15 Apr 1893) on light green paper with lettering, 2nd state (by 24 Feb 1893). Courtesy MSL coll., Delaware

One has only to compare this remarkable debut with the exit, Beardsley's obituary in the *Studio*'s May 1898 issue.[5] The article was two months late,[6] and Gleeson White, the *Studio*'s first editor, signed it with his initials only, as if it were unbecoming to fully claim it as his own. Moreover, its iconography was reduced to six drawings, none of which is disturbing or representative of the great books that the artist had decorated. Even worse, the last three pages yielded to a visual language altogether foreign to Beardsley, i.e., watercolours of Morocco by Walter Tyndale and numerous reproductions of medals. Given the context, such irrelevant iconography is a form of disrespect, if not grossness.

White was in no position to deny Beardsley the label of genius nor ignore his tremendous influence, but his personal reservations and doubts show in nearly every sentence: he referred to Beardsley's off-putting subject matter; his departure from drawing after life; his lack of schooling; and the fact that his art was offensive and inaccessible to the man in the street. While tracing the history of Beardsley's oeuvre, White focused on Beardsley's poster for John Todhunter's *A Comedy of Sighs!* and *The Land of Heart's Desire* by William Butler Yeats, catalogued as *Poster Design for the Avenue Theatre* (Zatlin 967), a work that was as revolutionary in its colouring, layout, and format as it was scandalising to passers-by (Fig. 4.2). Its central figure, in Margaret D. Stetz's words, "was clearly no lady – uncorseted, with loose hair, and with her clothes slipping off her shoulders."[7] White states that it made Beardsley "well known not only in the artistic society of both continents, but in a less[er] degree to the general public also" and recalls its parody after Dante Gabriel Rossetti's "The Blessed Damozel," the well-known Pre-Raphaelite poem, to ridicule the poster.[8] Rossetti's poem was modelled on the Beatrice of Dante's *Vita Nova* and celebrated a lost love. The parody desecrated it with trivial expressions and insisted on the

5 G. W. [Gleeson White], "Aubrey Beardsley: In Memoriam," *The Studio*, 13 (May 1898): 252–63.

6 The delay was all the more noticeable as the *Mercure de France* immediately announced Beardsley's demise in its "Échos," 26:100 (Apr 1898): 335, before transforming its May 1898 issue into a vibrant tribute to the deceased artist (see Chapter 5).

7 Margaret D. Stetz, *Aubrey Beardsley 150 Years Young* (New York: The Grolier Club, 2022), 39.

8 G. W. [Gleeson White], "Aubrey Beardsley: In Memoriam," 259.

drawing's so-called imperfections.[9] As far as obituaries go, the choice could hardly be more ambiguous.

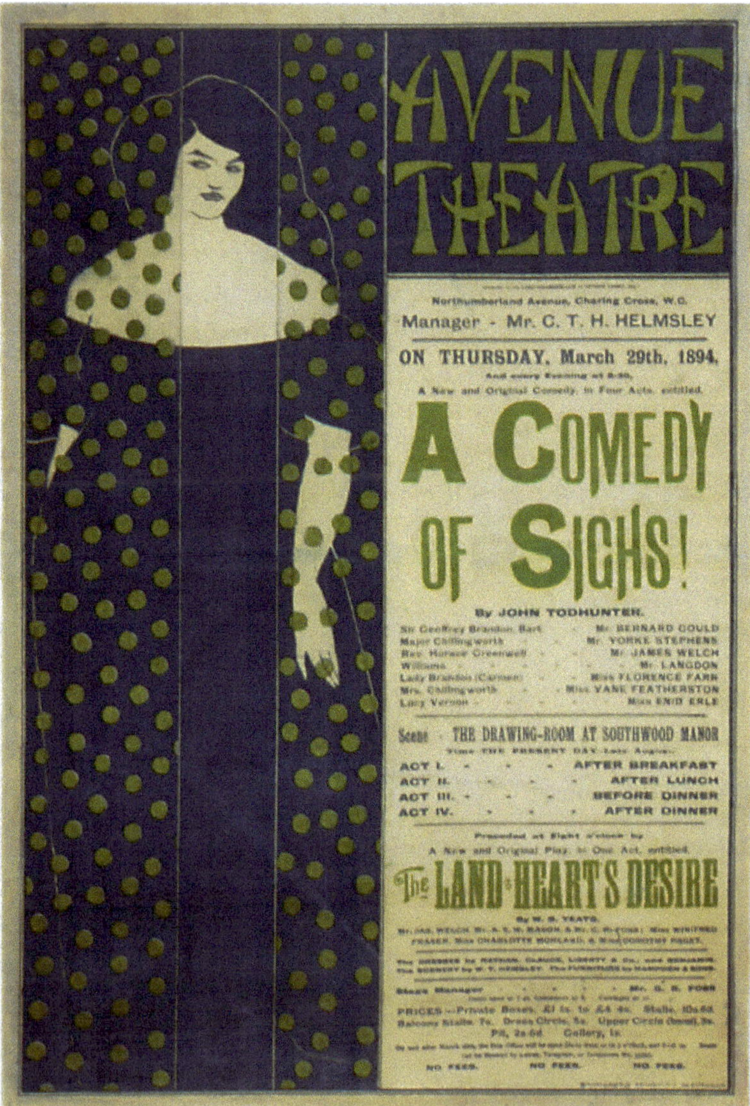

Fig. 4.2 Aubrey Beardsley, *Poster Design for the Avenue Theatre*, theatre poster for *A Comedy of Sighs!* by John Todhunter and *The Land of Heart's Desire* by William Butler Yeats (Jan–Feb 1894), colour lithograph. Courtesy MSL coll., Delaware

9 "Ars Postera," *Punch*, 106 (21 Apr 1894): 189.

Despite such a belittling farewell, the fact remains that the first *Studio* article established Beardsley in Europe with lasting effect: all articles presenting him for the first time referred to the *Studio*, from the Catalan *Joventut*[10] and the Russian *Mir iskusstva*,[11] to the German *Pan*[12] and, as shown in the next section, the Italian *Emporium*. In France, John Grand-Carteret's *Le Livre et l'Image*, a monthly journal focusing on bibliophilia and art which regularly presented new books and periodicals of note, echoed the *Studio* from August 1893. On three occasions, an anonymous contributor signing as "Un Book-Trotter" took over the first (disturbing) version of the *Studio* cover, finally used as prospectus (Zatlin 308a).[13] He further commented on Beardsley's style and reproduced *Merlin Taketh the Child Arthur into His Keeping*, a double-page drawing from *Le Morte Darthur* (Zatlin 344) previously featured in the English magazine, as a one-page design.[14] Like a seismograph, however, the French magazine lastly reflected the fluctuating fortunes of the artist: the third of these mentions welcomed the biting remarks of E[rnest] Knaufft, a former industrial art professor at Purdue University, art critic, art educator, and director of the Chautauqua Society for Fine Arts, on the "forty-three upturned noses" of *The Procession of Joan of Arc*, again from the *Studio*, judged too Pre-Raphaelite by the American commentator in his own New York magazine *The Art Student*.[15] *Le Livre et l'Image* retransmitted this humorous opinion, although in March 1894, barely a year after the

10 Alexandre de Riquer, "Aubrey Beardsley," *Joventut*, 1 (15 Feb 1900): 6–11.

11 A. N. [Al'fred Nurok], "Obri Berdslei," *Mir iskusstva*, 1:3–4 (1899): 16–17. Sergei Diaghilev further used two drawings by Beardsley to illustrate an article on the principles of artistic evaluation. See Sergei Diagilev, "Slozhnye voprosy: Osnovy khudozhestvennoi otsenki", *Mir iskusstva*, 1:3–4 (1899): 50–61.

12 Franz Blei, "Aubrey Beardsley," *Pan*, 5:4 (Nov 1899–Apr 1900): 256–60.

13 Un Book-Trotter, "L'Image: Titres réduits des nouveaux périodiques anglais," *Le Livre et l'Image*, 2:6 (Aug 1893): 57, https://gallica.bnf.fr/ark:/12148/bpt6k6118702f/f80.item

14 Un Book-Trotter. "L'Image: Mille moins un petits papiers. Les illustrations d'Aubrey Beardsley," *Le Livre et l'Image*, 2:7 (Sept 1893): 120, https://gallica.bnf.fr/ark:/12148/bpt6k6118702f/f149.item

15 Un Book-Trotter, "L'Image: Mille moins un petits papiers. Le 'Studio' critiqué," *Le Livre et l'Image*, 2:9 (Nov 1893): 249: "*quarante-trois nez retroussés*." Ernest Knaufft, himself a draughtsman, teacher, and lecturer, was the editor of the *Art Student: An Illustrated Monthly for Home Art Study*, or *A Monthly for the Home Study of Drawing and Illustrating*, published in New York from 1892 and a regular contributor to the *Review of Reviews*. See Peter Hastings Falk, ed., *Who Was Who in American Art, 1564–1975* (Sound View Press, 1999), 1871.

Studio, Grand-Carteret similarly opened his study on the illustrated book in three countries with Beardsley's decorative header for the title page of *Le Morte Darthur* catalogued as *Battling Knights* (Zatlin 511), and Beardsley himself only mentioned in passing.[16] It is in this context, highly laudatory, but also at times reserved or circumspect, that one may situate and gauge how he appeared in *Emporium*.

Emporium and the "Europe of Reviews"

Beardsley's presence in *Emporium*, a long-running Italian art magazine aimed at an educated readership (1895–1964), offers a unique opportunity to consider the construction of the artist's European fame. The editors, Paolo Gaffuri and Arcangelo Ghisleri, borrowed from English and American magazines and aimed at bringing the newest art, science, literature, and music to their readers. They sourced material for their magazine from across the European press via subscriptions, evidenced in preserved resources from the Istituto Italiano d'Arti Grafiche now at the Biblioteca Civica Angelo Mai in Bergamo.[17] *Emporium*'s three articles on Beardsley thus allow us to see the artist's image in the comparative context of a "Europe of reviews," as in two co-edited collections on European periodicals.[18]

Emporium's three articles date from September 1895, May 1898, and May 1904. The first, signed with the initials G. B., whose identity I have been unable to trace, is the very first on Beardsley in Italy. The second, unsigned, refers to the first, and must have originated from the same pen: it is an obituary, published two months after the artist's death on 15 March 1898. The last posthumous article, by Vittorio Pica, a leading figure in *Emporium* and advocate of numerous foreign avant-garde artists

16 John Grand-Carteret, "Le livre illustré à l'étranger: Angleterre – Allemagne – Suisse," *Le Livre et l'Image*, 3:13 (10 Mar 1894): 129–49 (header reproduced, 129), https://gallica.bnf.fr/ark:/12148/bpt6k5425700g/f154.item

17 Maria Elisabetta Manca, "Specchio di 'Emporium:' le riviste della biblioteca dell'Istituto Italiano d'Arti Grafiche di Bergamo," in *Emporium: Parole e figure tra il 1895 e il 1964*, ed. by Giorgio Bacci, Massimo Ferretti, Miriam Filetti Mazza (Pisa: Edizioni della Normale, 2009), 155–70.

18 Such enquiries have been led from 2006 in two collections edited by Évanghélia Stead and Hélène Védrine, *L'Europe des revues (1880–1920): Estampes, photographies, illustrations* (Paris: PUPS, 2008), repr. 2011, and *L'Europe des revues II (1860–1930): Réseaux et circulations des modèles* (Paris: PUPS, 2018).

in Italy,[19] reflects on Beardsley as well as on James Ensor and Edvard Munch, and was later included in Pica's well-known series *Attraverso gli albi e le cartelle*.[20]

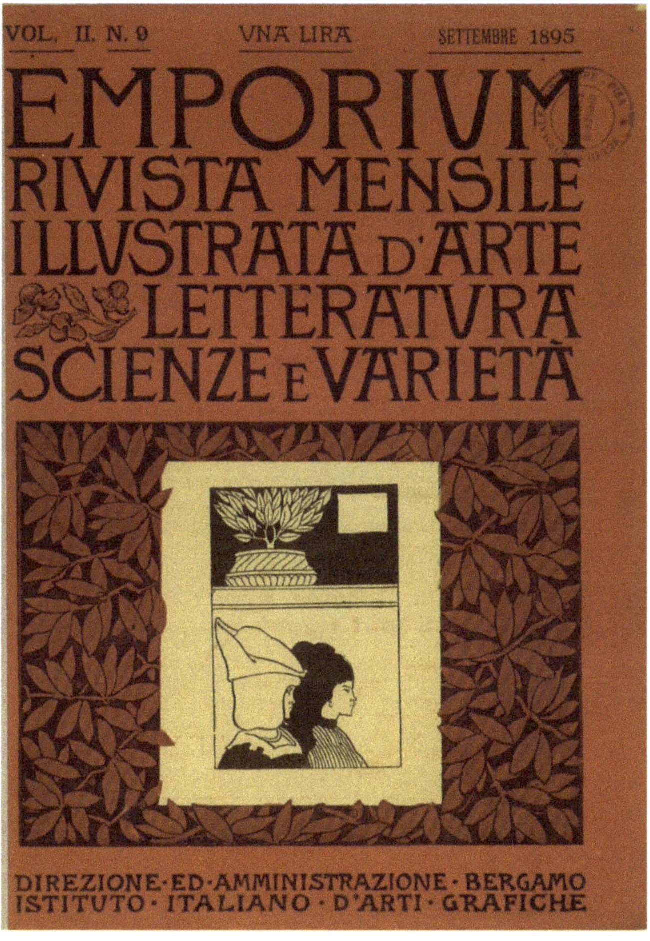

Fig. 4.3 *Emporium*, 2:9 (Sept 1895), cover of the issue with the first article on Beardsley showing a decorative vignette from *Le Morte Darthur* in foliage tributary of the *Studio* cover (see Fig. 4.1). Courtesy *DocStAr*, Scuola Normale Superiore di Pisa, Pisa. The vignette is *Man and Woman Facing Right* (Zatlin 528), from Bk. IX, chapter XVI

19 See Paola Pallottino, "'La finezza, il numero, la veracità delle illustrazioni:' l'opera pioneristica di Vittorio Pica su 'Emporium'," in *Emporium: Parole e figure tra il 1895 e il 1964*, 203–18.

20 See Vittorio Pica, *Attraverso gli albi e le cartelle: sensazioni d'arte, seconda serie* (Bergamo: Istituto Italiano d'Arti Grafiche, 1907), 89–135.

The first *Emporium* article owed much to the *Studio*.[21] It offered a similar layout, recycled several of the same images, and its cover – a vignette from *Le Morte Darthur* set within foliage – was strongly reminiscent of the *Studio*'s cover (Fig. 4.3, to compare with Fig. 4.1). The article opened impressively with a full-page reproduction of *The Lady of the Lake Telleth Arthur of the Sword Excalibur* (Zatlin 366),[22] and, like *The Studio*, reproduced Beardsley's *Les Revenants de Musique*, *The Procession of Joan of Arc*, the double-page drawing on Merlin from *Le Morte Darthur* reduced to a one-page layout as in *Le Livre et l'Image*, the Siegfried plate, *J'ai baisé ta bouche Iokanaan*, the two renowned frontispieces for Malory's narrative (which in the meantime had been completed in print), and a number of vignettes. It also reflected an evolution in the artist's style thanks to several drawings from the *Yellow Book*, launched in April 1894, from which Beardsley had been dismissed a year later, in particular the controversial covers of volumes one and three, and the red-light drawing *L'Éducation Sentimentale*, in which an old bawd sweet-talks a young apprentice.

Pennell, quoted and translated, provides in conclusion the main argument legitimising the Italian article itself: the risk taken in presenting a young artist. It is then fitting that the artist be shown in his prime: on the first and third page, two photographic portraits of Beardsley as a child (Fig. 4.4), with the caption "11½ years" ("*anni 11½*"), and of Beardsley as a young man (Fig. 4.5), are much more than a biographical illustration: they are proof of his precociousness. The article prosaically justifies it by discussing the English educational system that introduces graphic drawing as early as primary school alongside learning the alphabet and practising handwriting. There is no shortage of praise for Beardsley's work (rare inventive power, perfection of execution, intellectualism of subject, intensity of expression typical of true works of art), and no shortage of criticism either: this "product of a great centre of refined civility" (an expression that reflects the Anglomania well engrained in Italy since the eighteenth century)[23] is the author of the "too independent" plates for Wilde's scandalous *Salome*. With his

21 G. B., "Artisti contemporanei: Aubrey Beardsley," *Emporium*, 2:9 (Sept 1895): 192–204.

22 See https://emporium.sns.it/galleria/pagine.php?volume=II&pagina=II_009_192.jpg and ff.

23 See Arturo Graf, *L'Anglomania e l'influsso inglese in Italia nel secolo XVIII* (Turin: E. Loescher, 1911).

figures "out of the orbit with the work," he breaks free from illustration, which in the end captivates G. B.[24] His enthusiastic paragraph on *J'ai baisé ta bouche Iokanaan* transposes the work of art into a purple patch, i.e., a piece of ornate writing. Two months later, the November 1895 issue of *Emporium* echoes a similar fascination: the cover hosts one of the most disturbing *Salome* drawings, *The Dancer's Reward* (Zatlin 873), in which the lustful protagonist avidly takes possession of the prophet's head, while an opinion piece by "Neera" (Anna Zuccari) defends the primacy of idea over form in the work of art with the *Emporium* editors' blessing.[25] Uncommented iconography includes Beardsley's *Salome* drawing on the *Emporium* cover.

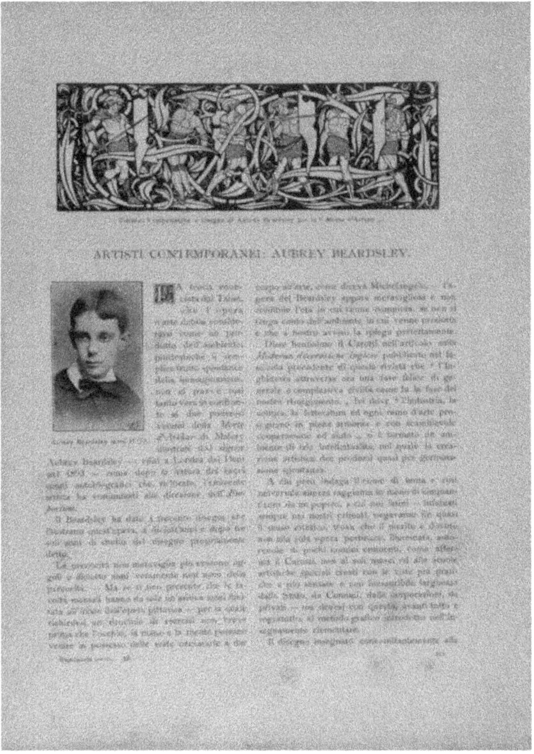

ARTISTI CONTEMPORANEI: AUBREY BEARDSLEY.

Fig. 4.4 Beginning of G. B.'s article on Beardsley, *Emporium*, 2:9 (Sept 1895): 192. Photograph of Beardsley at eleven and a half and decorative header for *Le Morte Darthur*. Courtesy *DocStAr*, Scuola Normale Superiore di Pisa, Pisa

24 G. B., "Artisti contemporanei: Aubrey Beardsley," 202–203: "*prodotto da un grande centro di civiltà*" (203); "*la sua tendenza a esorbitare dal mondo tangibile*" (202); "*opera d'arte autonoma ed indipendente*" (202).

25 Anna Zuccari Radius, "La coltura degli artisti," *Emporium*, 2:11 (Nov 1895): 337–43.

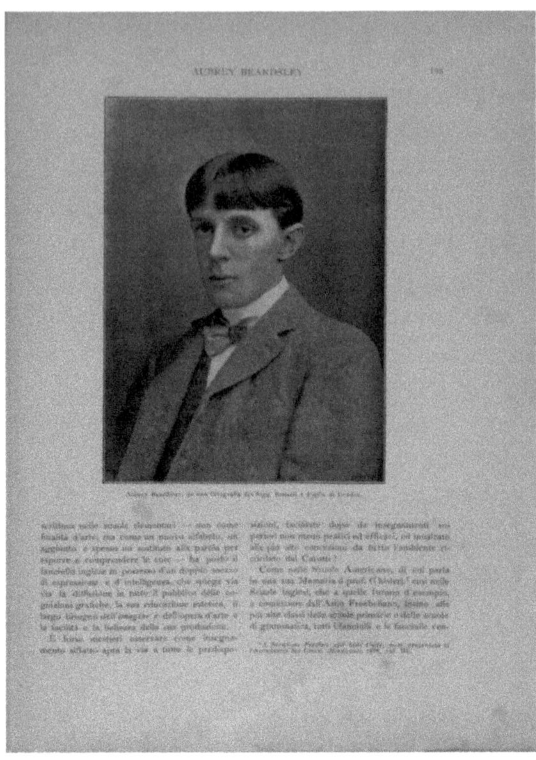

Fig. 4.5 A further page from G. B.'s article on Beardsley, *Emporium*, 2:9 (Sept 1895): 195. Photograph of the artist as a young man. Courtesy *DocStAr*, Scuola Normale Superiore di Pisa, Pisa

G. B.'s article shows that contact had been made with the artist himself (then working for Leonard Smithers after Lane had dismissed him from the *Yellow Book*): Beardsley had supplied the photographs as well as a brief biography, faithfully translated into Italian. Both photographs had appeared in London's *Sketch*, a general-public periodical that had published an interview with Beardsley at home under the title "An Apostle of the Grotesque." An infant Pierrot, drawn standing next to a bedridden woman, possibly his mother, accompanied the photos (Fig. 4.6). The latter, *Child at its Mother's Bed* (Zatlin 262), has autobiographical overtones.[26] It is also the oldest picture of Beardsley as Pierrot, ably stage-managing his *Sketch* interview as a one-man show. The entire page layout (with both photographs and drawing

26 Zatlin, *Catalogue Raisonné*, I, 158.

of *Child at its Mother's Bed*) reflected the article's opening sentence: "The youngest, and perhaps, taking one thing with another, the most original of latter-day geniuses..." The visuals show Beardsley, the ingenious child. Moreover, the set up is a response and delightful nod to Max Beerbohm's interview published four months earlier in this very same *Sketch* signalling his peer's precociousness and genius. Beerbohm, we remember, had illustrated his *Sketch* interview with his photograph as a ten-year-old child in a sailor's collar, the text emphasising the extreme youth he shared with Beardsley (see Fig. 2.9). Beardsley and Beerbohm, very close friends, cultivated artistic attitudes as they caricatured each other in mirror portraits with dogs. As artists they styled themselves as *enfants terribles*, bad yet gifted boys of the Nineties.

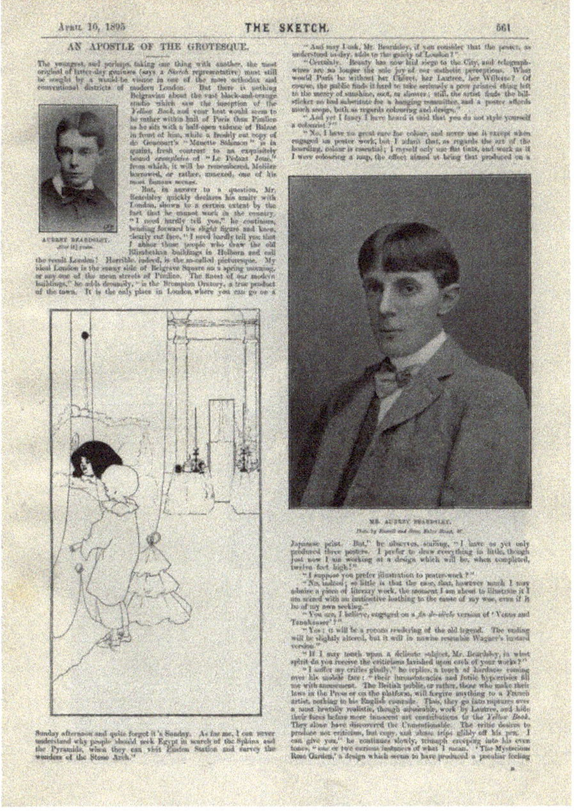

April 16, 1895 THE SKETCH. 561

AN APOSTLE OF THE GROTESQUE.

The youngest, and perhaps, taking one thing with another, the most original of latter-day geniuses (says a *Sketch* representative) must still be sought by a would-be visitor in one of the most orthodox and conventional districts of modern London. But there is nothing Belgravian about the vast black-and-orange studio which saw the inception of the *Yellow Book*, and your host would seem to be rather within hail of Paris than Pimlico as he sits with a half-open volume of Balzac in front of him, while a freshly cut copy of de Goncourt's "Manette Salomon" is in quaint, fresh contrast to an exquisitely bound *exemplaire* of "Le Pédant Joué," from which, it will be remembered, Molière borrowed, or rather, annexed, one of his most famous scenes.

AUBREY BEARDSLEY.
Aged [illegible] years.

But, in answer to a question, Mr. Beardsley quickly declares his amity with London, shown to a certain extent by the fact that he cannot work in the country. "I need hardly tell you," he continues, bending forward his slight figure and keen, clearly cut face, "I need hardly tell you that I abhor those people who draw the old Elizabethan buildings in Holborn and call the result London! Horrible, indeed, is the so-called picturesque. My ideal London is the sunny side of Belgrave Square on a spring morning, or any one of the mean streets of Pimlico. The finest of our modern buildings," he adds dreamily, "is the Brompton Oratory, a true product of the town. It is the only place in London where you can go on a Sunday afternoon and quite forget it's Sunday. As for me, I can never understand why people should seek Egypt in search of the Sphinx and the Pyramids, when they can visit Euston Station and survey the wonders of the Stone Arch."

"And may I ask, Mr. Beardsley, if you consider that the poster, as understood to-day, adds to the gaiety of London?"

"Certainly. Beauty has now laid siege to the City, and telegraph-wires are no longer the sole joy of our æsthetic perceptions. What would Paris be without her Chéret, her Lautrec, her Willette? Of course, the public finds it hard to take seriously a poor printed thing left to the mercy of sunshine, soot, or shower; still, the artist finds the bill-sticker no bad substitute for a hanging committee, and a poster affords much scope, both as regards colouring and design."

"And yet I fancy I have heard it said that you do not style yourself a colourist?"

"No, I have no great care for colour, and never use it except when engaged on poster work, but I admit that, as regards the art of the hoarding, colour is essential; I myself only use flat tints, and work as if I were colouring a map, the effect aimed at being that produced on a

MR. AUBREY BEARDSLEY.
Photo by [illegible] and [illegible], Baker Street, W.

Japanese print. But," he observes, smiling, "I have as yet only produced three posters. I prefer to draw everything in little, though just now I am working at a design which will be, when completed, twelve feet high!"

"I suppose you prefer illustration to poster-work?"

"No, indeed; so little is that the case, that, however much I may admire a piece of literary work, the moment I am about to illustrate it I am seized with an instinctive loathing to the cause of my woe, even if it be of my own seeking."

"You are, I believe, engaged on a *fin-de-siècle* version of 'Venus and Tannhauser'?"

"Yes; it will be a rococo rendering of the old legend. The ending will be slightly altered, but it will in nowise resemble Wagner's bastard version."

"If I may touch upon a delicate subject, Mr. Beardsley, in what spirit do you receive the criticisms lavished upon each of your works?"

"I suffer my critics gladly," he replies, a touch of hardness coming over his mobile face; "their inconsistencies and futile hypocrisies fill me with amusement. The British public, or rather, those who make their laws in the Press or on the platform, will forgive anything to a French artist, nothing to his English comrade. Thus, they go into raptures over a most brutally realistic, though admirable, work by Lautrec, and hide their faces before more innocent art contributions to the *Yellow Book*. They alone have discovered the Unmentionable. The critic desires to produce not criticism, but copy, and abuse trips glibly off his pen. I can give you," he continues slowly, triumph creeping into his even tones, "one or two curious instances of what I mean. 'The Mysterious Rose Garden,' a design which seems to have produced a peculiar feeling

Fig. 4.6 "An Apostle of the Grotesque," Aubrey Beardsley's interview with *Child at its Mother's Bed* and the two photographs republished in *Emporium* (see Fig. 4.4 and 4.5). *The Sketch*, 9 (10 Apr 1895): 561. University of Minnesota Libraries

With the artist's personal participation, *Emporium*'s article built on this stance, hardly aware that Beardsley was ably manipulating his image from a distance. Little known in Italy, Smithers's reputation as seller of erotica and books under the table, is not mentioned. The tone, however, becomes patronising when G. B. advises Beardsley not to pursue the path of childishness (*"puerilità"*). Had he grasped the irony of such a word, uttered out of the blue, when his article was illustrated by Beardsley's photograph as an eleven-and-a-half-year-old? Perhaps not... Besides, the objection *"puerilità"* is not originally G. B.'s, but Ernest Knaufft's, the censor of *The Procession of Joan of Arc* in the American *Art Student*, relayed by Grand-Carteret's French *Le Livre et l'Image*.

The *Emporium* article closely follows *Le Livre et l'Image*. It opens with *Battling Knights*, the very header from *Le Morte Darthur* reproduced in *Le Livre et l'Image* two years earlier (see Fig. 4.4), and offers the same *Morte Darthur* plate of Merlin. However, *Le Livre et l'Image* had also included the following comment by Knaufft, translated into French, with emphasis on no other term but childishness: "Aubrey Beardsley's work is *puerile* in its intellectual side. On seeing the May *Studio* [i.e., the full-size replica of *The Procession of Joan of Arc*], our humble opinion is that the young illustrator's technique can at times be *'puerilissimo'*..."[27] Inadvertently, the *Emporium* contributor had passed on the word at his own expense. And yet, he was fully aware of the hoaxes and pranks played by Beardsley on his English critics. Indeed, G. B. recalled the controversy surrounding a portrait of Andrea Mantegna in Mantegna-like style, published in volume three of the *Yellow Book*, which Beardsley had signed as "Philip Broughton" (Zatlin 905).[28] Several critics had praised Broughton's qualities by contrasting them with the horrors published in the magazine by... Aubrey Beardsley! The hoax had worked, and G. B. knew exactly why, having read in the *Sketch* how Beardsley let the cat out of the bag. Now, in *Emporium*, the prank on precociousness was at the expense of G. B. himself, bluffed by Beardsley and his photographs.

Trick aside, the first *Emporium* article on Beardsley illustrates how the network of magazines forms and operates: it is as much iconographic

27 Un Book-Trotter, "L'Image: Mille moins un petits papiers," *Le Livre et l'Image*, 2:9 (Nov 1893): 249, my emphasis: *"L'œuvre d'Aubrey Beardsley est* puérile *par son côté intellectuel. En voyant le Studio de Mai, notre humble opinion est que la technique du jeune illustrateur peut par moments être* 'puerilissimo'...."

28 *The Yellow Book*, 3 (Oct 1894): 9.

as it is textual; it borrows opinions, texts, images, and arguments from art periodicals (the *Studio*), fin-de-siècle quarterlies (the *Yellow Book*), general-public magazines (the *Sketch*), and books (*Le Morte Darthur*, *Salome*); it backs the artist's reputation for precociousness (sustained by childhood photographs) thanks to the *Sketch*, through the American *Art Student*, relayed by the French *Le Livre et l'Image*. The mix proved all-powerful from Britain to Italy, via the United States and France, and through it Beardsley became internationally renowned.

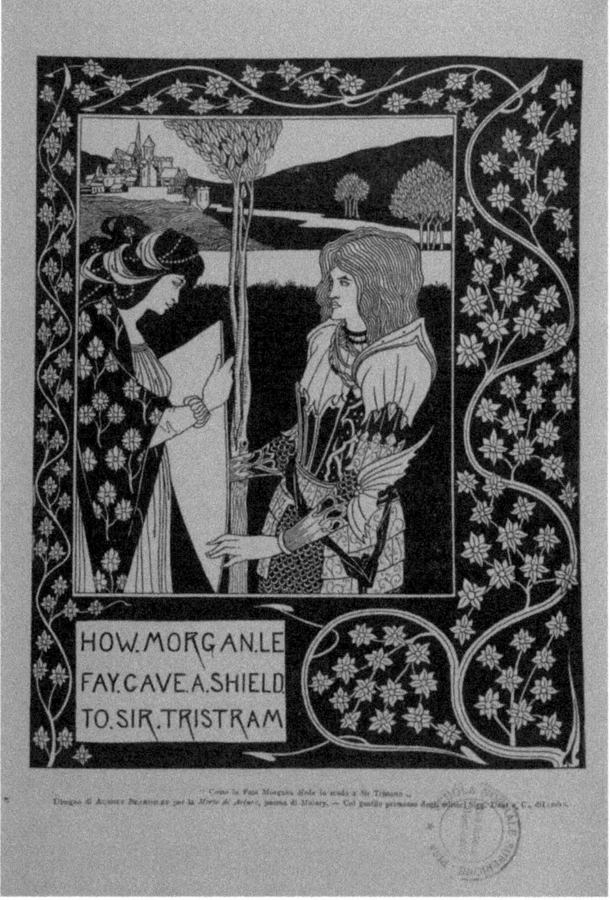

Fig. 4.7 Aubrey Beardsley, *How Morgan le Fay Gave a Shield to Sir Tristram* (by 3 Oct 1893), full-page plate from *Le Morte Darthur*, Bk. IX, chapter XL (Zatlin 539), repr. *Emporium*, 7:41 (May 1898): 322, issue frontispiece just after the advertisement pages. Courtesy *DocStAr*, Scuola Normale Superiore di Pisa, Pisa

Compared to the *Studio*'s unsympathetic obituary, *Emporium*'s (anonymous) version[29] stands out for its sobriety, its large frontispiece paying tribute to Beardsley (*How Morgan le Fay Gave a Shield to Sir Tristram*, a full-page plate from *Le Morte Darthur*, Fig. 4.7, Zatlin 539), but also its brevity (three and a half pages) and moderate iconography: none of the great final drawings are included, although reference is made to the refined plates of the *Savoy* and *The Rape of the Lock* (published by Smithers in 1896). The reproductions, mostly secondary – with the exception of *The Peacock Skirt* from *Salome* (Zatlin 866), and *The Wagnerites* (Zatlin 908), of great decorative force, hampered however by their quarter-page reproduction – adhered to the *Yellow Book*'s black-and-white idiom. Was this choice a result of caution? Restraint? A dearth of images? The article opens and closes with Beardsley's deathbed conversion to Catholicism, a reiteration that could not fail to move Catholic readers in the Italy of Umberto I, son of Vittorio Emmanuele, "*padre della patria.*" The obituary also recalls the first article in *Emporium*, albeit indirectly. The artist's precociousness is no longer justified by the English education system. However, opening the issue, an article by Helen Zimmern, a German-British writer and translator, "Il sistema Prang nell'insegnamento dell'arte," insists on the educational progress in American kindergartens,[30] a discreet reminder of the article three years earlier, which had allowed the prodigy Beardsley to blossom at the age of eleven and a half. In its tribute to an exceptional artist, *Emporium* failed, however, to explain why his art was so important and influential.

Pica's Aesthetic Choices

Vittorio Pica, though, had already been working on Beardsley in the Italian periodical. As early as February 1897, in an *Emporium* article on modern posters, Pica had pointed out Beardsley's originality: the warping of the human figure in his work, Pica argued, is neither gratuitous nor caricatural, but grants psychological complexity and a greater elegance to his figures. Thus, the woman on Beardsley's poster

29 "Artisti contemporanei: Aubrey Beardsley. In memoriam," *Emporium*, 7:41 (May 1898): 352–55. See https://emporium.sns.it/galleria/pagine.php?volume=VII&pagina=VII_041_352.jpg and ff.

30 Helen Zimmern, "Il sistema Prang nell'insegnamento dell'arte," *Emporium*, 7:41 (May 1898): 323–39.

for Todhunter's *A Comedy of Sighs!* (see Fig. 4.2) is remarkable for something both "leonardesque" (i.e., reminiscent of Leonardo da Vinci) and "Japanese-like." Anticipating the *Studio*'s disparaging obituary, which would strongly criticise that very poster, Pica's argument adopted an entirely different set of values.[31] Francesca Tancini has shown that the iconography and layout of Pica's article were partly borrowed from New York's *Scribner's Magazine*,[32] but the critical viewpoint and appreciation were entirely new. In a similar vein, in November 1902, Pica illustrated an article on Émile Zola with Beardsley's Japanese drawing of the writer (Zatlin 289) and his stylised "mask" by Félix Vallotton in *La Revue blanche*.[33] Pica's selection of visual material subtly connected Vallotton and Beardsley by way of their black-and-white graphics, showing how they mutually influenced each other.[34] They both used flat surfaces and strong outlines, stylised compositions, encouraged abstraction, and adapted their art to new printing technologies.

In May 1904, Pica's article, entitled "Tre artisti d'eccezione," was a celebration of Beardsley's, Ensor's and Munch's talents combined.[35] It began with a reference to what Pica calls in italics *"the Saturday plague"* ("il supplizio del sabato," emphasised): the two-penny illustrated weeklies that were seen to pollute the viewers' eyes and distort their taste. To alleviate the torment of the magazines' "brazen polychromatic coarseness" (*"la sfrontata loro grossolanità policroma"*), Pica turns to cerebral artists, whose refined and suggestive designs soothe the pain inflicted by the rampant expansion of the press. Recalling the *Studio*'s first article, Pica presents Beardsley as the first figure in a remarkable family, the article's trio, with supplementary reference to Charles Baudelaire, Jules Barbey d'Aurevilly and Paul Verlaine as avant-garde writers and artist Félicien Rops. Pica emphasises Beardsley's inventiveness, his

31 Pica, "Attraverso gli albi e le cartelle," *Emporium*, 5:26 (Feb 1897): 99–125, mainly 113–14. Reprinted in *Attraverso gli albi e le cartelle (sensazioni d'arte), prima serie* (Bergamo: Istituto Italiano d'Arti Grafiche, 1904), 279–324.

32 See Francesca Tancini, "L'ultimo dei pittori preraffaelliti: Walter Crane e 'Emporium,'" in *Emporium: Parole e figure tra il 1895 e il 1964*, 389–93, fig. 94 and 95.

33 Pica, "Letterati contemporanei: Émile Zola," *Emporium*, 16:95 (Nov 1902): 373–86 (Beardsley's drawing, 376). See https://emporium.sns.it/galleria/pagine.php?volume=XVI&pagina=XVI_095_376.jpg

34 See Jacques Lethève, "Aubrey Beardsley et la France," *Gazette des beaux-arts*, 68:1175 (Dec 1966): 347. Lethève argues that Beardsley was influenced by Vallotton's wood engravings.

35 Pica, "Tre artisti d'eccezione: Aubrey Beardsley – James Ensor – Edouard Münch [*sic*]," *Emporium*, 19:113 (May 1904): 347–68.

exceptional craftsmanship, his indisputable originality, and the role of the unconscious manifest in his work. He points out that the concern for style is predominant. Satire in Beardsley? Yes, undoubtedly, but animated by "a pitiless moralist's mind" ("*una mente di moralista spietato*"), that of the Goya of the *Caprichos*. Pica had read Arthur Symons's monograph on Beardsley, originally published in the *Fortnightly Review*, either in the magazine or in book form,[36] and recommended it to his readers, endorsing one of the most vivid tributes to the artist at the time. Finally, Pica responded to all those who objected to the abnormal, the artificial, the convoluted, with a strong argument, already made by Franz Blei in the first German article entirely devoted to the designer:[37] Beardsley cannot appeal to everybody. A year later, the *Mercure de France* would publish Pica's prose in full French translation without the images.[38]

However, Beardsley's images were relatively downplayed. Driven by a desire to make the other two artists better known,[39] Pica granted him only four figures against seven for Ensor, and nine for Munch. But the selection of images is well laid out and not prudish:[40] it opens with the first of the three drawings titled *The Comedy-Ballet of Marionettes, as Performed by the Troupe of the Théâtre-Impossible* (published in the *Yellow Book* and relayed by *Le Courrier français* as shown in the next chapter), continues full-page with *The Battle of the Beaux and the Belles*, one of the most accomplished plates from *The Rape of the Lock* (Zatlin 984), includes the powerful *Messalina Returning Home* after Juvenal's sixth satire (Zatlin 948), and closes with *The Death of Pierrot*, an emblematic drawing, as the next chapter shows (Zatlin 1015). The latter two are laid out centrally and facing each other on opposite pages. Beardsley's fine portrait by Jacques-Émile Blanche, already reproduced by Symons, accompanies the plates, reminding the reader that the talented artist

36 Arthur Symons, "Aubrey Beardsley," *The Fortnightly Review*, n.s., 63:377 (1 May 1898): 752–61; Symons, *Aubrey Beardsley* (London: At the Sign of the Unicorn, 1898).

37 Franz Blei, "Aubrey Beardsley," *Pan*, 5:4 (Apr 1900): 256–60.

38 Pica, "Trois artistes d'exception: Aubrey Beardsley, James Ensor, Édouard Münch [*sic*]," *Mercure de France*, 56:196 (15 Aug 1905): 517–30.

39 Two drawings by Ensor had already appeared in *Emporium*, in Pica's article "L'esposizione di bianco e nero a Roma," 16:91 (July 1902): 32–33, but no work by Munch. The only other articles to focus on them appear much later: 1935 for Munch (Antony De Witt, "Pittura norvegese moderna"), 1946 for Ensor, on the occasion of a retrospective.

40 See https://emporium.sns.it/galleria/libro.php?volume=XIX&pagina=XIX_113_347.jpg and ff.

was also an elegantly dressed dandy. An aesthetic tribute, illuminated with insight, the article is a curtain falling on a short play's din.

Pica amended the standpoint of the first two *Emporium* articles by G. B., yet his own *coup de coeur* did not have the polish of a final judgment either. The carefully balanced 1903 text given by the Danish art historian Emil Hannover to *Kunst und Künstle*r, a prestigious art journal focusing on European art and launched in 1902 in Berlin by Bruno Kassirer, easily takes the cake.[41] Its iconography pays tribute to three outstanding books, *Le Morte Darthur*, *Salome*, and *The Rape of the Lock*, each of which gets a characteristic full-page image. The frontispiece of *Le Morte Darthur* (*How King Arthur Saw the Questing Beast*, Zatlin 424) is replicated at the beginning of the article with great care, and is an especially difficult drawing to reproduce. The article's eight symmetrically arranged pages form a genuine composition, where images prevail over words, pausing at three key moments in the work: the medieval production, *Salome*'s black-and-white drawings tending towards abstraction, and the fine needlecraft inspired by Pope's poem.[42] By comparison, even though Pica's pen has done Beardsley justice with rare acuity, *Emporium*'s iconographic selection lets its critic down.

Humour and Advertisement

The smell of scandal that accompanied Beardsley – critiques, polemics, and facetious jabs – were all ultimately an asset to his work, and an incentive for members of the public to discover it for themselves. Beardsley himself deliberately provoked these outraged responses, as we have seen in the case of his portraits. *The Chap-Book: A Miscellany & Review of Belles Lettres* (1894–98), a refined American art and literature journal issued by art publishers Stone and Kimball in Chicago that would reach 16,500 subscribers, provides a good case study. The term *chapbook* suggests pedlars' literature and popular prints, but the Chicago review, a house organ and "a semi-monthly advertisement and regular prospectus for Stone and Kimball," verged on the deluxe.[43] Small in size and neatly

41 Emil Hannover, "Aubrey Beardsley," *Kunst und Künstler*, 1:11 (Nov 1903): 418–25.

42 See *Heidelberg Historic Literature*, https://digi.ub.uni-heidelberg.de/diglit/kk1902_1903/0427/image,info,thumbs#col_thumbs

43 See Alma Burner Creek, "Herbert S. Stone and Company," and "Stone and Kimball," in *American Literary Publishing Houses, 1638–1899*, Part 2, ed. by Peter Dzwonkoski and Joel Myerson (Detroit, Mich.: Gale Research Company, 1986),

printed, the periodical contained a range of very free uses of Beardsley's drawings. Beardsley certainly knew Stone and Kimball – he was frequently quoted or referred to in the periodical, and had been commissioned by the publishers to illustrate a deluxe edition of Edgar Allan Poe's works (Zatlin 926–29). Yet it is difficult to argue that he was himself involved in his multiple appearances in the *Chap-Book*. He had managed to manoeuvre and stage-manage his image in *Emporium* through *Sketch*, but allusions, skits, and iconography circulated beyond his control across the Atlantic. They were carried by his growing notoriety, granting him further publicity, and had a distinct commercial flavour.

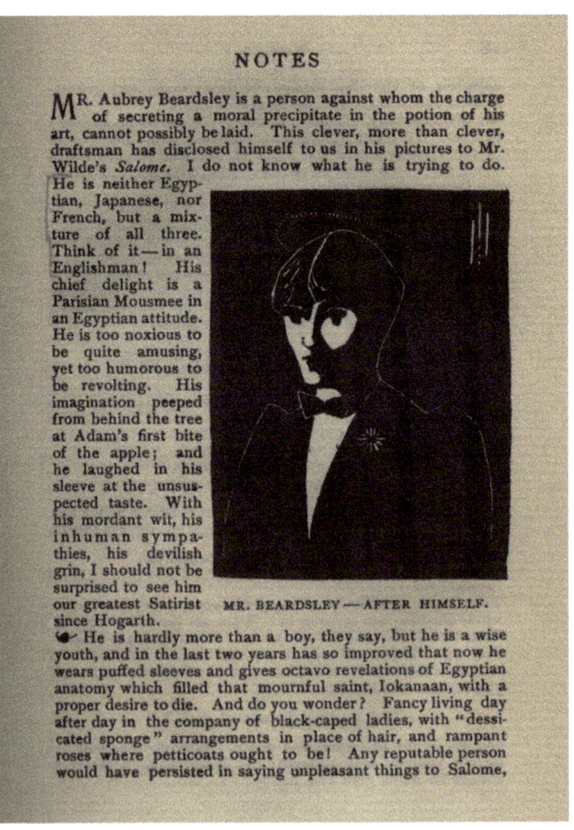

NOTES

MR. Aubrey Beardsley is a person against whom the charge of secreting a moral precipitate in the potion of his art, cannot possibly be laid. This clever, more than clever, draftsman has disclosed himself to us in his pictures to Mr. Wilde's *Salome*. I do not know what he is trying to do. He is neither Egyptian, Japanese, nor French, but a mixture of all three. Think of it — in an Englishman! His chief delight is a Parisian Mousmee in an Egyptian attitude. He is too noxious to be quite amusing, yet too humorous to be revolting. His imagination peeped from behind the tree at Adam's first bite of the apple; and he laughed in his sleeve at the unsuspected taste. With his mordant wit, his inhuman sympathies, his devilish grin, I should not be surprised to see him our greatest Satirist since Hogarth.

MR. BEARDSLEY — AFTER HIMSELF.

He is hardly more than a boy, they say, but he is a wise youth, and in the last two years has so improved that now he wears puffed sleeves and gives octavo revelations of Egyptian anatomy which filled that mournful saint, Iokanaan, with a proper desire to die. And do you wonder? Fancy living day after day in the company of black-caped ladies, with "dessicated sponge" arrangements in place of hair, and rampant roses where petticoats ought to be! Any reputable person would have persisted in saying unpleasant things to Salome,

Fig. 4.8 Beardsley's portrait with a saint's halo published with "Notes," *The Chap-Book*, 1 (15 May 1894): 17. University of Minnesota Libraries

436–40 and 440–43 (442). See also Giles Bergel, "*The Chap-Book* (1894–8)," in *The Oxford Critical and Cultural History of Modernist Magazines. II. North America 1894–1960*, ed. by Peter Brooker and Andrew Thacker (Oxford: Oxford University Press, 2012), 154–75.

In *Chap-Book*'s first issue, "Notes" is coupled with Beardsley's aesthetic and hagiographic portrait crowned with a halo.[44] The image showcases the artist's elegance and black-and-white technique (Fig. 4.8), but it is unclear whether it is apocryphal, a pastiche of *Portrait of Himself*[45] as the caption *Mr Beardsley – After Himself* signals, or an authentic work (signed top right with his Japanese signature). It is not credited in the table of illustrations, nor attributed to Beardsley in the catalogues of his work. Similarly, on his *Salome* designs, the second issue of 1 June 1894 includes a clever anonymous limerick, "The Yellow Bookmaker."[46] The title is a pun on the dealer of bets who determines odds, but also refers to the art editor and designer of the *Yellow Book*. It implied that Beardsley's major and winning bet was indeed this quarterly: his star had also risen thanks to the periodical press he so cleverly handled. The last verses included full purchasing instructions for those who would like to acquire *Salome* from Copeland and Day, the *Chap-Book* publishers also managing its sales for the American market:

> P. S. If you're anxious to see
> This most up to date Salomee
> Send over the way
> To Copeland and Day
> Cornhill, in the Hub, dollars three –
> And seventy
>   five
>   cents.[47]

These amusing, parodic contributions bow to a key fin-de-siècle rebellious spirit, foundational to the avant-garde reviews that challenged the editorial status quo and disputed attitudes of authority. They arise from a stance that uses parody and paradox as roundabout forms of manifesto.[48] Beardsley was no stranger to this. His *Sketch* interview hallowed him in half-reverential, half-mocking fashion, as "An Apostle of the Grotesque." It touted paradoxes wilfully cultivated, elaborated

44 Pierre La Rose, "Notes," *The Chap-Book*, 1:1 (15 May 1894): 17–18.

45 *The Yellow Book*, 3 (Oct 1894): 51. See Fig. 3.3 in this book.

46 Pierre La Rose, "The Yellow Bookmaker," *The Chap-Book*, 1:2 (1 June 1894): 41–42.

47 *Ibid.*, 42.

48 On this important point, see Linda Dowling, *Language and Decadence in the Victorian Fin de Siècle* (Princeton, NJ: Princeton University Press, 1986), 179–81, and Évanghélia Stead, *Le Monstre, le singe et le fœtus: Tératogonie et Décadence dans l'Europe fin-de-siècle* (Geneva: Droz, 2004), 22–23.

on his French culture and, of course, his precocity, with the childhood photographs as supporting evidence. Like the gargoyle shots by Evans (see Fig. 3.10 and Fig. 3.11a), they took part in a strategy to turn the Decadents into fin-de-siècle bad boys (*pueri*), promising yet already exhausted "elderly youths."[49] The *puer* produced naturally infantile drawings in a *puerilissimo* manner.

Singularity and Interchange

Avant-garde literature and art reviews were by nature malleable. They have been termed "small magazines," which has obfuscated their multifaceted identity and their relations with dominant periodicals and the mainstream press.[50] Nuances are necessary. The versatility and openness of the so-called "little reviews," as well as their undogmatic ideological and aesthetic positions, allowed avant-garde ideas to sift into larger-circulation magazines such as *Emporium*, designed *a priori* for a well-to-do bourgeois readership. In turn, *Emporium* expanded beyond its national and thematic borders by blending general-interest material and fine and applied art, with avant-garde literature and high art reviews.

Styled on the visual pattern of the *Studio*, and informed by both the fine art and general press of the time, the first *Emporium* article was subverted by the artist's own covert contributions. They model his persona on a more widely shared paradigm, alien to the earnestness and gravitas of the Italian periodical. Similarly, Pica's doubtless highly extensive art documentation does not fully explain all the iconographic choices of his last article, in particular the last plate, *The Death of Pierrot* (Zatlin 1015). Its symbolic weight is only fathomable if we consider Beardsley's obituaries in French art and literature reviews, as shown in the following chapter.

Comparison between periodical genres shows how Beardsley was portrayed and perceived across different journals and countries. A fine and applied art journal for educated readers, such as the *Studio*, was seminal in launching his career, crucial in disseminating his style and first images, and yet bordering on offensive in its epitaph. As a

49 See previously, Chapter 2.

50 See Evanghelia Stead, "Introduction," *Journal of European Periodical Studies*, special issue "Reconsidering 'Little' versus 'Big' Periodicals," 1:2 (2016): 1–17.

large-circulation magazine for the general public, the *Sketch* supported rumour and boosted its print run by publishing unsigned articles such as "An Apostle of the Grotesque," with Beardsley wittily staging himself as a child prodigy through an early photograph and an artwork. His precocity had nonetheless been sternly criticised in the American *Art Student* as *puerilità* – both (artistic) immaturity and juvenile irresponsibility, no doubt. Yet a detail of *The Procession of Joan of Arc* was taken seriously by *Emporium*, the anonymous G. B. falling unconsciously into the trap laid by Beardsley's prank. While *Emporium* voiced approval but also informed its readers of the Broughton controversy, the French *Le Livre et l'Image* and the German *Kunst und Künstler* served as European mediators of the artist's growing fame over the Continent. Contrariwise, over the Atlantic, the *Chap-Book* freely played with Beardsley's images and identities in gratifying satires to the point of counterfeiting him. Such a survey, however, is neither sufficient nor explains everything. Beyond the artist himself, affecting public opinion and iconography in a skilful way, the periodical press proves to be the major force in his myth making. His provocative work is media-supported and media operating. It further produces mock-hagiographic or parodic images styled on Beardsley's own (as in the *Chap-Book* here or E. T. Reed's skit in *Punch*, analysed in the previous chapter) that perpetuate and enhance his spirited stances.

Any network of periodicals may form and develop thanks to select personalities – journalists, editors, publishers – coming together in a specific place and time. They engage in mutual reading, critique, debate, acknowledgment, and/or acceptance around key images, which may not always correspond to their individual choices but to iconic representations moulded by press circulation. Such personalities foster a myth-creating iconography of talented artists like Beardsley, well aware of the images' symbolic value and function. Insightful critics such as Pica play a part in fostering Beardsley, as do the editors of *L'Ermitage*, Franz Blei in *Pan*, Sergei Diaghilev in *Mir iskusstva*, or Emil Hannover in *Kunst und Künstler*. And yet, these interpersonal relations may obscure the *exchange value* of periodicals *per se*, whether small, medium, or large, and their media performance. The exchange flow that produced immaterial ideas and linked them to material forms was a force behind Beardsley's images, his posing, and affectation. A reticular study of periodicals shifts the point of gravity of creations: it considers them not in themselves but rather in terms of *exchange* – visual, intellectual, symbolic, emotional, or relational. The periodical is not then a finished or stable object, but a *practice* (of texts, images, forms, shared by a community) and a *process*, which both privilege transfers and exchange. Beardsley's impish work took clear advantage of this from the heart of London to a distant *Emporium* of extensive influence.

5. Paris Performance Alive and Dead

"Si j'allais à Paris, je guérirais," so John Gray reminded French readers of his obituary in *La Revue blanche*, echoing Aubrey Beardsley's own words: "If I went to Paris, I would recover."[1] Beardsley's wishful thinking was not to be granted, although his art had repeatedly benefitted from a deeply rooted Francophile inspiration. As for Oscar Wilde, France was for Beardsley the land of free morals and free expression, as opposed to British prudery and conservatism. In his short life, the artist had enjoyed four lengthy stays in Paris. First in May 1892, when he first visited the Louvre, discovered the Salons and a wealth of exhibitions; then in May 1893, with his sister Mabel and the Pennells, to more Salons, the opera, the Latin Quarter, and the thrill of new acquaintances (including the poet Stéphane Mallarmé); then again in February 1896, initially with Leonard Smithers, when he went not only to parties and on other intoxicating adventures, but also to the *Salomé* premiere performed at the Comédie Parisienne by the Théâtre de l'Œuvre company, and was hard at work illustrating Alexander Pope's heroic-comic poem, amongst his masterpieces; lastly, from April 1897 to his death on 15 March 1898, he stayed partly in the capital and partly travelled around France. For the first part of this final visit, he experienced a brief improvement in health, was in exhilarating spirits, and met the novelist Rachilde and her Decadent protégés. He stayed in Saint-Germain-en-Laye and Dieppe, then returned to Paris. His last trip in 1897 took him to Menton, on the French Riviera, whence he would not return.

1 John Gray, "Petite gazette d'art: Aubrey Beardsley," *La Revue blanche*, 14 (May 1898): 68.

 https://doi.org/10.11647/OBP.0413.05

Early on he had shown his first work to Pierre Puvis de Chavannes, the symbolist painter, then President of the Champ de Mars Salon, who was also in the habit of drawing caricatures and grotesques.[2] An avid reader of French literature, Beardsley artfully employed French captions, usually with a naughty double entendre, in his drawings. He cultivated a French aesthetic when he decorated his rooms at 114 Cambridge Street, and put French inflections into the titles of his works. At the age of fifteen, he began applying the French article *La* to French or Frenglish words, paying no attention to the rules of gender. In a series of sketches caricaturing Ebenezer J. Marshall, headmaster of Brighton Grammar School, young Beardsley labelled them *La Apple, La Discourse, La Lecture, La Chymist* (Zatlin 89–92). At sixteen, he performed with his schoolmates in Thomas J. William's farce *Ici on Parle Français* on French travellers' linguistic exertions in England, and produced more sketches (Zatlin 98–103). Confined to bed by frequent haemorrhages between autumn 1889 and spring 1890, he read numerous French novels and drew a rich gallery of characters from Abbé Prévost's *Manon Lescaut*; Alexandre Dumas fils's *La Dame aux camélias*, the consumptive courtesan with whom he identified; Alphonse Daudet's *Tartarin de Tarascon*, *Sappho*, and *Jack*; Gustave Flaubert's *Madame Bovary*; Victor Hugo's *L'Homme qui rit*; Honoré de Balzac's *Le Curé de Tours*, *Le Cousin Pons*, and *Les Contes drolatiques*; and even Jean Racine's *Phèdre* (Zatlin 146–63, 165–67). He also often portrayed French writers in his own artwork: *Alphonse Daudet* (Zatlin 159), *Émile Zola* (Zatlin 288 and 289), *Henri Taine* (Zatlin 300r and 300v), and *Molière* (Zatlin 221). His early drawings and Japonesques used French titles and characters as in *The Birthday of Madame Cigale* (Zatlin 266) and *La Femme incomprise* (Zatlin 264). He slipped French words into his plates after Wilde's play (*Salome on a Settle, Maîtresse d'Orchestre; The Toilette of Salome*, Zatlin, 878, 871 & 877). Already in 1893, he had read it in its original French and his design and drawings for the English translation would establish him as a designer. The first drawing he made for it bears in French the tragedy's key line, "*J'ai baisé ta bouche, Iokanaan, j'ai baisé ta bouche*" ("I have kissed your mouth, Iokanaan, I

2 On this less known aspect of Puvis de Chavannes's work, see *Les Caricatures de Puvis de Chavannes, préface de Marcelle Adam* (Paris: C. Delagrave, 1906).

have kissed your mouth") (Zatlin 265), and startled the English public as it was published in the first article introducing his art.[3]

He excelled in hints and innuendos taken from French literature with a twist or a double meaning: if information is lacking on *Notre Dame de la Lune* (Zatlin 196), *Le Dèbris d'un poète* (Zatlin 244) relates to Beardsley himself an ironic quip from Flaubert's *Madame Bovary*, as shown in Chapter 3. *Il était une Bergère* (Zatlin 263) plays with Yvette Guilbert's spicy apex of a French folk song. *Les Revenants de Musique* (Zatlin 267) pictures a character, possibly Beardsley himself, haunted by the figures of Wagner's operas. In *Les Passades* (Zatlin 337), he projects onto two street-walkers the double meaning of the colloquial *la passade*, both "short-lived love affair" and "partner in such an affair." *L'Éducation Sentimentale* (Zatlin 889a) transposes the title of Flaubert's novel from Frédéric Moreau, Flaubert's "young man" (after the subtitle), to the lewd education of a young girl (see Fig. 5.4). Beardsley is supposed to have painted a portrait of Alfred Jarry's *Faustroll*, the inventor of "'pataphysics," and Jarry, impressed by *The Rape of the Lock* plates wrote an inspired piece in his honour, entitled "Du pays des dentelles" ("From the Land of Lace"). An admirer of the French language, Beardsley dreamt of importing French words into English, according to Blanche.[4] In a nutshell, he was "the first Englishman who turned whole-heartedly to France," as Julius Meier-Graefe put it.[5]

This chapter explores Beardsley's reception in French periodicals and the press. It is a subject that has already received significant critical attention: following a 1966 article by Jacques Lethève,[6] Jane Haville Desmarais has shown how Beardsley deliberately promoted his "French" and "Decadent" persona through press interviews.[7] Yet in her attentive

3 Joseph Pennell, "A New Illustrator: Aubrey Beardsley," *The Studio*, 1:1 (15 Apr 1893): 14–19, reproduced 19 (full page). On Pennell's article, see Chapter 4.

4 Jacques-Émile Blanche, "Aubrey Beardsley," *Antée: Revue mensuelle de littérature*, 3:11 (1 Apr 1907): 1106; Blanche, *Propos de peintre. De David à Degas, 1e série* (Paris: Émile-Paul Frères, 1919), 113.

5 Julius Meier-Graefe, "Aubrey Beardsley and his Circle," in *Modern Art: Being a Contribution to a New System of Aesthetics*, trans. by Florence Simmonds and George W. Chrystal, 2 vols. (New York: G. P. Putnam's Sons; London: William Heinemann, 1908), II, 253.

6 Jacques Lethève, "Aubrey Beardsley et la France," *Gazette des beaux-arts*, 68:1175 (Dec 1966): 343–50.

7 Jane Haville Desmarais, *The Beardsley Industry: The Critical Reception in England and France, 1893–1914* (Aldershot: Ashgate, 1998), 34–35, 46–48, 56–57.

comparative study of Beardsley's critical fortunes in Britain and France, Desmarais focuses on the text of these reviews, hardly mentioning the images. By contrast, I argue that reproductions of Beardsley's work were in fact a more potent and pliant means of diffusion and influence than any text. Although I give text due consideration, this chapter focuses specifically on the visual aspect of Beardsley's performance in French periodicals. Using new archival data, it explores the reproduction process he used so effectively, and analyses the impact of his images.

In doing so, it shows not only Beardsley's eagerness to shock Britain by his French publications, but also his readiness to adapt his work to a foreign magazine's varied contents and commercial considerations. His reception eludes expected patterns. Larger-circulation magazines wanted him more, and earlier, than avant-garde reviews. His death and the media chorus that mourned him gives final proof that Beardsley had lost control of his own image: although he did not wish to be associated with the potentially mawkish figure of Pierrot, it was the pathetic clown that became his posthumous symbol in the press. These two very different phases of Beardsley's representation in the French fin-de-siècle press – before his demise when he exercised some control, and after his death when he had none – have a common denominator: the centrality of images in understanding the artist's media performance and shaping his legend.

Entering the Stage

Beardsley's French reception through periodicals stands out for three reasons. First, it was rapid. It preceded the Italian *Emporium* (Sept 1895) by two years, the Berlin *Pan* and the Russian *Mir iskusstva* (1899) by five, and the Catalan *Joventut* (1900) by six. Second, it bears witness to personal relationships, which Beardsley harnessed to graft his personality and artistic persona onto Victorian clichés of French Decadents, French mores, and French literature. When first mentioned in John Grand-Carteret's *Le Livre et l'Image,* for instance, the magazine takes pride in implying direct contact: "a 20-year-old young artist, presently in Paris […]," although this is but a brief allusion to his effective presence in the capital.[8] Contrariwise, Theodore Wratislaw had styled "the precocious development of [his] brain before the hand has been sufficiently trained" as a result of French influence on his work. His drawings were the only ones to reflect "the modern neurosis, the delight in anything strange and depraved, the curiosity of a decadent style."[9] Yet his reception in France, surprising and free, is at odds with established ideas.

Such freedom shows in the type of magazine to first host his work on French soil for quite some time. Jules Roques's *Le Courrier français*, an illustrated Saturday weekly, founded in 1884 in Montmartre as an advertiser for Géraudel's cough and cold tablets, covered literature, fine art, theatre, and additionally but sparsely, also medicine and finance. It promoted spirited and risqué drawings and a range of authors from Paul Verlaine to Jean Lorrain. It opened with a "rhyming gazette," gossip in verse by Raoul Ponchon, a bohemian painter who loved songs, cabarets, and the bottle. Copies sold for 50 centimes with subscriptions at 12 francs 50 for six months and 25 francs for a year. The magazine served as a springboard for several new talents in illustration, as Roques constantly sought to renew its visual content by means of eye-catching effects, just as he used advertisement, literature, and politics.[10]

Le Courrier earned a reputation for being wicked: the writer Marcel Schwob's liberal family advised him against writing for *Le Messager français*, with his father describing it in an 11 March 1891 letter as "a competitor in pornography of *Le Courrier français*." He continued: "You are light-heartedly compromising your *agrégation* candidature, if you have not even dealt it a mortal blow. This is very, very unfortunate, and it almost seems as if you did it on purpose..."[11] Perhaps unsurprisingly, it was in Roques's journal that the first Beardsleys appeared in France in all their shocking variety. A book-enthusiasts' journal like *Le Livre et*

8 Un Book-Trotter, "L'Image: Titres réduits des nouveaux périodiques anglais," *Le Livre et l'Image*, 2:6 (Aug 1893): 57: *"un jeune artiste de 20 ans, actuellement à Paris [...]."*

9 Pastel [Theodore Wratislaw], "Some Drawings by Aubrey Beardsley," *The Artist and Journal of Home Culture*, 14 (1 Sept 1893): 259.

10 See Laurent Bihl, "Jules Roques (1850–1909) et *Le Courrier français*," *Histoires littéraires*, 12:45 (Jan–Feb–Mar 2011): 43–68; and Bihl, "*Le Courrier français*," *Ridiculosa*, special issue "Les revues satiriques françaises" (18 Nov 2011): 146–49.

11 Marcel Schwob, *Correspondance inédite précédée de quelques textes inédits*, ed. by John Alden Green (Geneva: Librairie Droz, 1985), 72.

l'Image, which had preceded Roques's by a year, had simply restrained itself to the medieval compositions of *Le Morte Darthur*.

There are two Beardsley seasons in *Le Courrier français*. The first, between November 1894 and April 1895, when Roques was the driving force, followed Roques's prolonged London stays between 1893 and 1894 to escape legal proceedings, after which he hosted a series on British graphic artists. Beardsley would be by far the most active and productive of these, though the extent of his involvement is ambiguous: for Jacques-Émile Blanche, who knew him closely, the artist either "collaborated" or "collaborated a little" with *Le Courrier français*.[12] The second period ran from February to July 1896, after a meeting in 1896 between Beardsley and two young men who would do much for him in French journals: the translator and critic Henry-D. Davray and the author and critic Gabriel de Lautrec, Henri de Toulouse-Lautrec's cousin.

Beardsley was first mentioned in *Le Courrier français* on 11 November 1894 in an article on a poster exhibition. Roques made reference to Beardsley's "uncommon weird imagination," and included three drawings that had made headlines in London.[13] Although evidence is lacking, it is safe to surmise that Roques's weekly developed into a scandal platform, ably used to respond to the barbed judgements of the British press that Beardsley went about liberally provoking. In order to accomplish this, a main weapon was the choice of images, as shown in the initial three drawings that appeared in the French periodical. The first, *Une femme bien nourrie* (Fig. 5.1), also known as *The Fat Woman* and titled *A Study in Major Lines* in the *catalogue raisonné* (Zatlin 932), had shocked Lane with its sexual explicitness (a prostitute waiting for customers at the Café Royal) and the allusion to Degas's *The Absinthe Drinker* then exhibited in London.[14] Lane had refused publication in the *Yellow Book* and the drawing had appeared in *To-Day* magazine on 12 May 1894. The second (Fig. 5.2), the frontispiece to John Davidson's *Plays* (Zatlin 331) drew on recent theatre events, a genre sponsored

12 Blanche, *Propos de peintre*, 113: "*collabora*." The first version, in the Bruges review *Antée*, 3:11 (1 Apr 1907): 1106, reads "with which he collaborated a little and in which he met with success right away" ("*auquel il collabora un peu et où il réussit du premier coup*").

13 Jules Roques, "Une exposition d'affiches artistiques à l'Aquarium'," *Le Courrier français*, 45 (11 Nov 1894): 2–5.

14 See Linda Gertner Zatlin, *Aubrey Beardsley: A Catalogue Raisonné*, 2 vols. (New Haven, Conn.: Yale University Press, 2016), II, 142 and 144.

by *Le Courrier français*, to create an ambiguous universe by mixing real people, magnified by their momentous fame, with mythological characters.[15] The *Daily Chronicle* had called it an "error of taste" because it displayed the easily recognisable portraits of Wilde and theatre manager Sir Augustus Harris. Beardsley had brazenly retorted that one of the gentlemen pictured was handsome enough to stand the test of portraiture (Wilde), the other owed him half a crown.[16] As for the third drawing (Fig. 5.2) – a poster for T. Fisher Unwin's "The Pseudonym and Autonym Libraries" (Zatlin 969) – it was, with its angular lines, Japanese perspective, and deliberately warped female figure, a comeback to the controversy caused by the poster for John Todhunter's play *A Comedy of Sighs!* pasted all over London. It had caused a stir, which would be relayed as far as Italy.[17]

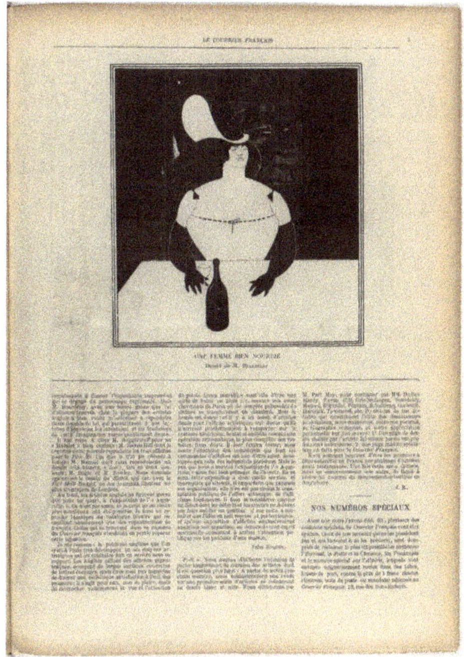

Fig. 5.1 Aubrey Beardsley, *Une femme bien nourrie* [*The Fat Woman*], catalogued as *A Study in Major Lines* (by Mar 1894), Tate collection, London, repr. *Le Courrier français*, 45 (11 Nov 1894): 5. BnF, Paris

15 *Ibid.*, 9.

16 See Aubrey Beardsley, *Under the Hill, and Other Essays in Prose and Verse* (London and New York: John Lane, 1904), 70.

17 See Chapter 4.

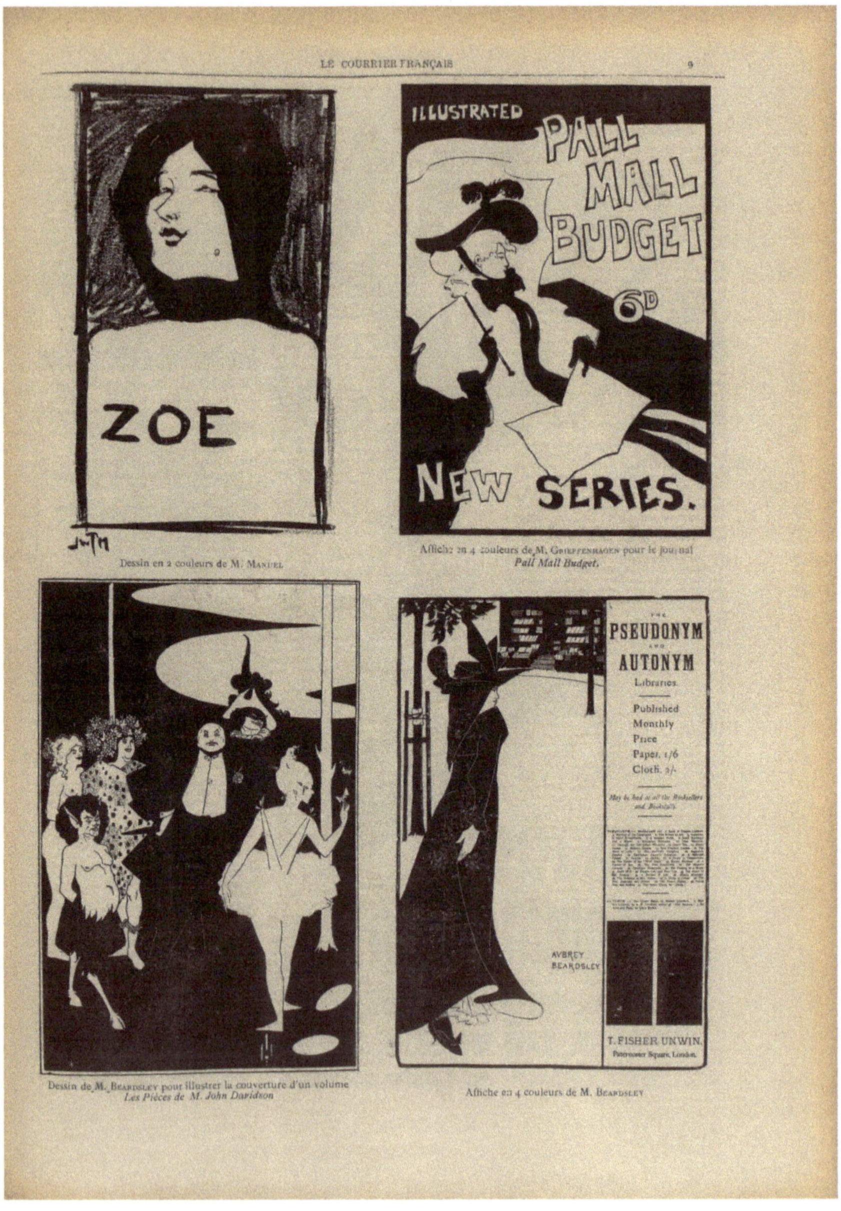
LE COURRIER FRANÇAIS 9

Dessin en 2 couleurs de M. Manuel

Affiche en 4 couleurs de M. Greiffenhagen pour le journal *Pall Mall Budget*.

Dessin de M. Beardsley pour illustrer la couverture d'un volume *Les Pièces de M. John Davidson*

Affiche en 4 couleurs de M. Beardsley

Fig. 5.2 *Le Courrier français*, 45 (11 Nov 1894): 9, reproducing bottom left Aubrey Beardsley, *Les Pièces de M. John Davidson* [*Frontispiece to John Davidson's Plays* (late Nov 1893)], and bottom right *Affiche en 4 couleurs de M. Beardsley* [*Poster for T. Fisher Unwin's The Pseudonym and Autonym Libraries* (early 1894)]. BnF, Paris

The next month, Beardsley was formally introduced by *Le Courrier français* as part of a series of articles on emerging British poster artists, painters and press illustrators. A dozen of them were reviewed, but most artists had a more realistic and literal style: Phil May, Dudley Hardy, Leonard Raven-Hill, Maurice Greiffenhagen, J. Wright T. Manuel, Oscar (?) Eckhardt, Fred Pegram, Edmund Sullivan, Alfred Chantrey Corboult, Archibald Standish Hartrick and Frederick Henry Townsend, the art editor of *Punch*.[18] In his general introduction to the series, Roques, conscious of the fact that previous lawsuits had granted his paper more than a whiff of scandal, took a stand on a recent London affair: the closing of the promenade and the ban on selling spirits at the Empire Theatre (similar to the Élysée-Montmartre, the venue he himself ran undercover and where the annual ball of *Le Courrier français* was held). He was looking for a promising new market in the English capital. He introduced English artists that he had personally met as the equals of "the most artistic of course, something like the equivalent of Messrs. Forain, Willette, Chéret, Legrand, Lunel, Anquetin, Grasset, L. O. Merson, Pille, Hermann Paul, Renouard, Raffaëlli, etc."[19]

By featuring Beardsley's interview in the 1894 Christmas issue (the series had started on 18 November with Dudley Hardy), Roques granted him a special place in the series (Fig. 5.3). The interview reflects Roques's astonishment at the young age of this much-publicised artist; the curiosity and discomfort triggered by his drawings; admiration for his unique style; Beardsley's acute feeling for distortion and the grotesque; and his ability to split a character into its real figure and its ghostly double. Some of these insights echo comments from the English press as steered by the artist himself. Others are more specifically French, such as references to Edgar Allan Poe, already used by Joris-Karl Huysmans in his art criticism

18 *Le Courrier français* presents them in the following order: Phil May on 18 Nov 1894, Dudley Hardy on 25 Nov, Chantrey Corbould on 2 Dec, Eckhardt on 9 Dec, Fred Pegram on 16 Dec, Beardsley on 23 Dec, J. W. T. Manuel on 30 Dec, Leonard Raven-Hill on 6 Jan 1895 (this issue also contains an invitation to exhibit, addressed by the Chelsea Arts Club artists to their French colleagues), A. S. Hartrick on 13 Jan, F. H. Townsend on 20 Jan, Edmond Sullivan on 27 Jan, Maurice Greiffenhagen on 3 Feb.

19 Roques, "Courrier de Londres," *Le Courrier français*, 44 (4 Nov 1894): 4a, "*les plus artistes bien entendu, quelque chose comme l'équivalent de MM. Forain, Willette, Chéret, Legrand, Lunel, Anquetin, Grasset, L. O. Merson, Pille, Hermann Paul, Renouard, Raffaëlli etc.*"

to comment on Odilon Redon's dark lithographs. Roques obviously borrowed from avant-garde journalism to comment on the British artist. His account, as delicate as it is fantastic, reveals fascination for Beardsley's personality and the prospect for Roques to choose drawings to reproduce at will. Beardsley's refusal to be paid for the interview (which must have delighted Roques) showed that he was ready to adapt in order to have his work published and diffused in France.

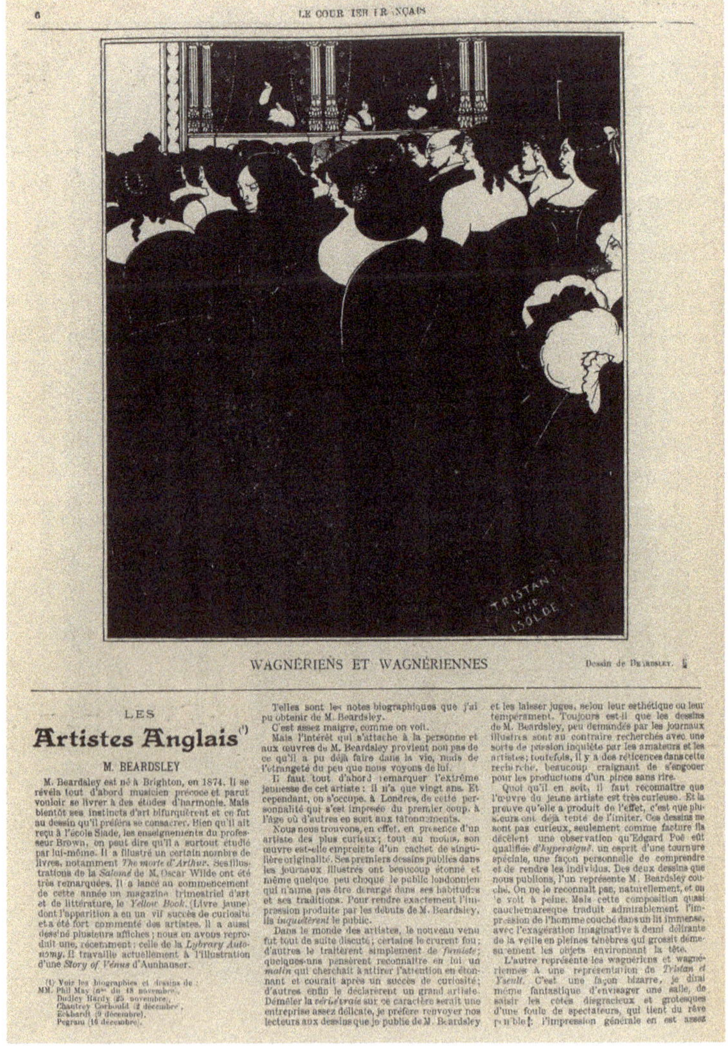

WAGNÉRIENS ET WAGNÉRIENNES

Dessin de BEARDSLEY.

LES

Artistes Anglais (1)

M. BEARDSLEY

M. Beardsley est né à Brighton, en 1874. Il se révéla tout d'abord musicien précoce et parut vouloir se livrer à des études d'harmonie. Mais bientôt ses instincts d'art bifurquèrent et ce fut au dessin qu'il préféra se consacrer. Bien qu'il ait reçu à l'école Slade, les enseignements du professeur Brown, on peut dire qu'il a surtout étudié par lui-même. Il a illustré un certain nombre de livres, notamment *The morte d'Arthur*. Ses illustrations de la *Salomé* de M. Oscar Wilde ont été très remarquées. Il a lancé au commencement de cette année un magazine trimestriel d'art et de littérature, le *Yellow Book*, (Livre jaune) dont l'apparition a eu un vif succès de curiosité et a été fort commenté des artistes. Il a aussi dessiné plusieurs affiches ; nous en avons reproduit une, récemment : celle de la *Lybrary Autonomy*. Il travaille actuellement à l'illustration d'une *Story of Vénus* d'Aunhauser.

(1) Voir les biographies et dessins de :
MM. Phil May (nº du 18 novembre),
Dudley Hardy (25 novembre),
Chantrey Corbould (2 décembre),
Eckhardt (9 décembre),
Pegram (16 décembre).

Telles sont les notes biographiques que j'ai pu obtenir de M. Beardsley.

C'est assez maigre, comme on voit.

Mais l'intérêt qui s'attache à la personne et aux œuvres de M. Beardsley provient non pas de ce qu'il a pu déjà faire dans la vie, mais de l'étrangeté du peu que nous voyons de lui.

Il faut tout d'abord remarquer l'extrême jeunesse de cet artiste : il n'a que vingt ans. Et cependant, on s'occupe, à Londres, de cette personnalité qui s'est imposée du premier coup, à l'âge où d'autres en sont aux tâtonnements.

Nous nous trouvons, en effet, en présence d'un artiste des plus curieux ; tout au moins, son œuvre est-elle empreinte d'un cachet de singulière originalité. Ses premiers dessins publiés dans les journaux illustrés ont beaucoup étonné et même quelque peu choqué le public londonnien qui n'aime pas être dérangé dans ses habitudes et ses traditions. Pour rendre exactement l'impression produite par les débuts de M. Beardsley, ils *inquiétèrent* le public.

Dans le monde des artistes, le nouveau venu fut tout de suite discuté ; certains le crurent fou ; d'autres le traitèrent simplement de *fumiste* ; quelques-uns pensèrent reconnaître *en* lui un *malin* qui cherchait à attirer l'attention en étonnant et courait après un succès de curiosité ; d'autres enfin le déclarèrent un grand artiste. Démêler la *vérité vraie* sur ce caractère serait une entreprise assez délicate, je préfère renvoyer nos lecteurs aux dessins que je publie de M. Beardsley et les laisser juges, selon leur esthétique ou leur tempérament. Toujours est-il que les dessins de M. Beardsley, peu demandés par les journaux illustrés sont au contraire recherchés avec une sorte de passion inquiète par les amateurs et les artistes ; toutefois, il y a des réticences dans cette recherche, beaucoup craignant de s'engouer pour les productions d'un pince sans rire.

Quoi qu'il en soit, il faut reconnaître que l'œuvre du jeune artiste est très curieuse. Et la preuve qu'elle a produit de l'effet, c'est que plusieurs ont déjà tenté de l'imiter. Ces dessins ne sont pas curieux, seulement comme facture ils décèlent une observation qu'Edgard Poë eût qualifiée *d'hyperaiguë*, un esprit d'une tournure spéciale, une façon personnelle de comprendre et de rendre les individus. Des deux dessins que nous publions, l'un représente M. Beardsley couché. On ne le reconnaît pas, naturellement, et on le voit à peine. Mais cette composition quasi cauchemaresque traduit admirablement l'impression de l'homme couché dans un lit immense, avec l'exagération imaginative à demi délirante de la veille en pleines ténèbres qui grossit démesurément les objets environnant la tête.

L'autre représente les wagnériens et wagnériennes à une représentation de *Tristan et Yseult*. C'est une façon bizarre, je dirai même fantastique d'envisager une salle, de saisir les côtés disgracieux et grotesques d'une foule de spectateurs, qui tient du rêve pénible : l'impression générale en est assez

Fig. 5.3 Beginning of Jules Roques's article, "Les artistes anglais: M. Beardsley," *Le Courrier français*, 51 (23 Dec 1894): 6, reproducing the drawing *The Wagnerites* (May 1893–June 1894), V&A, London, repr. *The Yellow Book*, 3 (Oct 1894): 55. BnF, Paris

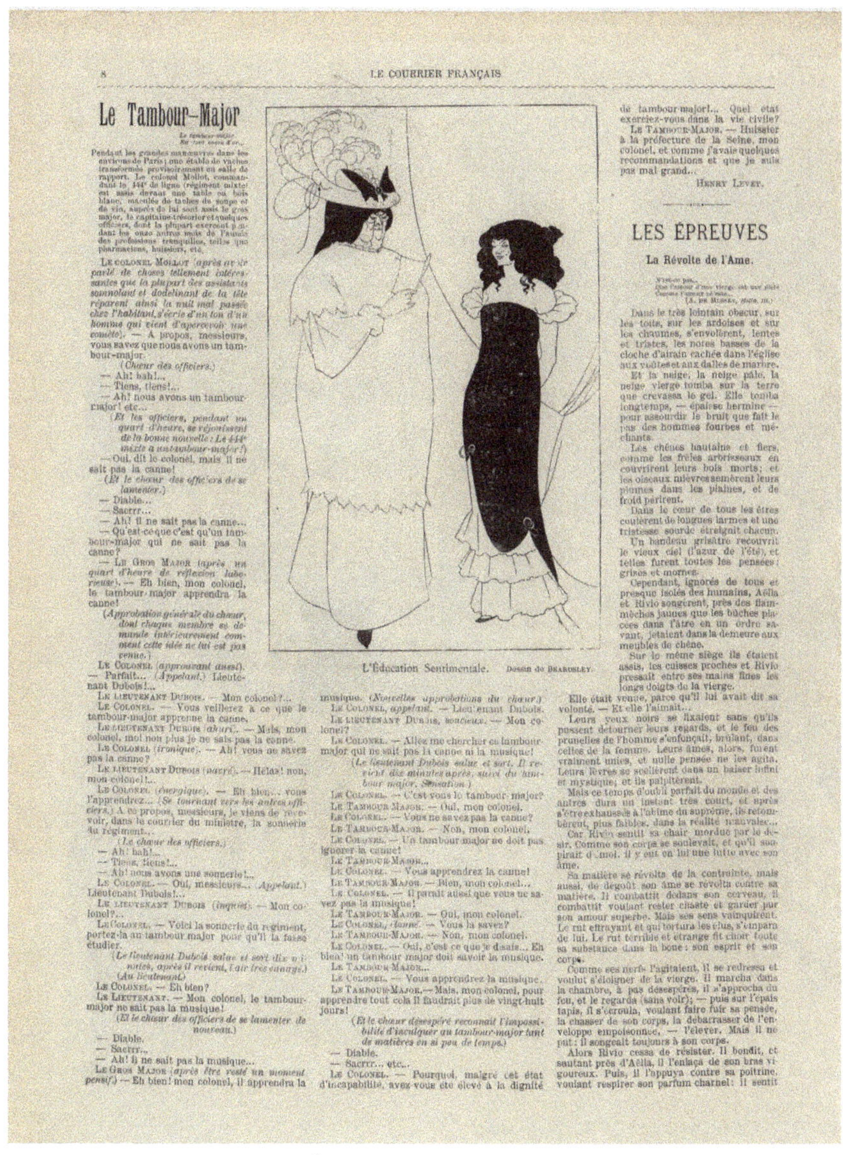

8 LE COURRIER FRANÇAIS

Le Tambour-Major

Pendant les grandes manœuvres dans les environs de Paris, une étable de vaches transformée provisoirement en salle de rapport. Le colonel Mollot, commandant le 144e de ligne (régiment mixte) est assis devant une table en bois blanc, maculée de taches de soupe et de vin, auprès de lui sont assis le gros major, le capitaine-trésorier et quelques officiers, dont la plupart exercent pendant les onze autres mois de l'année des professions tranquilles, telles que pharmaciens, huissiers, etc.

Le Colonel Mollot (*après avoir parlé de choses tellement intéressantes que la plupart des assistants somnolant et dodelinant de la tête réparent ainsi la nuit mal passée chez l'habitant, s'écrie d'un ton d'un homme qui vient d'apercevoir une comète*). — A propos, messieurs, vous savez que nous avons un tambour-major.

(*Chœur des officiers.*)

— Ah! bah!...

— Tiens, tiens!...

— Ah! nous avons un tambour-major! etc...

(*Et les officiers, pendant un quart d'heure, se réjouissent de la bonne nouvelle: Le 144e mixte a un tambour-major!*)

— Oui, dit le colonel, mais il ne sait pas la canne!

(*Et le chœur des officiers de se lamenter.*)

— Diable...

— Sacrrr...

— Ah! il ne sait pas la canne...

— Qu'est-ce que c'est qu'un tambour-major qui ne sait pas la canne?

— Le Gros Major (*après un quart d'heure de réflexion laborieuse*). — Eh bien, mon colonel, le tambour-major apprendra la canne!

(*Approbation générale du chœur, dont chaque membre se demande intérieurement comment cette idée ne lui est pas venue.*)

Le Colonel (*approuvant aussi*). — Parfait... (*Appelant.*) Lieutenant Dubois!...

Le Lieutenant Dubois. — Mon colonel?...

Le Colonel. — Vous veillerez à ce que le tambour-major apprenne la canne.

Le Lieutenant Dubois (*ahuri*). — Mais, mon colonel, moi non plus je ne sais pas la canne.

Le Colonel (*ironique*). — Ah! vous ne savez pas la canne?

Le Lieutenant Dubois (*navré*). — Hélas! non, mon colonel!...

Le Colonel (*énergique*). — Eh bien... vous l'apprendrez... (*Se tournant vers les autres officiers.*) A ce propos, messieurs, je viens de recevoir, dans le courrier du ministre, la sonnerie du régiment...

(*Le chœur des officiers.*)

— Ah! bah!...

— Tiens, tiens!...

— Ah! nous avons une sonnerie!...

Le Colonel. — Oui, messieurs... (*Appelant.*) Lieutenant Dubois!...

Le Lieutenant Dubois (*inquiet*). — Mon colonel?...

Le Colonel. — Voici la sonnerie du régiment, portez-la au tambour-major pour qu'il la fasse étudier.

(*Le lieutenant Dubois salue et sort dix minutes après il revient, l'air très ennuyé.*)

(*Au lieutenant.*)

Le Colonel. — Eh bien?

Le Lieutenant. — Mon colonel, le tambour-major ne sait pas la musique!

(*Et le chœur des officiers de se lamenter de nouveau.*)

— Diable.

— Sacrrr...

— Ah! il ne sait pas la musique...

Le Gros Major (*après être resté un moment pensif*). — Eh bien! mon colonel, il apprendra la musique. (*Nouvelles approbations du chœur.*)

Le Colonel, *appelant*. — Lieutenant Dubois.

Le Lieutenant Dubois, *soucieux*. — Mon colonel?

Le Colonel. — Allez me chercher ce tambour-major qui ne sait pas la canne ni la musique!

(*Le lieutenant Dubois salue et sort. Il revient dix minutes après, suivi du tambour-major. Sensation.*)

Le Colonel. — C'est vous le tambour-major?

Le Tambour-Major. — Oui, mon colonel.

Le Colonel. — Vous ne savez pas la canne?

Le Tambour-Major. — Non, mon colonel.

Le Colonel. — Un tambour-major ne doit pas ignorer la canne!

Le Tambour-Major...

Le Colonel. — Vous apprendrez la canne!

Le Tambour-Major. — Bien, mon colonel...

Le Colonel. — Il paraît aussi que vous ne savez pas la musique!

Le Tambour-Major. — Oui, mon colonel.

Le Colonel, *tonné*. — Vous la savez?

Le Tambour-Major. — Non, mon colonel.

Le Colonel. — Oui, c'est ce que je disais... Eh bien! un tambour-major doit savoir la musique.

Le Tambour-Major...

Le Colonel. — Vous apprendrez la musique.

Le Tambour-Major. — Mais, mon colonel, pour apprendre tout cela il faudrait plus de vingt-huit jours!

(*Et le chœur désespéré reconnaît l'impossibilité d'inculquer au tambour-major tant de matières en si peu de temps.*)

— Diable.

— Sacrrr... etc...

Le Colonel. — Pourquoi, malgré cet état d'incapabilité, avez-vous été élevé à la dignité de tambour-major!... Quel état exerciez-vous dans la vie civile?

Le Tambour-Major. — Huissier à la préfecture de la Seine, mon colonel, et comme j'avais quelques recommandations et que je suis pas mal grand...

Henry Lever.

L'Éducation Sentimentale. Dessin de Beardsley.

LES ÉPREUVES

La Révolte de l'Ame.

(A. de Musset.)

Dans le très lointain obscur, sur les toits, sur les ardoises et sur les chaumes, s'envolèrent, lentes et tristes, les notes basses de la cloche d'airain cachée dans l'église aux voûtes et aux dalles de marbre.

Et la neige, la neige pâle, la neige vierge tomba sur la terre que crevassa le gel. Elle tomba longtemps, — épaisse hermine — pour assourdir le bruit que fait le pas des hommes fourbes et méchants.

Les chênes hautains et fiers, comme les frêles arbrisseaux en couvrirent leurs bois morts; et les oiseaux mièvres semèrent leurs plumes dans les plaines, et de froid périrent.

Dans le cœur de tous les êtres coulèrent de longues larmes et une tristesse sourde étreignit chacun.

Un bandeau grisâtre recouvrit le vieux ciel (d'azur de l'été), et telles furent toutes les pensées: grises et mornes.

Cependant, ignorés de tous et presque isolés des humains, Aëlla et Rivio songèrent, près des flammèches jaunes que les bûches placées dans l'âtre en un ordre savant, jetaient dans la demeure aux meubles de chêne.

Sur le même siège ils étaient assis, les cuisses proches et Rivio pressait entre ses mains fines les longs doigts de la vierge.

Elle était venue, parce qu'il lui avait dit sa volonté. — Et elle l'aimait...

Leurs yeux noirs se fixaient sans qu'ils pussent détourner leurs regards, et le feu des prunelles de l'homme s'enfonçait, brûlant, dans celles de la femme. Leurs âmes, alors, furent vraiment unies, et nulle pensée ne les agita. Leurs lèvres se scellèrent dans un baiser infini et mystique; et ils palpitèrent.

Mais ce temps d'oubli parfait du monde et des autres dura un instant très court, et après s'être exhaussés à l'abîme du suprême, ils retombèrent, plus faibles, dans la réalité mauvaise...

Car Rivio sentit sa chair mordue par le désir. Comme son corps se soulevait, et qu'il soupirait d'émoi, il y eut en lui une lutte avec son âme.

Sa matière se révolta de la contrainte, mais aussi, de dégoût son âme se révolta contre sa matière. Il combattit dedans son cerveau, il combattit voulant rester chaste et garder pur son amour superbe. Mais ses sens vainquirent. Le rut effrayant et qui tortura les élus, s'empara de lui. Le rut terrible et étrange fit choir toute sa substance dans la boue: son esprit et son corps.

Comme ses nerfs l'agitaient, il se redressa et voulut s'éloigner de la vierge. Il marcha dans la chambre, à pas désespérés, il s'approcha du feu, et le regarda (sans voir); — puis sur l'épais tapis, il s'écroula, voulant faire fuir sa pensée, la chasser de son corps, la débarrasser de l'enveloppe empoisonnée, — l'élever. Mais il ne put: il songeait toujours à son corps.

Alors Rivio cessa de résister. Il bondit, et sautant près d'Aëlla, il l'enlaça de son bras vigoureux. Puis, il l'appuya contre sa poitrine, voulant respirer son parfum charnel: il sentit

Fig. 5.4 Aubrey Beardsley, *L'Éducation Sentimentale* (ca. Feb–Mar 1894), *The Yellow Book*, 1 (16 April 1894): 55, repr. *Le Courrier français*, 6 (10 Feb 1895): 8. BnF, Paris

The British series in *Le Courrier français* came to an end, yet Beardsley's drawings continued appearing. They ardently prolonged the provocation of the British establishment on an ethical and aesthetic level: *L'Éducation Sentimentale*, a drawing published in the first volume of the *Yellow Book* in April 1894 that re-appropriates the title of Flaubert's novel to name a brothel scene (Zatlin 889a), had incited the *Westminster Gazette* to demand "a short Act of Parliament to make this kind of thing illegal."[20] *Le Courrier français* reprinted it on 10 February 1895 (Fig. 5.4).

A fortnight later, Roques's magazine credited Beardsley with a portrait of Andrea Mantegna in the manner of the Flemish Primitives, which contrasted both with the designer's graphic style and the periodical's usual iconography.[21] It corresponded to another polemic: Beardsley had published it in the third volume of the *Yellow Book* (Oct 1894), signing it with the pseudonym Philip Broughton (Zatlin 905). The English press had admired it, contrasting it with works by Aubrey Beardsley, an illustrator "who could not draw." It was a good opportunity for the artist to reveal the hoax in England – a pleasure extended in France by attributing it to himself outright.

During this first phase, twenty Beardsley drawings, either in his new black-and-white manner or from *Le Morte Darthur*, ran through the pages of *Le Courrier français* over a six-month period, sometimes on a weekly basis. One of them, captioned *Wagnériens et wagnériennes* in the periodical (catalogued as *The Wagnerites*, see Fig. 5.3, Zatlin 908), was part of the *Courrier français* drawings sale on 18 February 1895 under the title "À une représentation de Tristan et Izeult." It fetched the price of 150 francs, amongst the highest. In terms of drawings selected for the journal, much depended on Roques's personal interests and taste. He approved of trestle theatre (two drawings from *The Comedy-Ballet of Marionettes, as Performed by the Troupe of the Théâtre-Impossible*) and privileged French subjects (two drawings of actress Réjane), but also piquant scenes such as Beardsley's frontispiece for John Davidson's novel *Earl Lavender* (Zatlin 944), a text inspired by Darwinian theories, which extols the virtues of flogging the weary souls of the time.

20 See preface by John Lane, in Beardsley, *Under the Hill*, vi; and Zatlin, *Catalogue Raisonné*, II, 79.

21 *Le Courrier français*, 8 (24 Feb 1895): 3 (reproduction).

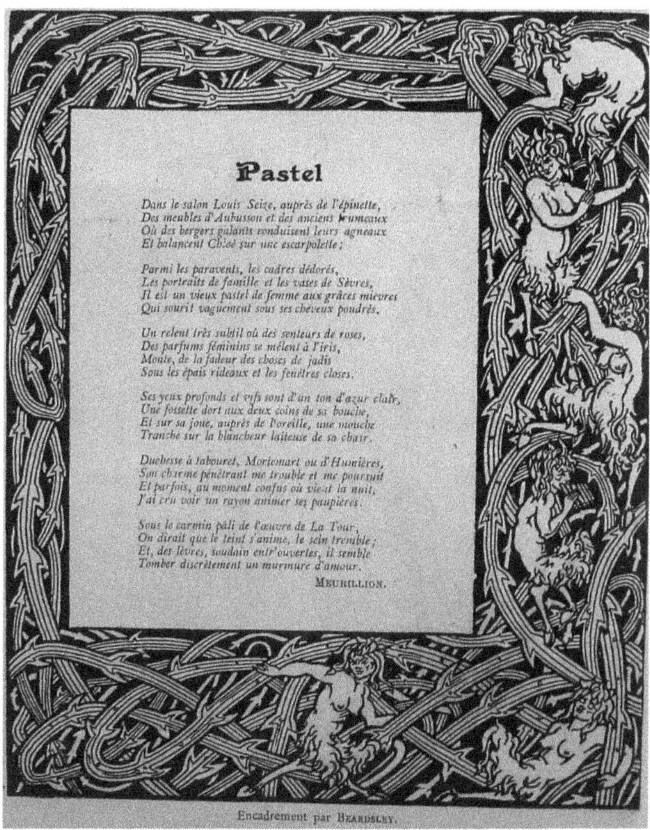

Pastel

Dans le salon Louis Seize, auprès de l'épinette,
Des meubles d'Aubusson et des anciens trumeaux
Où des bergers galants conduisent leurs agneaux
Et balancent Chloé sur une escarpolette ;

Parmi les paravents, les cadres dédorés,
Les portraits de famille et les vases de Sèvres,
Il est un vieux pastel de femme aux grâces mièvres
Qui sourit vaguement sous ses cheveux poudrés.

Un relent très subtil où des senteurs de roses,
Des parfums féminins se mêlent à l'iris,
Monte, de la fadeur des choses de jadis
Sous les épais rideaux et les fenêtres closes.

Ses yeux profonds et vifs sont d'un ton d'azur clair,
Une fossette dort aux deux coins de sa bouche,
Et sur sa joue, auprès de l'oreille, une mouche
Tranche sur la blancheur laiteuse de sa chair.

Duchesse à tabouret, Mortemart ou d'Humières,
Son charme pénétrant me trouble et me poursuit
Et parfois, au moment confus où vient la nuit,
J'ai cru voir un rayon animer ses paupières.

Sous le carmin pâli de l'œuvre de La Tour,
On dirait que le teint s'anime, le sein tremble ;
Et, des lèvres, soudain entr'ouvertes, il semble
Tomber discrètement un murmure d'amour.

MEURILLION.

Encadrement par BEARDSLEY.

Fig. 5.5 Aubrey Beardsley, framing with she-fauns from *Le Morte Darthur* reused for Meurillion's poem "Pastel," *Le Courrier français*, 12 (24 Mar 1895): 8 (detail). BnF, Paris. The frame is *Satyrs in Briars* (autumn 1892), from Bk. II, chapter I (Zatlin 371)

Roques exploited the drawings as he pleased, subjecting them to heavy-handed alterations and appropriating them into new contexts. A frame with female fauns in the 24 March 1895 issue, taken from *Le Morte Darthur* (*Satyrs in Briars*, Zatlin 371), hosts a Louis XVI "Pastel" signed Meurillion, an innocuous and obscure rhymer (Fig. 5.5). Another, on 14 April 1895, with a highly stylised cluster of grapes (*Hop Flowers on Vines*, Zatlin 666), houses a "Ballade du vieux buveur solitaire" by Émile Lutz. Lastly, on 17 February 1895, the first of the three *Comedy-Ballet of Marionettes, as Performed by the Troupe of the Théâtre-Impossible, Posed in Three Drawings*, changed into a poster (Zatlin 895), advertises the popular Géraudel cough tablets, the very *raison d'être* of Roques's paper.

Beardsley – who was more than willing for his work to be appropriated – had wonderfully adapted it to Roques's commercialism. In the first *Yellow Book* version (Fig. 5.6), the dwarf holds a mask in his hand. In *Le Courrier français*, the mask becomes a round box of lozenges, while an added inscription states in Frenglish: "If You Cough Take Géraudel's Pastilles" (Fig. 5.7).

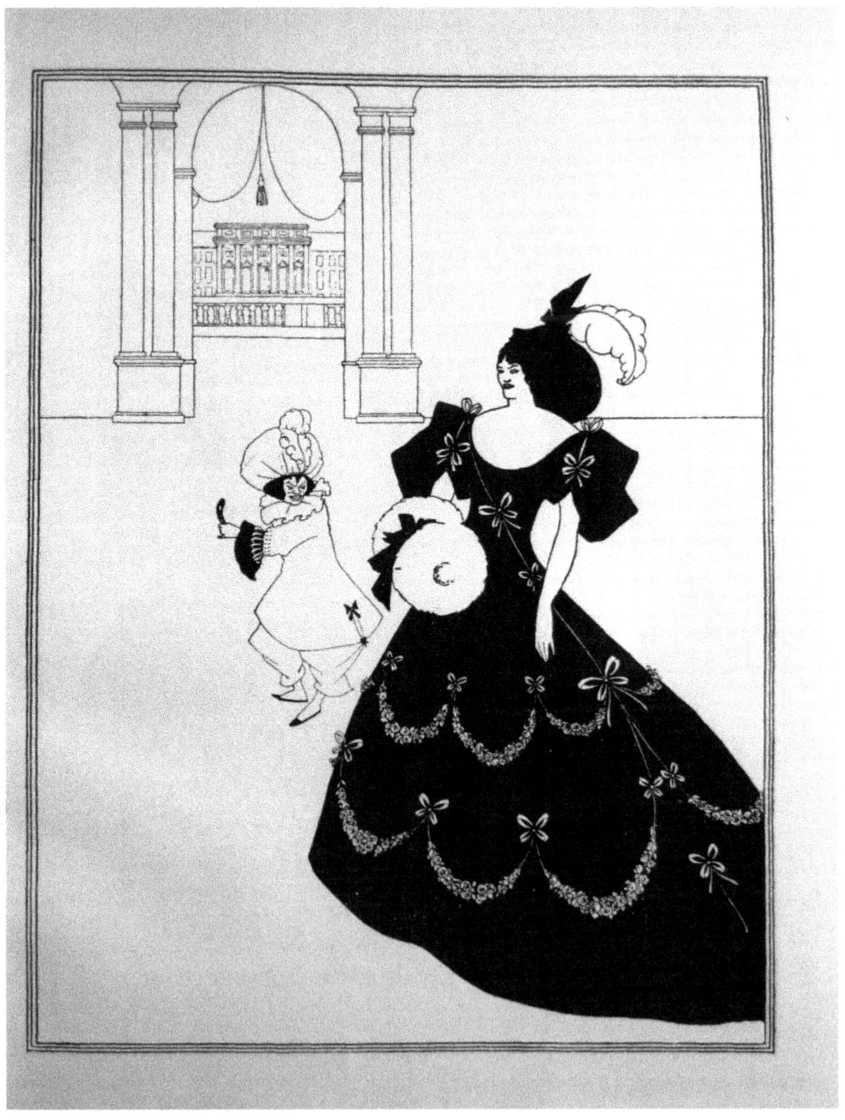

Fig. 5.6 Aubrey Beardsley, *The Comedy-Ballet of Marionettes, as Performed by the Troupe of the Théâtre-Impossible, Posed in Three Drawings, I* (by 27 June 1894), repr. *The Yellow Book*, 2 (July 1894): 87. Courtesy Y90s

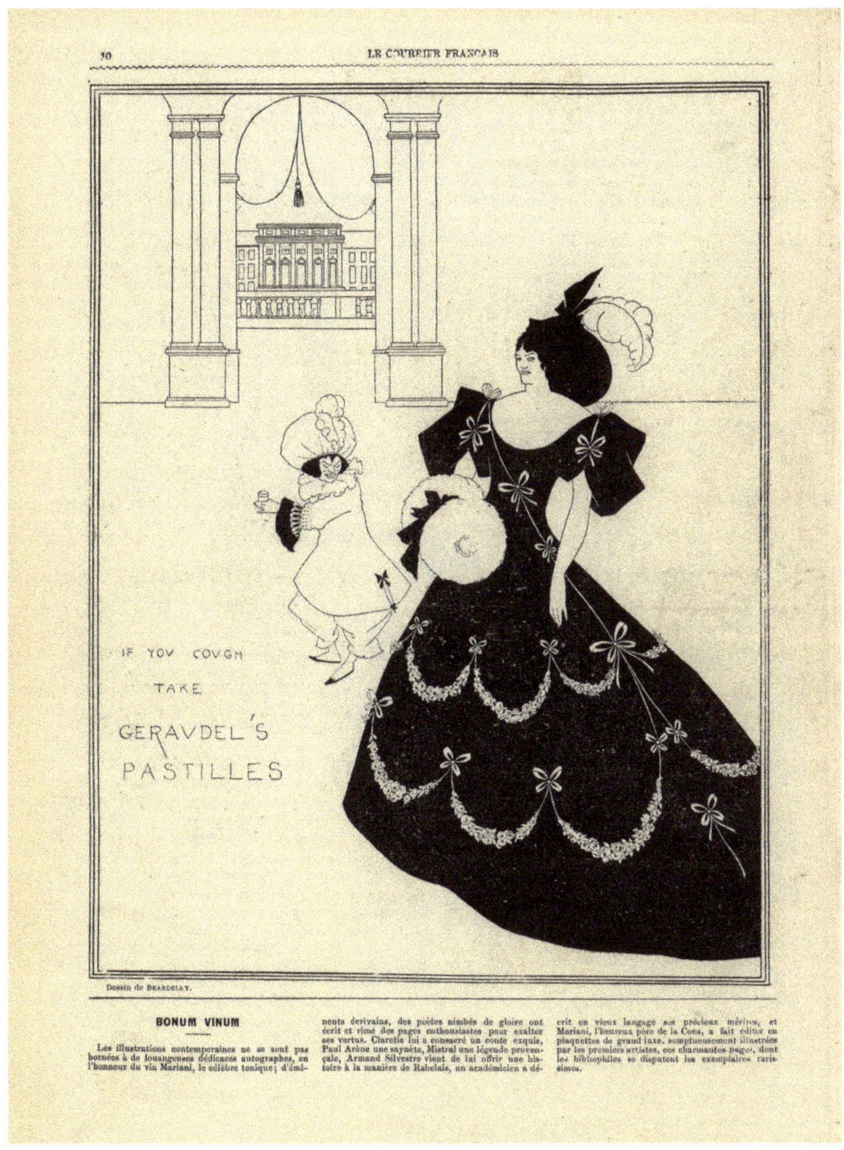

10 LE COURRIER FRANÇAIS

Dessin de BEARDSLEY.

BONUM VINUM

Les illustrations contemporaines ne se sont pas bornées à de louangeuses dédicaces autographes, en l'honneur du vin Mariani, le célèbre tonique; d'éminents écrivains, des poètes nimbés de gloire ont écrit et rimé des pages enthousiastes pour exalter ses vertus. Claretie lui a consacré un conte exquis, Paul Arène une saynète, Mistral une légende provençale, Armand Silvestre vient de lui offrir une histoire à la manière de Rabelais, un académicien a décrit en vieux langage ses précieux mérites, et Mariani, l'heureux père de la Coca, a fait éditer en plaquettes de grand luxe, somptueusement illustrées par les premiers artistes, ces charmantes pages, dont les bibliophiles se disputent les exemplaires rarissimes.

Fig. 5.7 Aubrey Beardsley, *The Comedy-Ballet of Marionettes I*, transformed into a billboard with the inscription "If you cough | take | Géraudel's | pastilles," *Le Courrier français*, 7 (17 Feb 1895): 10. BnF, Paris

Take offense? Why? The reproducibility and plasticity of Beardsley's works, their adaptability, were part and parcel of an expansion strategy, deliberately deployed in France. This country Beardsley loved to visit because, as John Gray's moving recollection put it after his demise, there one could see "*si nettement.*"[22] It little mattered that Roques's gazette often reproduced the drawings in quarter-page format, mingling them with a motley content, and with inking flaws that reproductions show. What mattered was that he published them. A strong aesthetic and ideological standpoint underpins this constraint-free use of images: to address the greatest number possible and educate the eye of the man in the street, as Beardsley's manifesto on the modern poster claimed.[23] Such reuse takes advantage of the forms' malleability in a press itself pliable and highly plastic. A case in point is the regular Beardsley spoofs in *Punch*. By parodying the artist, they propagated the "Beardsley style" and amplified it.[24] For an artistic personality such as Beardsley's, which changed styles with a speed rarely seen, and quickly turned every lit straw into a bonfire, such open-mindedness, if not open incitement, was crucial.

Adaptable, critical, and probably involving the draughtsman himself, the *Courrier français* reproduction of Beardsley's work was exceptional, and in terms of its flexibility and scope, outshone Beardsley's controlled presence in the British press. Roques's presentation of Beardsley was not devoid of blunders. He misconstrued an allusion by Beardsley to the novel he planned to write based on Wagner's *Tannhäuser*, and read Walter Sickert's signature on the artist's portrait as "sickest" ("*très malade*"), attributing the piece to Beardsley himself.[25] Later on, Franz Blei and Carl Sternheim's *Hyperion* would repeat the slip-up and publish this portrait as a work by Beardsley, made in Paris for *Le Courrier français*, which proves the pull of the Montmartre weekly to Viennese and German aesthetic circles.[26] The Russian *Mir iskusstva* reproduced the gaffe yet again.[27]

22 Gray, "Aubrey Beardsley," 68.

23 Beardsley, "The Art of the Hoarding," *The New Review*, 11 (July 1894): 53–55, collected in A. E. Gallatin, *Aubrey Beardsley: Catalogue of Drawings and Bibliography* (New York: The Grolier Club, 1945), 110–11, and in *Decadent Writings of Aubrey Beardsley*, ed. by Sasha Dovzhyk and Simon Wilson, MHRA Critical Texts 10, Jewelled Tortoise 78 (Cambridge: Modern Humanities Research Association, 2022), 188–89.

24 Further on this, see Chapter 3 and Chapter 4.

25 Roques, "Les artistes anglais: M. Beardsley," 8. Sickert's portrait of Beardsley, a sketch, is signed above right. The caption however reads: "Aubrey Beardsley, by himself" ("*Aubrey Beardsley, par lui-même*").

26 See *Selbstbildnis von Aubrey Beardsley aus dem Jahre 1894, Hyperion: Eine Zweimontasschrift*, 2 (1908), last plate but one with the indication: "*in Paris gezeichnet* für den 'Courier français' [*sic*]."

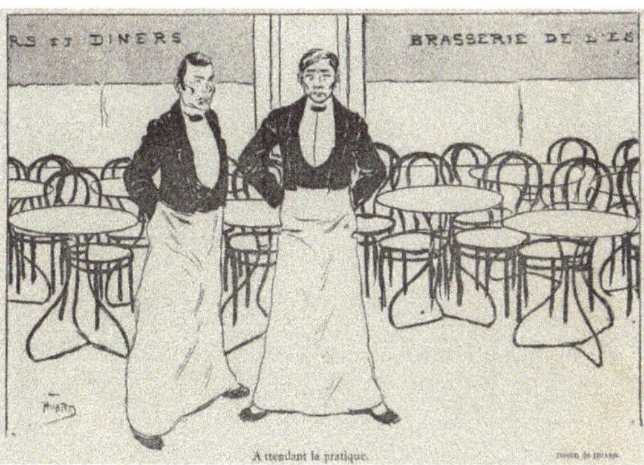

Fig. 5.8 Charles Huard, *En attendant la pratique* (*Waiting for the client*), repr. *Le Courrier français*, 10 (8 Mar 1896): 2 (detail). BnF, Paris

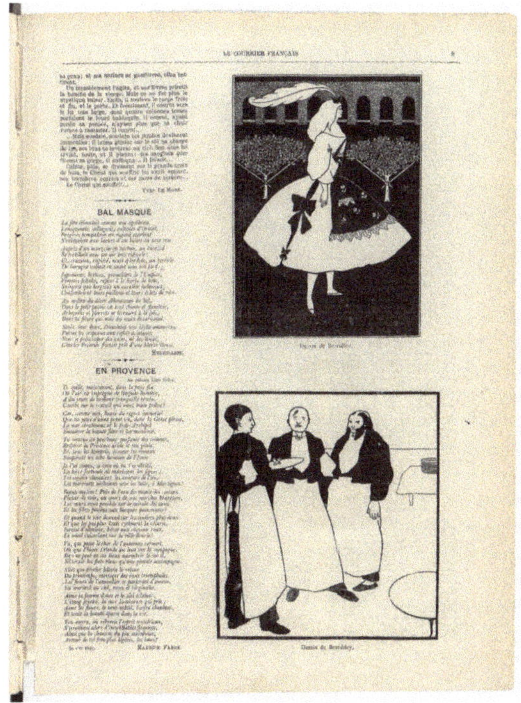

LE COURRIER FRANÇAIS

BAL MASQUÉ

EN PROVENCE

Fig. 5.9 Aubrey Beardsley, *Garçons de Café* (by June 1894), repr. *The Yellow Book*, 2 (July 1894): 93, catalogued as *Les Garçons du Café Royal*, repr. *Le Courrier français*, 6 (10 Feb 1895): 9. Above, reproduction of Beardsley, *The Slippers of Cinderella* (by 27 June 1894), MSL coll., Delaware, repr. *The Yellow Book* 2 (July 1894): 95 (Zatlin 899). BnF, Paris

27 O. Mek Koll', "Obri Berdslei," *Mir iskusstva*, 3:7–8 (1900): 84 (in Russian, without mentioning *Le Courrier français*).

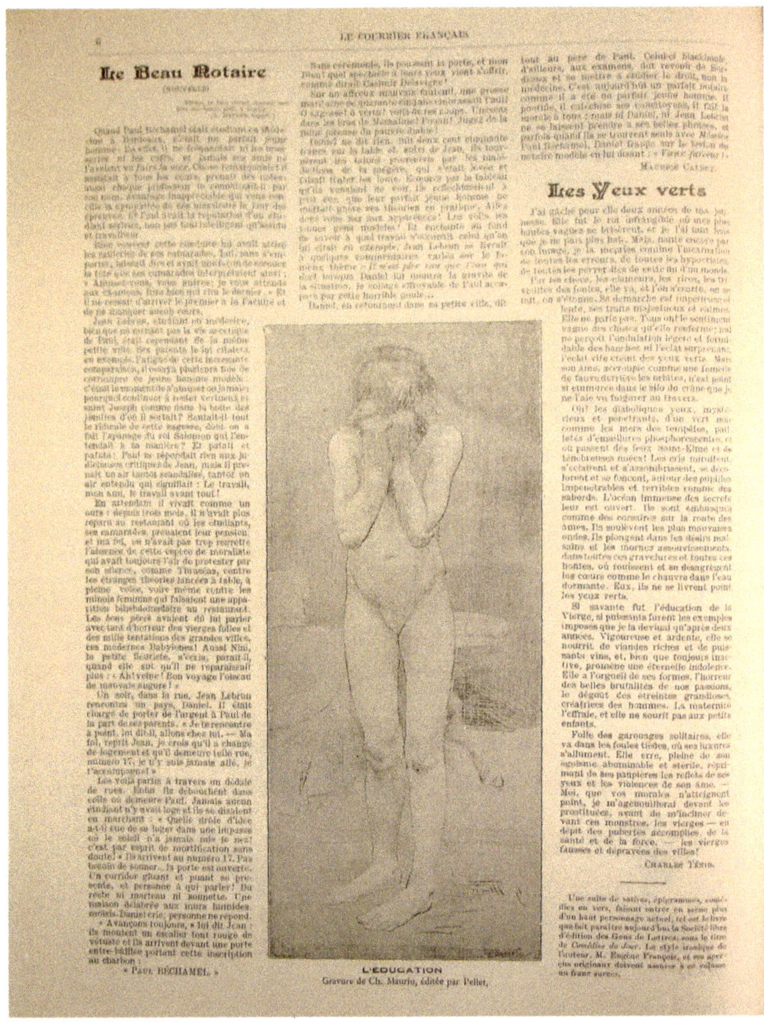

LE COURRIER FRANÇAIS

Le Beau Notaire

Les Yeux verts

L'ÉDUCATION

Gravure de Ch. Maurin, éditée par Pellet.

Fig. 5.10 Charles Maurin, Untitled plate from the series *L'Éducation sentimentale* (Gustave Pellet, 1896) repr. as *L'Éducation*, *Le Courrier français*, 23 (7 June 1896): 6. BnF, Paris

Still, *Le Courrier français* acted as a French podium and a mirror. Thanks to it, Beardsley influenced a number of French artists: Charles Huard's drawing *En attendant la pratique* (Fig. 5.8) was surely inspired by Beardsley's *Les Garçons du Café Royal* (Zatlin 898), published in the second volume of the *Yellow Book* as *Garçons de Café* (Fig. 5.9). *L'Éducation sentimentale* by Charles Maurin, a set of coloured etchings and dry-points issued by Gustave Pellet in 1896 with plates detailed in *Le Courrier français*, may have borrowed the idea of the title and the feminisation of the subject from Beardsley. In Beardsley's drawing, an old madam is educating a lewd young girl (see Fig. 5.4). In Maurin's, a young woman grooms a little girl, in delicate nudity, foregrounded in "a very remarkable sensual atmosphere."[28] In two of these engravings, the mother figure has disappeared. The print in which the naked child stands, her face hidden in her hands in an attitude of deep sorrow (Fig. 5.10a–b), has a rather blatant meaning in a journal in which painters like Adolphe Willette and Jean-Louis Forain overtly criticised the abuse of girls.[29] Yet Beardsley himself may have been inspired by continental artists, and Jacques Lethève has related his *Wagnerites* and *Garçons du Café Royal* to wood engravings by Félix Vallotton.[30]

Periodical Networking: *Le Courrier français* and the *Savoy*

Transfers, circulation of images, and extensive use of media formed the basis of the artist's strategy for self-promotion. As we saw in the previous chapter, reproductions of Beardsley's work challenge the supposedly watertight partition between large-circulation periodicals and art and literature reviews. The artificial divide is likely based more on the presumptions and constructs of literary history than on reality. This is certainly the case in France. From February 1896, Roques's weekly became the outlet for the *Savoy*, the aesthete art and literature journal, newly founded in London with Beardsley as art editor and Arthur Symons as literary editor. Once the *Savoy* had been introduced,[31] *Le Courrier français* regularly announced its contents and reproduced drawings, including those by Beardsley. A prose poem by Lautrec bears the inscription "Pour mon ami Aubrey Beardsley" as a tribute.[32]

28 *Charles Maurin, un symboliste du réel, textes de Maurice Fréchuret*, ed. by Gilles Grandjean (Lyon: Fage éditions; Le Puy-en-Velay: Musée Crozatier, 2006), 79: "*une atmosphère sensuelle très remarquable*." The print has sometimes be arbitrarily named *La Pudeur* (*Bashfulness*).

29 A lovely print of the original etching and drypoint with different coloured inks on pale green coloured paper may be seen here: https://www.navigart.fr/MAMC-saint-etienne-collections/artwork/charles-maurin-petite-fille-debout-nue-le-visage-cache-dans-les-mains-240000000005197

30 Lethève, "Aubrey Beardsley et la France," 347, fig. 5.

31 Gabriel de Lautrec, "Une nouvelle revue," *Le Courrier français*, 5 (2 Feb 1896): 8–9.

32 Lautrec, "Pour un Démon," *Le Courrier français*, 7 (14 Feb 1897): 6.

Shipments to Lautrec from Leonard Smithers, Beardsley's and the *Savoy*'s new publisher, were regular.[33]

One might be tempted to think that the bold drawings and spicy literature favoured by Roques reflected a bond with Smithers, notorious for his collection of erotica and books traded under the counter, disparaged by a conservative Britain, and known for having once displayed in his window the provocative notice "Smut is cheap today." Yet the artist's choice of both Roques and Smithers guaranteed above all freedom of expression. Rejected by John Lane, the rising and cautious *Yellow Book* publisher, Beardsley had readily been sponsored by Smithers. James G. Nelson's fine study has shown the central role Smithers played in promoting the avant-garde in prudish Britain.[34] Similarly, despite his opportunism, Roques was a patron of the avant-garde and a virtuoso of cultural networks.

As it happened, there was nothing particularly objectionable or controversial about Beardsley's drawings in *Le Courrier français* during his second phase of involvement. They were representative of his most beautiful and fine graphic style, the plates for Pope's heroic-comic masterpiece *The Rape of the Lock*. In May 1896, Lautrec gave the first French description of this book he had just received,[35] and which he may have lent to Jarry. "Du pays des dentelles," Jarry's splendid text inspired by Beardsley's plates after Pope, was published two years later in the *Mercure de France*. A central drawing in this series, *Le Rapt de la boucle*, an accurate translation of *The Rape of the Lock* (Zatlin 982), featured in *Le Courrier français* (Fig. 5.11), as did several other pieces: the cover of the first issue of the *Savoy*; Beardsley's mischievous self-portrait *A Footnote* (see Fig. 3.4); the drawing *L'Ascension de Sainte Rose de Lima* (*The Ascension of Saint Rose of Lima*, Zatlin 1005), taken from the first version of Beardsley's unfinished novel *Under the Hill*, published in instalments in the English magazine; and the plate *The Coiffing* (Zatlin 1009) accompanying Beardsley's poem "The Ballad of a Barber."[36]

---

33 *The Letters of Aubrey Beardsley*, ed. by Henry Maas, J. L. Duncan, and W. G. Good (London: Cassell, 1970), 231, letter dated 22 Dec 1896 to Smithers: "You generally send him [G. de Lautrec] (on account of the *Courrier Français*) a copy of my books."

34 See James G. Nelson, *Publisher to the Decadents: Leonard Smithers in the Careers of Beardsley, Wilde, Dowson* (University Park, Penn.: Pennsylvania State University Press, 2000).

35 Lautrec, "Envois de Londres," *Le Courrier français*, 22 (31 May 1896): 5–6.

36 *Le Courrier français*, 5 (2 Feb 1896): 9 (cover of the *Savoy*, no. 1); 20 (10 May 1896): 9 (*A Footnote*); 22 (31 May 1896): 5 (*The Ascension of Saint Rose of Lima*) and 6 (*The*

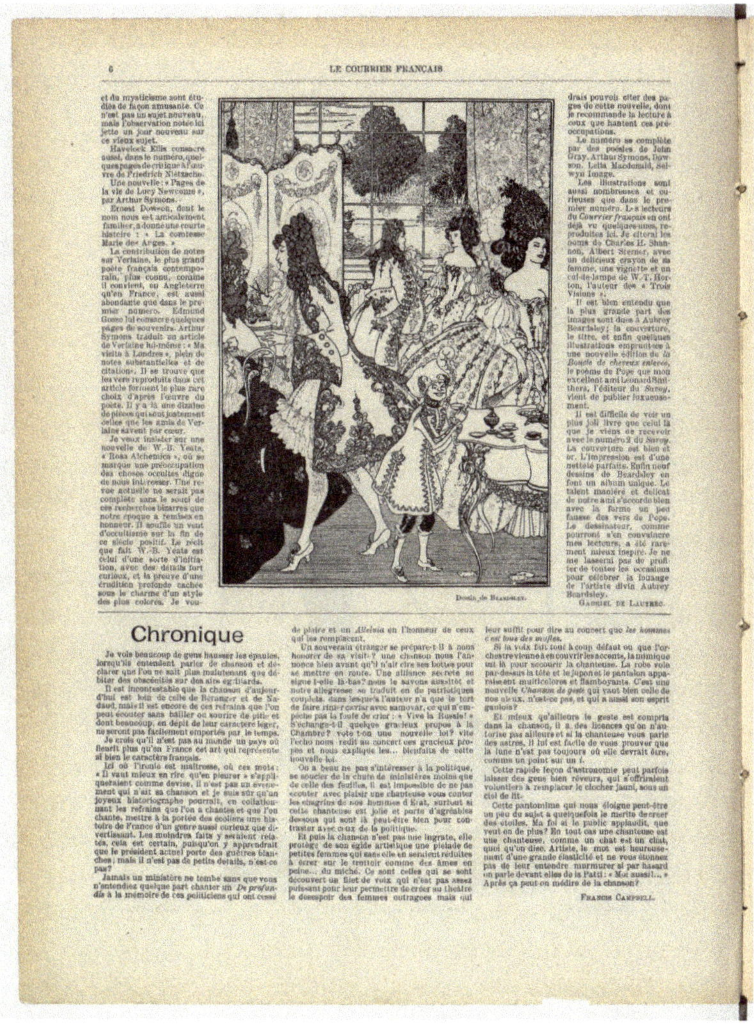

6 LE COURRIER FRANÇAIS

et du mysticisme sont étudiés de façon amusante. Ce n'est pas un sujet nouveau, mais l'observation notée ici jette un jour nouveau sur ce vieux sujet.

Havelock Ellis consacre aussi, dans le numéro, quelques pages de critique à l'œuvre de Friedrich Nietzsche.

Une nouvelle : « Pages de la vie de Lucy Newcome », par Arthur Symons.

Ernest Dowson, dont le nom nous est amicalement familier, a donné une courte histoire : « La comtesse Marie des Arges. »

La contribution de notes sur Verlaine, le plus grand poète français contemporain, plus connu, comme il convient, en Angleterre qu'en France, est aussi abondante que dans le premier numéro. Edmund Gosse lui consacre quelques pages de souvenirs. Arthur Symons traduit un article de Verlaine lui-même : « Ma visite à Londres », plein de notes substantielles et de citations. Il se trouve que les vers reproduits dans cet article forment le plus rare choix d'après l'œuvre du poète. Il y a là une dizaine de pièces qui sont justement celles que les amis de Verlaine savent par cœur.

Je veux insister sur une nouvelle de W.-B. Yeats, « Rosa Alchemica », où se marque une préoccupation des choses occultes digne de nous intéresser. Une revue actuelle ne serait pas complète sans le souci de ces recherches bizarres que notre époque a remises en honneur. Il souffle un vent d'occultisme sur la fin de ce siècle positif. Le récit que fait W.-B. Yeats est celui d'une sorte d'initiation, avec des détails fort curieux, et la preuve d'une érudition profonde cachée sous le charme d'un style des plus colorés. Je voudrais pouvoir citer des pages de cette nouvelle, dont je recommande la lecture à ceux que hantent ces préoccupations.

Le numéro se complète par des poésies de John Gray, Arthur Symons, Dowson, Leila Macdonald, Selwyn Image.

Les illustrations sont aussi nombreuses et curieuses que dans le premier numéro. Les lecteurs du *Courrier français* en ont déjà vu quelques-unes, reproduites ici. Je citerai les noms de Charles H. Shannon, Albert Sterner, avec un délicieux crayon de sa femme, une vignette et un cul-de-lampe de W.-T. Horton, l'auteur des « Trois Visions ».

Il est bien entendu que la plus grande part des images sont dues à Aubrey Beardsley ; la couverture, le titre, et enfin quelques illustrations empruntées à une nouvelle édition de *la Boucle de cheveux enlevée*, le poème de Pope que mon excellent ami Leonard Smithers, l'éditeur du *Savoy*, vient de publier luxueusement.

Il est difficile de voir un plus joli livre que celui là que je viens de recevoir avec le numéro 2 du *Savoy*. La couverture est bleu et or. L'impression est d'une netteté parfaite. Enfin neuf dessins de Beardsley en font un album unique. Le talent maniéré et délicat de notre ami s'accorde bien avec la forme un peu fausse des vers de Pope. Le dessinateur, comme pourront s'en convaincre mes lecteurs, a été rarement mieux inspiré. Je ne me lasserai pas de profiter de toutes les occasions pour célébrer la louange de l'artiste divin Aubrey Beardsley.

GABRIEL DE LAUTREC.

Dessin de BEARDSLEY.

Chronique

Je vois beaucoup de gens hausser les épaules, lorsqu'ils entendent parler de chanson et déclarer que l'on ne sait plus maintenant que débiter des obscénités sur des airs egrillards.

Il est incontestable que la chanson d'aujourd'hui est loin de celle de Béranger et de Nadaud, mais il est encore de ces refrains que l'on peut écouter sans bâiller ou sourire de pitié et dont beaucoup, en dépit de leur caractère léger, ne seront pas facilement emportés par le temps.

Je crois qu'il n'est pas au monde un pays où fleurit plus qu'en France cet art qui représente si bien le caractère français.

Ici où l'ironie est maîtresse, où ces mots : « Il vaut mieux en rire qu'en pleurer » s'appliqueraient comme devise, il n'est pas un événement qui n'ait sa chanson et je suis sûr qu'un joyeux historiographe pourrait, en collationnant les refrains que l'on a chantés et que l'on chante, mettre à la portée des écoliers une histoire de France d'un genre aussi curieux que divertissant. Les moindres faits y seraient relatés, cela est certain, puisqu'on y apprendrait que le président actuel porte des guêtres blanches ; mais il n'est pas de petits détails, n'est-ce pas?

Jamais un ministère ne tombe sans que vous n'entendiez quelque part chanter un *De profundis* à la mémoire de ces politiciens qui ont cessé de plaire et un *Alleluia* en l'honneur de ceux qui les remplacent.

Un souverain étranger se prépare-t-il à nous honorer de sa visite? une chanson nous l'annonce bien avant qu'il n'ait ciré ses bottes pour se mettre en route. Une alliance secrète se signe-t-elle là-bas? nous le savons aussitôt et notre allégresse se traduit en de patriotiques couplets, dans lesquels l'auteur n'a que le tort de faire rimer caviar avec samovar, ce qui n'empêche pas la foule de crier : « Vive la Russie! » S'échange-t-il quelques gracieux propos à la Chambre? vote-t-on une nouvelle loi? vite l'écho nous redit au concert ces gracieux propos et nous explique les... bienfaits de cette nouvelle loi.

On a beau ne pas s'intéresser à la politique, se soucier de la chute de ministères moins que de celle des feuilles, il est impossible de ne pas écouter avec plaisir une chanteuse vous conter les chagrins de nos hommes d'État, surtout si cette chanteuse est jolie et porte d'agréables dessous qui sont là peut-être bien pour contraster avec ceux de la politique.

Et puis la chanson n'est pas une ingrate, elle protège de son égide artistique une pléiade de petites femmes qui sans elle en seraient réduites à errer sur le trottoir comme des âmes en peine... du miché. Ce sont celles qui se sont découvert un filet de voix qui n'est pas assez puissant pour leur permettre de créer au théâtre le désespoir des femmes outragées mais qui leur suffit pour dire au concert que *les hommes c'est tous des mufles*.

Si la voix fait tout à coup défaut ou que l'orchestre vienne à en couvrir les accents, la mimique est là pour secourir la chanteuse. La robe vole par-dessus la tête et le jupon et le pantalon apparaissent multicolores et flamboyants. C'est une nouvelle *Chanson de geste* qui vaut bien celle de nos aïeux, n'est-ce pas, et qui a aussi son esprit gaulois?

Et mieux qu'ailleurs le geste est compris dans la chanson, il a des licences qu'on n'autorise pas ailleurs et si la chanteuse vous parle des astres, il lui est facile de vous prouver que la lune n'est pas toujours où elle devrait être, comme un point sur un i.

Cette rapide leçon d'astronomie peut parfois laisser des gens bien rêveurs, qui s'offriraient volontiers à remplacer le clocher jauni, sous un ciel de lit.

Cette pantomime qui nous éloigne peut-être un peu du sujet a quelquefois le mérite de créer des étoiles. Ma foi si le public applaudit, que veut-on de plus? En tout cas une chanteuse est une chanteuse, comme un chat est un chat, quoi qu'on dise. Artiste, le mot est heureusement d'une grande élasticité et ne vous étonnez pas de leur entendre murmurer si par hasard on parle devant elles de la Patti : « Moi aussi!... » Après ça peut-on médire de la chanson?

FRANCIS CAMPBELL.

Fig. 5.11 Aubrey Beardsley, *Le Rapt de la boucle* [*The Rape of the Lock* (by late Feb 1896), priv. coll., New York (Zatlin 982)], repr. *Le Courrier français*, 22 (31 May 1896): 6. BnF, Paris

It was therefore not avant-garde art and literature reviews that welcomed Beardsley in France, as one might have expected, but a weekly of broad circulation and dubious reputation, promoting graphic innovation. If Beardsley's own periodicals, the *Yellow Book* and the *Savoy*, welcomed and publicised modern art and literature, as did their French peers,

---

Rape of the Lock); 27 (5 July 1896): 11 (*The Ballad of a Barber*, taken from the July issue of the *Savoy*, reproduced without the poem).

the correspondence one might have expected between them is not confirmed. Media promotion was the keyword, and both Roques and Beardsley benefited from it in turn. Additionally, *Le Courrier français* also enabled Beardsley to feature alongside those who practised an art as demanding, innovative and disruptive as his own in France: Adolphe Willette, Jean-Louis Forain, Félix Vallotton, Jules Chéret, Armand Rassenfosse, Louis Legrand, and Henri de Toulouse-Lautrec for a time, as well as the American Will Bradley.

Baffling Associations

From a present-day standpoint, it might be assumed that French avant-garde journals would have followed *Le Courrier français* and discussed Beardsley's art much earlier. Yet, only in April 1897 did *L'Ermitage* grant him an article in his lifetime, three years after *Le Courrier français*, thanks to Henry-D. Davray.[37] A key translator of English texts, Davray wrote influentially in the *Mercure de France* on British literature, and spent time with Beardsley, whom he trained in oral French. An exclusive publication, *L'Ermitage* was in that phase open to Anglophone input (maybe encouraged by Stuart Merrill and Francis Vielé-Griffin, two Franco-American authors on its editorial team) and to images (under the artistic leadership of Jacques Des Gachons). In his *Ermitage* article on Beardsley, Davray himself aspired to comprehensive criticism, far from the hubbub, judging and defending a work of art because it is admirable though it may not please all. His efforts at completeness drew on a recent publication, Beardsley's album *A Book of Fifty Drawings* (issued by Smithers), which made gauging the artist's diverse styles possible. Davray's article included a single illustration, highlighted as a full-page plate, the openwork medallion concluding Ernest Dowson's *The Pierrot of the Minute* (Fig. 5.12, Zatlin 1043), on which Davray also commented in the *Mercure de France*.[38] Further exchanges with Davray show Beardsley's strong desire to participate in the illustrated edition of *L'Ermitage* in 1898.[39] His death prevented him from so doing.

37 Henry-D. Davray, "L'Art d'Aubrey Beardsley," *L'Ermitage*, 14 (Apr 1897): 253–61.
38 Davray, "Lettres anglaises," *Mercure de France*, 22:90 (June 1897): 582.
39 *The Letters of Aubrey Beardsley*, 419 (letter dated 7 Jan 1898): "Certainly I shall be only too pleased to let you have something for the new *Ermitage*."

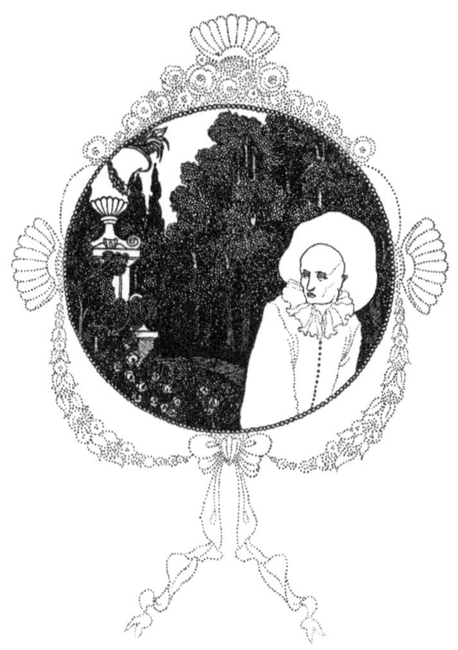

Fig. 5.12 Aubrey Beardsley, *Cul-de-lampe* (12–16 Nov 1896), Lessing J. Rosenwald coll., Library of Congress, Washington, DC, repr. as final plate in *Pierrot of the Minute*, 44. PE coll.

In the meantime, the artist had contributed to the Salon des Cent organised by yet another avant-garde review, *La Plume*, and several of his posters had appeared in a *Plume* special issue on this new art form that had launched a craze.[40] As shows a 13 August 1893 autograph receipt signed by Edward Bella,[41] he had made a colour cover for *La Plume*, which was never published.[42] Several French books in a variety of genres had

40 "Les affiches étrangères," *La Plume*, 155 (1 Oct 1895): 410 (*Affiche anglaise pour la galerie Goupil, à Londres*), 424 (Affiche pour la *Librairie Children's book* [*sic*]); "L'Affiche anglaise," *ibid.*, 428 (*Affiche "Autonym" pour une librairie*); "Supplément," 457 (affiche pour *A Comedy of Sighs!*), 459 (*Affiche anglaise*). Several of these will find their way into Uzanne's *Les Évolutions du bouquin*.

41 Edward Bella owned with his brother the paper firm "J. & E. Bella." He was a poster enthusiast, organiser of poster exhibitions, and the London correspondent for *La Plume*'s Salon des Cent. Further on Bella, see Philipp Leu, "Les revues littéraires et artistiques, 1890–1900. Questions de patrimonialisation et de numérisation," 2 vols. (PhD diss., Université Paris-Saclay, 2016), I, 103, n. 257, https://theses.hal.science/tel-03606156, and Zatlin, *Catalogue Raisonné*, II, 185, 191 and 194.

42 *The Gallatin Beardsley Collection in the Princeton University Library. A Catalogue Compiled by A. E. Gallatin and Alexander D. Wainwright* (Princeton, NJ: Princeton

mentioned him. Gabriel Mourey, the correspondent and manager-to-be of the *Studio* in France (from 1899), introduced him in *Passé le détroit*, his promenade on new art discoveries beyond the Channel.[43] Jean Lorrain mentioned him in his Parisian chronicles: commenting on the Parisian staging of Wilde's *Salomé*, he acclaims no other décor and costume designer than Beardsley, Wilde's "designated illustrator."[44] Following a Lautrec quote, Lorrain stressed the artist's "frail and tormented grace, the light and sometimes caricatural sensuality."[45] Octave Uzanne, who had met Beardsley three years earlier in London, commended him in *Les Évolutions du bouquin*, reproduced three drawings (praising the controversial *Comedy of Sighs!* poster, see Fig. 4.2), and announced a promising future.[46] Keen on new book genres and book design, he further introduced Beardsley in *L'Art dans la décoration extérieure des livres* with five covers and book bindings reproduced either in-text or as inserted plates.[47]

Unlike the Italian articles discussed in the previous chapter, which often included all sorts of biographical information at the expense of Beardsley's art – with ruminations on the British education system –, none of these numerous mentions in the French press offered witty or troubling comments on the artist's life. Except for a few sparse

---

University Library, 1952), 18.

43 Gabriel Mourey, "Quelques-uns et leurs œuvres: Aubrey Beardsley," in Mourey, *Passé le détroit: La Vie et l'art à Londres* (Paris: Paul Ollendorff, 1895), 268–71.

44 Jean Lorrain, "Pall-Mall semaine," *Le Journal* (16 Feb 1896): 2: *"l'illustrateur désigné pour les œuvres de Wilde."*

45 *Ibid.*: *"la grâce frêle et tourmentée, la sensualité légère et parfois caricaturale."* See also Lorrain, *Poussières de Paris* (Paris: Fayard frères, 1896), 150. Lorrain would also comment on Beardsley in *Poussières de Paris* (Paris: Paul Ollendorff, 1902), 100, reproducing "Pall-Mall Semaine," *Le Journal* (25 June 1899).

46 Octave Uzanne, *Les Évolutions du Bouquin. La Nouvelle Bibliopolis: Voyage d'un novateur au pays des néo-icono-bibliomanes, lithographies en couleurs et marges décoratives par H. P. Dillon* (Paris: Henri Floury, 1897), 41, 148, 151, 154, 161, 170, with four reproductions (two of which posters). See https://gallica.bnf.fr/ark:/12148/bpt6k8560074/f11.planchecontact

47 Uzanne, *L'Art dans la décoration extérieure des livres en France et à l'étranger, les couvertures illustrées, les cartonnages d'éditeurs, la reliure d'art* (Paris: Société Française d'Éditions d'Art, L. Henry May, 1898), 105 (cover for the *Savoy*), 108–109, 113, 147 (spine and front cover for *Le Morte Darthur*), 151 (binding for *A Book of Fifty Drawings*); insert plates between 96–97 (faun reading to a young lady), 104–105 (title page for the *Savoy*), 152–53 (blue printed boards on blue cloth for *Pierrot!* by H. de Vere Stacpoole). See https://gallica.bnf.fr/ark:/12148/bpt6k96299956/f8.planchecontact

allusions to his youth, comments focused on his art accomplishments. Art criticism prevailed in France, unlike in Italy, where personal data was mixed with limited comments on the art and rumour harvested from other magazines (although French newspapers were not above reporting scandalous anecdotes). It was only on Beardsley's death that French obituaries and posthumous celebrations led to a motley concert of biographical articles.

Tribute and Din

Obituaries are a tricky business. Two obituaries, closely following on Beardsley's demise that I discovered in the press and ascribed to their authors, were by men of taste who knew the artist well. The artist Jacques-Émile Blanche (only signing by his initials), who had painted a splendid 1895 portrait of Beardsley, penned the first in the supplement of *La Gazette des beaux-arts*.[48] Octave Uzanne, under the pseudonym Isis, contributed the second on the front page of *Le Figaro*, a widely distributed daily.[49] Curiously, their thoughtful tributes were offset by a racist anecdote on the front page of the *Journal des débats* a fortnight later: a poster by Beardsley is bought at a low price by an American, who then offers it to another as a specimen of modern art. Although this man takes the poster, he despises it, and uses it to wrap his dirty linen to take to the laundrette. The Chinese laundryman discovers the poster, marvels at it, hangs it up and has it admired. From one buyer to the next, its price rises to 500 dollars (2,500 francs). It ends up in the home of a wealthy Chinese gentleman in San Francisco, above an altar where a lamp burns night and day. "New prospects open up for misunderstood artists," concludes dryly the (unsigned) article.[50] Less than a month after the artist's demise, such a yarn sounds so inappropriate that neither prudery nor

48 J.-E. B., "Aubrey Beardsley," *La Chronique des arts et de la curiosité. Supplément à la Gazette des beaux-arts*, 13 (26 Mar 1898): 111.

49 Isis [Octave Uzanne], "Paris partout," *Le Figaro*, 89 (30 Mar 1898): 1. Attributed thanks to La Cagoule. Octave Uzanne, *Visions de notre heure. Choses et gens qui passent, notations d'art, de littérature et de vie pittoresque* (Paris: Henri Floury, 1899), 95–97, same text. Most of the chronicles included in this book were published in *L'Écho de Paris*, yet not the one on Beardsley.

50 "Au jour le jour," *Journal des débats*, 100 (11 Apr 1898): 1: "*Des horizons nouveaux s'ouvrent pour les artistes incompris.*"

narrow-mindedness exonerates it. The conventional French press had a field day over it, propagating it from one paper to the next.[51] The din went on, mocking the work in the absence of the self-jeering artist.

The anecdote had reached the French press from the British dailies and must be apocryphal. First published in the *Westminster Gazette* in August 1894, amid the Beardsley boom, it was repeated there on 17 March 1898, and relayed by the *Daily Mail* two days after the artist's death.[52] Its coarseness speaks volumes of the principles guiding press journalism at the time. Beardsley's oeuvre may have taken advantage of the uproar of outrage. Outrage turned against him at his departure. It took a year for the *Journal des débats*, and the publication of a new book of his drawings, to concede a fairer article to Beardsley, likened to Pierrot, "gay, mocking, suffering, doomed to die young."[53] The image springs from the work itself by way of the avant-garde journals. And it looks at an impressive future ahead albeit its meaning.

Pierrot Beside Himself: Exit Scenarios

The *Mercure de France* and *La Revue blanche* commemorated Beardsley in unison. The *Mercure* had announced Beardsley's passing already in April in a dense unsigned paragraph recalling the most important phases of his style.[54] The May 1898 *Mercure* issue turned to a plural tribute: Davray translated Wilde's "Ballad of Reading Gaol," by then in its sixth printing, whose poignant stanzas struck a melancholic chord, while Jarry published "Du pays des dentelles" celebrating Beardsley's last *ajouré* style after *The Rape of the Lock*, under the aegis of his *Faustroll* texts.[55] Davray's article on Beardsley was the issue's major

51 *La Justice* (12–13 Apr 1898): 3; *Le Radical* (16 Apr 1898): 2; *Le Bulletin de la presse*, 4:3, 54 (21 Apr 1898): 484 (abridged).

52 See Matthew Sturgis, *Aubrey Beardsley: A Biography* (London: Harper Collins Publishers, 1998), 121 (in note).

53 Charles Legras, "Au jour le jour: Aubrey Beardsley," *Journal des débats*, 87 (29 Mar 1899): 1: "*gai, moqueur, souffrant, destiné à mourir jeune.*"

54 "Échos," *Mercure de France*, 26:100 (Apr 1898): 335.

55 For an analysis of Jarry's tropes and the ways he gathers inspiration from Beardsley's work, see my article "Jarry et Beardsley," *L'Étoile-absinthe. Les Cahiers iconographiques de la Société des amis d'Alfred Jarry*, 95–96 (2002): 49–67, http://alfredjarry.fr/amisjarry/fichiers_ea/etoile_absinthe_095_96reduit.pdf

accolade, drafting the artist's intellectual portrait.[56] It was not illustrated but turned out to be almost as good as any illustration at proffering a poignant image of the artist's passing. Davray opened it and closed it in English and in italics, using at the opening Beardsley's full-length caption to *The Death of Pierrot* from the October 1896 *Savoy* (Zatlin 1015), and a few fragments of the same in his final words:

> As the dawn broke, Pierrot fell into his last sleep. Then upon tiptoe, silently up the stair, noiselessly into the room, came the comedians Arlecchino, Pantaleone, il Dottore, and Colombina, who with much love carried away upon their shoulders, the white frocked clown of Bergamo; whither, we know not.[57]

Both the caption and the absent plate staged the artist's exit, forlorn in his ultimate bunk, miles away from the cheek and vivacity of his mischievous portraits. Misfortune would have it that such a melodramatic curtain was at complete odds with the artist's own intentions, even though he had multiplied his Pierrot self-portraits from the very beginning. An early identification of the artist as the white-faced pining clown, in which Decadence saw the image of the poet, featured in an August 1893 letter to Robert Ross. Beardsley asked him for a prologue in verse for a projected book, *Masques*, which never materialised. It would have been spoken by Pierrot, i.e., himself.[58] A serious health crisis in 1896 surely encouraged the affinity. Yet Beardsley had clear reservations about associating himself with the potentially facile and overly maudlin image of Pierrot. He had deferred publishing *The Death of Pierrot* in the *Savoy*, unwilling for it to feature as an epitaph.[59] He would have been "seriously distressed" to see it published on its own, without any other accompanying drawings. It would have looked, he admitted to Smithers, like a confession of helplessness and illness.[60]

The *zeitgeist*, however, worked against him: Pierrot's enigmatic sadness and loneliness had grown hugely popular both in England and

56 *Mercure de France*, 26:101 (May 1898) includes Oscar Wilde, "Ballade de la geôle de Reading," 350–70, translated by Davray; Alfred Jarry, "Gestes et opinions du Dr Faustroll, pataphysicien: V. Du pays des dentelles, à Aubrey Beardsley," 399–400; Davray, "Aubrey Beardsley," 485–91.

57 *The Savoy*, 6 (Oct 1896): 32–33; *Mercure de France*, 26:101 (May 1898): 485.

58 *The Letters of Aubrey Beardsley*, 51.

59 See Zatlin, *Catalogue Raisonné*, II, 284.

60 *The Letters of Aubrey Beardsley*, 143 (ca. 11 July 1896 letter to Smithers).

in France.[61] In 1896, Lane published a series of four novels, "Pierrot's Library," with all volumes in identical front, back, and spine designs (but different colour by volume), title pages, front and back endpapers conceived by Beardsley (Zatlin 958–62). In 1897, Beardsley also designed the binding, ornaments, and plates for Ernest Dowson's melancholy fantasy, *The Pierrot of the Minute* issued by Smithers (Zatlin, 1040–43). The *Cul-de-lampe* for this shows a sad, aged Pierrot leaving a lush garden, the oval-shaped medallion set in an elaborate *ajouré* frame of garlands and roses with a mirror effect (see Fig. 5.12, Zatlin 1043). The *Cul-de-lampe* was no tailpiece but an ostentatious final image, a decorative oculus through which Pierrot looked back at the entire text itself.[62] Davray had publicised it in France as an openwork ornament set within his *Ermitage* article on Beardsley, the only text on the English artist to appear in a French avant-garde journal in his lifetime. A nearly blank page introduced it, bearing only its new title in French, *Le Pierrot d'aujourd'hui* (*The Pierrot of Today*).[63] White became Pierrot and blank announced his impending silence. Such an arrangement set the tone for Beardsley's farewell chorus. Davray's article in the *Mercure de France* did the rest.

With the help of the French press, *The Death of Pierrot* ended up becoming an inadvertent self-portrait and one of Beardsley's most iconic images. The drawing depicts several *commedia dell'arte* characters tiptoeing towards Pierrot on his deathbed, a finger against their lips (Fig. 5.13, Zatlin 1015). Pathos is at its highest but, nevertheless, impertinence is still present. The scrawny figure of Pierrot, lost under a swelling bedspread and an oversized bed, is the ultimate version of *Portrait of Himself* (see Fig. 3.3) minus the mischief. Fletcher notes "a bulging forehead that suggests the fetus image [...] with a bandage for headdress round the sharp contoured features of the dead face."[64] Half of the figures beckon at an audience: the unseen spectators, and ourselves, the viewers. Death has

61 See Andrew G. Lehmann, "Pierrot and Fin de Siècle," in *Romantic Mythologies*, ed. by Ian Fletcher (London: Routledge/Kegan Paul, 1967), 209–23; Robert F. Storey, *Pierrot: A Critical History of a Mask* (Princeton, NJ: Princeton University Press, 1978); Jean de Palacio, *Pierrot fin de siècle ou Les métamorphoses d'un masque* (Paris: Séguier, 1990).

62 See Zatlin, *Catalogue Raisonné*, II, 334–35.

63 Davray, "L'Art d'Aubrey Beardsley," 257.

64 Ian Fletcher, *Aubrey Beardsley* (Boston, Mass.: Twayne Publishers, 1987), 119.

become a performance enacted on a stage-like podium. The imaginative dimension of the drawing makes art even out of ultimate demise.

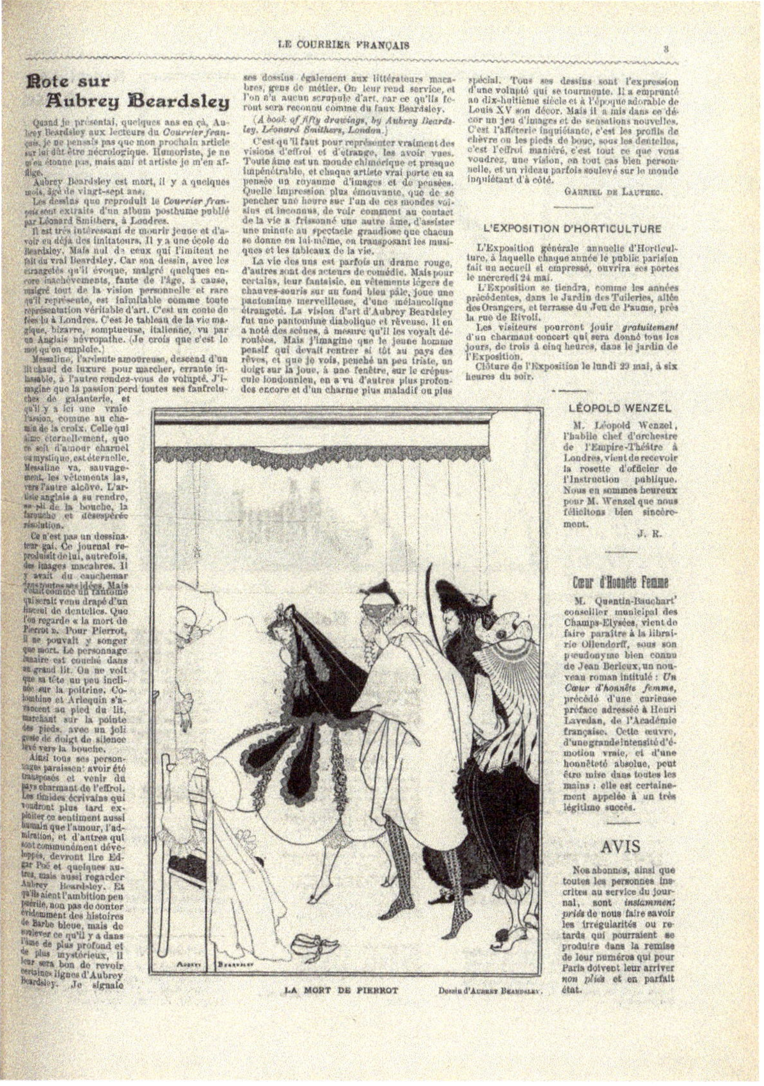

LE COURRIER FRANÇAIS 3

Note sur Aubrey Beardsley

Quand je présentai, quelques ans en çà, Aubrey Beardsley aux lecteurs du *Courrier français*, je ne pensais pas que mon prochain article sur lui dût être nécrologique. Humoriste, je ne m'en étonne pas, mais ami et artiste je m'en afflige.

Aubrey Beardsley est mort, il y a quelques mois, âgé de vingt-sept ans.

Les dessins que reproduit le *Courrier français* sont extraits d'un album posthume publié par Léonard Smithers, à Londres.

Il est très intéressant de mourir jeune et d'avoir eu déjà des imitateurs. Il y a une école de Beardsley. Mais nul de ceux qui l'imitent ne fait du vrai Beardsley. Car son dessin, avec les étrangetés qu'il évoque, malgré quelques encore inachèvements, faute de l'âge, à cause, malgré tout de la vision personnelle et rare qu'il représente, est inimitable comme toute représentation véritable d'art. C'est un conte de fées lu à Londres. C'est le tableau de la vie magique, bizarre, somptueuse, italienne, vu par un Anglais névropathe. (Je crois que c'est le mot qu'on emploie.)

Messaline, l'ardente amoureuse, descend d'un lit chaud de luxure pour marcher, errante inlassable, à l'autre rendez-vous de volupté. J'imagine que la passion perd toutes ses fanfreluches de galanterie, et qu'il y a ici une vraie Passion, comme au chemin de la croix. Celle qui aime éternellement, que ce soit d'amour charnel ou mystique, est éternelle. Messaline va, sauvagement, les vêtements las, vers l'autre alcôve. L'artiste anglais a su rendre, au pli de la bouche, la farouche et désespérée résolution.

Ce n'est pas un dessinateur gai. Ce journal reproduisit de lui, autrefois, des images macabres. Il y avait du cauchemar dans toutes ses idées. Mais c'était comme un fantôme qui serait venu drapé d'un linceul de dentelles. Que l'on regarde « la mort de Pierrot ». Pour Pierrot, il ne pouvait y songer que mort. Le personnage lunaire est couché dans un grand lit. On ne voit que sa tête un peu inclinée sur la poitrine. Colombine et Arlequin s'avancent au pied du lit, marchant sur la pointe des pieds, avec un joli geste de doigt de silence levé vers la bouche.

Ainsi tous ses personnages paraissent avoir été transposés et venir du pays charmant de l'effroi. Les timides écrivains qui voudront plus tard exploiter ce sentiment aussi humain que l'amour, l'admiration, et d'autres qui sont communément développés, devront lire Edgar Poë et quelques autres, mais aussi regarder Aubrey Beardsley. Et qu'ils aient l'ambition peu puérile, non pas de conter évidemment des histoires de Barbe bleue, mais de soulever ce qu'il y a dans l'âme de plus profond et de plus mystérieux, il leur sera bon de revoir certaines lignes d'Aubrey Beardsley. Je signale ses dessins également aux littérateurs macabres, gens de métier. On leur rend service, et l'on n'a aucun scrupule d'art, car ce qu'ils feront sera reconnu comme du faux Beardsley.

(*A book of fifty drawings, by Aubrey Beardsley. Léonard Smithers, London.*)

C'est qu'il faut pour représenter vraiment des visions d'effroi et d'étrange, les avoir vues. Toute âme est un monde chimérique et presque impénétrable, et chaque artiste vrai porte en sa pensée un royaume d'images et de pensées. Quelle impression plus émouvante, que de se pencher une heure sur l'un de ces mondes voisins et inconnus, de voir comment au contact de la vie a frissonné une autre âme, d'assister une minute au spectacle grandiose que chacun se donne en lui-même, en transposant les musiques et les tableaux de la vie.

La vie des uns est parfois un drame rouge, d'autres sont des acteurs de comédie. Mais pour certains, leur fantaisie, en vêtements légers de chauves-souris sur un fond bleu pâle, joue une pantomime merveilleuse, d'une mélancolique étrangeté. La vision d'art d'Aubrey Beardsley fut une pantomime diabolique et rêveuse. Il en a noté des scènes, à mesure qu'il les voyait déroulées. Mais j'imagine que le jeune homme pensif qui devait rentrer si tôt au pays des rêves, et que je vois, penché un peu triste, un doigt sur la joue, à une fenêtre, sur le crépuscule londonnien, en a vu d'autres plus profondes encore et d'un charme plus maladif ou plus spécial. Tous ses dessins sont l'expression d'une volupté qui se tourmente. Il a emprunté au dix-huitième siècle et à l'époque adorable de Louis XV son décor. Mais il a mis dans ce décor un jeu d'images et de sensations nouvelles. C'est l'afféterie inquiétante, c'est les profils de chèvre ou les pieds de bouc, sous les dentelles, c'est l'effroi maniéré, c'est tout ce que vous voudrez, une vision, en tout cas bien personnelle, et un rideau parfois soulevé sur le monde inquiétant d'à côté.

GABRIEL DE LAUTREC.

LA MORT DE PIERROT — Dessin d'AUBREY BEARDSLEY.

L'EXPOSITION D'HORTICULTURE

L'Exposition générale annuelle d'Horticulture, à laquelle chaque année le public parisien fait un accueil si empressé, ouvrira ses portes le mercredi 24 mai.

L'Exposition se tiendra, comme les années précédentes, dans le Jardin des Tuileries, allée des Orangers, et terrasse du Jeu de Paume, près la rue de Rivoli.

Les visiteurs pourront jouir *gratuitement* d'un charmant concert qui sera donné tous les jours, de trois à cinq heures, dans le jardin de l'Exposition.

Clôture de l'Exposition le lundi 29 mai, à six heures du soir.

LÉOPOLD WENZEL

M. Léopold Wenzel, l'habile chef d'orchestre de l'Empire-Théâtre à Londres, vient de recevoir la rosette d'officier de l'Instruction publique. Nous en sommes heureux pour M. Wenzel que nous félicitons bien sincèrement.

J. R.

Cœur d'Honnête Femme

M. Quentin-Bauchart' conseiller municipal des Champs-Elysées, vient de faire paraître à la librairie Ollendorff, sous son pseudonyme bien connu de Jean Berleux, un nouveau roman intitulé : *Un Cœur d'honnête femme*, précédé d'une curieuse préface adressée à Henri Lavedan, de l'Académie française. Cette œuvre, d'une grande intensité d'émotion vraie, et d'une honnêteté absolue, peut être mise dans toutes les mains : elle est certainement appelée à un très légitime succès.

AVIS

Nos abonnés, ainsi que toutes les personnes inscrites au service du journal, sont *instamment priés* de nous faire savoir les irrégularités ou retards qui pourraient se produire dans la remise de leur numéros qui pour Paris doivent leur arriver *non pliés* et en parfait état.

Fig. 5.13 Aubrey Beardsley, *La Mort de Pierrot* [*The Death of Pierrot* (by first week of July 1896), repr. *The Savoy*, 6 (Oct 1896): 33], here illustrating Gabriel de Lautrec's belated article, "Note sur Aubrey Beardsley," repr. *Le Courrier français*, 21 (21 May 1899): 3. BnF, Paris

Critics adored the stage-like quality of the piece, and claimed it as an ideal dénouement. Exploited to accompany many posthumous articles, it turned into a pathetic – and influential – symbol of the artist's early passing. *Le Courrier français* published it in 1899 with a Lautrec article (see Fig. 5.13), a tribute quite belatedly paid to the man who had much contributed to Roques's fortunes.[65] So did *Emporium* in 1904 under Vittorio Pica's seal.[66] As for *Kunst und Künstler*, in 1903 it replicated the Dowson *ajouré* Pierrot as a final image, this time a real tailpiece concluding Emil Hannover's article.[67] In their wake, Julius Meier-Graefe's study on Beardsley became an explicit farewell. It adopted as motto Beardsley's translation of Catullus's Latin farewell[68] and concluded with two Pierrot pictures, the Dowson *Cul-de-Lampe* and *The Death of Pierrot*, the latter, again detailed and dramatised in words.[69] The drama had been played out. Text and pictures grieved.

A similar mood prevailed in *La Revue blanche*. In a touching article, written and published in French on 1 May 1898, probably supervised by Félix Fénéon,[70] John Gray, a close friend of Beardsley's, called Pierrot "a sad biography" ("*une triste biographie*"). Additionally, Gray's opening sentence, "An artist has just died," echoed "M. Gustave Moreau has just died." Moreau had passed away on 19 April, following Beardsley. The first chronicle and its initial line, a tribute to the French artist, heralded the last, a homage to the British, under the common heading "Petite gazette d'art." Thadée Natanson, who had signed most of its entries, must have been no stranger to such an arrangement.[71] *La Revue blanche* thus expressed its dedication to two artists of stature, Gray's contribution being yet another shilling paid into the coffers of Franco-British

65 Lautrec, "Note sur Aubrey Beardsley," *Le Courrier français*, 21 (21 May 1899): 3.

66 Vittorio Pica, "Tre artisti d'eccezione," *Emporium*, 19:113 (May 1904): 351, see https://emporium.sns.it/galleria/pagine.php?volume=XIX&pagina=XIX_113_351.jpg

67 Emil Hannover, "Aubrey Beardsley," *Kunst und Künstler*, 1:11 (Nov 1903): 425, see https://digi.ub.uni-heidelberg.de/diglit/kk1902_1903/0434/image,info

68 See Catullus, "Carmen CI," in *Decadent Writings of Aubrey Beardsley*, 181.

69 Meier-Graefe, "Aubrey Beardsley and his Circle," 265–66, text 258–59.

70 In a letter to Gray, dated 17 Apr 1898 and authored on *La Revue blanche* paper, Fénéon writes to his friend Gray: "The lines you dedicate to his kind memory are exquisite, and you will find them printed as they stand, or nearly so." See Félix Fénéon – John Gray, *Correspondance*, ed. by Maurice Imbert (Tusson: Du Lérot, 2010), 76: "*Les lignes que vous consacrez à sa gentille mémoire sont exquises, et vous les trouverez imprimées telles quelles, ou à peu près.*"

71 "Petite gazette d'art," *La Revue blanche*, 16 (May 1898): 65–70 (the Moreau article opens the column, Gray's article on Beardsley ends it, 68–70).

friendship. Ironically, Moreau had shunned the public and eschewed clamour, quite the contrary to Beardsley.

Both the *Mercure* and *La Revue blanche* tempered, however, the pathos of that adieu. The *Mercure* article closes with a grotesque tailpiece by Joseph Sattler, who pictured a fancy grimacing Beardsley with faun's ears, ironically haloed with a crown adorned by a single laurel leaf (Fig. 5.14). In *La Revue blanche*, Beardsley's portrait by Vallotton, a black-and-white "mask," stands out against a black patch, a dripping ink blot that redrafts his profile in caricature (Fig. 5.15): the melancholic tribute is tempered by the grotesque in response to the artist who had stated that, if he was not grotesque, he was nothing.

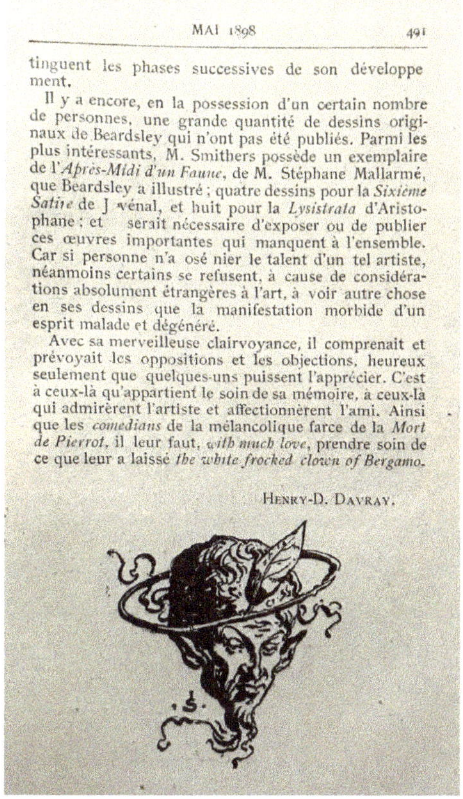

MAI 1898 491

tinguent les phases successives de son développement.

Il y a encore, en la possession d'un certain nombre de personnes, une grande quantité de dessins originaux de Beardsley qui n'ont pas été publiés. Parmi les plus intéressants, M. Smithers possède un exemplaire de l'*Après-Midi d'un Faune*, de M. Stéphane Mallarmé, que Beardsley a illustré ; quatre dessins pour la *Sixième Satire* de J vénal, et huit pour la *Lysistrata* d'Aristophane ; et serait nécessaire d'exposer ou de publier ces œuvres importantes qui manquent à l'ensemble. Car si personne n'a osé nier le talent d'un tel artiste, néanmoins certains se refusent, à cause de considérations absolument étrangères à l'art, à voir autre chose en ses dessins que la manifestation morbide d'un esprit malade et dégénéré.

Avec sa merveilleuse clairvoyance, il comprenait et prévoyait les oppositions et les objections, heureux seulement que quelques-uns puissent l'apprécier. C'est à ceux-là qu'appartient le soin de sa mémoire, à ceux-là qui admirèrent l'artiste et affectionnèrent l'ami. Ainsi que les *comedians* de la mélancolique farce de la *Mort de Pierrot*, il leur faut, *with much love*, prendre soin de ce que leur a laissé *the white frocked clown of Bergamo*.

HENRY-D. DAVRAY.

Fig. 5.14 Joseph Sattler, *Grotesque of Aubrey Beardsley*, tailpiece of Henry-D. Davray's article, "Aubrey Beardsley," repr. *Mercure de France*, 26:101 (May 1898): 491. Author's photograph

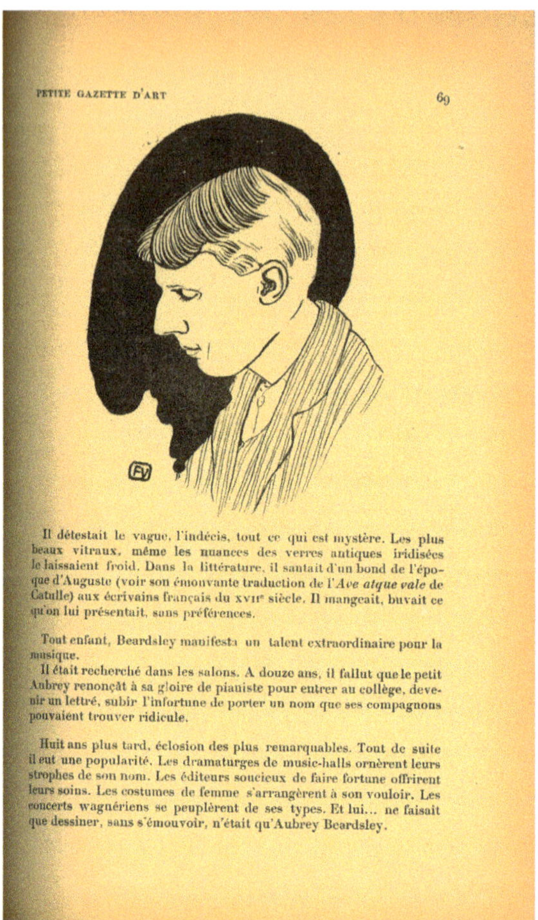
PETITE GAZETTE D'ART 69

FV

Il détestait le vague, l'indécis, tout ce qui est mystère. Les plus beaux vitraux, même les nuances des verres antiques iridisées le laissaient froid. Dans la littérature, il santait d'un bond de l'époque d'Auguste (voir son émouvante traduction de l'*Ave atque vale* de Catulle) aux écrivains français du XVIIe siècle. Il mangeait, buvait ce qu'on lui présentait, sans préférences.

Tout enfant, Beardsley manifesta un talent extraordinaire pour la musique.

Il était recherché dans les salons. A douze ans, il fallut que le petit Aubrey renonçât à sa gloire de pianiste pour entrer au collège, devenir un lettré, subir l'infortune de porter un nom que ses compagnons pouvaient trouver ridicule.

Huit ans plus tard, éclosion des plus remarquables. Tout de suite il eut une popularité. Les dramaturges de music-halls ornèrent leurs strophes de son nom. Les éditeurs soucieux de faire fortune offrirent leurs soins. Les costumes de femme s'arrangèrent à son vouloir. Les concerts wagnériens se peuplèrent de ses types. Et lui... ne faisait que dessiner, sans s'émouvoir, n'était qu'Aubrey Beardsley.

Fig. 5.15 Félix Vallotton, *Aubrey Beardsley's mask,* with John Gray's article in "Petite gazette d'art," repr. *La Revue blanche*, 16 (May 1898): 69. Author's photograph

It is therefore halfway between the white Pierrot and the grotesque vignettes that Beardsley's portrait as "dandy of the grotesque"[72] finally took shape in French and European periodicals. The white frock is but an evanescent bust. Yet a bust all the same. Witness Matthew Sturgis's Beardsley biography, which chooses no other image and no other heading to conclude. His last chapter is "The Death of Pierrot," and it

72 Partial title of Chris Snodgrass's study, *Aubrey Beardsley, Dandy of the Grotesque* (New York and Oxford: Oxford University Press, 1995).

uses the homonymous plate as chapter frontispiece.[73] Yet, Pierrot's loose white blouse and wide white pantaloons are perhaps nothing more than an ultimate mask enclosing nothing, a blank surface on which commiseration and pathos may glide and thrive. It brought the wide circulation of images of the "puerile" Beardsley to a stop, in obvious contradiction to an icon status long shaped by an aura of scandal and clever wit.

French Aftermath and Follow-Up

Two tributes in larger circulation periodicals addressed the general public at the time of Beardsley's death: Gabriel Mourey gave an overall approving evaluation of Beardsley's art, admiring his precociousness, in *La Revue encyclopédique*;[74] and Tristan Klingsor added a more descriptive piece in the *Revue illustrée*.[75] It was not until July 1899 that Davray wrote an "epitaph" in *La Plume*, echoing several English authors, and listing the print runs of the albums and the retail prices of several illustrated books.[76]

All the same, these articles signal a missed rendezvous. More often than not, the same facts and features about Beardsley passed from one author to the next, embellished with a few descriptions after reproduced drawings. The avant-garde reviews remained soberly illustrated. In these publications it was the work's originality and its boldness that moulded the words. The larger-circulation magazines had significant financial means, which the avant-garde journals could not compete with, so it was up to publications like the *Revue illustrée*, to provide reproductions of fine drawings requested from London. In this way, Beardsley's images reached a wider public through popular, general-interest magazines, guided by his legendary reputation. As Desmarais shows in her comparison of Beardsley's reception in England and France,

73 Sturgis, *Aubrey Beardsley*, 340–51.

74 Mourey, "Aubrey Beardsley," *La Revue encyclopédique*, 8:248 (4 June 1898): 520–21.

75 Tristan Klingsor, "Aubrey Beardsley," *Revue illustrée*, 13:13 (15 June 1898): n.p. The issue again relates Beardsley to Gustave Moreau under a cover showing Adolphe Willette in a Pierrot costume. Klingsor draws the Moreau/Beardsley parallel by calling Beardsley "some ingenious sorcerer's apprentice" ("*quelque ingénieux apprenti sorcier*"). The phrase refers to "Un maître sorcier" ("A Master Sorcerer"), the title of Jean Lorrain's opening article on Moreau in the same issue.

76 Davray, "Aubrey Vincent Beardsley," *La Plume*, 24:246 (15 July 1899): 449–51.

the French often stressed deformation, grotesqueness and perversity in their treatment of Beardsley.[77] A Robert de Montesquiou article, based on *A Book of Fifty Drawings* and *A Second Book of Fifty Drawings* is titled "Le Pervers,"[78] even though Montesquiou had no access to Beardsley's erotic work.

The beginning of the twentieth century extended this trend: Beardsley's work was troubling and potentially embarrassing, yet interest in it was still growing. His legend still held but was also receding in knowledgeable publications. Arthur Symons's book, one of the most thorough studies of Beardsley's art at the time, republished in 1905, was translated into French in 1906.[79] In February 1907, the Shirleys gallery, at 9 Boulevard des Malesherbes, organised a major exhibition of original drawings. Attendance was so large that it was extended by a week. On this occasion, an unexpurgated version of the *Salome* drawings was published in book form, as was the French translation of Beardsley's incomplete novel, *Under the Hill*. Robert de Montesquiou reviewed the exhibition on the front page of *Le Figaro*, describing Beardsley's line as "traced on a mirror with the edge of a diamond."[80] Jacques-Émile Blanche lengthily recorded his memories in the journal *Antée* and as a preface to the Paris and Bruges editions of *Under the Hill*.[81]

In 1907, the theatre manager Gabriel Astruc organised a grand production of Richard Strauss's *Salome* in its German version, with Strauss himself on the podium and Natalia Trouhanova and Aïda Bini

---

77 Desmarais, *The Beardsley Industry*, 117–22.

78 Robert de Montesquiou, "Le Pervers," in Montesquiou, *Professionnelles beautés* (Paris: Félix Juven, 1905), 85–104.

79 Arthur Symons, *Aubrey Beardsley, traduit par Jack Cohen, Édouard et Louis Thomas* (Paris: Floury, 1906).

80 Montesquiou, "Aubrey Beardsley," *Le Figaro* (21 Feb 1907): 1: "*un trait tracé sur une glace par la pointe d'un diamant;*" collected under the title "Beardsley en raccourci," in *Assemblée de notables* (Paris: Félix Juven, 1908), 19–27.

81 Blanche, "Aubrey Beardsley," *Antée*, 3:11 (1 Apr 1907): 1103–22; Blanche's text would serve as "Preface" to Beardsley's unfinished novel, "Sous la colline, une histoire romantique, traduit de l'anglais par A.-H. Cornette," published first in *Antée*, 2:6 (1 Nov 1906): 539–72, then by *Antée*'s publisher Arthur Herbert in Bruges with Blanche's preface, and finally in Paris (Floury, 1908) again with Blanche's preface. It was later included in Blanche's *Essais et Portraits* (Paris: Dorbon Aîné, 1912), 135–49, and *Propos de peintre. De David à Degas, 1e série* (Paris: Émile-Paul Frères, 1919), 111–31. Curiously the Bruges edition is not mentioned in Andries van den Abeele, "Une maison d'édition brugeoise: Arthur Herbert (1906-1907)," *Textyles*, 23 (2003): 95–101, https://doi.org/10.4000/textyles.796

alternating in the dance of the seven veils.[82] The press was again aflame with articles on Wilde and Beardsley. Despite this popularity, proper academic evaluation of the artist was slow to emerge. Armand Dayot's assessment in *La Peinture anglaise* in 1908 stands out from the crowd by concluding with the *Lysistrata* erotic drawings as the artist's masterpiece of synthesis.[83] This is more than unusual. However, still in the 1930s, a nostalgic view again emerged in an article by Edmond Jaloux for the newspaper *Le Temps*, on the occasion of another demise, that of Ellen Beardsley, the artist's mother, who had passed away in poverty.[84]

The French record is thus in keeping with what Roques had predicted in December 1894: "He will be excessively disparaged by some, frankly admired by others; he will be indifferent to no one."[85] This is apposite. The artist's choice of *Le Courrier français* was a lucky one when compared to other avant-garde reviews, which were moved by his death, but visually coy. Subscribers to *L'Ermitage* were estimated at 400 at best. *Le Courrier français*, for its part, may have run to 25,000 to 30,000 copies at its heyday between 1891 and 1896. Its fame, its distribution in the provinces and abroad, its longevity, its large number of illustrations, and the part it played in artistic life make it the "most important and most representative" paper of the nineteenth century's last decade.[86] All in all, the comparison shows, despite Beardsley's praise, a certain reserve and distance of the avant-garde journals regarding his radical graphic design, only imperfectly rendered by words. The divergence points to an antagonism between what appeals to the eye and what compels the intellect. Such is the paradox of Beardsley's ultimately intellectual art: to have imposed itself only through its own graphic form and the myths he himself fostered.

82 See Lynn Garafola, *Diaghilev's Ballets Russes* (New York and Oxford: Oxford University Press, 1989), 277.

83 Armand Dayot, *La Peinture anglaise de ses origines à nos jours* (Paris: Lucien Laveur, 1908), 339–41.

84 Edmond Jaloux, "L'époque de Beardsley," *Le Temps* (26 Feb 1932): 3.

85 Roques, "Les artistes anglais: M. Beardsley," 7: "*Il sera dénigré à outrance par les uns, franchement admiré par d'autres; il ne sera indifférent à personne.*"

86 Raymond Bachollet, "Les audaces du *Courrier français*," *Le Collectionneur français*, 218 (Dec 1984): 9.

Conclusion and Aftermath

In Aubrey Beardsley's entry for *The Oxford Dictionary of National Biography*, Alan Crawford states that "it is actually hard to see who Aubrey Beardsley was." Writing back in 2004, Crawford argues that the artist's legacy has been in the hands of academics, collectors, and connoisseurs, stifling significant progress in understanding him: he "has been parcelled out among different intellectual allegiances – biography, connoisseurship, cultural theory, bibliography, race and gender studies, reception studies," to ultimately stand "fragmented."[1] Twenty years later, such an evaluation feels decidedly out-of-date. Indeed, in 2016 Linda Gertner Zatlin's *Catalogue Raisonné* presented an outstanding piece of scholarship on Beardsley's artistic oeuvre. This comprehensive work allows for a well-informed and insightful assessment of Beardsley's drawings, piece by piece. The 2022 critical edition of his writings by Sasha Dovzhyk and Simon Wilson took another step forward by fully showing the claim of an unexpurgated version of *Under the Hill* to enter the Decadent literary canon, the extent of Beardsley's reading, the relation of his literary work to his art, and his ingenious way of co-opting the reader in contributing to his illustrations.[2] A further critical edition of his correspondence would make a highly significant tribute.[3]

Challenging and daring as an artist, Beardsley poses questions, throughout his wide-ranging production, regarding customary approaches to art and literature. By innovating tactics that Decadence employed to pave the way for avant-gardism, sophisticated creation, the

1 Alan Crawford, "Beardsley, Aubrey Vincent (1872–1898)" (23 Sept 2004), *Oxford Dictionary of National Biography*, https://doi.org/10.1093/ref:odnb/1821

2 *Decadent Writings of Aubrey Beardsley*, ed. by Sasha Dovzhyk and Simon Wilson, MHRA Critical Texts 10, Jewelled Tortoise 78 (Cambridge: Modern Humanities Research Association, 2022).

3 Such a critical edition was announced by Zatlin but has yet to materialise.

 https://doi.org/10.11647/OBP.0413.06

interrelation of the arts, and the intertwining of modes of expression, he stands as a central figure. He pioneered major aesthetic reversals, upturned the relation between periphery and centre and made margin significant in art. He promoted artwork printed in numbers as genuine and legitimate, extended and ousted the boundaries of the book by endorsing an "all margin" volume. And he revolutionised the canon by renewing the grotesque tradition as pivotal. His multifaceted talent, extensive literary knowledge, and resourceful use of press media call for an integrative, multidisciplinary approach inclined to de-fragment him. In this book, I endeavour to bring together seemingly dispersed views on Beardsley through interdisciplinary studies and differential comparison of the artist's work and persona. Although this book is no global reassessment of Beardsley, I will conclude by making explicit five modest principles I have applied in my attempt to fathom his art and its reception. These are not offered as unconditional precepts and unquestionable recommendations, but rather as the broad foci I have seen as most useful in exploring his legacy both closely and from a distance.

First, I found it fruitful to investigate one of Beardsley's innovative motifs, as I have done with the foetus, in a way that takes into account its entire aesthetic evolution. If one abides by Brian Reade's estimate (of the foetus as minor obsession) or Ian Fletcher's observation (its disappearance after 1893), it would be tempting to dismiss this complex motif as short-lived, and in doing so overlook its plasticity, malleability, and use as a graphic nucleus for other works. No less crucially, I have attempted to temper autobiographical readings – favoured by much previous scholarship – in order to privilege the motif's aesthetic weight. The influence of contemporaneous evolutionary theories, however implausible by modern standards, reinstates Beardsley's work outside the dominant autobiographical bias. It brings him closer to shared preoccupations of the period and highlights his attuned audacity and innovative talent. It further indicates how assumptions based on science expound aesthetic creativity and artistic breakthroughs.

Second, I think it is extremely useful to pay attention to aspects of Beardsley's oeuvre considered unimportant or secondary by conventional standards of "major" and "minor" works. The *Bon-Mots* vignettes are a good example. When seen through the lens of grand accomplishments, they seem insignificant. Yet, when reassessed through

Beardsley's reversal of centre and periphery, and his inversion of margin and centre, the grotesques open new aesthetic pathways fuelling his artistic experience far from his more famous work in, for example, *Le Morte Darthur*. His grotesques bring into being a rich test bed of new shapes, supply him with an ample scale of design possibilities, and equip his nib with accrued flexibility. They quarry foreign antecedents but often transmute them beyond recognition. They build a varied fin-de-siècle grotesque vocabulary, confirm the period's experiments with hybrid forms, and grow into a vital input of eccentric creation to nourish further a proto-form of surrealism. When set in perspective within fin-de-siècle print culture, they join the period's probing of novel ways to illustrate, think, and shape the book.[4]

Third, I think it is important to set Beardsley in context, read his work by comparison with others, and through the lens of shared preoccupations. Every period evolves under a galaxy. In fin-de-siècle skies speckled with numerous stars, he is a meteor no less dazzling. We can better grasp his avant-garde stances and the period's intellectual and aesthetic landscape when we explore his nuanced kinships with other artistic luminaries – as well as lesser-known contemporaries – to bring out similarities, parallels, and differences. Beardsley studies are still overwhelmingly monographic and centred on Britain. To reassess him in a wider and varied milieu reveals an international Beardsley, shining brightly across Europe and the United States.

Fourth, to truly understand Beardsley I think it is necessary to see him in the context of media-driven modernity and burgeoning print culture. He was the leading artist of a technical revolution, printing black-and-white drawings from line-blocks with images circulating rapidly for a low price in a mass market. His linear style opened new trajectories for graphic art and it is no coincidence that he incarnated the "Beardsley period," that is, a time characterised by the work of a young prodigy and the era of clear-cut black-and-white graphics that were easily reproducible. In the Victorian twilight, he also was a sophisticated book artist. Photomechanical engraving and cheap reproduction processes allowed his pen-and-ink drawings to be replicated next to letterpress to great advantage. Several of his drawings exist only in reproduction. He offered images that were not

4 On this more general question, see Évanghélia Stead, *La Chair du livre: Matérialité, imaginaire et poétique du livre fin-de-siècle* (Paris: PUPS, 2012), repr. 2013.

illustrations but freely related to text or inserted to texts in a way that still made them central to the book's meaning.

Finally, printed matter stands as the backbone of Beardsley work, and this was also reflected in his work's mass dissemination. His fame grew thanks to periodicals and I have often assessed journals, magazines, and the press in this book. The press allowed him to create his public persona, play with it, and broadcast it, in a way that ultimately went far beyond his control. Rather than critically assessing his art, press articles often simply spread it through endless duplication and international distribution, magnifying the artist's poses. The artist had chosen to shock and impress, using body art even before the term was coined. But his work also transmitted poignant semblances to critics moved to empathy by his untimely end. Differential comparisons between different types of periodicals across different countries within a "Europe of reviews" allow us to see how these images were shaped and disseminated.

Much of this book has focussed on Beardsley's reception during his lifetime and immediately after his death. This conclusion further points to the way Beardsley has been received and reinterpreted through multi-medial forms of expression and by other artists throughout the twentieth century. Beyond his iconic images, why was his legacy so prevalent? What outstanding contribution has he made to modern art? Performance, the claim of black-and-white to fine art status over and beyond traditional divisions, the international dimension of his influence, and a pervasive stimulus for other artists emerge as the foremost driving forces stemming from his work. When studied comparatively, these shed light on how the arts dialogued and co-created in the fin de siècle; and how Beardsley's appeal fuelled others' aesthetics and choices in wider-ranging contexts than usually perceived.

Multimedia Performance

The twentieth century has come to consider *performance art* as an artwork or exhibition invented by the artists themselves through their actions, attested in documentation, at a precise time, in space, and involving their body, presence, and relation with the public. Performance in Beardsley's case is threefold: he used his drawings as a stage to present fleeting fin-de-siècle shows and fictitious dramatic settings; he adopted exaggerated behaviour and a dandified stance to create a carefully directed public persona; he projected himself onto the social stage through his drawings and in photographs which were enthusiastically relayed by the press. As the Nicaraguan poet Rubén Darío put it in verse:

> Aubrey Beardsley glides
> like a disdainful sylph.
> Charcoal, snow and ash plied
> give the dream soul and skin.
>
> *Aubrey Beardsley se desliza*
> *como un silfo zahareño.*
> *Con carbón, nieve y ceniza*
> *da carne y alma al ensueño.*[5]

Beardsley's performance art did not develop in museums or the street, but in press interviews, periodicals, drawings, all published and widely circulated. Yet, its conceptual depth is evident, as shown by Evans's photographs. In its break away from convention and quest for new modes of expression, it foreshadows the performances of Dadaism by a couple of decades. It produced many reactions, mostly on paper, which Beardsley steered with a predilection for scandal but also a growing sense of aesthetics. Although his own differ from twentieth-century performances, since they are not live or publicly demonstrated (but for Beardsley's remarkable entrances or incarnations) and refrain from rebuke or social criticism, they are, however, piquantly related to his aesthetic experiences and aim to generate strong reactions. Even if his major accomplishment is the mark he left on the graphic arts, his black-and-white oeuvre tended to move away from paper, beyond books, and materialise in three dimensions.

In a little-known event on 2 June 1908, Beardsley's drawings escaped their book and bindings onto a stage at the grand studio of a Parisian princess who had decided to entertain her guests with a spectacle far from ordinary. Fernand Ochsé, multi-talented painter, stage-designer, composer, author and diseur, produced twelve tableaux vivants

5 Rubén Darío, "Dream," *El canto errante, ilustraciones de Enrique Ochoa* (1907); in *Obras Completas*, 22 vols. (Madrid: Administración Editorial "Mundo Latino," n.d. [1918]), XVI, 84, v. 16–20. Beardsley appears in good company: Shakespeare, Heine, Hugo, Verlaine, Nerval, Laforgue, and Mallarmé. He is the only one with Verlaine to earn a whole stanza.

named *Engravings* (*Eaux-fortes*) after poems by his brother, Julien Ochsé, inspired by Beardsley's plates.[6] Previously staged at the Ochsé household in Neuilly-sur-Seine, and become "popular in Paris society,"[7] the tableaux were performed for a hundred guests at the mansion of Princess Edmond de Polignac. A rich American, born Winnaretta Singer (of the sewing machine dynasty), the princess was a music and art lover, a well-known patron of the arts, and a Wagner enthusiast. If only for that detail, the Beardsley show may rival the German composer's idea of the *Gesamtkunstwerk*.

As in numerous other cases that capitalised on Beardsley, the event attracted the attention of the press. The tableaux were displayed in trios, each headed by a "frontispiece" and heralded by "invisible" music (replicating Julien Ochsé's title *L'Invisible Concert*) led by the young conductor and composer Désiré-Émile Inghelbrecht: "A foreword explains and introduces it [the show], and a musical prelude provides a harmonious opening, while the stanzas of the poem, recited by the author's brother, accompany and paraphrase each new vision. An interlude indicates the pauses between the different parts," wrote a press reviewer.[8] The black-and-white walls, flooring, and dark draperies of the stage were made after Beardsley's designs. The flats carried an array of his most recognisable hallmark motifs, including tall candles burning high. The three sequences, known as "The Black Page," "The Park," and "The White Page," grouped drawings from *Salome* and other works. They rose against the stage background, first in black, then in black-on-white, finally as on a white page, to the sound of Fernand Ochsé reciting and music. Then they came to life:

> And as if escaped [...] from the sheets of paper that usually hold them back and keep them still, fleetingly restored to life and taking on the form of real actors, the figures in these drawings emerge from the darkness

6 Julien Ochsé, "Eaux-fortes (à la manière d'Aubrey Beardsley)," in *L'Invisible Concert* (Paris: Bibliothèque Internationale d'Édition, E. Sansot et Cie, 1908), 101–14.

7 Sylvia Kahan, *Music's Modern Muse: A Life of Winnaretta Singer, Princesse de Polignac* (Rochester, NY: University of Rochester Press, 2003), 154.

8 Alexandre de Gabriac, "La Vie à Paris: Un spectacle d'art," *Le Figaro* (1 June 1908): 1: "*Un avant-propos l'explique et le présente, et un prélude musical lui fait une entrée harmonieuse, tandis que les strophes du poème récitées par le frère de l'auteur accompagnent et paraphrasent chaque nouvelle vision. Un interlude indique les haltes séparant les différentes parties.*"

and follow one another, casting their light or shadow over the white or black backdrops – human appearances that reveal the place they hold only by the mere outline of their contours, white on black and black on white.

Et comme échappées [...] des feuillets qui d'habitude les retiennent et les immobilisent, rendues à la vie passagèrement, et prenant corps sous la forme de véritables acteurs, les figures de ces dessins sortent de l'obscurité et se succèdent, promenant leur clarté ou leur ombre sur les fonds de blancheur ou de nuit – apparitions humaines n'accusant la place qu'elles occupent que par le seul tracé de leurs contours, blanc sur noir, et noir sur blanc.[9]

Fleshing out the plates, waking up the book, the actors (including "shaggy gnomes and hydrocephalic dwarfs") were costumed, made up and coiffed after Beardsley's drawings.

Select guests flocked to the entertainment. The audience included aristocrats, the upper crust, and some of the finest in letters and the arts: the Grand Duke Vladimir, uncle of Emperor Nicholas II; the Ambassador of the United States; Princess Murat; the Marquis and Marquise de Ganay; Prince and Princess Pierre de Caraman-Chimay; Countess Edmond de Pourtalès; Henri de Régnier and his spouse, Marie, known by the pen-name Gérard d'Houville; Jacques-Émile Blanche, Beardsley's portraitist; Marcel Proust and his friend Lucien Daudet; the Italian count Giuseppe Primoli; Lucien Muhlfeld of *La Revue blanche*; and artists Ernest Helleu and Leonetto Cappiello.[10] Freed into space out of the darkness, the printed word became a three-dimensional leafing through an imaginary volume while a musical recital gave the performance its tempo. As the avant-garde show followed a choice dinner, all senses were involved.

Period accounts compare it to "a suggestive album" with pages turned by a graceful hand,[11] or a silent masque of Beardsley's *fantoche* mannequins "emerging, morphing and melting into the night."[12] To others, such as Edmond Jaloux, *habitué* of Beardsley aesthetics and the Ochsé performances at their idiosyncratic Neuilly home, the show in the grandiose setting of the Polignac mansion seemed sad and sullen: "It is

9 *Ibid.*

10 See Ferrari, "Le Monde et la Ville," *Le Figaro* (4 June 1908): 2; Benoît Duteurtre, *La mort de Fernand Ochsé: Récit* (Paris: Fayard, 2018), 57–58.

11 Gabriac, "La Vie à Paris: Un spectacle d'art."

12 De Tanville, "Le Monde," *Gil Blas* (3 June 1908): 2: "*surgissant, évoluant et se fondant dans la nuit.*"

the funeral for Cythera," reportedly alleged Marie de Régnier.[13] Although appreciations diverge, the multimedia performance credits Beardsley's art with an aura that dispersed well beyond drawing and print culture. That evening, Winnaretta Singer's guests massively pledged Sergei Diaghilev and Gabriel Astruc's plan to free the famous-to-be ballet company from the dominance of the Russian Imperial Theatres. Thanks to the remarkable Beardsley soirée, Diaghilev's troupe "became an independent entity, henceforth known as the Ballets Russes."[14] Avant-garde performances flourished in interaction.

A silent film adaptation of Wilde's *Salome*, directed by Charles Bryant and Broadway star Alla Nazimova, who also played the heroine, extended Beardsley into yet another medium in 1922–23. The stylised costumes and minimal sets in black and white by talented set designer and art director Natacha Rambova were consciously designed after Beardsley's plates.[15] It was called at the time "a painting deftly stroked upon the silversheet,"[16] but proved a flop, at great financial expense. Yet, it has recently been rediscovered, considered as the first American art film, and favourably assessed: "Even by today's standards, the film's art direction reached for the outer limits of avant-garde."[17]

Collecting the Beardsley Pieces

These are but small, alluring scraps of evidence from period reviews and memoirs teeming with data, mentions, and allusions to the taste for showmanship and the spectacular that drove a whole era. Beardsley's creation had come to an early end, but his aftermath saw his production reused and reinterpreted by imitators, devotees, and ingenious artists. They adopted the same methods of appropriation, creative homage, and transformation that he himself had used, taking their very inspiration from his work even so far as to become part of life.

13 Edmond Jaloux, *Les Saisons littéraires: 1904–1914* (Paris: Plon, 1950), 51.

14 Kahan, *Music's Modern Muse*, 154.

15 See Carlos Carmila, "Salome de Oscar Wilde | Charles Bryant | Vose. | 1923" (25 Nov 2013), *YouTube*, https://www.youtube.com/watch?v=Pt0DSbnf7q8

16 "Little Hints," *Screenland* (Sept 1922): 41.

17 Martin Turnbull, "Salomé," *National Film Registry*, https://www.loc.gov/static/programs/national-film-preservation-board/documents/salome.pdf

Already in 1895, a Japanese critic remarked that Beardsley's drawings, particularly from the *Yellow Book*, had given rise "within a single year" to "a strong group of imitators," shaping interior decoration and public taste in the United States through "recent newspaper illustrations and obtrusive posters."[18] Coteries were branded "corrupt" after the *Yellow Book* crowd. Society belles lay in hospital beds "pillowed and counterpaned with a hundred muslin frills to look like Aubrey Beardsley's *Rape of the Lock*."[19] Writer Francis de Miomandre lived in an interior à la Beardsley, lace-bedecked, with black objects stationed on white ground and the artist's works in ebony frames.[20] Such *décor* was but a pretext to elaborate theories on the non-realist or oneiric novel. Indeed, Edmond Jaloux alluded to fiction as a domain "where I myself also carried the wrought-iron lantern that Beardsley suspends from the fist of his Mercuries in rose-spangled cloaks."[21]

Beardsley's influence on fin-de-siècle and avant-garde graphic design, beyond the manifesto appeal of several drawings, has not gone unheeded. Matthew Sturgis has made a useful distinction between mere "followers" who "tried to assume his mantle" and the "few who were able to transmute the influence of Beardsley's intensely personal vision into their own."[22] He counted among the latter Charles Rennie Mackintosh, the Macdonald sisters, Leon Bakst's early designs for the Ballets Russes, "Kandinsky, Klee, Matisse and Picasso."[23] Yet, there is prolific and productive middle ground in between such clear-cut categories in the intricate way some of Beardsley's so-called copiers and clones elaborated on his drawings. In this book, Karel de Nerée tot

18 Sadakichi, "Aubrey Beardsley from a Japanese Standpoint," *Modern Art*, 3:1 (Winter 1895): 22.

19 Diana Cooper, *The Rainbow Comes and Goes* (London: Rupert Hart-Davis, 1958), 82 and 140.

20 Jaloux, *Les Saisons littéraires*, 41–42.

21 Jaloux, *Correspondance avec Henri et Marie de Régnier: 1896–1939*, ed. by Pierre Lachasse (Paris: Classiques Garnier, 2019), 141: "*où j'ai promené aussi la lanterne en fer forgé que Beardsley suspend au poing de ses Mercures au manteau semé de roses*" (letter to Henri de Régnier, 12 Sept 1910). Jaloux alludes to *Le Boudoir de Proserpine* (Paris: Dorbon aîné, 1910), his collection of oneiric fictions where Beardsley appears in the conclusive text (p. 318).

22 Matthew Sturgis, *Aubrey Beardsley: A Biography* (London: Harper Collins Publishers, 1998), 357.

23 *Ibid.*, 358.

Babberich's piece after Beardsley's *Incipit Vita Nova*, analysed in Chapter 2, straddles new ground.

Many scholars have published lists of artists and writers influenced by Beardsley, but these usually provide little more than names and an occasional image. There is still much to explore and refine. What follows might also read as an overwhelming catalogue, and I could have limited it to a selection of examples in chosen directions. Nevertheless it is useful I think to conclude with such an imposing directory, even if devoid of analysis, in the hope of spurring detailed research, particularly beyond Britain and through comparison. The variety and length of the inventory testify at a glance to Beardsley's widespread impact.

In "The Long Shadow," Stanley Weintraub pioneered such an investigation on Beardsley's influence in 1976, suggestively recalling ballet (Diaghilev and Bakst), writing (Harley Granville-Barker, the young D. H. Lawrence, early James Joyce, Carl Van Vechten, Ronald Firbank, Roy Campbell, Rubén Darío, and William Faulkner), and mentioning pell-mell design, drawings, film, criticism, French literature, Matisse and Picasso, Charles Ricketts, Laurence Housman, Alan Odle, Eric Gill, Edward Gordon Craig, Arthur Rackham, Will Barnett, and others.[24] In his *Dictionary of 19th Century British Book Illustrators and Caricaturists*, first published 1978, among several "Schools of Illustration," Simon Houfe singled out a special list labelled "Arts Influenced by Aubrey Beardsley," the only one under an individual artist's name. Fourteen artists convene, ranging from American Will H. Bradley, to Irishman Harry Clarke, Dane Kay Nielsen, German Hans-Henning von Voigt (known as Alastair and commented in this book), and a large assembly of Brits of varied fame and achievement: Stewart Carmichael of Dundee, Annie French (alias Mrs G. W. Rhead), Fred Hyland, Francis Ernest Jackson, Gilbert James, John Kettlewell, William Brown Macdougall, Alan Elsden Odle, George Plank, and Austin Osman Spare.[25] Later Houfe added to the list Sidney H. Sime, Mabel Dearmer, Ilbery Lynch, Léon Solon for ceramics, James Hearn who signed himself "Weirdsley Daubery," the American Frank Hazenpflug, the Swiss Paul Klee, and Germans Thomas Theodor Heine,

24 Stanley Weintraub, "The Long Shadow," in Weintraub, *Aubrey Beardsley, Imp of the Perverse* (University Park, Penn., and London: Pennsylvania State University Press, 1976), 261–69.

25 Simon Houfe, *The Dictionary of 19th Century British Book Illustrators and Caricaturists* (Woodbridge: Antique Collectors' Club, 1996), 362.

Emil Preetorius, Marcus Michael Douglas Behmer, and Julius Diez.[26] In an appendix on a similar theme, a 1985 Italian exhibition on Beardsley added Ronald Egerton Balfour, Max Beerbohm, Edmond Xavier Kapp, Edgar Wilson, Heinrich Vogeler, Umberto Boccioni, Hermann-Paul (through *Le Courrier français*), Ephraim Moses Lilien, Nikolai Petrovich Feofilaktov, and Anatoli Afanasyevich Arapov.[27] The 2020–21 Tate/ Musée d'Orsay Beardsley exhibition added Edward Tennyson Reed, René Gockinga (who specialised in Decadent literature and was nicknamed the "Dutch Beardsley" for illustrating Wilde's *Salomé*), before expanding to several works, record sleeves, and even wallpaper from the 1960s,[28] as the 1998 V&A exhibition had already done.[29] In the Tate/ Musée d'Orsay catalogue, a contribution on "Beardsley and Russia" by Rosamund Bartlett signalled Konstantin Somov, Alexander Benois, Vsevolod Maksymovych, Nikolai Kalmakov, along with significant avant-garde theatre, dance, and literary events.[30] Joichiro Kawamura's insightful article on "Beardsley and Japan" further offered an entirely new harvest of Japanese affiliates with a telling frontispiece by Eitaro Takenaka and a vignette by Kiyoshi Hasegawa.[31]

Many more could join the ranks, from renowned Victorian illustrator Arthur Rackham (who, fascinated by Beardsley, had successfully parodied him)[32] to a French article on "Fine Art in the Army," mentioning in passing "lieutenant Dupouey's curious drawings recalling Aubrey Beardsley."[33] Such a fleeting mention shows the pervasive extent of Beardsley's art, which would have never achieved such a resounding reverberation if not for periodicals and reproduction. Much fine

26 Houfe, "Beardsley and his Followers," in Houfe, *Fin de Siècle. The Illustrators of the Nineties* (London: Barrie and Jenkins, 1992), 65-81, particularly 79–81.

27 *Aubrey Beardsley 1872–1898*, ed. by Brian Reade, Susan Lambert, and H. Lee Bimm (Rome: Fratelli Palombi Editori, 1985), particularly 216–29.

28 *Aubrey Beardsley*, ed. by Stephen Calloway and Caroline Corbeau-Parsons (London: Tate, 2020), 171–83.

29 See Stephen Calloway's last chapter, "The Aftermath and the Myth," in his *Aubrey Beardsley* (London: V & A Publications, 1998), 204–19.

30 Rosamund Bartlett, "Beardsley and Russia," in *Aubrey Beardsley 1872–1898*, 60–65.

31 Joichiro Kawamura, "Beardsley and Japan," in *ibid.*, 55–59.

32 Rackham's drawing was published in the *Westminster Budget*, 20 July 1894, with the comment "A Nightmare: Horrible result of contemplating an Aubrey Beardsley after supper." See Derek Hudson, *Arthur Rackham, His Life and Work* (London: Heinemann, 1974), 40 and 45.

33 Petrus Durel, "Les beaux-arts dans l'armée," *Le Monde illustré*, 2609 (30 Mar 1907): 203.

combing remains to be done. In a research article on relations between fin-de-siècle Hungary and Britain, Katalin Keserü mentioned "series of drawings by Lajos Kosma, Guyla Tichy, Attila Sassy (Aiglon)" under Beardsley's influence, which inaugurated a new genre in Hungarian art, i.e., a cycle of drawings on a specific theme. They followed a 1907 Beardsley exhibition at the Budapest Museum of Applied Arts and a detailed article on Beardsley in the periodical *Magyar Iparmüvészet*.[34] In Keserü's wake, Katalin Gellér extended the record mentioning Emil Sarkady, Mihály Rezsö, Sándor Nagy, and Guyla Tálos.[35]

All these brief mentions are useful in view of building a research network on Beardsley's continuous influence across Europe to Asia and over the Atlantic. The reverberation of his oeuvre, and the many ways it permeated not only his very period but later modern art, would be worth a global study. This could determine how deeply it stirred and marked graphic design, poster art, advertisement, illustration, interior decoration, and even fashion on one hand; and how it pollinated, impregnated, and fed into major artists' creativity on the other. It is easy to see that several countries are still under-represented and most of these allusions need further in-depth exploration. Any undertaking would need to build on thorough research and previous inputs such as Sasha Dovzhyk's 2020 article on Beardsley's influence on Leon Bakst and the World of Art's vision of modernity, their periodical *Mir iskusstva*, and the thematic "Beardsley issue" of the Moscow symbolist review *Vesy* (*Libra*).[36] Such research might further discuss such classifications as *plagiarist*, *parodist*, *imitator*, *follower*, *pasticheur*, *affiliated*, or *creatively related artist*.

More than a century after his passing, exhibitions and publications of Beardsley's work are still highly prized. The public flocks to admire his art and ponder the still-locked secrets of his drawings. Would the Beardsley craze of the 1960s and 1970s that gave birth to wallpaper, posters, T-shirts, record sleeves, and tea mugs after his work, still respond to contemporary curiosity? When Paris was in lockdown due

34 Katalin Keserü, "Art Contacts between Great Britain and Hungary at the Turn of the Century," *Hungarian Studies*, 6:2 (1990): 141–54 (145).

35 Katalin Gellér, "Hungarian Art Nouveau and its English Sources," *Hungarian Studies*, 6:2 (1990): 155–65 (156).

36 Sasha Dovzhyk, "Aubrey Beardsley in the Russian 'World of Art,'" *British Art Studies*, 18 (2020), https://doi.org/10.17658/issn.2058-5462/issue-18/sdovzhyk

to the Covid-19 pandemic, the Musée d'Orsay staged a short-lived Beardsley exhibition, open to the public for only three weeks, in which his grotesque photographic portraits by Frederick Evans welcomed the visitor as gigantic entrance panels. Nearly 130 years after they were taken, these images still intrigue and hold their power, symbols of avant-garde Decadence, which heralded contemporary art practices and a media-driven public life. The 2022 Grolier Club exhibition pertinently called Beardsley "150 Years Young."[37] It is thanks to artists like Beardsley, his brilliant and short career, and his sense of provocation, that we now welcome elements of the grotesque, marginality, and posturing in art. These have become central concerns, while in his time they were literally peripheral. Ultimately, it is to artists like him that we owe our current visual education.

37 Margaret D. Stetz, *Aubrey Beardsley 150 Years Young. From the Mark Samuels Lasner Collection University of Delaware Library, Museums and Press* (New York: The Grolier Club, 2022).

Bibliography and Iconography

Bibliography

Abeele, Andries van den. "Une maison d'édition brugeoise: Arthur Herbert (1906-1907)," *Textyles*, 23 (2003): 95–101, https://doi.org/10.4000/textyles.796

Acidini Luchinat, Cristina. "La grottesca," in *Storia dell'arte italiana*. 11. 3. *Situazioni, momenti, indagini*. 4. *Forme e modelli*, ed. by Federico Zeri. Turin: Giulio Einaudi, 1982, pp. 159–200.

Allais, Alphonse. "Le Bon Peintre," in Allais, (*Œuvres anthumes*) *À se tordre, histoires chatnoiresques*. Paris: Ollendorff, 1891, pp. 139–41; in *Œuvres anthumes*, ed. by François Caradec. Bouquins. Paris: Robert Laffont, 1989, pp. 50–51.

"An Apostle of the Grotesque," *The Sketch*, 9:115 (10 Apr 1895): 561–62.

"Ars Postera," *Punch, or The London Charivari*, 106 (21 Apr 1894): 189.

Art (L') au corps: Le Corps exposé de Man Ray à nos jours. Marseille: RMN, 1996.

"Artisti contemporanei: Aubrey Beardsley. In memoriam," *Emporium*, 7:41 (May 1898): 352–55.

Arwas, Victor. *Alastair: Illustrator of Decadence*. London: Thames and Hudson, 1979.

"Au jour le jour," *Le Journal des débats*, 100 (11 Apr 1898): 1.

Bachollet, Raymond. "Les audaces du *Courrier français*," *Le Collectionneur français*, 218 (Dec 1984): 9.

Baltrušaitis, Jurgis. "Le réveil du fantastique dans le décor du livre," in Baltrušaitis, *Réveils et Prodiges: le gothique fantastique*. Paris: A. Colin, 1960, pp. 195–234.

Barbou, Alfred. *Victor Hugo et son temps. Édition illustrée de 120 dessins inédits et d'un très grand nombre de dessins de Victor Hugo, gravés par Méaulle*. Paris: E. Hugues; G. Charpentier, 1881.

Bartlett, Rosamund. "Beardsley and Russia," in *Aubrey Beardsley*, ed. by Stephen Calloway and Caroline Corbeau-Parsons. London: Tate, 2020, pp. 60–65.

Baudelaire, Charles. "Le peintre de la vie moderne," *Le Figaro* (26 and 29 Nov, 3 Dec 1863). Collected in *L'Art romantique* (1868). Qtd. in *Œuvres complètes*, ed. by Claude Pichois, 2 vols. Bibliothèque de la Pléiade. Paris: Gallimard, 1976, II, pp. 683–724.

[Beardsley, Aubrey.] *A Book of Fifty Drawings by Aubrey Beardsley. With an iconography by Aymer Vallance*. London: Leonard Smithers, 1897.

Beardsley, Aubrey. *An Issue of Five Drawings Illustrative of Juvenal and Lucian*. London: Leonard Smithers, 1906.

[Beardsley, Aubrey.] *Decadent Writings of Aubrey Beardsley*, ed. by Sasha Dovzhyk and Simon Wilson. MHRA Critical Texts 10, Jewelled Tortoise 78. Cambridge: Modern Humanities Research Association, 2022, https://doi.org/10.2307/j.ctv33mgb1g

[Beardsley, Aubrey.] *The Early Work of Aubrey Beardsley*. With a Prefatory Note by H. C. Marillier. London and New York: John Lane, The Bodley Head, 1899.

Beardsley, Aubrey. "The Art of the Hoarding," *The New Review*, 11 (July 1894): 53–55. Collected in A. E. Gallatin, *Aubrey Beardsley: Catalogue of Drawings and Bibliography*. New York: The Grolier Club, 1945, pp. 110–11. Repr. in *Decadent Writings of Aubrey Beardsley*, ed. by Sasha Dovzhyk and Simon Wilson, pp. 188–89.

[Beardsley, Aubrey.] *The Letters of Aubrey Beardsley*, ed. by Henry Maas, J. L. Duncan, and W. G. Good. London: Cassell, 1970.

Beardsley, Aubrey. *The Story of Venus and Tannhäuser: A Romantic Novel, now First Printed from the Original Manuscript*. London: Printed for Private Circulation [L. Smithers], 1907.

Beardsley, Aubrey. "Sous la colline, une histoire romantique, traduit de l'anglais par A.-H. Cornette," *Antée*, 2:6 (1 Nov 1906): 539–72.

[Beardsley, Aubrey.] *The Uncollected Work of Aubrey Beardsley. With an Introduction by C. Lewis Hind*. London: John Lane, The Bodley Head, 1925.

Beardsley, Aubrey. *Under the Hill, and Other Essays in Prose and Verse*. London and New York: John Lane, 1904.

Beare, Geoffrey. "Alice B(olingbroke) Woodward (1862–1951)," *Yellow Nineties 2.0*, ed. by Lorraine Janzen Kooistra, https://1890s.ca/wp-content/uploads/woodward_bio.pdf

Beerbohm, Max. *Caricatures of Twenty-Five Gentlemen, with an Introduction by L. Raven-Hill*. London: Leonard Smithers, 1896.

Beerbohm, Max. "Diminuendo," first published as "Be it Cosiness," *The Pageant*, 1 (1896): 230–35. Repr. in *The Works of Max Beerbohm*, pp. 147–60.

Beerbohm, Max. *Letters to Reggie Turner*, ed. by Rupert Hart-Davis. London: Rupert Hart-Davis, 1964.

[Beerbohm, Max.] *The Works of Max Beerbohm, with a Bibliography by John Lane*. London: John Lane, The Bodley Head; New York: Charles Scribner's Sons, 1896.

Behmer, Marcus, and Max Meyerfeld, "Beardsleybriefe," *Kunst und Künstler*, 7:3 (1909): 134–38.

Benson, Edward Frederic. "Scenes from the Life of the Babe at Cambridge" (originally only eight chapters), published weekly in *The Granta*, 9:175–82 (18 Jan–10 Mar 1896).

Benson, Edward Frederic. *The Babe B.A., Being the Uneventful History of a Young Gentleman at Cambridge University*. London and New York: G. P. Putnam's Sons, 1897.

Benz, Richard. *Goethe und die romantische Kunst*. Munich: R. Piper and Co., 1940.

Bergel, Giles. "*The Chap-Book* (1894–8)," in *The Oxford Critical and Cultural History of Modernist Magazines*. II. *North America 1894–1960*, ed. by Peter Brooker and Andrew Thacker. Oxford and New York: Oxford University Press, 2012, pp. 154–75.

Bihl, Laurent. "Jules Roques (1850–1909) et *Le Courrier français*," *Histoires littéraires*, 12:45 (Jan–Feb–Mar 2011): 43–68.

Bihl, Laurent. "*Le Courrier français*," *Ridiculosa*, special issue "Les revues satiriques françaises," (18 Nov 2011): 146–49.

Bink, Sander, *Carel de Nerée tot Babberich en Henri van Booven: Den Haag in het fin de siècle, met een voorwoord van Caroline de Westenholz*. Zwolle: WBOOKS, 2014.

Bink, Sander, "Karel de Nerée tot Babberich's Forgotten Torture Garden," *The Rijksmuseum Bulletin*, 68:4 (2020): 335–58.

Birnbaum, Martin. "Marcus Behmer," in Birnbaum, *Jacovleff and Other Artists*. New York: Paul A. Struck, 1946, pp. 153–54.

[Blanche, Jacques-Émile.] B. J.-E. "Aubrey Beardsley," *La Chronique des arts et de la curiosité. Supplément à la Gazette des beaux-arts*, 13 (26 Mar 1898): 111.

Blanche, Jacques-Émile. "Aubrey Beardsley," *Antée: Revue mensuelle de littérature*, 3:11 (1 Apr 1907): 1103–22. Also published as "Preface" to the French translation of Beardsley's unfinished novel, *Sous la colline*. Bruges: Arthur Herbert éditeur, 1908. Included in Blanche's *Essais et Portraits*. Paris: Dorbon Aîné, 1912, pp. 135–49.

Blanche, Jacques-Émile. "Aubrey Beardsley: Préface à 'Under the Hill,'" in Blanche, *Propos de peintre. De David à Degas, 1e série*. Paris: Émile-Paul Frères, 1919, pp. 111–31.

Blei, Franz. "Aubrey Beardsley," *Pan*, 5:4 (Apr 1900): 256–60.

Bon-Mots of Charles Lamb and Douglas Jerrold, ed. by Walter Jerrold, with Grotesques by Aubrey Beardsley. London: J. M. Dent and Co., 1893.

Bon-Mots of Samuel Foote and Theodore Hook, ed. by Walter Jerrold, with Grotesques by Aubrey Beardsley. London: J. M. Dent and Co., 1894.

Bon-Mots of Sydney Smith and R. Brinsley Sheridan, ed. by Walter Jerrold, with Grotesques by Aubrey Beardsley. London: J. M. Dent and Co., 1893.

Booven, Henri van. "Karel de Nerée," *Elsevier's Geillustreerd Maandschrift*, 21:42 (July–Dec 1911): 6–18.

Booven, Henri van. *Witte Nachten*. Haarlem: Gebrs. Nobels, 1901.

Brophy, Brigid. *Beardsley and his World*. London: Thames and Hudson, 1976.

Buet, Charles. *Saphyr*. Paris: Calmann-Lévy, 1897.

Burdett, Osbert. *The Beardsley Period: An Essay in Perspective*. London: John Lane, 1925.

Calloway, Stephen. *Aubrey Beardsley*. London: V & A Publications, 1998.

Calloway, Stephen, and Caroline Corbeau-Parsons. eds. *Aubrey Beardsley*. London: Tate, 2020.

Champsaur, Félicien. *Dinah Samuel*, ed. by Jean de Palacio. Bibliothèque décadente. Paris: Séguier, 1999.

Champsaur, Félicien. *Lulu, roman clownesque*. Paris: Eugène Fasquelle, 1901.

Champsaur, Félicien. "Signature," in Champsaur, *Parisiennes*. Paris: A. Lemerre, 1887, p. 93.

Chastel, André. *La Grottesque. Essai sur l'"ornement sans nom."* Paris: Le Promeneur, 1988.

Cooper, Diana. *The Rainbow Comes and Goes*. London: Rupert Hart-Davis, 1958.

Crane, Walter, *Of the Decorative Illustration of Books Old and New*. London: George Bell and Sons, 1896.

Crawford, Alan. "Beardsley, Aubrey Vincent (1872–1898)," (23 Sept 2004), *Oxford Dictionary of National Biography*, https://doi.org/10.1093/ref:odnb/1821

Creek, Alma Burner. "Herbert S. Stone and Company," and "Stone and Kimball," in *American Literary Publishing Houses, 1638–1899, Part 2*, ed. by Peter Dzwonkoski and Joel Myerson. Detroit, Michigan: Gale Research Company, 1986, pp. 436–40 and 440–43.

Crépin-Leblond, Thierry. *La Cathérale Notre-Dame*. Paris: Éditions du Patrimoine, 2000.

Dacos, Nicole. *La Découverte de la Domus Aurea et la formation des grotesques à la Renaissance*. London: The Warburg Institute; Leiden: E. J. Brill, 1969.

Darío, Rubén. "Dream," *El canto errante, ilustraciones de Enrique Ochoa* (1907). Qtd. in *Obras Completas*, 22 vols. (Madrid: Administración Editorial "Mundo Latino," n.d. [1918]), XVI, pp. 81–85.

Davray, Henry-D. "Aubrey Beardsley," *Mercure de France*, 26:101 (May 1898): 485–91.

Davray, Henry D. "Aubrey Vincent Beardsley," *La Plume*, 24:246 (15 July 1899): 449–51.

Davray, Henry-D. "L'Art d'Aubrey Beardsley," *L'Ermitage*, 14:4 (Apr 1897): 253–61.

Davray, Henry-D. "Lettres anglaises," *Mercure de France*, 22:90 (June 1897): 582.

Dayot, Armand. *La Peinture anglaise de ses origines à nos jours*. Paris: Lucien Laveur, 1908, p. 339–41.

De Tanville, "Le Monde," *Gil Blas* (3 June 1908): 2.

Les Déliquescences, poèmes décadents d'Adoré Floupette, avec sa vie par Marius Tapora. Byzance [Paris]: Chez Lion Vanné [*sic* for Léon Vanier], 1885.

Desmarais, Jane Haville. *The Beardsley Industry: The Critical Reception in England and France, 1893–1914*. Aldershot: Ashgate, 1998.

Di Folco, Philippe. "*L'Estampe et l'Affiche*, une revue méconnue. 1897–1899," *La Revue des revues*, 52:2 (2014): 24–35.

Diaghilev, Sergei. "Slozhnye voprosy: Nash mnimyi upadok", *Mir iskusstva*, 1:1–2 (1899): 1–11; "Slozhnye voprosy: Vechnaia bor'ba", *Mir iskusstva*, 1:1–2 (1899): 12–16; "Slozhnye voprosy: Poiski krasoty", *Mir iskusstva*, 1:3–4 (1899): 37–49; "Slozhnye voprosy: Osnovy khudozhestvennoi otsenki", *Mir iskusstva*, 1:3–4 (1899): 50–61.

Dovzhyk, Sasha. "Aubrey Beardsley in the Russian 'World of Art'," *British Art Studies*, 18 (Nov 2020), https://doi.org/10.17658/issn.2058-5462/issue-18/sdovzhyk

Dovzhyk, Sasha. "The 'Artist Maks': The Ukrainian Disciple of Aubrey Beardsley," *British Library, European Studies blog* (21 Dec 2018), https://blogs.bl.uk/european/2018/12/the-artist-maks-the-ukrainian-disciple-of-aubrey-beardsley.html

Dowling, Linda. *Language and Decadence in the Victorian Fin de Siècle*. Princeton, New Jersey: Princeton University Press, 1986.

Dowson, Ernest. *The Pierrot of the Minute: A Dramatic Phantasy in One Act. With a Frontispiece, Initial Letter, Vignette and Cul-de-lampe by Aubrey Beardsley*. London: Leonard Smithers, 1897.

Durel, Petrus. "Les beaux-arts dans l'armée," *Le Monde illustré*, 2609 (30 Mar 1907): 202–3.

Duteurtre, Benoît. *La mort de Fernand Ochsé: Récit*. Paris: Fayard, 2018.

Easton, Malcolm. *Aubrey and the Dying Lady: A Beardsley Riddle*. London: Secker and Warburg, 1972.

"Échos," *Mercure de France*, 26:100 (Apr 1898): 335.

Eckmann, Otto. "Aubrey Vincent Beardsley," *Die Zukunft*, 7:40 (1 July 1899): 42–44.

Engelmann, Ines Janet, ed., *Alastair. Kunst als Schicksal*. Halle: Stiftung Moritzburg; Kunstmuseum des Landes Sachsen-Anhalt, 2004.

Engelmann, Ines Janet, ed., *Alastair. Kunst als Schicksal*. Munich: Bayerische Akademie der Schönen Künste, 2007.

Ernst, Max. *Écritures, avec cent vingt illustrations extraites de l'œuvre de l'auteur*. Paris: Gallimard, 1970.

Espey, John J. *Ezra Pound's "Mauberley": A Study in Composition*. Berkeley and Los Angeles, California: University of California Press, 1955.

Esswein, Hermann. *Aubrey Beardsley*. Munich and Leipzig: R. Piper and Co., [1908].

Evans, Frederick H. *Selected Texts and Bibliography*, ed. by Anne Hammond. Oxford: Clio Press, 1992.

Fénéon, Félix, and John Gray. *Correspondance. Avec les contributions de John Gray à "La Revue blanche"*, ed. by Maurice Imbert. Tusson, Charente: Du Lérot, 2010.

Ferrari, "Le Monde et la Ville," *Le Figaro* (4 June 1908): 2.

[Field, Julian Osgood] X. L. "A Kiss of Judas," *The Pall Mall Magazine*, 1:3 (July 1893): 339–66, with a drawing by Aubrey Beardsley.

Flaubert, Gustave. *Madame Bovary: mœurs de province, édition définitive suivie des requisitoire, plaidoirie et jugement intenté à l'auteur*. Paris: G. Charpentier, 1877.

Fletcher, Ian. "A Grammar of Monsters: Beardsley's Images and Their Sources," *English Literature in Transition, 1880–1920*, 30:2 (1987): 141–63.

Fletcher, Ian. *Aubrey Beardsley*. Boston, Massachusetts: Twayne Publishers, 1987.

Frayling, Christopher. ed. *Vampyres: Lord Byron to Count Dracula*. London: Faber and Faber, 1991. First published as *The Vampyre: Lord Ruthven to Count Dracula*, ed. by Christopher Frayling. London: Gollancz, 1978.

G. B. "Artisti contemporanei: Aubrey Beardsley," *Emporium*, 2:9 (Sept 1895): 192–204.

Gabriac, Alexandre de. "La Vie à Paris: Un spectacle d'art," *Le Figaro* (1 June 1908): 1.

[Gallatin, Albert Eugene.] *The Gallatin Beardsley Collection in the Princeton University Library. A Catalogue Compiled by A. E. Gallatin and Alexander D. Wainwright*. Princeton, New Jersey: Princeton University Library, 1952. Repr. from *The Princeton University Library Chronicle*, 10:2 (Feb 1949), 12:2 (Winter 1951), and 12:3 (Spring 1951).

Gallatin, Albert Eugene. *Aubrey Beardsley: Catalogue of Drawings and Bibliography*. New York: The Grolier Club, 1945.

Garafola, Lynn. *Diaghilev's Ballets Russes*. NewYork and Oxford: Oxford University Press, 1989.

Garbáty, Thomas Jay. "The French Coterie of the *Savoy* 1896," *PMLA*, 75 (1960): 609–15.

Gellér, Katalin. "Hungarian Art Nouveau and its English Sources," *Hungarian Studies*, 6:2 (1990): 155–65.

Gould, Charles. *Mythical Monsters, with Ninety-three Illustrations*. London: W. H. Allen and Co., 1886.

Graf, Arturo. *L'Anglomania e l'influsso inglese in Italia nel secolo XVIII*. Turin: E. Loescher, 1911.

Grand-Carteret, John. "Le livre illustré à l'étranger: Angleterre – Allemagne – Suisse," *Le Livre et l'Image*, 2:13 (10 Mar 1894): 129–49.

Grandjean, Gilles. ed. *Charles Maurin, un symboliste du réel, textes de Maurice Fréchuret*. Lyon: Fage Éditions; Le Puy-en-Velay: Musée Crozatier, 2006.

Gray, John. "Petite gazette d'art: Aubrey Beardsley," *La Revue blanche*, 14 (May 1898): 68–70.

Grewe, Cordula, *The Arabesque from Kant to Comics*. New York: Routledge, 2021.

Gustav Adolf Mossa. Catalogue raisonné des œuvres "symbolistes." Paris: Somogy, 2010.

Hannover, Emil. "Aubrey Beardsley," *Kunst und Künstler*, 1:11 (Nov 1903): 418–25.

Harris, Frank. "Lord Dunsany and Sidney Sime," in Harris, *Contemporary Portraits, Second Series*. New York: The Author, n.d. [1919], pp. 141–57.

Heidmann, Ute. "Pour un comparatisme différentiel," in *Le Comparatisme comme approche critique*, ed. by Anne Tomiche in cooperation with Kelly Morckel, Pauline Macadré, Léa Lebourg-Leportier *et al.*, Rencontres. Série Littérature générale et comparée. Paris: Classiques Garnier, 2017, pp. 31–58.

Heneage, Simon, and Henry Ford, *Sidney Sime, Master of the Mysterious*. London: Thames and Hudson, 1980.

Heyd, Milly. *Aubrey Beardsley: Symbol, Mask and Self-Irony*. New York: Peter Lang, 1986.

Houfe, Simon. "Beardsley and his Followers," in Houfe, *Fin de Siècle. The Illustrators of the Nineties*. London: Barrie and Jenkins, 1992, pp. 65–81.

Houfe, Simon. *The Dictionary of 19th Century British Book Illustrators and Caricaturists*. Woodbridge: Antique Collectors' Club, 1996. First published 1978, revised ed. 1981, 1996.

Hudson, Derek. *Arthur Rackham, His Life and Work*. London: Heinemann, 1974.

Hugo, Victor. *Notre-Dame de Paris, illustrations de Luc-Olivier Merson*, 2 vols. Paris: A. Ferroud, 1889–90.

Hugo, Victor. *Notre-Dame de Paris: 1482. Nouvelle édition illustrée*, 2 vols. Paris: Eugène Hugues, 1876–77.

Hugo, Victor. *Notre-Dame de Paris*. Paris: Garnier-Flammarion, 1967.

Huysmans, Joris-Karl, *À Rebours*. Paris: G. Charpentier et Cie, 1884.

Huysmans, Joris-Karl. "Le Monstre," *Certains*. Paris: Tresse et Stock, 1889, pp. 137–54.

Jackson, Holbrook. *The Eighteen Nineties: A Review of Art and Ideas at the Close of the Nineteenth Century*. London: Grant Richards, 1913. Repr. 1922.

Jaloux, Edmond. "L'époque de Beardsley," *Le Temps* (26 Feb 1932): 3.

Jaloux, Edmond. *Correspondance avec Henri et Marie de Régnier: 1896–1939*, ed. by Pierre Lachasse. Paris: Classiques Garnier, 2019.

Jaloux, Edmond. *Les Saisons littéraires: 1904–1914*. Paris: Plon, 1950.

Jankélévitch, Vladimir. "La Décadence," *Revue de métaphysique et de morale*, 90:4 (Oct–Dec 1950): 435–61.

Jarry, Alfred. "Du pays des dentelles," *Mercure de France*, 26:101 (May 1898): 399–400.

[Jossot] La Direction, "Nos Illustrations. Jossot," *L'Estampe et l'Affiche*, 10 (15 Dec 1897): 233.

Jossot, Henri Gustave. "L'Affiche caricaturale," *L'Estampe et l'Affiche*, 10 (15 Dec 1897): 238–40.

Jossot, Henri Gustave. *Le Foetus récalcitrant*, ed. by Henri Viltard. [Bordeaux]: Finitude, 2011.

Kahan, Sylvia. *Music's Modern Muse: A Life of Winnaretta Singer, Princesse de Polignac*. Rochester, New York: University of Rochester Press, 2003.

Kawamura, Joichiro. "Beardsley and Japan," in *Aubrey Beardsley*, ed. by Stephen Calloway and Caroline Corbeau-Parsons. London: Tate, 2020, pp. 55–59.

Keserü, Katalin. "Art Contacts between Great Britain and Hungary at the Turn of the Century," *Hungarian Studies*, 6:2 (1990): 141–54.

Klein, Rudolf. *Aubrey Beardsley*, 2nd ed. Berlin: Julius Bard, [1902].

Klingsor, Tristan. "Aubrey Beardsley," *Revue illustrée*, 13:13 (15 June 1898): n.p.

Plume (*La*), 155 (15 Oct 1895). Special issue "L'affiche internationale illustrée." Beardsley mentioned at pp. 410, 424, 428, 457, 459.

La Rose, Pierre, "Notes," *The Chap-Book*, 1:1 (15 May 1894): 17–18. With the drawing *Mr Beardsley–After Himself*. Text attributed by the table of contents.

La Rose, Pierre, "The Yellow Book," *The Chap-Book*, 1:7 (15 Aug 1894): 161–65. Plates by Beardsley published independently, *A Drawing*, p. 106, and *The Masque of the Red Death*, p. 158.

La Rose, Pierre. "The Yellow Bookmaker," *The Chap-Book*, 1:2 (1 June 1894): 41–42.

Labruyère [pseud. of Albert Millaud]. "Le Décadent," *Physiologies parisiennes: 120 dessins de Caran d'Ache*. Paris: À la Librairie Illustrée, 1886, p. 173–78.

Laforgue, Jules. "Pierrots, I," *L'Imitation de N.-D. la Lune*. Paris: Léon Vanier, 1886 [1885]; ed. by Pascal Pia. Poésie. Paris: Gallimard, 1979, pp. 28–29.

Langenfeld, Robert. ed. *Reconsidering Aubrey Beardsley, with an Annotated Secondary Bibliography by Nicholas Salerno. Foreword by Simon Wilson*. Ann Arbor, Michigan, and London: U.M.I. Research Press, 1989.

Lautrec, Gabriel de. "Envois de Londres," *Le Courrier français*, 22 (31 May 1896): 5–6.

Lautrec, Gabriel de. "Note sur Aubrey Beardsley," *Le Courrier français*, 21 (21 May 1899): 3.

Lautrec, Gabriel de. "Pour un Démon," *Le Courrier français*, 7 (14 Feb 1897): 6.

Lautrec, Gabriel de. "Une nouvelle revue," *Le Courrier français*, 5 (2 Feb 1896): 8–9.

Lawrence, Arthur H. "Mr. Aubrey Beardsley and His Work," *The Idler*, 11 (Mar 1897): 189–202. Repr. in Stanley Weintraub, *Aubrey Beardsley, Imp of the Perverse*, pp. 218–23.

Legras, Charles. "Au jour le jour: Aubrey Beardsley," *Le Journal des débats*, 87 (29 Mar 1899): 1.

Lehmann, Andrew G. "Pierrot and Fin de Siècle," in *Romantic Mythologies*, ed. by Ian Fletcher. London: Routledge and Kegan Paul, 1967, pp. 209–23.

Lethève, Jacques. "Aubrey Beardsley et la France," *Gazette des beaux-arts*, 68:1175 (Dec 1966): 343–50.

Leu, Philipp. "Les revues littéraires et artistiques, 1890–1900. Questions de patrimonialisation et de numérisation." 2 vols. PhD diss., Université Paris-Saclay, 2016, https://theses.hal.science/tel-03606156

Leverson, Ada. *Letters to the Sphinx from Oscar Wilde, with Reminiscences of the Author*. London: Duckworth, 1930.

[Leverson, Ada.] "A Few Words with Mr. Max Beerbohm," *The Sketch* 8:101 (2 Jan 1895): 439. With the photograph "Max Beerbohm in 'Boyhood'."

[Leverson, Ada.] "Letters from a Débutante," *Punch, or The London Charivari*, 107 (6 Oct 1894): 168, and (13 Oct 1894): 180.

"Little Hints," *Screenland* (Sept 1922): 41.

Locke, George. *From an Ultimate Dim Thule: A Review of the Early Works of S. H. Sime*. London: Ferret Fantasy, 1973.

Locke, George. *The Land of Dreams: A Review of the Work of Sidney H. Sime, 1905 to 1916*. London: Ferret Fantasy, 1975.

Loos, Adolf. "Ornament und Verbrechen," in Ulrich Conrads, *Programme und Manifeste zur Architektur des 20. Jahrhunderts*. Bauwelt: Fundamente, 1964, pp. 15–21.

Lorrain, Jean [Raitif de la Bretonne]. "Pall-Mall Semaine," *Le Journal* (15 Feb 1896): 2.

Lorrain, Jean. *Poussières de Paris*. Paris: Fayard Frères, n.d. [1896].

Lorrain, Jean. *Poussières de Paris*. Paris: Paul Ollendorff, 1902.

Loti, Pierre. *La Troisième Jeunesse de Madame Prune*. Paris: Calmann Lévy, 1905.

Lucian's True History, Translated by Francis Hickes, Illustrated by William Strang, J. B. Clark and Aubrey Beardsley. London: Privately Printed [Lawrence and Bullen], 1894.

Lyden, Anne M. *The Photographs of Frederick H. Evans, with an Essay by Hope Kingsley*. Los Angeles, California: The J. Paul Getty Museum, 2010.

Mac-Nab, Maurice. "Les Fœtus," in Mac-Nab, *Poèmes mobiles: Monologues, avec illustrations de l'auteur et une préface de Coquelin cadet*. Paris: Léon Vanier, 1886, pp. 15–22, with vignettes.

MacColl, D[ugald] S[utherland]. "Aubrey Beardsley", in *A Beardsley Miscellany*, ed. by R. A. Walker. London: The Bodley Head, 1949, pp. 15–32.

[MacColl, D. S.] Mek Koll, O. "Obri Berdslei," *Mir iskusstva*, 3:7–8 (1900): 73–84 (with twelve illustrations and a portrait); *Mir iskusstva*, 3:9–10 (1900): 97–120. Russian version of the above, commissioned by Sergei Diaghilev and first published in Russian.

Manca, Maria Elisabetta. "Specchio di 'Emporium:' le riviste della biblioteca dell'Istituto Italiano d'Arti Grafiche di Bergamo," in *Emporium: Parole e figure tra il 1895 e il 1964*, ed. by Giorgio Bacci, Massimo Ferretti, and Miriam Filetti Mazza. Pisa: Edizioni della Normale, 2009, pp. 155–70.

Meier-Graefe, Julius. "Aubrey Beardsley and his Circle," *Modern Art: Being a Contribution to a New System of Aesthetics*, trans. by Florence Simmonds and George W. Chrystal, 2 vols. New York: G. P. Putnam's Sons; London: William Heinemann, 1908, II, pp. 252–66.

Mercure de France, 26:101 (May 1898). The issue brings together Oscar Wilde, "Ballade de la geôle de Reading,"translated by H.-D. Davray, p. 350–70; Alfred Jarry, "Gestes et opinions du Dr Faustroll, pataphysicien: V. Du pays des dentelles – à Aubrey Beardsley," pp. 399–400; Henry-D. Davray, "Aubrey Beardsley," pp. 485–91.

Montesquiou, Robert de. "Aubrey Beardsley," *Le Figaro*, 52 (21 Feb 1907): 1. Collected under the title "Beardsley en raccourci," in Montesquiou, *Assemblée de notables*. Paris: Félix Juven, 1908, p. 19–27.

Montesquiou, Robert de. "Le Pervers (Aubrey Beardsley)," *Professionnelles beautés*. Paris: Félix Juven, 1905, pp. 85–104.

Morel, Philippe. *Les Grotesques. Les Figures de l'imaginaire dans la peinture italienne de la fin de la Renaissance*. Paris: Flammarion, 2001. First published in 1997.

Mourey, Gabriel. "Aubrey Beardsley," *La Revue encyclopédique*, 8:248 (4 June 1898): 520–21.

Mourey, Gabriel. "Quelques-uns et leurs œuvres: Aubrey Beardsley," in Mourey, *Passé le détroit: La Vie et l'Art à Londres*. Paris: Paul Ollendorff, 1895, pp. 268–71.

N. A. [Nurok, Al'fred], "Obri Berdslei," *Mir iskusstva*, 1:3–4 (1899): 16–17.

[Natanson, Thadée?], "Petite gazette d'art," *La Revue blanche*, 16 (May 1898): 65–70.

Nelson, James G. *Publisher to the Decadents: Leonard Smithers in the Careers of Beardsley, Wilde, Dowson*. University Park, Pennsylvania: Pennsylvania State University Press, 2000.

"New Publications," *The Studio*, 1 (15 July 1893): 162–67.

Newhall, Beaumont. *Frederick H. Evans: Photographer of the Majesty, Light and Space of the Medieval Cathedrals of England and France*. New York: Aperture, 1973.

Ochsé, Julien. "Eaux-fortes (à la manière d'Aubrey Beardsley)," in Ochsé, *L'Invisible Concert*. Paris: Bibliothèque Internationale d'Édition, E. Sansot et Cie, 1908, pp. 101–14.

Palacio, Jean de. "La cathédrale hystérique: monstre hybride et repaire de monstres," in *La Cathédrale*, ed. by Joëlle Prungnaud. Lille: UL3, Travaux et Recherches, 2001, pp. 137–45.

Palacio, Jean de. *Pierrot fin de siècle ou Les métamorphoses d'un masque*. Paris: Séguier, 1990.

Pallaske, Christophe. "Luther – kein Teufels Dudelsack | zur Fehlinterpretation einer Karikatur" (21 Nov 2021), *Hypotheses: Historisch Denken | Geschichte machen,* https://historischdenken.hypotheses.org/5409

Pallottino, Paola. "'La finezza, il numero, la veracità delle illustrazioni:' l'opera pioneristica di Vittorio Pica su 'Emporium,'" in *Emporium: Parole e figure tra il 1895 e il 1964*, ed. by Giorgio Bacci, Massimo Ferretti, and Miriam Filetti Mazza. Pisa: Edizioni della Normale, 2009, pp. 203–18.

Pantazzi, Michael. "Du stryge au gratte-ciel," *Livraisons de l'histoire de l'architecture*, 20 (2010): 91–112, https://doi.org/10.4000/lha.261

Pastel [Theodore Wratislaw]. "Some Drawings by Aubrey Beardsley," *The Artist and Journal of Home Culture*, 14 (1 Sept 1893): 259–60.

Pennell, Elizabeth Robins. *The Life and Letters of Joseph Pennell*, 2 vols. Boston, Massachusetts: Little, Brown, and Company, 1929.

Pennell, Joseph. "A New Illustrator: Aubrey Beardsley," *The Studio*, 1:1 (15 Apr 1893): 14–19. With several reproduced drawings that exceed the textual bounds of the article.

Pennell, Joseph. *The Adventures of an Illustrator, mostly in Following his Authors in America and Europe*. Boston, Massachusetts: Little, Brown, and Company, 1925.

[Pennell, Joseph.] "The Devils of Notre-Dame, by Mr Joseph Pennell with a Comment by R. A. M. Stevenson," *The Pall Mall Budget* (14 and 21 Dec 1893). See also *The Devils of Notre-Dame* (deluxe edition).

[Pennell, Joseph.] *The Devils of Notre-Dame, A Series of Eighteen Illustrations by J. Pennell, With Descriptive Text by R. A. M. Stevenson*. London: Pall Mall Gazette, 1894. Separately published as a deluxe elephant folio folder on Japanese paper, limited ed. of seventy copies only fifty of which were for sale.

Pica, Vittorio. "Artisti d'eccezione," in Pica, *Attraverso gli albi e le cartelle: sensazioni d'arte, seconda serie*. Bergamo: Istituto Italiano d'Arti Grafiche, 1907, pp. 89–135 (on Beardsley, see particularly pp. 89–108). With a richer iconography than in the 1904 corresponding article. It still ends with *The Death of Pierrot*.

Pica, Vittorio. "Attraverso gli albi e le cartelle (sensazioni d'arte): V. I cartelloni illustrati in America, in Inghilterra, in Belgio ed in Olanda," *Emporium*, 5:26 (Feb 1897): 99–125 (on Beardsley, see particularly pp. 113–14). Collected in *Attraverso gli albi e le cartelle (sensazioni d'arte), prima serie*. Bergamo: Istituto Italiano d'Arti Grafiche, 1904, pp. 279–324.

Pica, Vittorio. "Letterati contemporanei: Émile Zola," *Emporium*, 16:95 (Nov 1902): 373–86. With a Beardsley drawing, p. 376.

Pica, Vittorio. "Tre artisti d'eccezione: Aubrey Beardsley – James Ensor – Edouard Münch [*sic*]," *Emporium*, 19:113 (May 1904): 347–68.

Pica, Vittorio. "Trois artistes d'exception: Aubrey Beardsley, James Ensor, Édouard Münch [*sic*]," *Mercure de France*, 56:196 (15 Aug 1905): 517–30.

Pierre et Paul [Léon Vanier]. "Maurice Mac-Nab, dessin de Fernand Fau," *Les Hommes d'aujourd'hui*, 6:295, n.d. [1887].

Pope, Alexander. *The Rape of the Lock*, ed. by Geoffrey Tillotson, 3rd ed. London, Methuen Educational Ltd., 1971.

[Pope, Alexander.] *The Rape of the Lock: An Heroi-Comical Poem in Five Cantos Written by Alexander Pope. Embroidered with Eleven Drawings by Aubrey Beardsley*. London: Leonard Smithers, 1897.

Posters in Miniature. [A Well-known Collection of Posters together with Some Portraits of the Artists]. With an Introduction by E[dward] Penfield. London: John Lane; New York: R. H. Russell and Son, 1896.

Pound, Ezra. *Hugh Selwyn Mauberley by E. P.* London: The Egoist Ltd., 1919. Qtd. in Pound, *Poems and Translations*, ed. by Richard Sieburth, The Library of America 144. New York: The Library of America, 2003, pp. 547–63.

Pre-Raphaelites (*The*). London: The Tate Gallery; Penguin Books, 1984.

"Precocious Baby (The), A Very True Tale (To be Sung to the Air of the 'Whistling Oyster')," *Fun*, n.s. 6 (23 Nov 1867).

Princesse Sapho [Léon Genonceaux]. *Le Tutu: mœurs fin de siècle, avec une planche de musique céleste et une composition symbolique de Binet*. Paris: L. Genonceaux, 1891.

Prospectus. *The Yellow Book*, 1 (Apr. 1894). *Yellow Book Digital Edition*, ed. by Dennis Denisoff and Lorraine Janzen Kooistra. *Yellow Nineties 2.0*, Toronto Metropolitan University Centre for Digital Humanities, 2011, https://1890s.ca/wp-content/uploads/YB1-prospectus.pdf

Rancy, Catherine. *Fantastique et Décadence en Angleterre, 1890–1914*. Paris: Éditions du CNRS, 1982, https://www.cairn.info/fantastique-et-decadence-en-angleterre-1890-1914—9782222031178.htm

Reade, Brian. *Aubrey Beardsley*. London: V & A Museum, Her Majesty's Stationery Office, 1966.

Reade, Brian. *Beardsley, Introduction by John Rothenstein*, revised ed. Woodbridge: Antique Collectors' Club, 1987, repr. 1998. First published London: Studio Vista, 1967, repr. Studio Vista, 1971.

Reade, Brian. "Enter Herodias: Or, What Really Happened?," *Los Angeles County Museum of Art Bulletin*, 22 (1976): 58–65.

Reade, Brian, Susan Lambert, and H. Lee Bimm. eds. *Aubrey Beardsley 1872–1898*. Rome: Fratelli Palombi Editori, 1985.

Recht, Roland. *La Cathédrale de Strasbourg*. Strasbourg: La Nuée bleue, 1993.

Riquer, Alexandre de. "Aubrey Beardsley," *Joventut*, 1 (15 Feb 1900): 6–11.

Robins, Anna Gruetzner. 1999. "Demystifyng Aubrey Beardsley," *Art History*, 22 (Sept 1999): 440–44.

Roques, Jules. "Courrier de Londres," *Le Courrier français*, 11:44 (4 Nov 1894): 4.

Roques, Jules. "Les artistes anglais: M. Beardsley," *Le Courrier français*, 11:51 (23 Dec 1894): 6–8. Reproducing two drawings by Beardsley (*The Wagnerites*, *A Portrait of Himself*) and his portrait by Walter Sickert, wrongly attributed to Beardsley himself.

Roques, Jules. "Une exposition d'affiches artistiques à l''Aquarium'," *Le Courrier français*, 11:45 (11 Nov 1894): 2–5.

Rosen, Elisheva. *Sur le grotesque: l'ancien et le nouveau dans la réflexion esthétique*. Saint-Denis: Presses Universitaires de Vincennes, 1991.

Ross, Robert, *Aubrey Beardsley, with Sixteen Illustrations and a Revised Iconography by Aymer Vallance*. London: John Lane, The Bodley Head; New York: The John Lane Company, 1909.

[Rossetti, Dante Gabriel.] *Dante and His Circle, with the Italian Poets Preceding him. A Collection of Lyrics*, ed. and trans. in the original metres by D. G. Rossetti. London: Ellis and White, 1874 [1873].

[Rossetti, Dante Gabriel.] *The Early Italian Poets from Ciullo d'Alcamo to Dante Alighieri, together with Dante's 'Vita Nuova,'* trans. by Dante Gabriel Rossetti. London: Smith, Elder & Co., 1861.

Rossetti, Dante Gabriel. "Lilith (For a Picture)," in Rossetti, *Poems*. London: F. S. Ellis, 1870, p. 269. Republished as "Body's Beauty" within the section "The House of Life: A Sonnet Sequence," in Rossetti, *Ballads and Sonnets*. London: Ellis and White, 1881, p. 240.

Rossetti, Dante Gabriel. "Sibylla Palmifera (For a Picture)," in *Poems*. London: F. S. Ellis, 1870, p. 270. Republished as "Soul's Beauty," within the section "The House of Life: A Sonnet Sequence," in *Ballads and Sonnets*. London: Ellis and White, 1881, p. 239. This sonnet precedes "Lilith" in both collections.

Rossetti, Dante Gabriel. *The New Life of Dante Alighieri. Translations and Pictures by Dante Gabriel Rossetti*. New York: R. H. Russell, 1901.

Rümann, Arthur. *Das illustrierte Buch des XIX. Jahrhunderts in England, Frankreich und Deutschland, 1790–1860*. Leipzig: Im Insel Verlag, 1930.

Sadakichi, "Aubrey Beardsley from a Japanese Standpoint," *Modern Art*, 3:1 (Winter 1895): 22–24.

Salerno, Nicholas A. "An Annotated Secondary Bibliography," in *Reconsidering Aubrey Beardsley*, ed. by Robert Langenfeld. Ann Arbor, Michigan, and London: U.M.I. Research Press, 1989, pp. 267–493.

Savoy (*The*). Nos. 1–8 (1896). London: Leonard Smithers.

Savoy Digital Edition (The), ed. by Christopher Keep and Lorraine Janzen Kooistra, 2018–20. *Yellow Nineties 2.0*, Ryerson University Centre for Digital Humanities, 2021, https://1890s.ca/savoy-volumes/

Schatz, Dr Christian Friedrich. *Die Griechischen Götter und die Menschlichen Mißgeburten. Vortrag gehalten im Docentenverein der Universität Rostock am 3. Mai 1901, mit 62 Abbildungen im Text*. Wiesbaden: J. F. Bergmann, 1901, https://archive.org/details/diegriechischen00schagoog

Schwob, Marcel. *Correspondance inédite précédée de quelques textes inédits*, ed. by John Alden Green. Genève: Librairie Droz, 1985.

[Seaman, Owen.] Unsigned. "Lilith Libifera, (*After Rossetti*)," *Punch, or The London Charivari*, 107 (3 Nov 1894), p. 205. Later collected in Owen Seaman, *The Battle of the Bays*. London and New York: John Lane, 1896, p. 57 (with variants).

Sharp, Evelyn. "A New Poster," *The Yellow Book*, 6 (June 1895): 123–63.

Sharp, Evelyn. *Unfinished Adventure: Selected Reminiscences from an Englishwoman's Life*. London: John Lane, 1933.

Sidney H. Sime, Master of Fantasy, Compiled by Paul W. Skeeters. Pasadena: Ward Ritchie Press, n.d. [1978].

Small, Herbert. "Book Illustrators: X. Aubrey Beardsley," *The Book Buyer*, n.s. 12:1 (Feb 1895): 26–29.

Snodgrass, Chris. "Beardsley Scholarship at His Centennial: Tethering or Untethering a Victorian Icon?," *English Literature in Transition*, 42:4 (1999): 363–99.

Snodgrass, Chris. *Aubrey Beardsley, Dandy of the Grotesque*. New York and Oxford: Oxford University Press, 1995.

Stead, Évanghélia. "Aubrey Beardsley dans *Emporium* (1895–1904) et l'Europe des revues," in *Emporium, II: Parole e figure tra il 1895 e il 1965*, ed. by Giorgio Bacci and Miriam Filetti Mazza. Pisa: Edizioni della Normale, 2014, pp. 323–46.

Stead, Évanghélia. "Autoportraits grotesques d'Aubrey Beardsley: l'humour, la marge, le monstre," *Humoresques*, special issue "Rires marginaux, rires rebelles," 19 (Jan 2004): 131–56.

Stead, Évanghélia. "*Encor Salomé*: entrelacs du texte et de l'image de Wilde et Beardsley à Mossa et Merlet," in *Dieu, la chair et les livres. Une approche de la Décadence*, ed. by Sylvie Thorel-Cailleteau. Paris: Honoré Champion, 2000, pp. 421–57, fig. 1–12. Revised and enlarged version published as "Triptyque de livres sur Salomé," in Stead, *La Chair du livre: matérialité, imaginaire et poétique du livre fin-de-siècle*, pp. 157–203.

Stead, Evanghelia. "Introduction," *Journal of European Periodical Studies*, special issue "Reconsidering 'Little' versus 'Big' Periodicals," I:2 (2016), 1–17, https://ojs.ugent.be/jeps/issue/view/480.

Stead, Evanghelia. "Introduction", in *Reading Books and Prints as Cultural Objects*, ed. by E. Stead. New Directions in Book History. Cham: Palgrave/Macmillan, 2018, pp. 1–30.

Stead, Évanghélia. "Jarry et Beardsley," *L'Étoile-absinthe. Les Cahiers iconographiques de la Société des amis d'Alfred Jarry*, 95–96 (2002): 49–67, 9 fig., http://alfredjarry.fr/amisjarry/fichiers_ea/etoile_absinthe_095_96reduit.pdf

Stead, Évanghélia. *La Chair du livre: matérialité, imaginaire et poétique du livre fin-de-siècle*, Histoire de l'imprimé. Paris: PUPS, 2012. Repr. in 2013.

Stead, Évanghélia. *Le Monstre, le singe et le fœtus: Tératogonie et Décadence dans l'Europe fin-de-siècle*. Genève: Droz, 2004. Published version of a PhD thesis defended in 1993.

Stead, Évanghélia. "Les grotesques d'Aubrey Beardsley (*Bon-Mots*)," *L'Étoile-absinthe, les cahiers iconographiques de la Société des amis d'Alfred Jarry*, 95–96 (Autumn 2002): 5–47, 132 fig. *Bon-Mots* grotesque vignettes first time catalogued and full reproduced, http://alfredjarry.fr/amisjarry/fichiers_ea/etoile_absinthe_095_96reduit.pdf

Stead, Évanghélia. "Les perversions du merveilleux dans la petite revue ; ou, comment le Nain Jaune se mua en Yellow Dwarf dans treize volumes jaune et noir," in *Anamorphoses décadentes, Études offertes à Jean de Palacio*, ed. by Isabelle Krzywkowski and Sylvie Thorel-Cailleteau. Paris: Presses de l'Université de Paris-Sorbonne, 2002, pp. 102–39. Revised version entitled "Nain Jaune and Yellow Dwarf dans *The Yellow Book*: Un kaléidoscope," in É. Stead, *Sisyphe heureux. Les revues littéraires et artistiques, approches et figures*. Rennes: PUR, 2020, pp. 195–218.

Stead, Évanghélia, and Hélène Védrine. eds. *L'Europe des revues (1880–1920): Estampes, photographies, illustrations*. Histoire de l'imprimé. Paris: PUPS, 2008. Repr. in 2011.

Stead, Évanghélia, and Hélène Védrine. eds. *L'Europe des revues II (1860–1930): Réseaux et circulations des modèles*. Histoire de l'imprimé. Paris: PUPS, 2018.

Stetz, Margaret D. *Aubrey Beardsley 150 Years Young. From the Mark Samuels Lasner Collection University of Delaware Library, Museums and Press*. New York: The Grolier Club, 2022.

Storey, Robert F. *Pierrot: A Critical History of a Mask*. Princeton, New Jersey: Princeton University Press, 1978.

Sturgis, Matthew. *Aubrey Beardsley: A Biography*. London: Harper Collins Publishers, 1998.

Symons, Arthur. "Aubrey Beardsley," *The Fortnightly Review*, n.s. 69:377 (1 May 1898): 752–61.

Symons, Arthur. *Aubrey Beardsley*. London: At the Sign of the Unicorn, 1898. A new edition of Symons's *Fortnightly Review* article with a preface. Reprinted and expanded in 1905.

Symons, Arthur. *Aubrey Beardsley*, new edition revised and enlarged. London: J. M. Dent and Co., 1905. Repr. John Baker, 1966.

Symons, Arthur. *Aubrey Beardsley, traduit par Jack Cohen, Édouard et Louis Thomas*. Paris: Floury, 1906.

Tancini, Francesca. "L'ultimo dei pittori preraffaelliti: Walter Crane e 'Emporium'," in *Emporium: Parole e figure tra il 1895 e il 1964*, ed. by Giorgio Bacci, Massimo Ferretti, and Miriam Filetti Mazza. Pisa: Edizioni della Normale, 2009, pp. 379–401.

Tavel, Hans Christoph von. *Die Randzeichnungen Albrecht Dürers zum Gebetbuch Kaiser Maximilians*. Munich: Prestel Verlag, 1966.

Turnbull, Martin. "Salomé," *National Film Registry*, https://www.loc.gov/static/programs/national-film-preservation-board/documents/salome.pdf

Un Book-Trotter. "L'Image: Mille moins un petits papiers. Le 'Studio' critiqué," *Le Livre et l'Image*, 2:9 (Nov 1893): 249–50.

Un Book-Trotter. "L'Image: Mille moins un petits papiers. Les illustrations d'Aubrey Beardsley," *Le Livre et l'Image*, 2:7 (Sept 1893): 120.

Un Book-Trotter. "L'Image: Titres réduits des nouveaux périodiques anglais," *Le Livre et l'Image*, 2:6 (Aug 1893): 57–58.

Uzanne, Octave. [as Isis.] "Paris partout," *Le Figaro*, 89 (30 Mar 1898): 1.

Uzanne, Octave. [as La Cagoule.] *Visions de notre heure. Choses et gens qui passent, notations d'art, de littérature et de vie pittoresque*. Paris: Henri Floury, 1899, pp. 95–97.

Uzanne, Octave. *L'Art dans la décoration extérieure des livres en France et à l'étranger, les couvertures illustrées, les cartonnages d'éditeurs, la reliure d'art*. Paris: Société Française d'Éditions d'Art, L. Henry May, 1898.

Uzanne, Octave. *Les Évolutions du bouquin. La Nouvelle Bibliopolis: Voyage d'un novateur au Pays des Néo-Icono-Bibliomanes, lithographies en couleurs et marges décoratives par H. P. Dillon*. Paris: Henri Floury, 1897.

Vallance, Aymer. "List of Drawings by Aubrey Beardsley, compiled by Aymer Vallance," in Robert Ross, *Aubrey Beardsley, with Sixteen Illustrations and a Revised Iconography by Aymer Vallance*. London: John Lane, The Bodley Head; New York: The John Lane Company, 1909, pp. 59–112.

Vallès, Jules. "Les Exercices du corps," *L'Événement* (5 Feb 1866): 3c.

Vareilles, Pierre. "Silhouettes décadentes: I. Georges Toulouse," *Le Décadent*, 1 (10 July 1886): 2.

Vergine, Lea. *Body Art e storie simili*. Milan: Skira, 2000.

Verlaine, Paul. "Gosses [Mômes-monocles]," *Art et Critique*, 2:76 (8 Nov 1890). Repr. in *Œuvres en prose complètes*, ed. by Jacques Borel. Bibliothèque de la Pléiade. Paris: Gallimard, 1984, pp. 227–32.

Vilain, Jean-François, and Philip R. Bishop. *Thomas Bird Mosher and the Art of the Book*. Philadelphia, Pennsylvania: F. A. Davis Company, 1992.

Walter, Robert. *Histoire anecdotique de la cathédrale de Strasbourg*. Strasbourg: Erce, 1992.

Weintraub, Stanley. *Aubrey Beardsley, Imp of the Perverse*. University Park, Pennsylvania, and London: The Pennsylvania State University Press, 1976.

[White, Gleeson.] G. W. "Aubrey Beardsley: In Memoriam," *The Studio*, 13 (May 1898): 252–63.

Wilde, Oscar. *Das Bildnis des Dorian Gray: Roman aus dem Englischen übertragen von Alastair*. Konstanz: Lingua Verlag, 1948.

Wilde, Oscar. *L'Anniversaire de l'infante, illustrations par Alastair*. [Preface by Harry Crosby.] Paris: The Black Sun Press, Éditions Narcisse, 1928.

Wilde, Oscar. *The Picture of Dorian Gray*. Harmondsworth: Penguin Books, 1949, repr. 1981. First published London: Ward, Lock and Co., 1891.

Wilde, Oscar. *Salomé, drame en un acte*. Paris, Librairie de l'Art indépendant; London: Elkin Mathews and John Lane, The Bodley Head, 1893. Purple cover with silver lettering.

Wilde, Oscar. *Salomé, drame en un acte. Dessins de Alastair*. Paris: Les Éditions G. Crès et Cie, 1922.

Wilde, Oscar. *Salome, Tragödie in einem Akt, übertragen von Hedwig Lachmann, mit 10 Zeichnungen, Ornamentrahmen im Doppelinnentitel, Vorsatz- und Einband-Dekor von Marcus Behmer*. Leipzig: Insel, 1903.

Wilde, Oscar. *Salome. A Tragedy in One Act: Translated from the French of Oscar Wilde [by Lord Alfred Douglas]. Pictured by Aubrey Beardsley*. London: Elkin Mathews and John Lane; Boston, Massachusetts: Copeland and Day, 1894.

Wilde, Oscar. *The Sphinx Illustrated and Decorated by Alastair*. London: John Lane, The Bodley Head; New York, John Lane Company, 1920.

Wilson, Simon. *Beardsley*. Revised and enlarged edition. Phaidon Colour Library. Oxford: Phaidon Press, 1983. First published in 1976. Trans. into French by Laurent Gonzalez. [Gennevilliers]: Ars Mundi, 1987.

Wright, Thomas. *A History of Caricature and Grotesque in Literature and Art, with Illustrations Drawn and Engraved by F. W. Fairholt*. London: Chatto and Windus, 1875. First published London: Virtue Brothers, 1865. Trans. into French by Octave Sachot with a Note by Amédée Pichot, 2nd ed. Paris: A. Delahays, 1875.

Yellow Book (The). "Introduction to Volume 6 (July 1895)" *The Yellow Book Digital Edition*, ed. by Dennis Denisoff and Lorraine Janzen Kooistra, 2012.

Yellow Nineties 2.0, Ryerson University Centre for Digital Humanities, 2019, https://1890s.ca/yb-v6-introduction/

Yellow Book (The). Nos. 1–13 (Apr 1894–Apr 1897). London: Elkin Mathews and John Lane (until Sept 1894); then John Lane. In parallel Boston, Massachusetts: Copeland and Day, nos. 1–10; then New York: John Lane.

Yellow Book Digital Edition (The), ed. by Dennis Denisoff and Lorraine Janzen Kooistra, 2011–2014. *Yellow Nineties 2.0*, Ryerson University Centre for Digital Humanities, 2020, https://1890s.ca/yellow-book-volumes/

"Yellow Bookmaker (The)," *The Chap-Book*, 1:2 (1 June 1894): 41–42. The text, unsigned, appears as "Book-Maker" in the table of contents.

Zatlin, Linda Gertner, *Aubrey Beardsley: A Catalogue Raisonné*, 2 vols. New Haven, Conn. and London: Yale University Press, Published for the Paul Mellon Centre for Studies in British Art, 2016.

Zatlin, Linda Gertner. *Beardsley, Japonisme, and the Perversion of the Victorian Ideal*. Cambridge: Cambridge University Press, 1997.

Zimmern, Helen. 1898. "Il sistema Prang nell'insegnamento dell'arte," *Emporium*, 7:41 (May 1898): 323–39.

Zuccari Radius, Anna. "La coltura degli artisti," *Emporium*, 2:11 (Nov 1895): 337–43.

Iconography

The following list comprises artworks in this book used in comparison with Beardsley's yet not Beardsley's own. For full information, a historical record, and critical appreciations of Beardsley's artworks, the reader may refer to Linda Gertner Zatlin's *Aubrey Beardsley: A Catalogue Raisonné*, 2 vols. (New Haven, Connecticut, and London: Yale University Press, 2016), referenced throughout my study.

Alastair. *Dorian Gray in Catherine de Medici's Mourning Bed*, early 1920s, Indian ink and watercolour, 16.8 × 11.5 cm, Victor and Gretha Arwas coll., London. Courtesy and © Gretha Arwas. Published as *The Picture of Dorian Gray* in Victor Arwas, *Alastair: Illustrator of Decadence*, 86, no. 71.

Behmer, Marcus. 9th plate in Oscar Wilde, *Salome, Tragödie in einem Akt, übertragen von Hedwig Lachmann, mit 10 Zeichnungen, Ornamentrahmen im Doppelinnentitel, Vorsatz- und Einband-Dekor von Marcus Behmer*. Leipzig: Insel, 1903, repr. 1999, no. 9.

Behmer, Marcus. *Figure in Black Mantle*, full-page drawing, the third of "Sechs Grotesken," repr. *Die Insel*, 3:7–8 (Apr–May 1902): 135.

Behmer, Marcus. *Fœtus and Skeleton*, full-page drawing, the first of "Sechs Zeichnungen," repr. *Die Insel*, 3:10 (July 1902): 107.

Behmer, Marcus. Full-page Illustration for Paul Ernst's Fantasy Piece (*Fantasiestück*), "Der Schemen," repr. *Die Insel*, 2.1:1 (Oct 1900): 81, text 68–83.

Behmer, Marcus. *Hydrocephalic Pierrot Biting into a Mask*, full-page drawing, repr. *Die Insel*, 3:5 (Feb 1902): 245.

Behmer, Marcus. *Newborn Babe and Fly*, full-page drawing, the first of "Zwei Zeichnungen," repr. *Die Insel*, 2.4:10 (July 1901): 127.

Behmer, Marcus. *Oversize Silhouette*, full page drawing, the first of "Drei Zeichnungen", repr. *Die Insel*, 1.3:9 (June 1900): 375.

Behmer, Marcus. *Spindly Diver*, the last of "Drei Zeichnungen," repr. *Die Insel*, 1.3:7 (Apr 1900): 93.

Cam. *Design for New Cover of the "Granta." (à la BEARDSLEY)*, repr. *The Granta*, 8:155 (23 Feb 1895): 212.

Evans, Frederick H. *Aubrey Beardsley* (1894), platinum print, 15 × 10 cm, acquired by the Musée d'Orsay in 1985. © GrandPalais-RMN (Musée d'Orsay) / Christian Jean, PHO1984-57. Repr. as *The Gargoyle*, in Herbert Small, "Aubrey Beardsley," *The Book Buyer*, n.s. 12:1 (Feb 1895): 29.

Evans, Frederick H. *Aubrey Beardsley* [photographed as Meryon's *Le Stryge*] (ca. 1894), framed platinum print, titled, dated and signed by Evans, 15 × 10 cm, acquired by the Musée d'Orsay in 1985. © GrandPalais-RMN (Musée d'Orsay) / Christian Jean, PHO1985-351.

Fairholt, Frederick William. *The Music of the Demon*, vignette drawn and engraved after Erhard Schön's *Des Teufels Dudelsack*, repr. in Wright, *A History of Caricature and Grotesque in Literature and Art*, p. 252, fig. 145.

Fairholt, Frederick William. *The Spirit of Evil* [*sic*], vignette drawn and engraved after Charles Meryon's *Le Stryge*, repr. in Wright, *A History of Caricature and Grotesque in Literature and Art*, p. 74, fig. 44.

Hammond, Gertrude D. *The Yellow Book*, repr. in *The Yellow Book*, 6 (June 1895): 119. See *Yellow Book Digital Edition*, https://1890s.ca/yb6-hammond-yellow/

Huard, Charles. *En attendant la pratique* (*Waiting for the client*), repr. *Le Courrier français*, 10 (8 Mar 1896): 2.

Hyland, Fred. *Two Pictures: I. The Mirror*, repr. *The Yellow Book*, 6 (June 1895): 279. See *Yellow Book Digital Edition*, https://1890s.ca/yb6-hyland-mirror/

Hyland, Fred. *Two Pictures: II. Keynotes*, repr. *The Yellow Book*, 6 (June 1895): 281. See *Yellow Book Digital Edition*, https://1890s.ca/yb6-hyland-keynotes/

Jossot, Henri Gustave. *Two-headed Monster with Webbed Feet and a Rooster's Tail Biting into a Child's Body*, left-hand top vignette with Jossot's text "L'Affiche caricaturale," repr. in *L'Estampe et l'Affiche*, 10 (15 Dec 1897): 240, text pp. 238–40.

Mac-Nab, Maurice. *Fœtus Vignette in Evening Dress*, accompanying Mac-Nab's monolog "Les Fœtus," in Mac-Nab, *Poèmes mobiles*, p. 17, text pp. 15–22.

Maurin, Charles. *L'Éducation sentimentale*, set of coloured dry-points (Paris: Gustave Pellet, 1896), plates republished and detailed in *Le Courrier français*.

Merson, Luc-Olivier. *Notre-Dame de Paris* (ca. 1881), pen and black ink, brush and black wash, white gouache and graphite on light brown wove paper, sheet 32.6 × 21.7 cm, Bequest of Muriel Butkin 2008, The Cleveland Museum of Art, Cleveland, Ohio, USA. The CMA Open Access Initiative, https://www.clevelandart.org/art/2008.359

Meryon, Charles. *Le Stryge* (1853 and later), engraving, 5th state, 16.9 × 13 cm, in portfolio *Eaux-fortes sur Paris*. Paris: Charles Meryon, 1853, pl. 6, numbered 1. © BnF, Estampes, Paris.

Mossa, Gustav Adolf. *Le Fœtus* (ca. 1905), watercolour, graphite, ink, gouache relief and gilding on paper, 50 × 32 (34 × 19) cm, Nice, Musée des Beaux-Arts. See *Gustav Adolf Mossa. Catalogue raisonné des œuvres "symbolistes"*, pp. 152–53 (A 68).

Nerée tot Babberich, Karel de. *Sourire* (1901), pen drawing in Indian ink, 34 × 21 cm, Paris, Musée d'Orsay, inspired by Henri van Booven's collection *Witte Nachten* (1901). Département des Arts Graphiques du musée du Louvre, Paris, acquired in 1987, RF 41471. © PE for a high-resolution scan made from a © RMN photograph acquired in 1990.

Pennell, Joseph. Humorous sketch in ink after Beardsley's drawing depicting him as Meryon's *Stryge* (Dec 1893), in letter to Helen J. Robins, repr. in Elizabeth Robins Pennell, *The Life and Letters of Joseph Pennell*, I, 264.

Reed, Edward Tennyson. Unsigned pastiche of *Portrait of Himself* by Beardsley, repr. *Punch, or The London Charivari*, 107 (3 Nov 1894): 205.

Revault, Étienne. Photograph of Viollet-le-Duc's statue as Thomas the Apostle on Notre-Dame, in Thierry Crépin-Leblond, *La Cathédrale Notre-Dame*, 46.

Rossetti, Dante Gabriel. *Beata Beatrix* (ca. 1864–70), oil on canvas, 86.4 × 66 cm, London, Tate Britain, N01279. CC BY-NC-ND.

Rossetti, Dante Gabriel. *Lady Lilith* (1866–68, reworked 1872–73), oil on canvas, 96.5 × 85.1 cm, Delaware Art Museum, Wilmington, Delaware, USA.

Rossetti, Dante Gabriel. *Sibylla Palmifera* (1866–70), oil on canvas, 98.4 × 85 cm, Lady Lever Art Gallery, Port Sunlight, UK.

S. T., *A Cambridge Night-Piece (with Apologies to Mr. Aubrey Beardsley)*, repr. *The Granta*, 9:169 (2 Nov 1895): 37.

Sattler, Joseph. *Grotesque of Aubrey Beardsley*, tailpiece of Henry-D. Davray's article, "Aubrey Beardsley," repr. *Mercure de France*, 26:101 (May 1898): 491.

Schön, Erhard. *Des Teufels Dudelsack* (*The Devil's Bagpipe*), ca. 1530–35, coloured woodcut, coll. Schloss Friedenstein Gotha, Inv. Nr. 37,2. Wikipedia commons https://commons.wikimedia.org/wiki/File:Teufels_Dudelsack.gif#/media/File:A_monk_as_devil's_bagpipe_(Sammlung_Schloss_Friedenstein_Gotha_Inv._Nr._37,2).jpg

Sime, Sidney Herbert. *Black Fiend Squeezing Paint onto an Oversized Palette and Tiny Laurel-wreathed Artist Enclosed in Black Whirls*, grotesque tailpiece to G. S. Street's "From a London Attic," repr. *The Pall Mall Magazine* 18 (July 1899): 432b.

Sime, Sidney Herbert. *Famished Author and Wastepaper Basket*, grotesque vignette in G. S. Street's "From a London Attic," repr. *The Pall Mall Magazine* 18 (July 1899): 430b.

Sime, Sidney Herbert. *Miniature Imps Sharpening a Gigantic Quill on a Grindstone*, grotesque tailpiece to G. S. Street's "From a London Attic," repr. *The Pall Mall Magazine* 18 (June 1899): 288b.

Sime, Sidney Herbert. *Sime Abandons his Palette*, grotesque vignette in G. S. Street's "From a London Attic," repr. *The Pall Mall Magazine* 18 (July 1899): 430a.

Sime, Sidney Herbert. Sime's version of *Beardsley's Comedy of the Cuckold Husband*, grotesque vignette in G. S. Street's "From a London Attic," repr. *The Pall Mall Magazine* 18 (May 1899): 140b.

Sime, Sidney Herbert. *Yawning Author Pointing to an Arabesque-bordered Void and Imp Running away with Manuscript*, grotesque tailpiece to G. S. Street's "From a London Attic," repr. *The Pall Mall Magazine* 17 (Apr 1899): 576.

Vallotton Félix. *Aubrey Beardsley's mask*, with John Gray's article in "Petite gazette d'art," *La Revue blanche*, 16 (May 1898): 69, text pp. 68–70.

Vignette of terracotta head no. 769 from the Myrina excavations kept in the Louvre Museum, repr. in Jean-Martin Charcot and Paul Richer, *Les difformes et les malades dans l'art*. Paris: Lecrosnier et Babé, 1889, p. 9.

Vignette of the Notre-Dame stryge, in Charcot and Richer, *Les difformes et les malades dans l'art*, 7.

List of Illustrations

Index

Note: Given the richness of entries pertaining to Aubrey Beardsley himself, the entry for "Beardsley, Aubrey" follows a thematic classification system, organised under four categories: I. Cultivation of public persona; II. Beardsley as innovator; III. Reception and influence; IV. Works quoted.

About the Team

Alessandra Tosi was the managing editor for this book.

Adèle Kreager proof-read this manuscript and compiled the index. The author created the Alt-text.

Jeevanjot Kaur Nagpal designed the cover. The cover was produced in InDesign using the Fontin font.

Cameron Craig typeset the book in InDesign and produced the paperback and hardback editions. The main text font is Tex Gyre Pagella and the heading font is Californian FB.

Cameron also produced the PDF and HTML editions. The conversion was performed with open-source software and other tools freely available on our GitHub page at https://github.com/OpenBookPublishers.

Jeremy Bowman created the EPUB.

Raegan Allen was in charge of marketing.

This book was peer-reviewed by Margaret D. Stetz, professor of Women's Studies, University of Delaware, and an anonymous referee. Experts in their field, these readers give their time freely to help ensure the academic rigour of our books. We are grateful for their generous and invaluable contributions.

This book need not end here...

Share

All our books — including the one you have just read — are free to access online so that students, researchers and members of the public who can't afford a printed edition will have access to the same ideas. This title will be accessed online by hundreds of readers each month across the globe: why not share the link so that someone you know is one of them?

This book and additional content is available at:
https://doi.org/10.11647/OBP.0413

Donate

Open Book Publishers is an award-winning, scholar-led, not-for-profit press making knowledge freely available one book at a time. We don't charge authors to publish with us: instead, our work is supported by our library members and by donations from people who believe that research shouldn't be locked behind paywalls.

Why not join them in freeing knowledge by supporting us:
https://www.openbookpublishers.com/support-us

You may also be interested in:

William Rimmer

Champion of Imagination in American Art

Dorinda Evans

https://doi.org/10.11647/obp.0304

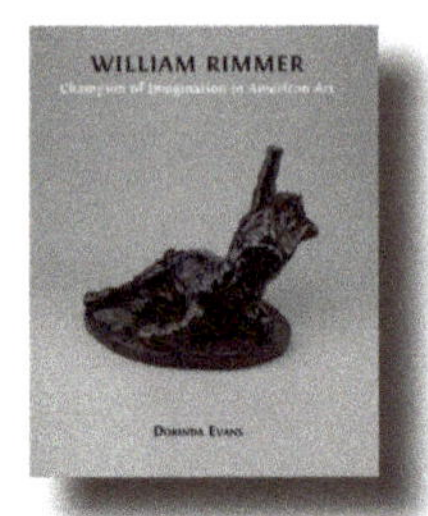

Modernism and the Spiritual in Russian Art

New Perspectives

Louise Hardiman and Nicola Kozicharow(eds.)

https://doi.org/10.11647/obp.0115

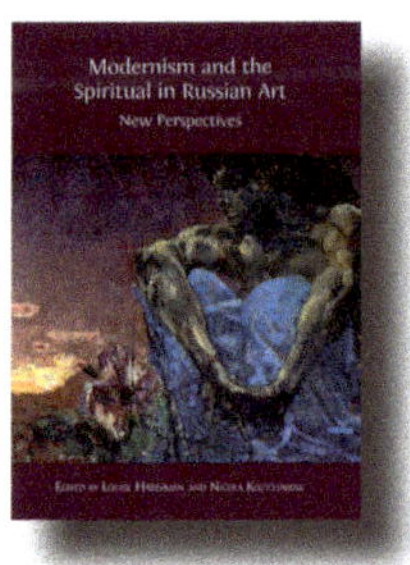

William Moorcroft, Potter

Individuality by Design

Jonathan Mallinson

https://doi.org/10.11647/obp.0349

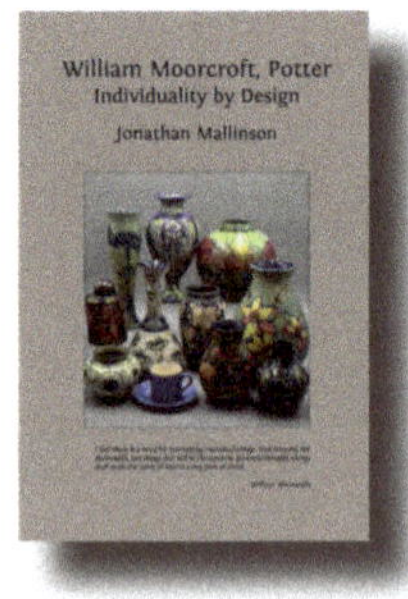

www.ingramcontent.com/pod-product-compliance
Lightning Source LLC
LaVergne TN
LVHW052350100826
845147LV00013B/806

9781805113454